ESSAYS ON
CONTEMPORARY
AMERICAN
DRAMA

edited by

HEDWIG BOCK

AND

ALBERT WERTHEIM

Max Hueber Verlag

1. Auflage
3. 2. 1.
1984   83   82   81

© 1981 Max Hueber Verlag München

Book Design: Stephanie Wicks
Printed in U.S.A.

ISBN 3-19-00.2232-1

CONTENTS

INTRODUCTION

The essays in this volume, written by scholars from the United States and Europe, are meant to be a useful introduction to the playwrights and drama of the United States during the last twenty years. Most of the essays concern themselves with major playwrights, but some are meant to provide the reader with a general overview of important works and developments in contemporary black, Chicano and women's theatre. The annotated bibliography at the close of the volume is not meant to be exhaustive but to offer a starting point for further reading.

Unlike European dramatists who benefit from a long tradition of drama and theatre, American dramatists work within a native tradition that has barely passed its infancy. In the years to come, some of the playwrights in this volume will have achieved a long-lived reputation, while others may well fall into obscurity. What is recorded here is a series of essays covering a period of change and development for a drama still growing to maturity.

The editors wish to make special mention of the agreement concluded by President John Ryan of Indiana University and Präsident Peter Fischer-Appelt of the Universität Hamburg for the regular exchange of scholars, personnel, and research activities between the two universities. That agreement expedited this joint venture immeasurably. We wish to thank as well the Fulbright Commission, the Deutscher Akademischer Austauschsdienst (DAAD), and the office of John V. Lombardi, Dean for International Programs at Indiana University for their kind and generous assistance.

Hedwig Bock, Universität Hamburg
Albert Wertheim, Indiana University

Tennessee Williams, Southern Playwright

HEDWIG BOCK

Tennessee, born Thomas Lanier, Williams in Columbus, Mississippi in 1911, is justly considered in America as well as in Europe, one of the leading American playwrights since World War II. His fame is mainly based on the success of his two plays *The Glass Menagerie* and *A Streetcar Named Desire*. These two plays have been staged, filmed, and TV versions have frequently been shown as part of Tennessee Williams revivals. Interest in him does not seem to have slackened at all. After the first staging of these two plays in the nineteen-forties, however, Tennessee Williams' talent seems to have faded gradually, and his latest plays, sometimes rewritten from earlier versions of plays for which he had found no publisher, are regarded as failures.

Together with the works of writers like William Faulkner, Carson McCullers, and Thomas Wolfe, Tennessee Williams' plays have been mainly shaped and coloured by the traditions and legends of the American Old South and the reality of an aggressive New South. The action of his plays takes place very often either in the Mississippi Delta Country south of Memphis, or in the Gulf area of New Orleans. When the action of his plays is set abroad, Tennessee Williams' characters still are definitely southerners in their character structure and behaviour. Moreover, Europeans' and Americans' views of the South have been greatly influenced by Tennessee Williams' gothic descriptions of that part of the United States.

His plays mainly deal with the "fugitive kind", misfits of modern society, who often cling to their own views of a society, the ante-bellum South, which no longer exists and perhaps never existed. Their behaviour is deformed by their refusal to accept a modern reality as it is, and by their clinging to the dream of a life that is non-existent. This clash between a dream of freedom, gentility, and wealth, and the reality of inescapable poverty and vulgarity or vulgar wealth exposes his characters to a battle for survival, which they almost always lose. Madness, disease, and death is their only alternative. "Murder, cannibalism, castration, madness, incest, rape, adultery, nymphomania, homosexuality. There exists no savage act about which my son has not written", says Tennessee Williams' mother about his plays,[1] but Tennessee Williams declared: "I write out of love for the South. But I can't expect southerners to realize that my writing about them is an expression of love. It is out of regret for a South that no longer exists that I write of those forces that destroyed it."[2]

What Williams' drama, therefore, reflects, is the society of the South, but at the same time he wrote compulsively to "escape from madness. His sister, Rose, was not as fortunate, for she became forever lost in mental illness, not strong enough to combat the horror she felt threatening her life."[3] She did not have the talent her brother Tom had. He escaped her fate through the therapeutic effect of writing. What we discover of Southern society in Tennessee Williams' drama, is a transmission of social attitudes through his own experiences, as well as through internalized codes of behaviour mainly through the women who surrounded him: his mother and his sister Rose, to whom he was deeply attached and with whom he identified. Concomitantly he hated his father, who did not know how to deal with his introvert son. This conflict of identification resulted in an insoluble ambivalence: his admiration and longing for strong masculinity, as he portrays it in Stanley Kowalski and Big Daddy, both of them men who can cope with life. At the same time his best portrayals, his protagonists, are all women, whom he understood so well because of his own female identification. There is probably more of Tennessee Williams' psychic condition in his Blanche Dubois of *A Streetcar Named Desire* than in his Tom of *The Glass Menagerie*.

Far more important, however, is the reflection of the human condition through these characters, outsiders in a modern society, who still cling to internalized values of a no longer existent society and still act out a sociologically narrow superstructure of the "Southern Lady", the "lovely woman of the Southland, as pure and chaste as this sparkling water, as cold as this gleaming ice",[4] whose frequent frigidity was called purity. White male supremacy and the survival of the white race in a patriarchial system of the Old South depended on keeping those women in complete economic subjugation. This produced a double morality which gave white men all the power and an oriental freedom concerning women. In Tennessee Williams' drama this appears as a longing for saintly purity as well as a deep involvement in sex. His presentation of extremely infantile women also reflects this double morality: these women were unable to grow up to full and responsible maturity in a newly emancipated South. Their neurosis was generally hysteria.

In *Sweet Bird of Youth* (1959),[5] Tennessee Williams presents a most negative picture of the decaying Old South with its race hatred, sex envy, and double standard of morality, whilst in *The Glass Menagerie* he shows tremendous understanding, sympathy and love for Amanda and Laura, the main characters of his most delicate play. Boss Finley of *Sweet Bird of Youth*, one of Tennessee Williams' overpowering and destructive fathers, presides at the head of a family of infantile, weak women and a weak son. His will to gain power, but also his fear of losing power, have turned him into one of the most unscrupulous male characters in Tennessee Williams' dramas. His political platform is "the threat of desegregation to the women's chastity in the South" (p. 65), "white youth in danger" (p. 66). He portrays himself as "all that stands between the South and the black days of reconstruction" (p. 66) and "all of them that want to adulterate the pure white blood of the South" (p. 67). He forces his daughter, Heavenly, for him a mere object for gaining power, to stand up with him on the platform, "wearing the stainless white of a virgin" (p. 66), even though everybody knows that a "whore's operation" (p. 55) was performed on her. He forbade her to marry the man she loved, not because he thought Chance Wain incapable of taking care of her—which he would obviously never have been—but to try and force Heavenly to marry "a fifty-year-old money bag" (p. 63) from whom he expected some favour. He himself does not live up to the standards of purity he preaches. Even though he may have married his wife for love, he keeps a mistress in a "fifty-dollar-a-day hotel suite at the Royal Palms" (p. 60). He does not stand up against the lynching of a negro whom "they picked out . . . at random and castrated the bastard to show they mean business about white women's protection in this state" (p. 80).

Sweet Bird of Youth is Tennessee Williams' only play which criticizes political power, and the will to gain it and to keep it, as the most destructive element in life. If this play depicts Southern society, Tennessee Williams' *Glass Menagerie* (1945),[6] the play that first made him world-famous, is a play that shows life as a personal and private microcosm (a St. Louis flat with a fire escape as entrance and exit), with a universal background of a macrocosm on fire: "when the huge middle class of America was matriculating in a school for the blind" (p. 234), when "Franco triumphs" (p. 265) and Guernica was destroyed. It shows the three members of the Wingfield family, none of whom is fully able to realize the meaning of reality. Each one has his or her own idea of escape: Laura into the world of her "glass menagerie"; Amanda into a dream of youth and the Old South; Tom into the land of film and adventures and finally out to the sea, Tennessee Williams' everlasting symbol of birth and death. The father "fell in love with long distances" (p. 235) leaving Amanda helpless, for "Southern ladies was never brought up to manage finanshul affairs".[7] They always depended on the help of relatives (p. 245) or "the kindness of strangers,"[8] and all Amanda learnt was baking Angel Cakes. Since Amanda was psychically unable to marry the "right" man, that is a rich planter, she is now left destitute with a crippled daughter and a son who is a dreamer. Amanda, the pathetic Southern belle, whose beauty faded long ago, sees her situation quite clearly, but tries to cope with it according to an internalized code of Southern behaviour. Both her children are grown up, but she clings to them, and especially treats the son Tom as her baby, since the role of a mother was the only one she was allowed to play since she had got married and her beauty had faded. On the one hand, she constantly directs and castrates Tom, who is over 20 years old; on the other hand, she completely relies on him as the man to take care of her financially, to take over the role of her runaway husband. His scanty interest in his job upsets her: "What right have you to jeopardize your job? Jeopardize the security of all of us? How do you think we'd all of us manage?" (p. 251). He hands her the money he earns, she gives him pocket money, and if she considers it necessary, a little extra to take the streetcar home.

However, Amanda and Tom seem to have found a way which enables them to cope with life even as outsiders of society. The most pitifully unsuccessful member of the Wingfield household is Laura, Tom's sister. As the whole Wingfield family is a portrait of Tennessee Williams' own family, so the character of Laura is the tender portrait of his sister Rose, the only woman in his life whom he loved dearly, and one of the few female characters in his plays created with understanding and love, not hatred. Because of the portrait of helpless and crippled Laura and the scenic devices Tennessee Williams uses to present her, *The Glass Menagerie* is Tennessee Williams' most gentle play, lacking the violence and crude sex of his other plays. He characterizes Laura more through the stage devices of his "plastic theatre" and more through symbols than through actions. Most of the time she sits helplessly on the sofa; the fire escape does not offer her any escape from the imprisonment in her own psychic condition. She resists, with fits of hysterical vomiting, her mother's efforts to have her trained for a job, although the fear of facing her mother and telling her the truth gives her the strength to wander around the park on cold winter days without catching a cold. The coat she wears on these occasions does not fit her and is old; she inherited it from Amanda, like the code of behaviour which does not fit into reality and makes her helpless. Her key symbol is the transparent pieces of her glass menagerie. Washing and drying them—an act of purification—is her only occupation during the days she spends in her room. The light upon her has a "peculiar pristine clarity such as light used in early religious portraits of female saints and madonnas" (p. 231). Her favourite in the menagerie is the unicorn, which is as different from the other glass animals as Laura is from other people. In the complexity of its meaning it suggests the Virgin Mary and a phallic symbol at the same time.

As Jim breaks off its horn, he awakens Laura. He goes down the fire escape. She stays behind, mentally and physically crippled.

The most pathetic of Tennessee Williams' figures is Blanche Dubois in his *A Streetcar Named Desire* (1949),[9] his most famous play, and surely his best. Blanche's portrait — the swan song of a Southern lady — induces us to pity her helplessness in a male-dominated Southern world of school inspectors, poker players, and Stanley Kowalskis; a world, whose code of purity and helplessness she has internalized but cannot act out. She is unable to accept the ambivalence between her sexual needs and desires, and the society-imposed super-ego of the image of the Southern belle. Her name means "white", she prefers to wear dainty white clothes, but spills Coca Cola, the drink of modern American reality, on her skirt. She continually takes baths to wash off the dirt of the world surrounding her.

In her relation with Mitch, which she sees as a last chance to find a refuge from the dangers of this world, she plays the role of the Southern lady. She tries to please and entertain him, in order to catch him for life as her protector and breadwinner, until he discovers her past and therefore decides that she is not "clean enough to bring in the house with my mother" (p. 207).

Since she has been brought up with the double standard of purity, meaning frigidity, and sex, meaning "epic fornications" (p. 140) and dirt, she has the choice of either being "pure", as in her relations with her young husband (a homosexual) and with Mitch, or acting out her desires in the most chaotic way, even as a prostitute. Her desires make her throw herself at Stanley until he rapes her. Sexual satisfaction, through her own instigations, is forbidden fruit, "unwashed grapes" (p. 220), and dirty, and therefore includes the punishment. Her only way out of these conflicts which she is unable to solve, is insanity, the asylum, withdrawal from this world into peace and infantility until death, the last refuge of purity. She arrives in New Orleans in a dainty white suit; on the poker night she wears a wrapper of fiery and aggressive red; when Stanley rapes her, her white gown is soiled; and she chooses a dress of Della Robbia blue, "the blue of the robe in the old Madonna pictures" (p. 219), when she finally retreats.

In Elia Kazan's film version of *A Streetcar Named Desire* there seem to be some concessions to the taste and to the sexual taboos of the early nineteen-fifties. The film is an obviously bowdlerized version of the play, but except for the ending it is very much in keeping with the spirit of the play. The opening scene of the play presents the chaotic atmosphere of prostitution, "red hot" sex and hell fire in the French Quarter of New Orleans. The film's opening scene presents a view of the Mississippi River. In myth, rivers take on the meaning of the borderline between life and death. Blanche crosses this borderline on her way from Desire to Cemetries. In the drama water is related to cleanliness and death: Blanche takes many baths; she remembers a "moonlight swim at the old rock quarry" (p. 208) at the bottom of which looms death; her young husband committed suicide at Moon Lake; she expects Shep Huntley to take her on a Caribbean Cruise; she even dreams that death will come in the shape of a very young, nice looking ship's doctor: "And I'll be burried at sea sewn up in a clean white sack and dropped over board—at noon—in the blaze of summer—and into an ocean as blue as ... my first lover's eyes!" (p. 220). Hers is a narcissistic dream of final regression into the protection of the mother's womb.

In his portrait of the Stanley/Stella relationship, Williams presents us with what is to him a successful overcoming of loneliness, the full integration of sex into life: the sole basis of their "love" is the pleasure they derive from sex. Tennessee Williams cannot help displaying an obvious admiration for Stanley, "a one hundred per cent American, born and raised in the greatest county on earth" (p. 197) under the sign of the Capricorn, the goat, symbol of a lecherous man: he is a phallic symbol personified. On the morning after the poker night and because of the pleasure he got from sex with Stella, he gives her ten dollars. Their marriage appears to be hardly more than legalized prostitution. There is, however, a child born. New life springs from this marriage of Stella, the descendant of the Old South, and Stanley, the representative of modern America.

In this respect the end of the film does not cohere to the meaning of the drama. Stella and Stanley depend on each other, and since Blanche interferes with this successful marriage and becomes a rival of Stanley for Stella, Stanley has the choice of either destroying Blanche or giving up Stella. But Stella cannot afford to leave Stanley, as she seems to do at the end of the film. Her life depends on him, economically as well as for the pleasure she gets with him. Also, the central meaning of the transformation of an old society is thus lost.

What makes Tennessee Williams' *A Streetcar Named Desire* one of the great modern American plays is the poetic devices of the plastic theatre as well as the imagery and symbols used to explicate the often subconscious levels of meaning in the play: the meaning of colours, lighting, noises, the clothes people wear and the water symbolism. They are not used in a decorative sense, but, as shown above, create the deeper meaning of the play. In no other of his later or earlier plays has Tennessee Williams achieved this poetic level of dramatic explication.

Summer and Smoke (1948)[10] followed immediately after *A Streetcar Named Desire*. In his *Memoirs* (1975) Tennessee Williams says about this play: "the play was a tough nut to crack. Miss Alma Winemiller may very well be the best female portrait I have drawn in a play. She simply seemed to exist somewhere in my being and it was no effort to put her on paper.

However, the boy she was in love with all her youth, Johnny Buchanan, never seemed real to me but always a cardboard figure and I knew it and it distressed me but I kept at the play for a couple of months, I wrote several drafts of it. Then, one evening, when I thought it completed, I read it aloud to a young man who was friendly to me. He kept yawning as I read... 'how could the author of *The Glass Menagerie* write such a bad play as this?' "

In Alma, Spanish for soul, Tennessee Williams again portrays the ambivalence of the spirit and puritanism versus the body and sex. He presents Alma as the hysteric daughter of a puritanic minister and a mother, who repeats Tennessee Williams' portrayal of childishly demented mothers—the "cross" of their families.

Like Blanche, Alma cannot conceive of her body and soul as one unity. She moves from an existence of purity —that is hysteric frigidity —to prostitution. She is juxtaposed to young Dr. Buchanan, who first is shown acting out his bodily impulses violently, but longing for the spiritual existence he sees in Alma. The shock of his father's death mysteriously transforms him, and he marries a rather silly young woman, who, like the new John Buchanan makes no distinction between purity and sex.

If Stella of *A Streetcar Named Desire*, who is a weak personality and an incarnation of the genteel traditions of the Old South, manages to cope with life successfully, Maggie of *A Cat on a Hot Tin Roof* (1955)[12] is, according to Tennessee Williams' standards, successful in life. She is at the same time a person of strong willpower, able to solve the conflict which Amanda of *The Glass Menagerie* is unable to solve and which, though only on the surface, causes Blanche's downfall; the conflict of love versus money. Her characterization reflects the same ambivalent admiration Williams had for Stanley Kowalski. Both have the aggressive strength and willpower to achieve their aim of surviving. Both, however, are flawed: they brutally use their power to oust anyone who gets in their way. This is most obvious in "Maggie the Cat". The play's theme is "mendacity, and the disgust with mendacity" (p. 92), but it ends with a lie through which Maggie achieves her aim of inheriting Big Daddy's money. The play's plot construction is also very efficient and excites the audience. This may be the reason for the repeated staging and filming of *Cat on a Hot Tin Roof*. Tennessee Williams says about this play: "I realize how very old-fashioned I am as a dramatist to be so concerned with classic form but this does not embarrass me, since I feel that the absence of form is nearly always, if not always, as dissatisfying to an audience as it is to me. I persist in considering *Cat* my best work of the long plays because of its classic unities of time and place and the kingly magnitude of Big Daddy."[13]

The plot of the play is about the birthday of Big Daddy, one of the richest plantation owners in the Delta Country,[14] who at the age of 65 has severe cancer and will soon die without having made a will. He has two sons, competent Gooper with his wife Mae and their five children, and Brick, an alcoholic and perhaps a homosexual, married to Maggie the Cat. They have no children. There is a strong sibling envy between the two sons, because both parents have always loved Brick, their youngest, better than their first born, but have, through this treatment, also spoiled him and not given him the chance to grow up mentally: Big Mama calls him "my precious baby" (p. 50), or even "my only son" (p. 106). Since sex was all that existed between the old couple, they have transferred their emotions to their youngest son. Thus the struggle arises over who will inherit the plantation: the avaricious Gooper and Mae, or Maggie through a Brick who does not care.

The audience's attention is focused on Maggie, young, beautiful and seductive, who, unfortunately, originally was too poor to lead the carefree dream life of a Southern lady, though she comes from good, old Southern stock: "...I've been so God damn disgustingly poor all my life!...Always had to suck up to people I could not stand because they had the money and I was poor as Job's turkey. You don't know what that's like ... [to] have to suck up to relatives that you hated because they had the money and all you had was a bunch of hand-me-down clothes...And my poor Mama, having to maintain some semblance of social position, to keep appearances up, on an income of 150 dollars a month on those old government bonds. When I came out, the year I made my debut, I had just two evening dresses! One mother made from a pattern in Vogue, the other from a snotty rich cousin I hated! ... You can be young without money, you can't be old without. You've got to be old with money..." (pp. 41–42). This attitude explains her unscrupulous battle for Brick and against his homosexual friend Skipper. Her husband refuses to sleep with her to punish her, for she proved to him that Skipper was a homosexual. For this reason she will not have children and thus envies her fertile sister-in-law and at the same time hates Mae's five children. She finds a way out of the dilemma by the announcement at the end of the play that she is pregnant, an announcement that has no foundation in truth, even though Tennessee Williams makes us believe that she will be successful and beget a child with Brick.

The end of the play makes us believe that Maggie really loves her husband. The question of whether she would have loved him if he had been poor does not arise. In what might be called an earlier version but also a sequel to the play, the short story "Three Players of a Summer Game",[15] Margaret and Brick are both older, and Margaret Pollit has completely taken over, since Brick's only love is his liquor. She has taken on the androgynous quality of several of Tennessee Williams' characters. "Her beauty has turned into a wonderful male assurance" (p. 30). She chauffeurs home her completely drunk husband, who has lost his driver's license for drunk driving.

Big Daddy and Big Mama are a repetition of the theme of the up-start man of an aggressive New South, marrying a woman who is a representative of the Old South. Big Mama, at the age of 63 too old to be a sex object, is again a representation of one of Tennessee Williams' great but pitifully ridiculous mother characters. She is of limited horizon but also lovingly faithful throughout a long marriage, although Tennessee Williams, and in this case Big Daddy and Brick, do not seem to believe in any woman's lasting love. "Wouldn't it be funny if that was true", says Big Daddy about Big Mama's confession of love (p. 59), and Brick repeats this to Maggie at the end of the play after her statement of her love for Brick's beauty and weakness (p. 123). Since love means sex to drown loneliness, the shock of the revelation of his near death brings Big Daddy to the conclusion that he will buy sex and prove his virility with the money he has made in a lifetime.

Cat on a Hot Tin Roof lacks the subtle beauty of *Streetcar*'s poetic language and symbolism. Blanche's extreme narcissism was evidenced both in her behaviour and in her attitude towards others. It was beautifully defined in the meaning of colours, light and the water symbolism, while Brick's narcissistic attitude is merely present in his actions and behaviour (good looks, drinking). The antagonism between Brick and Gooper obviously represents Tennessee Williams' own ambivalent attitude towards his younger brother. Brick, the drunken son, who was spoiled by father, mother and wife, attains what he never made an effort for: money which will give him a chance to buy more drink. Gooper's sober efforts to save the plantation for himself are juxtaposed with the reader's disgust with Gooper's lack of charm and selfish behaviour. Williams himself is in Gooper's position as the older brother,[16] and yet Williams' own wishful thinking is concentrated on Brick. Through him the audience identifies with Brick. Also, Gooper, his fertile wife, and the ever present briefcase, are the incarnation of the competent and aggressive New South which will survive, while Brick represents the Old South, charming, incompetent, but loved by Tennessee Williams himself, and without much chance of survival.

Maggie is not only Tennessee Williams' strongest woman, but also unique in her ability to envision the future from the experience of her past. Most other Tennessee Williams women have their roots in a past or past experiences which they have suppressed, so that there is no chance for them for active creativity in the present and also no hope for the future. Laura withdrew into her mother's home, Blanche found shelter in an asylum, and what will happen to Alma Winemiller, is not stated, but pretty certain. In *Night of the Iguana* (1961)[17], Hannah as well as Maxine and Shannon will continue their life's journey in a world that is on fire and in which life does not seem to make sense at all.

In *Night of the Iguana*, Tennessee Williams presents us with a group of American outcasts. They are isolated individuals in Mexico, at the foot of a hill. Those who reach the hilltop, will go through a process of rebirth, suggesting spiritual enlightenment. They are confronted with the knowledge of their own situation in life and also with the problem of choosing which further directions they will take. As it turns out, their only choice is to accept the path on which they have already started to move, which leads to the sea, which can be seen from the hilltop, and which symbolizes birth, death, and purity. There are those who do not have the intention of making the pilgrim's progress up the narrow footpath to the top: a busload of schoolteachers from Baptist Female College in Blowing Rock, Texas, "a football squad of old maids" (p. 10), and the German family who spend most of their time drinking beer down at the beach. These are the people who attain no spiritual enlightenment.

Those, who reach the top, are Shannon, the defrocked priest; Hannah Jelkes, an artist; and Nonno, her 98 year old grandfather, a poet. All three reach the peak at a critical point in their lives. It was the grandfather, who in the face of his oncoming death, made the decision for himself and his granddaughter to make the journey to Mexico and the hilltop with the view over the sea. The arrival for him means a last moment of creativity, a poem which he knows will be his last one after 20 years of sterility and before he dies. This however, places his daughter Hannah, "a real lady, a real one and a great one" (p. 69) in a borderline situation in which to continue life on her own. She, like Laura in *The Glass Menagerie*, is one of Tennessee Williams' saintly figures, "remarkable looking—ethereal, almost ghostly. She suggests a Gothic cathedral image of a medieval saint, but animated... she is totally feminine and yet androgynous looking—almost timeless" (pp. 17–18). As a saint, she is timeless and anthropologically a unity of male and female. She is pure and the Platonic incarnation of the spirit. She neither searches for nor needs the other half. Through her work as an artist, she has looked closely at the faces of the living and the dying, and she has discovered human loneliness and suffering. As she looked out at others, she discovered herself in a ritual passage through a dark tunnel and final birth in a new, white light:

> HANNAH: ... and gradually, at the far end of the tunnel,
>   that I was struggling out of, I began to see this
>   faint white light—the light of the world outside
>   me—and I kept climbing towards it. I had to.

SHANNON:	Did it stay a grey light?...
HANNAH:	No, it stayed only white, but white is a very good light to see at the end of a long black tunnel you thought would never be ending, that only God or Death could put a stop to, especially when you... since I was... far from sure about God. (p. 99)

She has experienced that a home is "a thing that two people have between them in which each can...well, nest—rest—live in, emotionally speaking" (p. 101). Through her ability to reach out to other people and to reach them without the need for sex, there is in her a deep trust in her future paths, since she knows that nobody ever has to go alone.

Her deep insight into her own and other people's endurances and afflictions enable her at this critical moment to serve Shannon as guide for his rites of passage. Like the Iguana, Shannon is still tied to a rope, he cannot yet reach out fully to discover the existential meaning of his own life and of God. As a God-seeker, Shannon moves away from the idea of a puritanical Old-Testament God who "brutally punish[es] all he created for his own faults in construction" (p. 52), to a personal idea of a God in thunder and lightning. He discovers, through the initiation of Hannah, in a third stage of development, the meaning of a human life, a life without violence, resting in compassion and acceptance of one's weakness as part of the human condition. He will therefore not travel with Hannah, but, after freeing the Iguana, he finds refuge and protection with Maxine, the mother figure, and the partner to complete the male-female unity. Maxine gives him, what Hannah, the saintly woman, will not be able to give him.

By the end of the night, all three people have chosen to accept life in all its ambivalence. They will therefore be able to live.

The Night of the Iguana is Tennessee Williams' last play to reach out to his audience through a deeper meaning. The 1960s brought Tennessee Williams' own deep collapse, the end of his ability to write for his own therapeutic liberation and at the same time create images of the human condition through outsiders in an otherwise inhuman world.

The Milk Train Doesn't Stop Here Any More (1962)[18] contains the same symbols as *The Night of the Iguana*, the rock above the sea, the path up to the rock; it also presents Tennessee Williams' own search for a meaning in life. This time, however, he fails to present this quest as a general circumstance of the human condition. In *The Milk Train Doesn't Stop Here Any More* he paints a very vivid picture of the American abroad. Mrs. Goforth, who does not want to die, has the path up to her rock "above the oldest sea in the Western world" (p. 7) defended by bloodhounds. Her life has been a constant striving upwards, from the bottom of the social ladder into the social register and into great wealth. But her climb was accompanied by constant death. Her life now is complete loneliness and she orders her servants about by pushing buttons on an intercom. Her only human contact is with the Witch of Capri, also American, who only pretends to be friendly. Unwilling to die, Mrs. Goforth distrusts everybody until a young American beatnik, as the Angel of Death, passes the bloodhounds on the narrow goatpath up to her house. She dies. Who will inherit or steal her immensely valuable possessions, is left open.

With *The Night of the Iguana* Tennessee Williams won his fourth New York Drama Critics Circle Award. *The Milk Train Doesn't Stop Here Any More* was first produced at the Spoleto Festival in Italy. What followed after these plays were no more than variations on a theme: Southern women, now aging considerably; overpowering mothers; spinsters hungry for sex, sometimes saints, sometimes devils, sometimes both, but definitely one-sided; male studs, whose only aim in life is sex; or weaklings and homosexuals but all characters, male as well as female, are used by Tennessee Williams to exhibit and cry out to the world his own severe psychic problems. The problems of American society of the 1960s and 1970s do not seem to have touched him at all.

His *Slapstick Tragedy* of 1966[19] closed after only seven performances. Occasionally, as in *The Seven Descents of Myrtle* (1968)[20] he repeats his theme of Old South versus New South. This time the Old South is suggested by Lot, homosexual transvestite with bleached hair and the usual oedipal syndrome, whose "wife" is taken over by his half-brother Chicken, whose mother was black. Chicken is the strong healthy male in the Williams sense of the word: the New South, who wins, gets the woman, inherits the old farm and escapes the deluge of the great flood.

In 1969 *Die Stuttgarter Zeitung* (25 May, 1969) refers to the New York performance of *In a Bar of a Tokyo Hotel* (1969)[21] as *"Endstation Sack-gasse"* (Destination Dead-End, the German title of *A Streetcar Named Desire* is *Endstation Sehnsucht*). Finally, after several more failures in the 1970s, *Die Welt* (24 March, 1979) in an article for his 65th birthday calls Tennessee Williams "the greatest dramatist of contemporary American literature", but asks: *"Wurde der Katze das Blechdach zu heiß?"* (Did the tin roof become too hot for the cat?). The article suggests that Tennessee Williams might have received the Nobel Prize, had he stopped writing in 1954, the year he wrote *Cat on a Hot Tin Roof*.

Tennessee Williams' pursuit of a meaning in life has led him on a long and crooked journey. In the beginning of his career he definitely reached "a poet's vocation to influence the heart in a gentler fashion than you have made your mark on that loaf of bread".[22]

Life's journey in his plays turns out to be the streetcar's rattling along a track with no chance of escape, neither for him nor for his characters. Rebellion is useless: Laura has to stay at home and Tom knows that he will return to her. The destiny always is loneliness. Brutal desire or death are the only alternatives. Stella's relations with Stanley do not allow a different interpretation either.

Still, Tennessee Williams in *The Night of the Iguana* comes very near to realizing that sex and love are distinct. "Maxine: I know the difference between loving someone and just sleeping with someone".[23] There is in this play a deep longing to reach out to somebody near, but finally no hope that "the violets can break the rocks".[24] There is also a deep rooted existential fear, a primal distrust of any lasting human contact: "We have to distrust each other ... It is our only defence against betrayal".[25]

Only in *The Night of the Iguana* does Tennessee Williams come to a kind of final answer in his quest for identity and meaning in life. To understand and help each other is the essence of life, and to choose and accept life as it is leads to a deeper insight into the human condition. Sex, for Tennessee Williams, has no room in this concept of life, since it always includes chaos.

In the plays following *The Night of the Iguana*, Tennessee Williams leaves the path upwards, and turns back to infantility and the inability to reach out to other people, seeing the self as the center of a world, narrow-minded and imprisoned. This includes his own inability to reach out to an audience to which he no longer has anything to say, and also his failure to use writing as his own therapy.

NOTES

1. Edwina Dakin Williams, *Remember Me to Tom* (New York: G. P. Putnam, 1963), p. 213.
2. *Ibid*. p. 213.
3. *Ibid*. p. 14.
4. Carl Cramer, *Stars Fell on Alabama*, in W. J. Cash, *The Mind of the South* (New York: Vintage Books 1941), p. 340.
5. Tennessee Williams, *Sweet Bird of Youth, A Streetcar Named Desire, The Glass Menagerie* (Harmondsworth: Penguin Books, 1962).
6. *Ibid*.
7. Tennessee Williams, *27 Wagons Full of Cotton* (New York: New Directions, 1966), p. 91.

8. Tennessee Williams, *Sweet Bird of Youth, A Streetcar Named Desire, The Glass Menagerie* (Harmondsworth: Penguin Books), p. 225.

9. *Ibid*.

10. Tennessee Williams, *Summer and Smoke* (New York: James Laughlin, 1948).

11. Tennessee Williams, *Memoirs* (Garden City, New York: Doubleday, 1975), p. 109.

12. Tennessee Williams, *Cat on a Hot Tin Roof* (New York: Signet Books, 1955).

13. Tennessee Williams, *Memoirs* (Garden City, New York: Doubleday, 1975), p. 234.

14. This is between Memphis and Vicksburg, and not South of New Orleans, which is "the mouth" of the Mississippi. Memphis is a thriving industrial town and in this play suggests the "New South". New Orleans in Tennessee Williams' plays always suggests the "Old South".

15. Tennessee Williams, *Three Players of a Summer Game and Other Stories* (Harmondsworth: Penguin Books, 1965).

16. See Tennessee Williams, *Cat on a Hot Tin Roof* (New York: Signet Books, 1955), p. 113; *Memoirs* (Garden City, New York: Doubleday, 1975), p. 220.

17. Tennessee Williams, *The Night of the Iguana, Orpheus Descending* (Harmondsworth: Penguin Books, 1964).

18. In *The Theatre of Tennessee Williams* (New York: New Directions Books, 1976), vol. V.

19. In Tennessee Williams, *Dragon Country: Eight Plays* (New York: New Directions Books).

20. In *The Theatre of Tennessee Williams* (New York: New Directions Books, 1976), vol. V.

21. In Tennessee Williams, *Dragon Country: Eight Plays* (New York: New Directions Books).

22. Tennessee Williams, *The Rose Tattoo, Camino Real* (Harmondsworth: Penguin Books, 1958), p. 179.

23. Tennessee Williams, *The Night of the Iguana, Orpheus Descending* (Harmondsworth; Penguin Books, 1964), p. 75.

24. Tennessee Williams, *The Rose Tattoo, Camino Real* (Harmondsworth: Penguin Books, 1958), p. 192.

25. *Ibid.*, p. 191.

Arthur Miller:
After the Fall and After

ALBERT WERTHEIM

There is an hiatus of nearly eight years between the first production of Arthur Miller's revised two-act version of *A View from the Bridge* and the opening of *After the Fall* on January 23, 1964. During that period he wrote a number of short stories; a children's book entitled *Jane's Blanket* (1963); the filmscript for *The Misfits*, based on one of his stories; and a number of magazine essays. During that period he also faced the inquisitors of the House Un-American Activities Committee, was convicted by them for contempt of Congress (1957), and saw that conviction reversed a year later; he married (1956) and divorced (1960) Marilyn Monroe, married the photographer Inge Morath (1962), and suffered the death of Marilyn Monroe (1962). The events in Miller's life in those years between *View from the Bridge* and *After the Fall* were to have a profound impact on the subject matter and themes of what one could label the second flowering of Arthur Miller's playwriting career, a flowering that includes *After the Fall, Incident at Vichy* (December 3, 1964), *The Price* (February 7, 1968), and *The Creation of the World and Other Business* (November 30, 1972). All these plays deal with the theme of insight and responsibility, the loss of innocence and its consequences. And all these plays, with the possible exception of *The Price*, imply a sense of universal allegory, setting the drama of individuals against the spectre of the Nazi death camps or the monumental events of the first four chapters of *Genesis*.

   After the Fall has found few true admirers among the critics. Gerald Weales urges us to recognize Miller's total achievement despite the disappointment felt toward *After the Fall* and the plays that follow.[1] Ruby Cohn recognizes that the play "must have been written at some personal cost to Miller," but that it does not reflect his dramatic skill.[2] And Harold Clurman argues that the play was a necessary psychological catharsis for Miller, who, "had he not written this play he might never have been able to write another."[3] There is an almost universal sense of embarrassment about *After the Fall* often stemming from the recognition that, coming from the pen of the same man who wrote such masterworks as *Death of a Salesman*, *All My Sons*, and *The Crucible*, *After the Fall* seems the work of a young playwright signifying something but full of too much sound and fury nonetheless. The reviewers for their part fixed on the autobiographical content particularly on the figure of Maggie, who clearly bears many similarities to Marilyn Monroe. Coming as it did so soon after Marilyn Monroe's untimely death, *After the Fall* was seized upon by the reviewers as Arthur Miller's rendition of the Marilyn Monroe story, a reputation that continues to dog the play.[4] But *After the Fall* is not a play about Marilyn Monroe. It is a complex work marking a new direction in Miller's playwriting. Comparisons with Miller's earlier dramatic works can serve to cloud the discussion of *After the Fall*, which, though not the work of a young playwright is nonetheless the work of a playwright attempting, sometimes awkwardly, to move in what is for him a new direction.

Quentin is both protagonist and antagonist in *After the Fall*, for the play centers on the self-imposed mental trial of Quentin, who is at once both his most incisive accuser and most eloquent defender. As Gerald Weales has noted, *The Inside of His Head*, Miller's original title for *Death of a Salesman*, might well be an alternate title for *After the Fall*,[5] since the play is written in the form of Quentin's confessional directed to an unseen Listener, who, according to the stage directions, "would be sitting just beyond the edge of the stage itself." In his Foreword to the play, Miller explains that the Listener might be regarded by some as a psychoanalyst or God but "is Quentin himself turned at the edge of the abyss to look at his experience, his nature and his time."[6] Important, however, is the location of the Listener (one side of Quentin) within the audience section of the theatre. Looming behind Quentin, rising above the set and "dominating the stage" is the ever-present tower of a German concentration camp. And surely the terrifying brutality and evil represented by the tower is also an aspect of Quentin's personality. Quentin the man on stage is, then, literally pitted between two aspects of himself, the frequently illuminated tower of the German concentration camp and the sympathetic Listener identified with the audience and with whom the audience identifies. The medieval Everyman acted his role between the extremities of Heaven and Hell-Mouth. Miller so uses the audience section that his Everyman, Quentin, acts out his struggle between the extremities of living humanity and the stony edifice of radical inhumanity. Quentin's dramatized internal psychological dialectic is further heightened by the stage set. Since *After the Fall* aptly locates its episodes within the convolutions of Quentin's brain, this is made manifest onstage through the use of free-form sculpted areas, whose "effect is neolithic, a lava-like, supple geography in which, like pits and hollows found in lava, the scenes take place" (p. 1).[7]

The structure of the medieval morality play was frequently based upon the idea of the pilgrimage of human life. The human soul journeyed between the extremes of Paradise and Hell, which were often, as in the famous drawing of the Valenciennes theatre,[8] actually present on stage. In the morality play a final judgment is made and the main character, like Mankind in *The Castle of Perseverance*, is taken into Paradise or, like Marlowe's Doctor Faustus, cast into Hell. The final speech of God in *The Castle of Perseverance* nicely explicates the final judgments of the old plays:

> Et qui bona egerunt, ibunt in vitam eternum; qui vero mala, in
> ignem eternum.
> And they that well do in this world here, wealth shall a-wake;
> In heaven they shall heynd be in bounty and in bliss.
> And they that evil do, they shall to hell lake,
> In bitter balës burnt: my judgement it is.

The problem explored in *After the Fall* is that the pilgrimage of modern life is not informed with such ultimate and knowable consequences. Grace and Evil, the humane Listener and the Concentration Camp, do exist but they are not points on a linear plane at which man can arrive. They are instead an axis around which the three-dimensional locus of human existence revolves.

Quentin is Miller's contemporary Everyman, for whom the moral issues that confront him in life turn out not to be the easy black-and-white, either/or issues of the medieval protagonist. Nor is there a deity, a judge, who renders pellucid decisions about guilt and innocence:

> But underlying it all, I see now, there was presumption. That I
> was moving on an upward path toward some elevation,
> where—God knows what—I would be justified, or even
> condemned—a verdict anyway. I think now that my disaster
> really began when I looked up one day—and the bench was
> empty. No judge in sight. And all that remained was the endless
> argument with oneself—this pointless litigation of existence
> before any empty bench. Which, of course, is another way of
> saying—despair. And, of course, despair can be a way of life;
> but you have to believe in it, pick it up, take it to heart, and move
> on again. Instead, I seem to be hung up. (p. 3)

Quentin's dilemma is not merely theological; as a professional lawyer he must question the validity of legal judgments and laws in a world in which the final Judge is not in sight and no final judgments forthcoming. More important, Quentin is a man who in the course of the play is constantly faced with moral situations and who has to make consequent decisions, a man whom his wife Maggie disparagingly calls "Judgey." The absence of a judge on high renders him embroiled in his own interior debate, "the endless argument with oneself," carried on within the context of the unseen, sympathetic Listener in the foreground and the searchlights of hell on earth, the concentration camp, in the background.

At first, Quentin, like the poet in Henry Vaughan's "The Retreat" or Wordsworth's *Intimations* ode, looks back longingly to earlier days of innocence, simplicity and clear knowledge of right and wrong:

> And I keep looking back to when there seemed to be some duty
> in the sky. I had a dinner table and a wife—a child and the world
> so wonderfully threatened by injustices I was born to correct! It
> seems so fine! Remember—when there were good people and
> bad people? And how easy it was to tell! The worst son of a
> bitch, if he loved Jews and hated Hitler, he was a buddy. Like
> some kind of paradise compared to this. Until I began to look at
> it. (pp. 22–23)

The title *After the Fall* refers of course to the loss of Paradise in *Genesis* (the main subject also of *The Creation of the World and Other Business*) and Quentin here romanticizes his position as a post-lapsarian punishment. It was all Edenic "until I began to look at it." Quentin has bitten the apple and knowledge has brought suffering. Quentin's simplistic view is, however, quickly abrogated by the moral contradictions inherent in having "the worst son of a bitch" become "a buddy" or by having "the worst son of a bitch" hate Hitler. It is abrogated as well by the knowledge that Quentin's marriage to Louise was from the outset beset by moral complexity, with attempts to do right resulting in injuries, with compliments taken as insults, and with actions seen by Quentin as eminently justifiable taken by Louise as injustices.

The triumph of Miller's technique in *After the Fall* is that by using a free form set and by making the play a dramatized interior monologue free from the constraints of time and space, Miller is able to have Quentin juxtapose significant and sometimes analogous moments drawn from relations with his parents, wives, Socialist friends, clients, and his new love and prospective third wife to illustrate Quentin's striving for moral rectitude, his search for "an upward path toward some elevation," and his necessary recognition that life is not mapped by either straight-and-narrow or primrose paths. Quentin must come to terms with the admixture of good and evil in human affairs, with the fact that his mother's love for him is in part based on hostility toward her husband, that her disdain for her husband's illiteracy must be countered by the fact that her intellectually superior family are ne'er-do-wells supported by her husband, and that his love for his mother must be tempered by the remembrance of psychological betrayal as she screamed "You are an idiot" (p. 20) when his father lost his monies in the Depression. Likewise in his own marriages to Louise and Maggie, Quentin must face the truth behind the acrimonious accusations of his wives as well as feeling the injuries they have inflicted upon him. And, surely echoing Miller's own appearance before HUAC and the inner trials it must have brought him, Quentin must face up to the fact that 1930s socialism and communism proved a false paradise; that much as he would like to feel a loyalty born out of pure love for his friends of that era, his attitude toward them is shaped by a constellation of different emotions that includes love but also includes a loveless sense of duty, fear for his own professional position, a martyr's elation for putting his professional career heroically in jeopardy, disillusionment and pity. Human relationships and motivations, in short, are all played out in life as they are on Miller's symbolic stage: between the polarities of the death camp and the unseen judge or Listener.

Quentin must acknowledge that much as he would like to be totally innocent, he never can be; that love and betrayal are not mutually exclusive but coexist. He is forced, therefore, seeing the concentration camp tower to acknowledge, "Even this slaughterhouse! Why does something in me bow its head like an accomplice in this place!" (p. 30). There is even guilt in knowing one is relieved to have escaped death in a concentration camp, dying with one's brothers, for in feeling that relief one tacitly affirms fraternity with those who condemned the victims of the camps to death:

> And I am not alone, and no man lives who would not rather be
> the sole survivor of this place than all its finest victims! What is
> the cure? Who can be innocent again on this mountain of skulls?
> I tell you what I know! My brothers died here — but my brothers
> built this place; our hearts have cut these stones! (p. 113)

In *After the Fall* the post-lapsarian terror, the knowledge of good and evil and the knowledge that good and evil coexist within man and within the human situation, is projected within the mind and life of Quentin, a contemporary Everyman. What the plays offers in the face of this knowledge is the insight and vision of Holga, the play's most enlightened character, who tells Quentin:

> I dreamed I had a child, and even in the dream I saw it was my
> life, and it was an idiot, and I ran away. But it always crept onto
> my lap again, clutched at my clothes. Until I thought, if I could
> kiss it, whatever in it was my own, perhaps I could sleep. And I
> bent to its broken face, and it was horrible ... but I kissed it. I
> think one must finally take one's life in one's arms, Quentin.
> Come, they play *The Magic Flute* tonight. You like *The Magic
> Flute?* (p. 22)

For Holga acceptance replaces judgment: acceptance of the deformity and idiocy in life; acceptance of the fact that the environs of Salzburg can house the disgrace of a concentration camp and the achievement of Mozart; and that one can go from the complex feelings engendered by a visit to the edifice of evil, the concentration camp, to the simplistic triumph of pure good as Mozart's Pamina and Tamino witness the disappearance of the Queen of the Night, become part of the sanctified world of Sarastro and hear intoned, "Die Strahlen der Sonne vertreiben die Nacht,/Zernichten der Heuchler erschlichene Macht." Quentin's visit to Salzburg, then, captures the spirit of *After the Fall* and the play's vision of life, for Quentin sees there both the unreality of pure evil manifested in the concentration camp and the equal unreality of the triumph of pure good as purveyed in the libretto of *Die Zauberflöte*. Likewise throughout *After the Fall*, Quentin acts and re-enacts his life framed by the concentration camp searchlight and the unseen, unheard Listener who is meant to help Quentin annihilate his guilt and his culpability.

On December 3, 1964, slightly more than ten months after the opening of *After the Fall*, Miller's *Incident at Vichy*, directed by the late Harold Clurman, premiered in New York. Like *After the Fall*, *Incident at Vichy* treats the questions of evil and raises the spectre of the Nazi concentration camps. Although the play takes place in Vichy during the Nazi occupation, although it does present a group of people who are mostly Jews and more than likely on their way to Auschwitz and other concentration camps, it is not a play about Nazism nor is it, as Robert Brustein's vitriolic and shockingly short-sighted review would have it, merely Hannah Arendt's *Eichmann in Jerusalem* revisited.[9] Brustein compares *Incident at Vichy* to Robert Sherwood's *Petrified Forest*. On the surface, Sherwood's *There Shall Be No Night* (1940) would be a more apt analog. One needs to see, however, that *Incident at Vichy*, written nearly two decades after the close of World War II, only uses the incident it portrays as an example, as an incident of human beings facing evil and facing an evil from which they can never wholly divorce themselves.

Miller's metier is usually seen as the family drama, as in *All My Sons* (1947) and *Death of a Salesman* (1949). In *Incident at Vichy*, however, as in that brilliant (perhaps Miller's best) and much neglected play *A Memory of Two Mondays* (1955), Miller presents a panorama of social types, a cross-section of European civilization, gathered together in a non-descript room for interrogation by the Nazi SS and the subservient French police. As the stage directions make clear, the audience sees some boxes and a bench, grimy windows, and the entrance to a private room within "a large empty area whose former use is unclear but which suggests a warehouse, perhaps, an armory, or part of a railroad station not used by the public"

(p. 1).[10] The set provides no clues either to the audience or to the characters of the play as to what this location is meant to be. The definition of the place relies, then, on what the characters make of it. The characters likewise must come to define themselves as a group, for on the surface they are extremely diverse: a merchant, an artist, an electrician, a physician, an actor, a young boy, an Old Jewish man, an Austrian prince, a waiter and a gypsy. Without the Nazis having to say it, the motley group soon categorizes itself as Jews and a gypsy, racial groups marked by the Nazis as culpable and marked by them for extermination. The Austrian prince, Von Berg, has been picked up by mistake and is, in the course of the play, removed from the aloofness that his name suggests and forced to act. The merchant, who ironically has the supposedly classic Jewish vocation, is quickly discovered to have been erroneously detained and is set free. The others have little in common. Except for the Old Jew who is identifiable by his garments, beard and sidelocks, the various characters show no visible Jewishness or resemblance to one another. Likewise, they are from dissimilar walks of life and share no common attitudes. And yet they quickly know that they are marked men and they quickly acknowledge why they have been gathered for interrogation, thereby partially assenting to and coöpting with those who rounded them up.

The horror of *Incident at Vichy* is that the presence of Evil is strongly felt but never made manifest. The audience sees the characters only before they are interrogated. What happens inside the private room is never shown, but none of the victims except Marchand and Von Berg, who are neither Jews nor gypsies, ever emerges from that room. Never knowing for a fact how the victims are treated or what their fate will be, heightens the terror, leaving the audience with thoughts they dare not think and the outlines of scenes that defy definition by human reason. The characters themselves exemplify the tragic comedy of human reason, of rationalization, in the face of faceless Evil. As economic forces, as capitalist culpability, as lower class vulgarity, as short-sighted parents, as a nagging wife, and as foolish error are blamed for having brought the characters to the pass they are in, it is clear that each reason is laughably inadequate in the face of total Evil, which, by its very nature is the embodiment of irrationality itself. As Leduc, the physician and most incisive thinker of the group, insists, "Is there a rational explanation for your sitting here? But you are sitting here, aren't you?" (p. 39).

One by one the disparate characters enter the interrogation room but do not emerge from it, until only the two most sensitive and thoughtful figures, Leduc and Baron Von Berg (with obvious hints of regality in both their names), are left onstage debating. Both men are curiously idealists or purists insofar as Leduc cynically argues that man is by nature ignoble and

Von Berg optimistically asserts that man is by nature noble. Leduc explains his view exclaiming:

> I am only angry that I should have been born before the day when man accepted his own nature; that he is not reasonable, that he is full of murder, that his ideals are only the little tax he pays for the right to hate and kill with a clear conscience. I am only angry that, knowing this, I still deluded myself. That there was not time to truly make part of myself what I know, and to teach others the truth. (pp. 67–68)

This wholly negative idealism is countered by Von Berg, who answers:

> There are ideals, Doctor, of another kind. There are people who would find it easier to die than stain one finger with this murder. They exist. I swear it to you. People for whom everything is not permitted, foolish people and ineffectual, but they do exist and will not dishonor their tradition. (p. 68)

Although Leduc tries to make the Baron unearth his complicity with the Nazis, it is Leduc himself whose view of man is the more congruent with that of his captors. By destroying the Baron's idealism and by affirming the supposedly irrational basic nature of humankind, Leduc casts himself as an innocent victim in a world that is by definition evil; yet to affirm evil and the irrational is by extension to assent to Nazism and the death camps.

Incident at Vichy ends with the Baron forced to admit that he is not wholly untainted by evil but then acting with a positive idealism, giving Leduc an exit pass and thereby sacrificing his life. At that moment, however, Leduc, in accepting the exit pass, acknowledges his willingness to escape from what he has just characterized as inescapable irrationality. He must acknowledge, too, Von Berg's positive concept of man; and he must leave guilty of Von Berg's inevitable death. As Leduc leaves, the stage direction states, "Leduc backs away, his hands springing to cover his eyes in the awareness of his own guilt" (p. 72). The final recognition, then, is a recognition not about Nazis and concentration camps but about the nature of life. The play affirms the existence and frequent triumph of evil as a fact of life but not as the definition of life. Likewise, and frequently with as much irrationality, good exists and triumphs. *After the Fall* and *Incident at Vichy* should perhaps be considered together, for they are close in production date and nearly identical in theme. The first focuses the idea of good and evil's existence through the psyche of an individual man, Quentin; the second reveals it through a panoramic cross-section of mankind.

After the panorama of characters contained in *Incident at Vichy* and after the rather free form and sprawling nature of *After the Fall*, Miller's next play, *The Price* (first produced February 7, 1968), marks a return to the more focused and controlled form and style of Miller's earlier dramas. Even the Aristotelian unities are upheld. It contains only four characters and like *All My Sons* and *Death of a Salesman* it uses one of Arthur Miller's favorite dramatic devices: two brothers. *The Price* reflects once more Miller as well-schooled in the techniques of Ibsen's dramaturgy, and the result is surely one of Miller's masterworks. Picking up from a muted strand of plot in *After the Fall* concerning the uneasy relations between Quentin and his brother Dan and between Quentin's parents, *The Price* explores the choices one makes about the direction of one's life, the rationalizations for those choices, and the price that must be paid whatever the choice.

At the heart of *The Price* is the stage set itself, the mass of parental furniture that Victor and Walter Franz, after not having had contact for sixteen years, must now dispose of. The building in which the furniture is stored is marked for demolition and their parents' furniture, which has stood about for decades, must be removed. The long opening stage direction describing the set in detail, and that the audience faces the set from the moment the theatre is entered, both stress the importance of the stage picture, "the chaos of ten rooms of furniture squeezed into this one" (p. 3).[11] Quickly the hodge-podge of furniture makes itself felt as an expressionistic metaphor for Victor and Walter Franz's past; the empty, overstuffed armchair and the solitary gilt harp become inanimate actors giving powerful performances in the roles of Victor and Walter's father and mother. Quickly, too, Miller makes it clear that the demolition of the building and the disposal of the furniture is a dramatized simile for the fact that Victor and Walter must dispose of, face up to, and evaluate the past and its effect on their respective lives. The myths, the rationalizations about the past, will be demolished along with the building in which the play takes place, disposed of along with the furniture.

The brothers Franz have chosen disparate professions and consequent lifestyles. Victor is a civil servant, a policeman in a relatively safe, non-violent position at the airport. His means are modest, his son a scholarship student at M.I.T., and his wife loving but chronically disappointed with her husband's status and income. Walter, by contrast, is affluent, having chosen surgery, one of the more lucrative and bloody aspects of medicine. He has money, success, and respect but his marriage has ended in divorce, his children are unsuccessful and estranged from him, and he has suffered but recovered from a nervous breakdown. The two brothers have not seen one another for sixteen years because, it would seem from Victor's view in Act I, Walter has callously neglected his brother as he had likewise neglected his father. And yet, from the very beginning of the play, Victor and Walter seem like an inseparable pair, two aspects of one problem. As Esther points to an attractive chest of drawers, Walter's name is tellingly first introduced into the play when Victor replies, "That was mine. The one over there was Walter's. They're a pair" (pp. 6–7). This idea is echoed repeatedly when, for example, Walter says to the used furniture dealter, "He can't conclude any deal without me, Solomon, I'm half owner here" (p. 69) or when Walter sums up their lives saying, "...we're brothers. It was only two seemingly different roads out of the same trap. It's almost as though we're like two halves of the same guy. As though we can't quite move ahead—alone" (p. 112). The impossible division of the brothers is reinforced by the two-act structure of *The Price*. Act I is Victor's act, for Walter does not appear until the final moment; Act II is dominated by Walter and Walter's point of view. The two acts of the play, like the two brothers, are necessary for Miller's unified dramatic statement. And who better to preside over the two but a furniture dealer named Solomon, the descendent of the famous biblical king who demonstrated his wisdom by presiding over the impossible division of the child?

Their attitudes toward the furniture onstage and toward Solomon, the old furniture dealer who is close in age to their father, reiterate the choices the Franz brothers have made in their lives and the ways they treated and were treated by their father. Furniture style and lifestyle become synonymous as the wise Solomon explains:

> I ask you to remember—with used furniture you cannot be emotional (p. 32)
> Officer, you're talking reality; you cannot talk reality with used furniture. (p. 33)
> Because the price of used furniture is nothing but a viewpoint, and if you wouldn't understand the viewpoint is impossible to understand the price. (p. 37)

There are no right and wrong life choices. Victor is not the moral victor his name implies or that he sees himself to be in Act I, nor was Walter's severity toward his father as justified as Walter wishes in Act II to prove it was. Rather, for better and for worse, each man has followed his taste, his psychological inclination; and the play is meant to place the brothers in juxtaposition without favoring one's choice over the other's. By meeting to evaluate the furniture of their youth, the men meet more importantly to evaluate each other, to point out the truth to one another, and, finally to discover truth in themselves, to determine what price they have paid for their lives. That this is the aim of the play is made explicit and pellucid in the production note Miller appended to the playscript:

> A fine balance of sympathy should be maintained in the playing
> of the roles of Victor and Walter. ... The production must

therefore withhold judgment in favor of presenting both men in all their humanity and from their own viewpoints. Actually, each has merely proved to the other what the other has known but dared not face. At the end, demanding of one another what was forfeited to time, each is left touching the structure of his life. (p. 119)

The Price, however, turns on a secret and since that secret is largely relevant to Victor's life, Miller's desired equilibrium is somewhat tilted toward Victor and it is he more than Walter who is racked by the pain of truth and whose understanding of the price he has paid for his life is the more harrowingly won.

Victor's life lie is that he gave up a promising career in science, became a policeman, to support a father left nearly penniless and emotionally crippled by the economic and psychological catastrophe of the Depression. Walter reminds Victor that when Victor had wanted to borrow money for medical school tuition, Walter had told him that his father had the money. What becomes clear, however, is that even without Walter's information Victor could well have guessed his father's true financial circumstances. The answer was there, as it still is, on the stage: the mass of costly furniture which could have been sold, which could have provided medical school tuition money as well as a protection against total indigence. The truth that emerges is that Victor created a life of self-sacrifice to prove to himself that love and fellowship can bind men and families, that there is more to relationships than mere loveless economic dependence. And the response from Victor's father sitting in his overstuffed chair was only enigmatic laughter. Again in the present tense of *The Price*, Victor repeats the past making the same choice once more. Moved by the feistiness, old age and shabbiness of Solomon, Victor parts with the furniture for a paltry sum. Victor can then, however, carry away the warm feelings that he has brought hope to the aging Solomon and that he has convinced the antique dealer that life still has meaning. Unlike Walter, Victor cannot treat Solomon callously and make a profit by taking the furniture as a tax write-off. He likewise seems willfully to ignore Solomon's impressive diamond ring, large enough for him to use for cracking his hardboiled eggs, large enough for the audience to estimate its obvious value and recognize that Solomon is no beaten man. Solomon is, moreover, the present day proxy for Victor's father. This is made manifest at the close of the play as Solomon places himself amid the furniture, sits in the father's chair and laughts enigmatically as the curtain slowly falls.

Since *The Price*, Miller has written and produced *The Creation of the World and Other Business* (1972), *The Archbishop's Ceiling* (1977), and a television play, *Fame* (aired November 30, 1978). His new play *The*

American Clock, having had trial stagings in New York and at the Spoleto Festival in South Carolina (May, 1980), is slated to have its official premiere in New York late in 1980. *The Creation of the World* was not well received and is often dismissed as a failure. In *The Creation*, the biblical reference in the title of *After the Fall* is the idea of the play, for it concerns Adam and Eve before and more largely after their fall. It treats the postlapsarian lives of Adam, Eve, Abel and Cain as well as the problems of good and evil, knowledge and ignorance, and constructive and destructive human impulse already rehearsed in *After the Fall.*[12] What is special about *The Creation,* however, is its comic tone. That Arthur Miller, the official serious American playwright, the American heir to the mantle of Ibsen, should suddenly reveal a talent for the comic and try on the mantle of George Bernard Shaw is indeed surprising. That surprise may well have helped to prompt the negative reviews. Certainly *The Creation* cannot be counted among Miller's finest plays,[13] but Miller's Lucifer is a comic triumph, a cousin-german to Shaw's Mephistophelean Andrew Undershaft. That Miller is able to treat the serious subject of *After the Fall* with comedy and with Shavian wit in *The Creation* is something of a breakthrough and a triumph for Miller. Perhaps *The Creation* should not be judged in the context of the other plays but as a first try at serious comedy and thus containing the expected weaknesses of a first play.

Miller continued to develop his skills as a comic dramatist in the television play *Fame,* which contains three very loosely connected comic sketches (the first of which is based on his short story "Fame") held together by Richard Benjamin as the comic protagonist Meyer Shine. *Fame* treats Meyer Shine's attempt to come to grips with a life that has become unreal after his several successful plays have made him a public figure and have altered his financial circumstances almost beyond his own comprehension. Shine's most recent success, moreover, a comedy entitled *Mostly Florence*, is about a woman whose beauty is so astonishing that she becomes unreal to herself. Shine's character Florence like Shine himself are Maggie of *After the Fall* (and perhaps Marilyn Monroe and Arthur Miller) seen through a comic focus. Although *Fame* is little more than a pleasantry and although *Fame* seems like a televised stage play rather than a teleplay, the fact that Miller is developing skills as a comic playwright may bode well for Miller's future work. Perhaps toward the end of his career, Miller, like Shakespeare, may be able to combine his comic and tragic insights to create new plays in a tragicomic mode.

The Archbishop's Ceiling, produced at the Kennedy Center in Washington was not a success, has not been revived or published. Miller's new play, *The American Clock* should wed Miller's two dramatic structures, the family play and the panoramic play. Based in part on Studs Terkel's *Hard*

Times, an oral history of the Depression, *American Clock* will treat a family, probably much like the Franz family, painted against a panoramic treatment of the Depression. In an interview about *The American Clock* with Studs Terkel, Miller explained his technique concluding, "I've attempted a play about more than simply overheard voices in the dark. It's a story of the United States talking to itself."[14] Miller says as well in the interview that *The American Clock* "ends on a very positive note" and that it contains "cheerfulness" and "humor."[15] *The American Clock* may well show Miller having gone beyond the tragedy of the common man and the Shavian comedy of *The Creation* to find a new, perhaps tragicomic, style. It may show as well his mastery of the focussed plot structure inherited from Ibsen together with his mastery of the plot structure, perhaps inherited from Clifford Odets and Elmer Rice, that emphasizes a cross-section of society and a panoramic view. What is clear, however, in viewing the dramatic output of Arthur Miller from *After the Fall* to the present is that he is a playwright who has not stood still. He continues to develop new ideas as well as a new dramaturgy to convey them.

NOTES

1. Gerald Weales, "Arthur Miller's Shifting Image of Man," in *The American Theater Today*, ed. Alan S. Downer (New York: Basic Books, 1967), p. 98.

2. Ruby Cohn, *Dialogue in American Drama* (Bloomington: Indiana University Press, 1971), p. 90.

3. Harold Clurman, "Arthur Miller's Later Plays," In *Arthur Miller: A Collection of Critical Essays*, ed. Robert W. Corrigan (Englewood Cliffs: Prentice-Hall, 1969), p. 152.

4. See for example Benjamin Nelson, *Arthur Miller* (New York: David McKay Co., 1970), pp. 240–249.

5. Weales, p. 97.

6. "Foreword to *After the Fall*," *Saturday Evening Post*, 237 (Feb. 1, 1964), p. 32, rpt. in Robert A. Martin, ed., *The Theatre Essays of Arthur Miller* (Harmondsworth: Penguin Books, 1978), p. 257.

7. Arthur Miller, *After the Fall* (New York: Viking Press, 1964). All quotations are from this edition. Page numbers are indicated in parentheses.

8. A particularly good color reproduction appears in Phyllis Hartnoll, *The Concise History of the Theatre* (New York: Harry N. Abrams, n.d.), pp. 42–43.

9. Robert Brustein, *Seasons of Discontent* (New York: Simon & Schuster, 1967), p. 261.

10. Arthur Miller, *Incident at Vichy* (New York: Viking Press, 1965). All quotations are from this edition. Page numbers are indicated in parentheses.

11. Arthur Miller, *The Price* (New York: Bantam Books, 1968). All quotations are from this edition. Page numbers are indicated in parentheses.

12. See Rolf Högel, *"The Creation of the World and Other Business:* Arthur Millers Spekulationen über die Ursprünge des Bösen," *Literatur,* 12 (1979), 37–48.

13. Robert F. Moss, "Arthur Miller Reaches for Glory," *Saturday Review*, Sept., 1980, 22–23.

14. "Studs Terkel Talks with Arthur Miller," *Saturday Review*, Sept., 1980, 27.

15. *Ibid.,* 26.

Edward Albee:
Playwright of Evolution

KATHARINE WORTH

Albee is a playwright whose great distinctiveness is peculiarly hard to name and define. He has been claimed for the Absurdists and linked with Ionesco on the strength of his early plays, *The Zoo Story* (1958) and *The American Dream* (1960)[1]; comparisons with Strindberg have been prompted by his relish for comic/ferocious sex battles, as in *Who's Afraid of Virginia Woolf?* (1961); and his use of polite social rituals to convey psychological malaise has called up thoughts of T.S. Eliot and Noel Coward. He has strong affinities with some of his American predecessors, notably with the O'Neill of *Dynamo* and *Welded*, and with Thornton Wilder, who has the same feeling for the poignant brevity of human life and the rapid passing of generations. In *The Long Christmas Dinner* Wilder represents this by an accelerated ageing process: as the members of the family join and leave the endless Christmas dinner, they put on wigs from time to time to indicate their movement from one generation to another. Albee's use of a wig in *Tiny Alice* (1964) to conceal the youth of Miss Alice and then as adornment on a phrenological head, as Julian dies, makes a similar suggestion of instability and mortal change. At the end of that same play the Butler goes round the room placing dust covers over the furniture, a prelude to Julian's death. We could hardly fail to think of *Endgame* at such a moment — and Albee, no less than other major modern playwrights, shows his awareness of Beckett in many subtle echoes of this kind.

To be aware of these affinities and resemblances is not of course to diminish Albee[2]. On the contrary, whatever he takes he distils into a style which is entirely his own: no American playwright has a more distinctive voice. Its special quality comes partly from its ease in moving between an intellectual and an aggressively physical mode. Albee's characters usually belong to a well-to-do, educated middle class: typical is the Long Winded Lady in *Quotations from Chairman Mao Tse-Tung* (1968), described as 'very average and upper middle class. Nothing exotic, nothing strange'. We might question how 'average' she is in her reading tastes — Trollope and

Henry James — but my point is that this cultivated, literate lady is the sort of person Albee favours. He is the most intellectual and literary of American playwrights. But he combines the cerebral with an extraordinary emphasis on the physical. His characters talk with often outrageous candour about their sexual and bodily activities: we are never allowed to forget that we live in an animal world. His plays are full of animals, from the dogs, cats and parakeets of *The Zoo Story*, the 'little zoo', as Jerry mockingly describes them, to the talking lizards in *Seascape* (1975) who come on to land to join with a human couple in a symposium on the nature of human beings and animals. Like Jerry in *The Zoo Story* Albee seems inspired by the desire 'to find out more about the way people exist with animals, and the way animals exist with each other, and with people too'. He often uses people's relations with animals to measure their relation with each other and he can give a terrifying impression of the thin line dividing one world from the other, as when in *All Over* (1971) the Wife and Mistress relapse into animal fury, driving the newsmen out of the room, or in the same play, a woman who has had a mental collapse is said to have been sent 'spinning back into the animal brain'.

The seemingly comfortable position of his characters, their sophistication and self-consciousness, are useful to Albee, partly because he can quite naturally enrich the dialogue with the widely ranging cultural references and quotations his theme requires, partly because it allows him to 'disturb' his characters in interesting ways. Disturbance is above all Albee's theme, or as I am calling it 'evolution'. And it is that aspect of his drama I want to examine in this essay. He is an expert in contriving shocks and explosions to break up surfaces, façades, carapaces, and in so doing create new lines of direction. With increasingly fine instruments, as his art develops, he records what happens after these disturbances. Fine degrees of change, as well as spectacular ones, are recorded with the exactitude of a seismograph: it may be a collapse, as in *Listening* (1975) or a cataclysmic upheaval as in *Tiny Alice*, or a series of small adjustments resulting in the restoration of the status quo along with an almost imperceptible change as in *Who's Afraid of Virginia Woolf?* and *A Delicate Balance*. Albee himself sometimes talks so as to suggest his evolutionary interests. *The American Dream*, he said, was a 'stand against the fiction that everything in this slipping land of ours is peachy-keen'. The word 'slipping', so interestingly unexpected, surely suggests the sort of geophysical associations which underlie the intricate movements of Albee's dramatic action: earthquakes, tidal erosions, continents adrift.

When he was asked in 1968 what was the subject of his new play, Albee said he supposed it was about evolution.[3] The play, *Seascape*, does indeed give an impression of the great stretch of human evolution, opening with

the noise of jet planes screeching over the beach and ending, in one of
Albee's most endearing and poignant scenes, with the creatures who have
just come out of the sea contemplating their next movement:

NANCY:	You'll have to come back ... sooner or later. You don't have any choice. Don't you know that? You'll have to come back up.
LESLIE:	(*Sad smile*) Do we?
NANCY:	Yes!
LESLIE:	Do we have to?
NANCY:	Yes!
LESLIE:	Do we have to?
NANCY:	(*Timid*) We could help you, please?
LESLIE:	(*Anger and doubt*) How?
CHARLIE:	(*Sad, shy*) Take you by the hand? You've got to do it—sooner or later.
NANCY:	(*Shy*) We could help you.
	(*Leslie pauses; descends a step down the dune; crouches; stares at them*)
LESLIE:	(*Straight*) All right. Begin.

There is a wonderful ring to this 'begin'. It has some of the heroic
quality of the evolutionary drama of Shaw which is bound to come to mind
when one contemplates Albee's absorbed interest in human development.
Shaw's 'metabiological pentateuch', *Back to Methuselah*, begins in the
Garden of Eden and ends with a scene showing how human beings have
extended their life span indefinitely, and have become wise enough to win
the approval of the Life Force: 'And because these infants that call themselves ancients are reaching out towards that [i.e. wisdom], I will have
patience with them still; though I know well that when they attain it they
shall become one with me and supersede me ... '. This last play in the
pentateuch is called 'As Far as though can Reach'. Albee's characters
indulge a great deal in this kind of thinking, stretching their minds to
contemplate the future of the race as well as their own. The conversation of
Charlie and Nancy in *Seascape*—touching on everything from jet planes
and world travel to sex, ageing, mortality and the meaning of things—is
only one of many such dialogues where the characters' probing of themselves and each other opens up speculation on society and human life in
general. Albee is often thought of as a pessimistic playwright, and certainly
he depicts some pessimistic moods and situations, but there is a kind of
Shavian optimism all the same in the spirited energy his characters bring to
the contemplation of their own lives and to the puzzle of the world.

Albee's characters do not have much prospect of becoming supermen,
like the Ancients of *Back to Methuselah*, but in their anything-but Arca-

dian world they do succeed in making readjustments which change their own lives and may, he sometimes seems to hint, be contributing, if almost imperceptibly, to evolutionary change on a grander scale. Of course he is more interested in the dark undergrowth of his characters' psychology than Shaw; despite their wit and comic stylisations, his plays are often nearer to the tragic mood of O'Neill, the other American who shares with Albee and Shaw a preoccupation with the mysteries of evolution.

At its strongest, their urge to dramatise these mysteries drives them all into more or less fantastic modes which allow the non-human elements in the universe a vital role in the proceedings. Shaw has his talking snake in the Garden of Eden scene of *Back to Methuselah*, and in *Too True to be Good* the audience is addressed by a disgruntled microbe which, we are told, resembles a human being but in substance suggests 'a luminous jelly with a visible skeleton of short black rods'. O'Neill ends *The Hairy Ape* with a deathly encounter between man and ape in the zoo (anticipations here of *The Zoo Story*) and in *Dynamo* makes a destructive Mother Goddess out of electrical machinery. Similarly, Albee puts microcosm and macrocosm on stage in *Tiny Alice* and in *Seascape* brings out of the sea the creatures with unequivocal tails who identify themselves with such charming absurdity as Leslie and Sarah.

The function of Shaw's microbe is to draw attention to the wrong-headedness of human beings, the doctors, patients and fussy mothers who infect innocent microbes with measles and spoil their own lives by the unhealthy way they live them. Once the patient is set free from her genteel domestic prison by the anarchic Burglar her whole way of thinking changes totally, a change Shaw expresses through an instant physical change: in one scene a querulous girl wrapped up in blankets; in the next a beautiful animal, with hard, glistening muscles. The rebellious daughter eventually evolves to the point where she can accept her mother on terms which give them both an exhilarating new freedom. In the extraordinary last scene where one character after another is shown taking stock of his or her past life and making a choice for the future, the Elderly Lady announces her decision to change herself, move on to a different phase of evolution: 'The world is not a bit like what they said it was. I wasn't a bit like what they said I ought to be. I thought I had to pretend. And I needn't have pretended at all'.

This is very much the kind of activity Albee's characters are engaged in, a struggle to recognise what the world really is, what they really are and then to survive and evolve in the light of the knowledge they acquire or have thrust upon them. The aim is harder to realise in Albee's world than in Shaw's. Albee has in much higher degree a modern sense of the instability of the self, its lack of control over the deep movements of the psyche. There is certainly an abundance of strong-willed characters on his stage: we are always aware of the desperate will behind the 'fun and games' played out by Martha and George and the more deadly charades constructed by the unholy trio in *Tiny Alice*. But we are constantly aware too of the world beneath the will; the biological instincts, the subconscious, the many unknown forces that drive the human individual and the strange universe he finds himself in, along with all those animals. There is a much less strong illusion of mind controlling events than in the evolutionary comedy of Shaw or the evolutionary tragedy of O'Neill. The latter's battling characters often feel themselves driven in ways they cannot understand but they never really lose their heroic will; they retain a sense of purpose and meaning even when they are defeated, perhaps then most of all. Yet all three playwrights are linked by their fascination with the notion of tides sweeping men on to some unknown future and with their function as humans in a world which seems in a way better adjusted to animals, vegetables and inorganic elements. 'It was a great mistake, my being born a man', muses O'Neill's Edmund Tyrone in *Long Day's Journey into Night*, 'I would have been much more successful as a sea-gull or a fish'; while Shaw's Ancients in *Back to Methuselah* are steadily approaching the time when they will transmute themselves into a vortex of pure intelligence. One of the adolescents (newly born from an egg) puts the question, 'But if life is thought, can you live without a head?' 'Not now perhaps', replies the He-Ancient, 'But prehistoric men thought they could not live without tails. I can live without a tail. Why should I not live without a head?' The newly born then unwittingly helps to make the point by her innocent question, 'What is a tail?'; drawing from the Ancient a declaration of his evolutionary faith. The tail was a habit, no more, of which the human ancestors managed to cure themselves, and that is what must now happen with the whole body, the 'machinery of flesh and blood' which, he says, 'imprisons us on this petty planet and forbids us to range through the stars': men must free themselves from that tyranny and become the masters of matter, not its slaves.

Shaw plays with the evolutionary theme in witty argument, O'Neill uses it to fuel the tragic endeavours of his characters to rise above themselves and acquire heroic status. Albee incorporates it into the small change of life. The accidental, physical side of things looms much larger in his plays than in those of the other two: we hear more about the ordinary vicissitudes of the body, the 'machinery of flesh and blood'; in its various phases, health and illness, sexual excitement and frustration, need for procreation and disappointment in it, ageing and dying. Albee has really made himself the playwright of ageing: he studies with fascination the evolution of personality from one phase of life to another. He is interested in transitions and in the fineness of the line between different states of mind; between the vegetable and the animal, between real calm and the sinister quietness of malaise which is so often, in his plays, the stillness before the earthquake or the exhaustion following the after-shock when the troubled substance settles down again. He is acutely aware of the fragile equilibrium of the mind: no accident that one of his plays is called *A Delicate Balance*. His characters have this awareness too: they fear madness or question whether they are hallucinated. Often they really are 'disturbed' in the common modern sense of being mentally unstable or ill, liable to break down altogether as a result of some clinical condition, like the suicidal girl in *Listening*.

They also, however, need to be disturbed. The games they play, the social strategies they devise, are a form of self-protection but also a means—perhaps unconscious—of galvanising themselves into the new situations which almost always seem of impasse. Like O'Neill's Dion Anthony in *The Great God Brown*, Albee is interested in the sort of doubt and disturbance which enters into the system, a germ which 'wriggles like a question mark of insecurity, in [the] blood, because it's part of the creative life ...'.

In this drama of 'evolvings', death plays a major role. No playwright has paid more attention to the business of dying or to death as an ordinary part of life. In the early plays the deaths tend to be outrageous and symbolic; Grandma's playful exit with the Angel of Death in *The Sandbox* (1959), the ritual shooting of Julian in *Tiny Alice*. But in the later plays the focus is on more commonplace and quiet forms of dying, often protracted so that we are obliged to see this too as process, part of life's movement. 'Is he dead?' asks the Wife in *All Over*, as they sit and wait for the man to die (on stage but out of view). The Mistress refuses the expression, quoting the man himself on the inappropriateness of the verb to be to a state of non-being: 'one could be dying or have died...but could not...be...dead'. Language itself insists on death becoming an activity.

There are many different kinds of active death on Albee's stage. *All Over* shows us one kind. The dying man is in one way peculiarly helpless; until they brought him home from hospital he had been hooked up to a machine and was totally dependent on it for life. Looking at him, his wife conceived the strange fantasy that he had become part of the machine and that the machine had become organic, 'an octopus: the body of the beast, the tentacles electric controls, recorders, modulators, breath and heart and brain waves...'. For a moment it seemed to her that 'he was keeping it ... functioning. Tubes and wires'. The image is painful and shocking but it keeps the man not only in life but powerfully so. And it is a true image, for by the power of his personality he has brought these characters together and holds them to him with the tentacles of feeling; memory, grief, hostility, desire. They are 'hooked up' to him, as one critic has said, as irresistibly as he to the machine.

Though his dying is so active and we can tell that he will continue to inhabit the minds on the stage, the man ceases to breathe at the close of *All Over*. Other kinds of death on Albee's stage are more metaphorical, deaths which contribute to the making of lives. As one of the characters says, 'Goodness, we all died when we were thirty once'. There is the little death of sexual consummation, the death of feelings, the deaths of the selves discarded in moving from one stage of life to the next. Albee shows us some bleak 'little deaths' but his characters pick themselves up and begin again; 'Well, we can exist with anything, or without. There's little that we need to have to go on ... evolving'.

I want now to look at some of the methods Albee uses to show these 'evolvings', drawing on plays from different phases of his own evolution as a playwright.

Perhaps one of the most striking features of the early plays is Albee's youthful amazement at the difficulty of shaking people up, at their imperviousness to new thoughts or anything that might disturb their self-satisfaction. Along with this goes a profound feeling for the sense of loss and uncertainty which can be experienced in human relationships, especially the parent/child relationship. It is hard to avoid thinking of his own situation as an adopted child who has admitted to antagonistic feelings towards the natural parents who abandoned him at two weeks old. His achievement is to take up the personal distress into the dramatic structure of plays like *The American Dream* and use it to humanise the surrealist caricatures through which he satirises bourgeois complacency. What emerges in the end is a moment of good change, an 'evolving'. I want now to look at the working out of these changes in the first of his plays.

The satire in *The Sandbox* and *The American Dream*—the two plays in which Mommy, Daddy and Grandma figure—begins by being very funny, though with the touch of nightmare the theme of imperviousness requires. Mommy is the epitome of self-satisfaction. To poor browbeaten Daddy's choral comment 'That's the way things are today; you just can't get satisfaction; you just try', she replies with triumph, 'Well, I got satisfaction' and we can see she does. She dismisses anything likely to disturb her with the simple 'I won't think about it' and ruthlessly stamps on anyone who does not conform with her chosen way, as she has done, we are told in *The American Dream*, with the adopted child, 'the bumble of joy'. The horrific account of the dismemberment and castration of this child which is given by Grandma to the Young Man who appears out of the blue is the moment when the derisive glee aroused by the Ionesco-like stereotypes,

Mommy, Daddy and Mrs. Barker, turns into something more human and more deeply disturbing. What Grandma describes, in her dry, laconic style, as a far-off fabulous event, is felt by the Young Man as a real nightmare, somehow associated with his lost twin, or perhaps, other self: without knowing how it happened, he has felt himself drained, emasculated and hollow. Grandma and the Young Man are victims of Mommy and this remains the Young Man's function: physically perfect but inwardly hollow he is absorbed into the family as their American Dream. But Grandma has another role to play. She enlists his aid in her escape plan, and gathers together all her boxes, full of memories and dreams, and walks out on them, reappearing on the side of the stage, unseen by the dreadful family, to tell the audience:

> Well, I guess that just about wraps it up. I mean, for better or worse, this is a comedy, and I don't think we'd better go any further. No, definitely not. So, let's leave things as they are right now...while everybody's happy...while everybody's got what he wants...or everybody's got what he thinks he wants. Good night, dears.

What everybody thinks he wants is not perhaps what he would really want if he could be brought to understanding of himself, so Grandma implies. To be left with Mommy can be no happy ending for the Young Man, nor is there much prospect of happiness for Mommy with the 'clean-cut', midwest farm boy type, almost insultingly good-looking in a typically American way, as he detachedly describes himself. As for Grandma's exit, critics have been inclined to see this as a way of representing her death: reacting like the social worker, muddled Mrs. Barker, they feel incredulous about the possibility of a departure for a new life at her age: 'But old people don't go anywhere; they're either taken places, or put places.' Albee, however, corrects that view. Grandma dies, perhaps, but not in the usual sense: rather, he says, she moves 'out of the death within life situation that everybody else in the play was in'.[4] She takes her boxes with her, loaded with the past—'eighty six years of living...some sounds...a few images'— but she has a lively sense of the future too, as her delighted reaction to the handsome young man suggests. 'Well, now, aren't you a breath of fresh air!', she says, and 'Yup...yup. You know, if I were about a hundred and fifty years younger I could go for you'. 'Yes, I imagine so', he spiritlessly replies, pointing up the sad difference between the young man who has become fixed in a deadly stereotype and the old lady who is still, despite all expectations, 'evolving'.

Evolution is a more painful matter in *The Zoo Story*. The complacent bourgeois here is not a monstrous caricature like Mommy, but a mild, well-mannered, believable man who attracts considerable sympathy for the plight he finds himself in: accosted while enjoying a quiet read, on a bench in Central Park on Sunday afternoon, by a youthful version of the Ancient Mariner looking for someone to listen to his story. The unwelcome apparition begins without preamble, 'MISTER, I'VE BEEN TO THE ZOO' and then proceeds to force on his reluctant auditor elaborate stories about squalid encounters with his landlady who pesters him with her 'foul parody of sexual desire' and with her dog, a 'black monster of a beast'.

Jerry is an alarming figure, sardonic and intense. When he says later in the play, as he drives Peter on, 'I'm crazy, you bastard,' we must wonder whether it is not in fact so. In the end he kills himself in a peculiarly whimsical way, forcing the unfortunate Peter to defend his place on the bench by thrusting a knife into his hand as a weapon, and then running on to it. Yet his is the perspective that triumphs. Though Jerry is clearly in a process of breakdown, it is equally clear that Peter is too undisturbed. He shares something with Mommy after all: despite, or because of, his interest in fiction as ordinary reader and as professional publisher, he finds it hard to face the harsh realities of life. His reaction to Peter's horrific tale of his landlady is to shrink away: 'It's so ... unthinkable. I find it hard to believe that people such as that really are.' 'It's for reading about?' asks Jerry. He is mocking but Peter takes it seriously. 'Yes', he says.

He has to be jolted out of this inability to imagine the plight of others — 'what other people need', in Jerry's phrase; Jerry's object from the start is to force him into a vital relationship. All this can be seen (and partly has to be) in psychological terms, simply as the effort of a lonely, suicidal outcast to find someone to really listen to him, and perhaps gain the impetus to finish himself off. But Albee takes pains to stress the biological and evolutionary aspects of the action. The two contrasting lives are expressed partly through their situation vis-à-vis animals. Peter is seemingly master of an orderly world where cats and two parakeets fit into a tidy scheme of things along with two daughters. The fact that he has no son and knows that he will have no more children is a flaw in the biological perfection which comes to the surface under the pressure of his encounter with Jerry. Jerry on the other hand seems unable to draw any line between the human and the animal world: dog and landlady equally rouse his loathing. We are made to think about what it is to be human by Jerry's emphasis on the hierarchy of evolution. The well-adjusted Peter is in Jerry's view no more than a vegetable: this is the insult he flings at him when goading him into defending his park bench (and by implication, of course, his way of life). The two men fight over territory like beasts — Jerry's dying scream 'must be the sound of an infuriated and fatally wounded animal' — and when Peter is at last enraged enough to fight he is paid the compliment, '... You're not really a vegetable; it's all right, you're an animal. You're an animal too'.

It is the highest term of praise the action allows, for both these characters are found imperfect in terms of the human culture they both in their different ways aspire to. Jerry is the more imaginative but he has found it impossible to establish a relationship with anyone, dog or human: hating and loving all end up as indifference. His efforts are admirable and pathetic: he is trying to climb the evolutionary ladder, one might say, when he confides in Peter, 'If you can't deal with people, you have to make a start somewhere. WITH ANIMALS!' But he also has to be seen as an evolutionary failure, who falls out of the system. In his death he provokes Peter into a livelier awareness of 'others': this is presented as an achievement of a kind, which takes some of the depressing futility out of his life. Whether we can place much confidence on Peter's ability to advance as a human being is another question, but he has been given the chance: it is a moment of evolutionary choice.

The next two plays I want to consider form a 'pair' in the sense that the earlier two did, offering strikingly contrasting treatments of a similar theme. *Who's Afraid of Virginia Woolf?* operates within the naturalistic convention, though with a degree of stylisation which extends its possibilities. *Tiny Alice* on the other hand is a much more arcane piece which trumpets its symbolism from the start and indeed could hardly be interpreted on any but a symbolic level.

Yet there is one striking affinity between the two plays. In each we must be struck by the remarkably elaborate nature of the preparations for the drastic change we feel preparing from the start: in one play it is a next step in the evolution of a relationship, in the other in an individual consciousness. In each play too there is a strong element of consciously histrionic performance. Martha and George act out their most intimate feelings in bold, exaggerated form for the startled benefit of their naive audience, the younger couple who seem to understand nothing of what is really going on until the very end. And in *Tiny Alice* the conspirators who change Julian's life flaunt their acting ability throughout, from Miss Alice's bravura impersonation of an old woman in her first meeting with Julian to the thoroughly professional 'blocking' of the death scene from a scenario the performers evidently know by heart and have played many times. As in a permanent ensemble company, they even take it in turns to play the lead: Butler and Lawyer have no names, only functions (though Butler claims to derive his function from his name) and they both give orders to and take them from Miss Alice, whose servant/lovers they are.

What is the purpose of all this play-acting? In each play it is implied that a momentous psychic change is under way: something that has been gathering in the unconscious has reached a level of intensity that forces it out into the conscious, where it has to find theatrical form for expression, since it does not really belong in the world it has invaded. One part of the mind is acting another part, one might say.

The differences of form between the two plays relate to the difference in the balance of conscious and unconscious elements. George and Martha have a pretty shrewd understanding of their own and the other's mental processes. This 'sensitive and intelligent couple', as Albee calls them[5], have lived together for so long that they can interpret pretty well every move in the games they play to exorcise their daemons. They share a language rich in private jokes, quotation and allusion, as they demonstrate at the start when they come home, rather drunk, and laughing, at two in the morning and go straight into one of their double acts. 'What a dump', says Martha, looking round, and, to George:

MARTHA: ... 'What a dump'! Huh? What's that from?
GEORGE: I haven't the faintest idea what ...
MARTHA: Dumbbell! It's from some goddamn Bette Davis picture ... some goddamn Warner Brothers epic ...
GEORGE: I can't remember all the pictures that ...
MARTHA: Nobody's asking you to remember every single goddamn Warner Brothers epic ... just one! One single little epic! Bette Davis gets peritonitis in the end ... She's got this big black fright wig she wears all through the picture and she gets peritonitis, and she's married to Joseph Cotten or something ...
GEORGE: ... Some**body** ...
MARTHA: Some**body** ... and she wants to go to Chicago all the time, 'cos she's in love with that actor with the scar ...

George comes up with the answer: **'Chicago!** It's called **Chicago.'** 'Good grief! Don't you know **anything?'** she taunts him, **'Chicago** was a 'thirties musical, starring little Miss Alice **Faye**. Don't you know **anything?'** But he wins the round, taking the opening she gives him to get in a customary tart reminder of their respective ages: *Chicago* was probably before his time. Every conversational movement, even the effort to remember an old film, affords them opportunities for the marital argument they both understand so well. Albee points up their high degree of self-awareness by contrast with the young guests, Honey and Nick, who are at the opposite extreme, quite without self-knowledge and very much out in the cold altogether: the audience is presumably a few steps ahead of them in their struggles to catch the true drift of the caustic, funny and eliptical conversations between George and Martha.

In *Tiny Alice* the balance is the other way. The point here is that Julian does not understand himself. Among characters who are nothing but function, he alone has none: he is a lay brother, committed to the celibacy of a priest but without a priest's power. He is in a kind of limbo, not knowing which of his experiences are real, unlike George and Martha who know their imagined child is a fantasy (though that does not prevent them from thinking of him sometimes as real). Julian is much more confused: he is at the mercy of something he does not understand when he comes to the castle to be 'brought up' to Miss Alice. The first thing he does there, despite his conscious intention, is to confide in the Butler the traumatic tale of his six years' lapse of faith, when he had himself voluntarily committed to a mental institution. And the next is to confess to Miss Alice, at the moment of first meeting how, in that confused period, he had a sexual experience of great strangeness and intensity which he does not know whether to think of as dream, hallucination or reality. He lost his virginity, so it seemed, with a woman patient who imagined herself the immaculate Mother of God—but what she was bearing in her womb was a cancer. The dream, if such it was, is to be acted out in a new form with Miss Alice. It is as if he were meeting his own unconscious, in the romantically confused and sinister forms imposed by his imagination. The three who manage the machine (to borrow a phrase from Eliot's *The Cocktail Party*, a play with some obvious resemblances to *Tiny Alice*) make it clear enough that they in their turn are controlled from some other dimension. Miss Alice refers to herself as a 'surrogate' for the Miss Alice who resides in the model and the model itself is a perpetual reminder that the action is being conducted on more than one level. It stands there throughout, a man-sized replica of the castle, lighting up from time to time in its different rooms, following—or perhaps initiating—changes of location in the macrocosm. Albee had planned to have Julian bound to the model in the death scene; in the event he was made only to collapse against it, but the point is made, that in the end nothing but this would be left to him.

The process of effecting change is difficult, in one play because of the middle age of the characters, in the other because of immaturity. In *Who's Afraid of Virginia Woolf?* it seems at first as though there could be no breaking out of the fixed pattern of life George and Martha have established over many years: she is in her fifties, he is somewhat younger. Yet into their tired rituals—weariness is a feature of the proceedings—Albee artfully manages to insert growth points. Martha breaks the rules of the marital game by speaking to someone in the outside world of their fantasy son: she takes the young wife upstairs, confides in her, and then remains behind, disconcertingly, to change her clothes. George senses what this might mean. He dissuades the young couple from leaving, as they embarrassedly feel they should:

> Oh no, now...you mustn't. Martha is changing...and Martha is
> not changing for me. Martha hasn't changed for me in years. If
> Martha is changing, it means we'll be here for...days.

It is the experience not of days but of years that is packed into the remaining small hours: George destroys the son who never was and perhaps in doing so frees himself from the obsessive dream or memory of a murderous relation between son and father which he tells of in the form of a story and seems to relate in some way to his own past. We cannot be sure of this, but there is a sense of relief as well as sadness in the ending. Perhaps Martha, despite all her bluster, knew at some deep level, as George does, that the change had to come. As he says, 'It was...time'. She receives the verdict with doubt and apprehension, but still, it is clear, with a readiness to move on with him to a new stage in their marriage: there has been an 'evolving' and it was necessary.

In *Tiny Alice* the difficulties are more obscure but are clearly to do with Julian's immaturity. At one point of his adventure, Julian muses about the possibility of avoiding experience:

> What may we avoid! Not birth! Growing up? Yes. Maturing?
> Oh, God! Growing old, and?... yes, growing old; but not the
> last; merely when.

In his proud demand for abstract perfection he shrinks from life, refuses procreation (except in dreams), resists the idea of God in man's image, although it is the idea on which his Church rests. 'Don't you teach your people anything?', sneers the Lawyer to the Cardinal. He has to unlearn his certainties, learn to know, as the Lawyer says, that 'We do not know. Anything'. He has to be 'brought up' to Miss Alice: the sexual/religious punning, like everything in the play, contradicts his idea that man can separate God from nature. In embracing Alice he accepts mortality (always implicit in the beauty of the flesh) and perhaps too the mystery he rejects: at the moment when they come together, she stretches out arms enclosed in very full sleeves so that the effect is of enfolding him 'in her great wings'.

Julian's is a martyrdom of a kind. The 'agents' leave, their work done, Alice telling him she is 'the illusion', the Lawyer counselling him to resign himself to the mysteries. Like the man in the story from which Albee said the play was derived (he was imprisoned in a room inside another room), Julian is left to die by the model, unable to tell whether he is in microcosm or macrocosm. The model is a world without human figures in it and it is a horror. 'THERE IS NO ONE THERE', he calls in agony: the flesh and blood Alice is what he needs, after all. Some critics have taken this to be the moral of the piece; Julian, for them, is forcibly converted by secular evangelists who have proved to him sardonically that there is no world other than that experienced by the senses. That would be, however, to destroy the insistent ambiguity which is surely meant to convey something quite different, the necessity for symbols. As Miss Alice puts it, 'We must ... represent, draw pictures, reduce or enlarge to ... to what we can understand.'

And is there another dimension? In the play it is inescapable. Butler, Lawyer and Alice all assume it: the Lawyer is sarcastic about 'the mouse in the model' but he also promises Alice in the model, with 'no sarcasm', Albee says: 'You will have your Julian'. And Alice prays to the model to save the chapel when it seems in danger of burning down. 'Don't destroy!', she cries, and 'Let the resonance increase'. Though Julian cries in his agony 'THERE IS NO ONE THERE', yet as he dies we see on the empty stage lights descending the staircase of the model and 'the shadow of a great presence filling the room', while exaggerated heartbeats are heard. Audiences were inclined to rationalise these as Julian's own, but Albee has said that he expected people to think of this 'enormous' sound that engulfs Julian either as his hallucination or as the personification of an abstract force. There is no way of resolving the ambiguity. That is the painful truth Julian has to learn and the learning is an advance in maturity; he dies in the attitude of crucifixion—which in the religious imagery of the play must imply the possibility of resurrection. Though so cryptic and in many ways unpleasant and distasteful, the process has to be seen, I think, as evolution rather than catastrophic collapse.

The next play I want to consider, *A Delicate Balance*, draws into a new pattern threads from earlier plays. Again, as in *The Zoo Story*, animals are used to measure degrees of refinement in human consciousness. Tobias' story about the cat he grew to hate because it became indifferent to him tells us much about his self-mistrust: when Claire wants to convey the reality of her sordid experience as an alcoholic, she describes it as becoming more like an animal every day (to be an animal in this play is to go down in the evolutionary hierarchy). The structure resembles that of *Virginia Woolf*; a conversation among married couples (with complications in the form of a sister and daughter) goes on and on, with the aid of drink, through the hours of two nights, ending with breakfast, still intermixed with drinking, on the third day. As in *Virginia Woolf*, the talk is confessional in a thoroughgoing American style which makes one wonder how there could be anything left unrevealed, how indeed there could be any real movement or change. The play opens with Agnes confiding in Tobias her suspicion that she might one day go out of her mind and moves on to Tobias' confession to Claire that he had killed (or 'put down' as she softens it) the cat which grew to dislike him. Other more commonplace revelations come thick and fast; the whole idea of the confessional is indeed parodied in Claire's self-mocking account of how she rose to make a grand public confession at a meeting of Alcoholics Anonymous and turned it into bathos. 'I am Claire and I am a alcoholic', she said in her little girl's voice, then sat down.

These confessions are too easy, too familiar a feature of their daylight world. Albee wants to move in on the night, that limbo where thoughts are struggling out from the unconscious and the anxieties lie deeper, are kept closer. He brings this about by a brilliant invention, the arrival of Harry and Edna, the twin couple to Agnes and Tobias, their best friends, whose lives are 'the same'. These two have left their own home because they became frightened—of what they cannot say. They can only repeat: 'WE WERE FRIGHTENED ... AND THERE WAS NOTHING'. The scene of their arrival is comic in its lack of explanation and childlike suddenness, as when Edna says 'Can I go to bed now? Please?'. But they have brought into the house a disturbing sense of generalised anxiety relating to fears of darkness, nothingness and death. At the end of the play Edna articulates the unlocalised dread: 'It's sad to come to the end of it, isn't it, nearly the end, so much more of it gone by ... than left.' Under the pressure of this unease they all experience a revelation of their limits and breaking points. Agnes brings up from the abyss a misery she was not able to voice at the start, the memory of the time when her son died and Tobias refused her another child. She lay at night pleading, 'Please? Please, Tobias? No, you wouldn't even say it out: I don't want another child, another loss'.

Through it all runs a helpless longing to be safe and at home: the much married daughter hysterically claims her girlish room; Harry and Edna settle into it, like cuckoos in the nest. Yet changes occur, despite the characters' efforts to resist them: perhaps they occur because of that. Both married couples return perforce to the single room they had given up, Agnes expressing the shy hope that it may not be simply a temporary change: an elegiac tribute is paid to the sexuality that is leaving them. Various adjustments of feeling are made among the individuals in the group and finally Tobias, by enormous effort of will, looks at himself and forces himself to come out with an honest statement to the 'best friend' who has come to him for succour:

I DON'T WANT YOU HERE!
I DON'T LOVE YOU!
BUT BY GOD ... YOU STAY!

A deep obligation, running underneath all questions of personality, is faced and acknowledged under pressure of the night fears, the 'plague' that Harry and Edna have brought with them. Daylight returns, the intruders depart and Agnes is left contemplating what has happened—'They say we sleep to let the demons out'—and preparing to return to normal: 'Come now; we can begin the day'. Some critics have found this ending sentimental but there is no reason why it should have to be so taken: the tone is dry, matter-of-fact: the 'day' has its own problems, as we have seen. Beginning it again is all that can be done—yet the play makes us feel respect for the human resilience which allows for these routine adjustments.

In the plays that follow *A Delicate Balance* there is less room for radical changes of situation. The emphasis is on another kind of evolution, the development of finer understanding. Increasingly the characters watch and listen to each other with the sort of care and detachment described by Tobias when he tells Agnes of his reverie in the small hours: 'look at it all, reconstruct, with such...detachment, see yourself...look at it all...play it out again, watch'. The style becomes increasingly delicate and oblique as Albee moves closer to the concept of 'static' drama most famously enunciated by Maeterlinck in his plea for recognition of the dramatic interest in an old man sitting in the lamplight[6]. Maeterlinck is indeed referred to in *All Over*, where the Mistress tells us that he was once a topic of conversation for her lover, the man now dying. It is an appropriate reference for a play so Maeterlinckian in its situation—waiting for death—but in the other plays too Maeterlinck is brought to mind, especially by the musicality which becomes so marked a feature of the dramatic structure. In *Box* and *Quotations from Chairman Mao Tse-Tung* (1968) Albee makes a point of his concern with the 'the application of musical forms to dramatic structure': he explains in his introduction that he has notated the dialogue on musical lines with an exceptionally precise use of punctuation, commas, semicolons and so on, with stage directions, with devices such as capitalising and italicising.

We have to listen exceptionally hard to follow this intricate dialogue, with its mesh of half-finished allusions, quotations, ambiguous sayings, ironies and fugue-like repetitions. It seems natural that in this phase of his art Albee should produce a play for radio called simply *Listening* (1975). Characters at this time tend to lose their names and be represented by function, like notes in music. The Wife amusingly calls attention to this phenomenon in *All Over* when she demands of Mistress, 'Me! Wife! Remember?'

Box and *Chairman Mao* are the first two plays constructed on Albee's new musical principle. They were written separately and can be so performed, Albee says, though surely he must be right in finding them more effective when 'enmeshed'.

The action of *Box* involves only a view of a box, or cube, and a Voice reflecting on it: the reflections widen out into a Jungian stream-of-consciousness which opens up beyond the personal life into 'the memory of what we have not known'. Throughout runs a theme of decline and loss—in art and craft (no one could make such a box now), in social responsibility (milk deliberately spilt when children are starving), and in understanding. Continually Voice returns to the sense of direction in art and the pain it can cause by contrast with loss of direction in life: 'When art hurts. That is what to remember'. Finally human artefacts and ideas give way to a vision of the sea, with birds skimming over it and only the sound of bell buoys in the fog to remind us of human presence.

When the second play begins, the outline of the box is still visible, creating the impression that the thoughts we now hear are taking place within the other consciousness: everything flows into and out of that empty space. The leading character in *Chairman Mao*, the Long-Winded Lady, is haunted by a memory she cannot assimilate, of falling into the sea from the deck of an ocean liner (such as she is now travelling on) after the death of her much-loved husband. The play ends with her repetition of the questions she was asked: 'that I may have done it on purpose?...thrown myself off?' Then, in one of Albee's delicate punctuation hints, she drops the question mark, turns 'tried to kill yourself' into a statement she has to deal with herself and arrives at the sad conclusion: 'Good heavens, no; I have nothing to die for'.

With her thoughts (they are supposedly voiced to a totally silent auditor, a Minister, who gives her no comfort) are interwoven the thoughts of two others. The Old Woman also tells a sad story of family loss, but in the more distant form of a poem, Will Carleton's ballad, 'Over the Hills to the Poor-House'. And in contrast to this limited personal view of history come the vast assertions of Chairman Mao proclaiming the class war and calling for revolution. The three lines of thought are separate but occasionally touch; the Old Woman nods approvingly from time to time when Mao refers to the hard life of the poor, but she also indicates silent sympathy with the unhappiness of the upper class lady. Mao's optimistic political simplifications are both reinforced and undermined by the experiences conveyed in the women's thoughts. His thoughts are crude and bracing, providing a strong upward thrust, a necessary counterpoint to the pessimism of Voice in *Box*. He does indeed at one point use an image of her kind. It is not a bad but a good thing, he says, that China's six hundred million people are 'poor and blank' because poverty stimulates the desire for change and 'on a blank sheet of paper free from any marks, the freshest and most beautiful characters can be written'.

Of course there is irony in this: the image of the box perpetually filling up with inherited and fresh thoughts tells us that there is no such thing as a 'blank' human character. Still, even if it is an illusion, there is a need for the dream of 'beginning again'. Even the Long-Winded Lady feels it: whimsically she pictures herself 'falling up!' and reflects that 'One never returns from a voyage the same'. There is a suggestion of an 'evolving' here, and certainly there is an antidote to the emptiness portrayed by Voice in the complex texture of consciousness woven by the voices. When they die away, the light comes up again upon the empty box and we return to the Voice's elegy, to the contemplation of the painful beauty of a partita and the mystery of those memories we did not know we had. Voice reminds us that she could recognise the sound of bell buoys in the fog though she had never seen the sea: 'Landlocked, never been, and yet the sea sounds ... '. It is with the miracle of the sea that the play ends and with the sense of mysterious direction: the birds are flying all in one direction, in 'a black net', only one 'moving beneath ... in the opposite way'. What may be the direction for human evolution? This is Albee's large theme. He makes it dramatically gripping through his mastery of form and his ability to interest us in the small changes and in the real lives of his people; even in the disembodied or fragmented shape which is all they have in this play, they come through as vivid personalities.

As so often, we can see in these two plays the germ of the next one. The Long-Winded Lady sees one prospect of comfort: she might be able to forget the bitter detail of her husband's last illness; perhaps it is 'all over'. The phrase provides the title for the next play, *All Over* (1971), which explores the impact of a death about to happen on the five people closest to the dying man. We go in and out of their thoughts and memories in a pattern of engagement and disengagement which is something they have been painfully conscious of in their past lives. The Wife has been separated from her husband for thirty years and is alienated from the Daughter, seems indeed to be on better terms with the Mistress. The Mistress, though treated as a friend, is disengaged from them all and yet it is she who can best tell them about the phases in the dying man's withdrawal from life, the 'faint shift from total engagement'. The mood is one of 'languor' and exhaustion. The stories they tell to fill in the time of waiting tend to turn on various kinds of dying, including the sort of death which is to do with feeling: the Wife tells of a woman who died when she was twenty-six, 'died in the heart that is, or in whatever portion of the brain contains the spirit'.

A paradox develops. The little life the man has left is the source from which they draw: they are fired by him; and as they talk of him and more of their past life pours out, they become deeply and bitterly engaged with each other. There are moments of understanding and of violent hostility, till at last the Wife, looking into the landscape of the future, abandons her calm and acknowledges her need to 'feel something'. 'I'm waiting to' she says, and 'I have no idea what I'm storing up. You make a lot of adjustments over the years, if only to avoid being eaten away'. The cool politeness she has observed with the Mistress drops away, she accuses her: 'You've usurped'. And though she immediately apologizes, the frustration of thirty years at last erupts. 'I LOVE MY HUSBAND', she calls out in pain and in relief: we have an impression of parched land being flooded. Then it is, as we hear the doctor saying, 'All over'. But for the people waiting everything goes on; Albee has made us feel, through the unease of their conversational adjustments, something of the effort involved in that simple 'going on': it is an achievement.

Albee has commented that after a certain age arthritis of the mind sets in and 'change becomes impossible finally.' No sign of this with him: his later plays continue to show his own capacity to 'evolve'. In *Listening* and *Counting the Ways* (1976) he interestingly applied a vaudeville method — laconic, quick-firing cross talk and scenes punctuated by signs descending from the flies or a voice counting — to very different material, creating in one play a deeply sombre, in the other a genial, high-spirited mood. *Listening* was written for radio: it is about the need to listen and the difficulty of doing so. In the grounds of a one-time mansion, now a mental institution, by a dried up fountain, two of the staff, a Woman and a Man, meet to explore each other — and the Girl who is the Woman's charge — through strange, intense talk, weighing words, testing nuances. The Girl has slipped half out of the human world; she reacts, we are told, like an animal, tensing and sensing her surroundings, then 'humanising' intermittently. 'You don't listen', she complains, 'Pay attention, rather, is what you don't do'. 'I listen', says the Woman, 'I can hear your pupils widen'. But she does not pay the attention the Girl needs; she and the Man abstract themselves, pursuing sexual memories they may or may not have shared, while the Girl takes her chance to find some broken glass and cut her wrists. Her last words are: 'Then ... you don't listen'. She is an evolutionary failure, arousing pity and giving a dark colouring to the struggle — experienced in a bitter-sweet way by the other two — of listening to others in a fully human way.

In *Counting the Ways* also, a couple cross-question each other, listening hard for the implications in every reply. But this time the mood is happy, even though strains and small shocks occur. The play begins with her asking, 'Do you love me?' and ends with him answering that he does and then asking the question of her. In between, they count the ways — as in the poem from which the play takes its title, 'How do I love thee? Let me count the ways.' Whole phases of married life are traversed in a series of swift duologues: they count the petals of a rose, ask of each other en passant 'How many children do we have?', move into a new stage when she remarks of the roses that they should be in a vase on the table between their beds and there is a double-take before he realises the implications. 'When did that happen?' he asks, in comic anguish, and later, 'When did our lovely bed . . . split and become two?' 'Well, it happens sooner or later,' she says, and then, soothing him, 'Maybe we'll be lucky and it won't go any further'. He is left reeling from the impact of a new shock — 'separate rooms'. But he picks himself up again. Despite the charming lightness of touch, the preoccupations are as serious as in *Listening*; all feelings are fragile and uncertain. When he asks 'Do you love me?' at the close, her 'I think I do' is a curtain line which leaves everything open: nothing can be done about the fragility of life.

The subsequent variation on the marriage theme, *Seascape,* opens with a similar marital cross-questioning act. Nancy and Charlie, lazing on the beach, are involved in one of Albee's typical stock-taking sequences — current state of feeling, hazy plans for the future now their children are grown up. It is the evolution of a marriage, treated in a gently, bantering naturalistic style. Then suddenly it widens out, through the alarming, only half-comic arrival of the animal couple, into a view of the whole of human evolution, seen entirely in terms of what these well-meaning intelligent but limited, groping individuals can make of it.

It is one of Albee's most touching moments when the animals achieve realisation of what it means to be human through learning of death, which must one day separate them from each other. 'I want to go back', wails Sarah, 'I don't want to stay here any more. I want to go back'. But there is no going back. The play ends with the creatures recognising this and preparing, with the aid of those of a little further on the way, to take the great evolutionary step: 'All right. Begin'.

It is a heroic assertion, unusual for our times, of faith in the capacity of human beings to learn from each other and evolve in good ways. And although nothing is more certain than that he will strike out in a different direction with other plays, this must all the same be a particularly appropriate point to conclude a discussion of Albee as the playwright of evolution.

NOTES

1. As C. W. E. Bigsby, *Albee* (Edinburgh: Oliver and Boyd, 1969), p. 16 points out, this claim has been exaggerated: "Critic after critic has tried to force Albee into the theatre of the absurd."

2. Some critics have thought otherwise. Robert Brustein, for instance, in *Seasons of Discontent* (New York: Simon and Schuster, 1965), p. 308, makes pejorative reference to Albee's "theatrical echo chamber." The charge is refuted by Ruby Cohn in her *Edward Albee* (Minneapolis: University of Minnesota Press, 1969).

3. Interview with M. E. Rutenberg in *Edward Albee* (New York: DBS Publications, 1969), p. 257.

4. *Ibid.*, p. 236.

5. *Ibid.*, p. 230.

6. The passage occurs in "The Tragical in Daily Life," an essay in Maeterlinck's *The Treasure of the Humble*, London 1897 (first edition, in French, Brussels 1896).

Arthur Kopit:
Dreams and Nightmares

JÜRGEN WOLTER

With Arthur Lee Kopit another American playwright has found his way from Harvard Square to Broadway. Before him, such well-known dramatists as Anderson, Barry, Sheldon, Sherwood and, most important of all, O'Neill travelled this path, providing an ancestry sufficient to burden any young playwright and at the same time a reason why Kopit should not be assessed from this perspective but rather within the context of contemporary American theater. Although only nine of the more than twenty plays he has written to date are available in print,[1] these are evidence enough to rank him among the best American playwrights of the 1960's and 1970's. They give us an adequate picture of his art and of his dominant themes and techniques. On closer inspection, they show a strong coherence in their subject matter: in almost all of his published plays to be analyzed in this article Kopit is concerned with an individual's interior landscape and the question of his identity; the protagonist's visionary self-portrait is tested and exposed as a fallacious dream which, revealing his true soul, turns into an apocalyptic nightmare.

Kopit called *The Questioning of Nick* (1957) "the only realistic play I have written", and on the surface this is certainly true. The basketball player Nick Carmonatti is subjected to a police interrogation, which, however, is only superficially concerned with penal offences, i.e. with the question whether Nick brutally wounded his fellow player Stanikowski and whether he accepted money for throwing a game. Less superficially, the play questions Nick's personality. He is extremely egocentric; proudly but ambiguously he boasts: "I'm the center on the team" (p. 44)[2]. His egocentricity determines his behavior during the interrogation and leads to his exposure and failure. Whenever the policemen pretend to have lost their interest in him, he is desperate to reattract their attention and abandons all caution and cunning. When, e.g., Carling wants to send him home, because he is not only "a big, big nothing" (p. 52) in his team but even useless as an informer to the police, Nick has to fight back his tears; in this moment of self-realization he has to acknowledge his weakness and failure, and he is willing to cooperate and give evidence. In the light of his egocentricity, however, one rightly doubts the truth of his statement; it is more probable that he only wants to grasp his last chance to triumph. But even his desire to have at least a grand exit, to be jailed as the gang leader and hero is not fulfilled. He remains a harmless braggart, who grossly overestimates his importance even in his confession, which turns out to be a self-commendation, since he would like to make the policemen—and himself—believe that he was the "one and only" who pulled the strings:

> I threw the game.... I was the guy who got paid.... I'm the only one that ever got paid.... I'm the guy who thought up the Black Angels!... I busted 'em up.... I'm the only one in this town that got into *Sport Magazine*. (p. 53)

The dream of his importance and influence does not stand the test of reality. He is a cheat, imposter, and a rowdy. Thus, in the course of the cross-examination he reveals not his guilt but his true inner self. Just when he wants to demonstrate his glory ("I'm gonna show ya how stupid you guys are" [p. 53]), he proves himself the biggest of failures. The dream of his greatness turns into the nightmare of his futility, so that he can only stare "in horror" (p. 54) at the open door to the world outside, the door which he has slammed in his own face. One can be sure that he will not leave the room, because outside, face to face with the gang, he would now feel the nightmare all the more. The self-made hero has deceived himself and is paralyzed by the revelation of his soul.

Thus, even this supposedly realistic drama demonstrates Kopit's art of progressing from a matter-of-fact surface to the depiction of an inner landscape; from a seemingly objective reality to the subjective dreams and individual conceptions which constitute the life and truth of his protagonists. The merging of these two levels is the central concern in all of Kopit's plays.

If *The Questioning of Nick* is Kopit's most realistic play, *Sing to Me Through Open Windows* (1959, rev. 1965) can justifiably be called his most surrealistic work. The probably adolescent Andrew Linden dreams of a visit he, as a boy, pays an ex-magician. The framework structure makes clear that the visit is only a vision, i.e. that the action takes place in the subconscious of the dreaming Andrew Linden. The dream dramatizes the fall of an aging magician, Ottoman, who cannot accept the loss of his youth and art; he shrinks back from the recognition of his true situation and continually waits for spring, that is to say, for a recovery of his power and public appeal. For a long time, the boy's visit does not effect any change in his mood of resignation, and Ottoman is unable to establish contact with this visitor from an outside world which he observes through the windows with eager eyes but which at the same time he wants to shut out from his microcosm. In his talk with the boy he is either "not conscious of the boy's presence" (p. 65) or stares blankly out of a window, the contrast between his age and isolation and the boy's youth causing him to reconsider his life and to search for some elixir through which he might regain his past magic. He hopes to find it in telling stories about times and places "fabulous beyond your wildest dreams" (p. 65) and, for a brief moment, again experiences his former strength and personality as "Ottoman the Great, Master Magician: Man of a Thousand Disguises, Man of a Thousand Tricks" (p. 66). But all his tricks somehow fail, and he has to admit: "I am vanishing" (p. 68). His partner, the clown, is eager to take over, but his tricks, too, are more or less unsuccessful. Finally Ottoman is convinced that the search for his past greatness is futile, and he sends the boy home despite the latter's wish to stay. This, and the fact that he is now able to put his arm round the boy, signifies that at the end of the visit, which is at the end of the dream, he has come to accept his situation. In this way, the inner conflict between youth and age, past and future, life and death is solved. He asks the clown to close the windows and withdraws into his isolated microcosm, where he dies. However, he does not vanish from this visionary dream without revealing his inner feelings: "Fear is like regret. Only with fear there's not much time left", and: "all my life it was someone else, standing there in the dark, watching me ... and laughing". (p. 76) All his life he had been out of contact with the people around him and afraid of failing. Regretting the loss of his past youth, he at the same time feared the uncertain and, as he thought, brief future. If we take into account the fact that in our dreams we furnish the landscape of our soul with images of our feelings, the magician could well be a personification of Andrew Linden's subconscious, his regrets and fears. Linden, in a personality crisis and afraid of failure, craves for somebody who, as a messenger from the outside, sings a song of spring, of life and encouragement to him. He opens the window and is eager to listen. In his dream Andrew Linden has a vision of his greatness (here for him "the impossible is the commonplace" [p. 66]), but also experiences the death of his magic and personality. This certainly is a nightmare.

Kopit here stretches the possibilities of the stage to its limit. He presents a dream-within-a-dream structure, which is sometimes rather bewildering. But it is an exciting experiment with spatial and visual effects, to some extent a preparatory exercise for *Indians* and *Wings*.

After his most realistic and surrealistic works Kopit achieved his first international success with his most absurd and humorous play *Oh Dad, Poor Dad, Mamma's Hung You in the Closet and I'm Feelin' So Sad*

(1960). Like its predecessors it was severely criticized, despite its popularity with theater audiences. If critics praised anything at all, it was its fascinating stage fun. A close analysis, however, shows that beneath its farcical surface *Oh Dad* is a serious play which deals with some of Kopit's favorite themes, nor is it so absurdly unrealistic that it could not be approached on conventional terms; our logic must not necessarily be discarded for an adequate analysis, as the play still makes good sense within the traditional pattern of literary symbols and metaphors.

Oh Dad presents the story of a woman who has been completely disillusioned by life and, in consequence, withdraws with singular consistency and resolution from a world which she accuses of greed and hypocrisy. She refuses to accept any values apart from pecuniary ones and is resolved to dominate, if not tyrannize, everybody around her. Her pets, two carnivorous Venus Flytraps and the speaking piranha Rosalinda are symbols of her unrestrained urge to suppress and devour everything and everyone. Searching for an alternative life, she has built her own microcosm and jealously guards it against all intruders, all representatives of the outside world. For instance, in a potential love affair she subjects Commodore Roseabove, who appears to be head over heels in love with her, to deromanticizing shock therapy. She prepares their sentimental tête-à-tête in an extremely calculating manner so that she has complete power over him; this is represented symbolically by the chairs, which he cannot move but which are manipulated by some magic hand. She openly admits that she is only interested in his money and rebuffs his advances curtly: "Feelings are for animals" (p. 48).[3] She tells him about her husband's corpse in the closet, and her kiss almost chokes the life out of the asthmatic Commodore, who soon gives up his romantic dream of adventure. At the height of his disillusionment he is eager to take to his heels, completely shocked. His dream has become a nightmare from which he wants to escape by whatever means possible.

Thus, Mrs. Rosepettle leads the Commodore through the same process of knowing which she had herself to go through before and during her marriage. Her first experiences with men were not of the kind which arouse dreams of "handsome princes and enchanted maidens; full of love and joy and music, tenderness and charm" (p. 52). On the contrary, her meeting with a man destroyed all latent dreams of romantic love:

> And then, one night, when I was walking home I saw a man standing in a window. I saw him take his contact lenses out and his hearing aid out of his ear. I saw him take his teeth out of his thin-lipped mouth and drop them into a smiling glass of water. I saw him lift his snow-white hair off of his wrinkled head and place it on a gnarled wooden hat-tree. And then I saw him take

his clothes off. And when he was done and didn't move but stood and stared at a full-length mirror whose glass he had covered with towels, then I went home and wept. (p. 53)

It was the dismantling of a dream, the revelation of naked reality, and in order to avoid contact with this kind of life and its lies she married an outsider of whom she thought she could at least be sure. But they did not develop a relationship of love and understanding, and in the end she shut herself off from the world and built her own microcosm. Now she wants to protect her son Jonathan from the evil influences of that life and tries to keep nocturnal lovers on the beach from making foolish mistakes. She explains her conception of life outside, in the Commodore's world, in vivid words:

And I feel sorrier for you! For you are nothing! While my son is mine. His skin is the colour of fresh snow, his voice is like the music of angels, and his mind is pure. For he is safe, Mr. Roseabove, and it is I who have saved him. Saved him from the world beyond that door. The world of you. The world of his father. A world waiting to devour those who trust in it; those who love. A world vicious under the hypocrisy of kindness, ruthless under the falseness of a smile. Well, go on, Mr. Roseabove. Leave my room and enter your world again — your sex-driven, dirt-washed waste of cannibals eating each other up while they pretend they're kissing. Go, Mr. Roseabove, enter your blind world of darkness. My son shall have only light! (p. 59)

She does not even grant this world the corpse of her husband, preferring to keep it in her isolated microcosm as a trophy of her fight with the outside. However, by giving up the hope of realizing her dreams within the world, she indulges in the equally false vision of fulfillment in isolation, for in the long run she is not able to keep the outside out of her life. This is exemplified at the beginning of the third scene, where the French windows, which are supposed to shut out the world and its joyful, but also derisive laughter, fall to the floor. The walls of her ivory tower crumble continually.

The world outside and its vitality constantly intrude upon Mrs. Rosepettle's dead microcosm, especially through Rosalie, who gives Jonathan enough self-confidence and courage to consider escaping from this self-made prison. At the climax of his alienation from his mother he kills the symbols of maternal suppression, the Venus Flytraps and the piranha. The more he frees himself from her, the less he stutters. Finally he can even complain to Rosalie about his being kept in entire dependence. But in the course of his affair with Rosalie he realizes that she is as possessive as his mother. Thus, at the end of the play we see two worlds fighting for an immature adolescent, two attitudes towards life tearing at his soul; his mother's microcosm of lifeless isolation competes with Rosalie's world of passion, with all its love and squalor. During this struggle the dream of life in opulence and of a seemingly idyllic retirement from the harshness of a bewildering reality is put to the test of contact with this reality; it turns into nightmare, which is so depressing that Jonathan tries to keep up the dream, to save his mother's world by killing Rosalie. He buries her under the symbols of his microcosm, his stamps, coins and books. It is significant that in his small world they represent isolation, whereas outside they are means of human communication. This restriction of their symbolic connotations emphasizes the lifelessness of his existence. Like his mother at about his age, he has now had his nightmarish experience of life and love. Another representative of what the two Rosepettles consider the world's dreadfulness is dead, and we ask ourselves if they will hang a second trophy in the closet. Mrs. Rosepettle has explained the relationship between her life and her husband's corpse in the closet to the Commodore:

> Life, my dear Commodore, is never funny. It's grim! It's there every morning breathing in your face the moment you open your red baggy eyes. Worst of all, it follows you wherever you go. Life, Mr. Roseabove, is a husband hanging from a hook in the closet. Open the door without your customary cup of coffee and your whole day's shot to hell. But open the door just a little ways, sneak your hand in, pull out your dress, and your day is made. Yet he's still there, and waiting—your husband, hanging by his collar from a hook, and sooner or later the moth balls are gone and you've got to clean house. It's a bad day, Commodore, when you have to stare Life in the face, and you find he doesn't smile at all; just hangs there ... with his tongue sticking out. (pp. 50/51)

Jonathan will now hang Rosalie's corpse on a hook as his trophy of his encounter with Life, as a monument which sarcastically sticks its tongue out at everybody who opens the door too wide, who seeks too close a contact with the world.

Oh Dad thus asks the question if and in what way we may shut ourselves off from Life and indulge in an almost ideological isolation, dreaming of our greatness and the baseness and depravity of the outside (Kopit treats a similar subject in *The Day the Whores Came Out to Play Tennis*). Despite all its humor and horseplay *Oh Dad* poses the problem of a ruthless fight between accepting and refusing life's inconsistency and sordidness, between integration and isolation, life and death, a fight in which our dreams might suddenly become nightmares, because we will not always win. Sometimes our laughter sticks in our throats, when the comedy reveals its macabre humor and we recognize ourselves on the stage. *Oh Dad* is not a farce full of slapstick but, as Bradish rightly pointed out in his introduction to the original edition, it is "the logical fusion of the comic and the serious facets of Kopit's imagination".[4] To date critics have completely neglected these "serious facets" and commented solely on the funny wrapping.

Chamber Music (1963) also treats a serious subject beneath an absurd surface. In a mental institution the "Duly Elected Grievance and Someday-Governing Committee of Wing Five, Women's Section" meets to discuss their problems and those of their electorate. The eight members of the committee have changed their identities and are now the wife of W. A. Mozart, the explorer and authoress Osa Johnson, the writer Gertrude Stein, the film actress Pearl White, the aviatrix Amelia Earhart, Isabella I Queen of Spain, Joan of Arc and the suffragette Susan Brownell Anthony. The group at first consists of eight separate personalities, but when Mrs. Mozart insists too much on her individuality, the other women unite in an act of collective aggression. Unnoticed by the others, Mrs. Mozart plays a record, sings to it and throws open the window; thus she finds her identity not in the group but in the music and searches for contact with the world outside (cf. the same metaphor in *Sing to Me Through Open Windows*). By this act she openly leaves the group and accepts the position of an outsider, a step which cannot be tolerated by the women nor by the authorities, because it is against "decorum" (p. 17). At once the others relinquish their individualities and unite in order to prosecute the offence and destroy the means of Mrs. Mozart's flight from the group, i.e. the record. Throughout the play all the women show a latent aggressiveness which expresses itself in verbal attacks; but now at last they have the welcome outlet of collective hysteria. Their aggression compensates for an inner tension, which itself results from their being under continuous supervision by the authorities. So, when the doctor approaches their room, they comply with decorum and feign "mock innocence" and harmony.

After the interruption by the doctor's routine visit, the action of the first half of the play is repeated on a higher level of intensity and aggression. Now the group is not only threatened by the authorities and the excessive individuality of one of its members, this time Amelia Earhart, but especially by the Men's Ward. The women indulge in the fixed delusion of being persecuted by the men and expect a brutal attack, which they want to forestall by demonstrating their strength. However, since they cannot externalize their paranoid tension through open hostility against the authorities or the Men's Ward, they turn on the weakest in their group, Amelia

Earhart, who proves herself an outsider by still considering their changes of identity as a problem, not as a fact. She even critically comments: "I said it's just incredible.... All this nonsense" (p. 23, also p. 28). Apparently the sanest of the committee, she does not join in the general battle of words and is "bored with it all" (p. 27). Consequently, she is soon treated as a representative of the world outside and thus has to be sacrificed to their insanity. Again, for a short time, the women unite for the cathartic ritual of destroying the outsider, accompanied by a "tribal beat" (p. 34). It is an act of mobbish hysteria, during which each woman gives up her identity, subordinates herself to the ritual ceremony and is completely in the power of the collective unconscious. Only after the murder do they realize the consequences of their deed, "that something is wrong" (p. 37). In close similarity to the first scene of collective aggression, the representative of authority now returns and admonishes them to stick to the rules, i.e. to close the windows and forget about the outside.

Chamber Music was certainly not written in order to find fault with American mental institutions. On the contrary, it is a metaphor of our societies, which are not too different from the group of the women. Like Pinter, Kopit here describes a world where the individual lives in constant fear of a threat from outside and where he externalizes this fear by outward aggressiveness—as Mrs. Rosepettle says at the end of *Oh Dad:* "This place is a madhouse", a mental home where obsessions, manias, fixed ideas and uncertain identities lead to open hostilities and where the attempt to step outside is punished by society in legalized rituals. But the explosion of the collective unconscious, the act of brutality, does not change anything. Like the women in the ward we live in a vicious circle escalating in aggressiveness. In governing our affairs we are as insane as the women, and it is only our compliance with decorum and our fear of the threat from outside which stabilizes our human relationships. At the end of the play the patients are about to take over the institution. The former authorities are dethroned because of their failure, and the reign of timeless night, of the darkness of insanity, is announced. Sanity has not helped the world, insanity will not be any worse. The play defines as insanity what we suppose to be our sanity, because we are actually part of the committee; the women's world is our world and some will feel like Amelia Earhart: "I want to get out of here. One of the main reasons for this is the fact that I'm not insane. In fact, I'm not even exceptionally neurotic" (pp. 11/12). And is it not a nightmarish and traumatic experience to recognize that our logic basically works like that of the mentally ill:

> ... these reports all prove that no source can be found for the various feelings of hatred, hostility, jealousy, be-lli-gerency ...

and revenge known to exist. The conclusion then. The source must come from outside our ward. Or, in other words, the Men's Ward! Which none of us have ever seen. And is therefore, most likely. (p. 22)

Are we so encased in our "normal" and "sane" logic that we cannot recognize that we are our biggest problem? Do we not prove ourselves insane by laughing about the women and taking our sanity and our identity for granted? By posing these questions and implicitly doubting the fundamentals of our existence, *Chamber Music* is Kopit's most pessimistic play. Again he presents a serious subject in an absurdly unrealistic, sometimes enigmatic and on the whole very funny wrapping with side-splitting slapstick elements.

One of Kopit's most favorite themes is the questioning of our concept of heroism. It is not only the central concern of *The Questioning of Nick, Sing to Me Through Open Windows* and, most obviously, *Indians,* but also of the two shortest plays he has published to date. *The Conquest of Everest* and *The Hero* were both written on a single day in 1964. *The Conquest of Everest* shows strong traces of its hasty composition. On the whole, it is a satire on the suppression of man by scientific or ideological programs; man can achieve much greater feats by mere spontaneity. A hero is not made by a plan but by man's natural impulses. Furthermore, the drama is a satire on the legend of the American superman, whose sole aim of life is "phys. ed." (p. 89), but also on the hypocrisy of a puritan morality and on some excesses of tourism. But the play lacks unity of effect.

The pantomime *The Hero* is much more to the point and is a disconcerting metaphor of our life. After a long journey through the world, i.e. after a severe test of his heroism by reality, the hero, exhausted and in rags, has reached the desert, the final test of his pseudo-existence. No real nourishment to sustain his heroism is left, his last sandwich is rock hard. Nevertheless, he desperately tries to maintain his world of pretence and paints an oasis on a scroll which he then uses as a billboard to advertize the false dream of his heroism. When a woman comes along, he succeeds in making her believe in his vision. She abandons her initial skepticism and seeks fulfillment in his fictive world. The vision is stronger than reality, since it offers more security and human contact than the world, which is just a life-destroying desert. For the audience, the dream of heroism, which the woman indulges in although she knows it to be false, turns into nightmare, because we realize that, according to the play, life can only be endured with the help of a visionary illusion. Human contact is established because of our common fight with a grim reality, and we find fulfillment in our common dream of a better world, an oasis in the desert. Thus, heroism in our world is not dependent upon extraordinary deeds, but upon the ability to paint an imaginary world of which we can dream and in which we can endure our real existence in the heat of the desert. One of the heroes who was (and still is) able to transpose us into a visionary world of heroism and greatness is, of course, Buffalo Bill, the central figure in Kopit's most successful play, *Indians*.

The Day the Whores Came Out to Play Tennis (1965) also dramatizes the failure of a dream when tested by reality. The Committee of the exclusive Cherry Valley Country Club meets in the club's nursery early in the morning to find a way out of a major catastrophe: 18 women, non-members, are playing tennis on the club's courts and, even worse, they do not wear the proper dresses but basketball shoes and plaids, without underpants! The club's reputation and respectability is at stake, and during this crisis all its pretences to superiority are unmasked. The harmony of the men reveals itself as completely utilitarian, their friendship now breaks up and their latent aggressiveness becomes manifest in the vulgarity of their language. Even their strong morality is hypocrisy. The catastrophe is brought about by the women's threat to destroy the club's world of superiority which existed only in their dreams and whose walls are now being pulled down by the tennisballs that the women pelt at the edifice of would-be respectability. In accordance with the predominant atmosphere of decline, Herbert reads Hemingway's *The Sun Also Rises*, whose title is a quotation from *Ecclesiastes* 1:5, a chapter also appropriate for the vanity of the world Kopit depicts. All previous ideals of the club collapse during this crisis. For example, the men have always considered tennis to be the sport of an aristocratic elite; now they have to admit that the whores, who represent the masses, are better than the world champions. Symbolically anticipating the destruction of their world, the "huge and glorious castle... made entirely of children's blocks" (p. 99), is smashed to pieces. The club tried to establish a reputation of high-society exclusiveness by employing an authentic English butler, who, however, has not come to serve but to teach them an aristocratic diction. And even the dream of being morally superior to the vulgar mass breaks down, for Kuvl's and Herbert's wives have evidently acted in a rather whorish manner. During the crisis the men realize that by withdrawing into their imaginary world of false values and ideals they have lost contact with reality, a fact symbolized by torn telephone wires. Their dream turns into nightmare because they cannot guard their aristocratic exclusiveness against reality, against the world outside which fiercely knocks on the walls of their castle and demands admission. The masses want to participate in the dream of a better life, but they knock so hard that they destroy this dream. Certainly it is a nightmarish experience for the members of the club, but the men have to learn to face reality and its problems instead of isolating themselves. For such a learning process they chose the proper room: the nursery of the club. They are naive children indulging in fairy tales. From the nursery they have the best view out onto the world visiting them: a vulgar place but one teeming with vitality. Rudolph is the only one to realize that in the course of the crisis the club not only faces extinction, but is also offered a unique chance: "the place has come to life" (p. 118).

Indians (1968) is Kopit's most mature play to date. All this previous works were exercises for this climax in his playwriting career and it is certainly one of the best American plays of the 1960's and 70's. In *Indians* Kopit uses most of the themes, metaphors and stage tricks tried out in his former plays, but now he is particularly successful in combining them in a unique play on his favorite theme, the destruction of a dream, which he dramatizes with admirably lucid and poignant metaphors and which he transforms from an individual to a collective vision—and nightmare. And in *Indians* Kopit is especially good in correlating his theatrical techniques with the central theme, which he defined in an interview with John Lahr: "But our dream of glory wasn't the nightmare of destruction, of willfulness, of greed, of perjury, of murder, which it has become."[5]*Indians* depicts why and how the dream of glory turned into nightmare.

Kopit uses a contrapuntal structure and alternates scenes in which Sitting Bull's Indians present their complaints to a Senate committee with scenes from Cody's Wild West Show. These two plots of the drama characterize each other, and it becomes clear that Cody's show as well as the hearing is based on lies. For although Cody wants to persuade the president to negotiate personally with the Indians, because "A committee won't be able to help!" (Scene 10), he tries to make the Indians believe that talking to the senators "will be the same as talking to him" (Scene 2). The negotiations are not only bound to fail because of the personal lies of a man whose reputation as a Wild West hero is founded upon deception, but also because of the collective improbity of the nation and its representatives, who feign a desire to help the Indians, although basically all they want is that the Indians adopt the white man's ways, give up their aboriginal identity and culture, and cede their land. Sitting Bull reveals the paradox of the official Indian policy:

> We had land. You wanted it. You took it. That . . . I understand
> perfectly. What I cannot understand . . . is why you did all this,
> and at the same time . . . professed your love. (Scene 13)

This is a reproach for Buffalo Bill as well as for the whole nation. It was the premise of the American policy that the Indians had to be treated like children, as they could not support themselves within the economic system of white capitalism. Such a condescending arrogance was typical of white attitudes and is reflected in the senatorial hearing in *Indians*. In his 1875 report, Commissioner of Indian Affairs Edward P. Smith justified this policy along with the illegal occupation of the Black Hills:

> They are children, utterly unable to comprehend their own great necessities just ahead; they cannot, therefore, see that the country which now only furnishes them lodge-poles and a few antelope has abundant resources for their future wants, when they shall cease to be barbarous pensioners upon the Government and begin to provide for their own living. Their ignorance of themselves and of true values makes the stronger appeal to our sense of what is right and fair.[6]

In the hearing and in the show scenes Buffalo Bill cuts a very poor figure. The contradiction between his wish to redress the wrongs done to the Indians and the uncontrolled course of events reveals the hypocrisy of his role as mediator, even to himself, so that whenever he comes to recognize the failure of his intentions and dreams he is speechless, stunned, feels dizzy, rubs his eyes as if he wanted to soothe a headache, or squints as if in pain. The change from dream to nightmare is the central theme of nearly every scene and is expressed by the frequent use of visual, especially lighting, effects, whenever we leave the stage of historical reality and enter the landscape of Cody's soul. Actually, the play is not about Indians, as its title suggests, but about white Americans, the WASPs, the heirs to Cody's dream. Originally Kopit planned to give his play the perhaps more appropriate title *Cody's Will*. In Buffalo Bill Kopit connects an individual life with national history; Cody's psyche represents the collective subconscious of the whole nation. Kopit is especially interested in a psychological analysis of America's history, and this he can do much better by dealing with an individual functioning as concretized metaphor. Cody's split personality represents the national schizophrenia, and his dream and nightmare is that of the nation as a whole. The multidimensional structure resulting from the interplay of individual and collective history and individual and collective subconscious is in some scenes quite confusing. *Indians* appeals to the audience with obvious didacticism and shocks it out of its self-complacency; it uses neo-Brechtian alienation devices to set us thinking about what we see and experience.

When the audience take their seats, there is no curtain, because the drama is already well under way, both inside and outside the building. The theater has been transformed into a museum where three showcases display symbols of the westward movement. A "larger-than-life-size effigy" shows Buffalo Bill as the legendary hero of the Wild West, the unrealistically enlarged and glamorized representative of the victorious white race and culture. By contrast, Sitting Bull's effigy is unadorned, as he stands for the defeated race. The brutality of the relationship between their worlds is symbolically expressed by a blood-stained Indian shirt, an old rifle, and a buffalo skull, which, significantly enough, is not the genuine bone but just an artifact — this points to the historical fact that the species became so rare that man had to produce imitations for his museums. The inconsistencies in American history are likewise expressed acoustically, by a strange background music which is supposed to evoke a "sense of dislocation". Kopit wants the music to prevent any visitor from indulging in a glorifying dream of heroic exploration of the continent; on the contrary, the spectator should experience "something musically amorphous, and viscerally disturbing, like a bad dream".[7] When the lights fade out on these three cases, the first scenic unit of the play and a symbolic anticipation of the whole drama in nuce ends; like a framework it is repeated at the end of *Indians*.

Out of this tableau the drama proper develops in slow motion: only gradually do light, music, scenery and action coalesce in the usual effects of the Wild West show. This technique reflects the fact that Cody only hesitatingly enters the world of his show. He has to be caught by the lights and admonished by the director. Obviously he finds it difficult to adopt his role, because it does not reflect his true self and the real world outside the show and the museum. Only when everything (music, lights, and scenery) adds up to the accustomed show can William Cody change to Buffalo Bill. As such he is the superhuman hero of the museum, "effortlessly in control of the whole world, the universe; eternity". But evidently he has recently experienced a crisis of identity, for he has to persuade himself that this is the place where he belongs and he tries to defeat his fear by quoting encouraging words from another national hero, General Custer, who once advised him: "'Bill! If there is one thing a man must never fear, it's makin' a personal comeback'". Much as he would like to, Cody cannot prevent the beginning of his false show life, for this is demanded of him, but he is anxious to postpone it if possible; so he starts to tell a trifling story about a previous engagement, but is interrupted: Indians appear on the stage of his consciousness and remind him of his guilt. They are monuments to the nation's history and to his own failure and frighten him so much that now, at last, he is eager to seek refuge from the bewildering and accusing reality: he willingly adopts the false role of the hero, for as such he is above all doubts. He feels guilty and thinks it necessary to defend himself: "I am a fine man. And anyone who says otherwise is WRONG!... My life is an open book; I'm not ashamed of its bein' looked at!"

The rest of the drama is, to use his metaphor, concerned with opening the book of his life, so that all the other scenes are retrospective. The fact that Cody in the first scene deems it important to define his attitude towards his show and his and the nation's history, proves how much he is caught up in the contradictions between his myth-generating role in the show and grim reality. Both worlds assail him and neither grants him the individual freedom he as the hero of the frontier is supposed to embody. The hero doubts his fictive glory, the Indians attack him on the stage of his subconscious. The dream of his superiority and infallibility becomes the nightmare of his guilt and failure. But he is desperate to keep up the dream, to defeat his conscience and truth: "I *believe* [my italics] I ... am a hero. ... A GODDAMNED HERO!" Thus, in the first scene, as in all those that do not present the senatorial hearing, the actual drama takes place on the stage of Cody's soul.

The nature of the myth he personifies is explicitly formulated in the third scene; Cody explains it to Spotted Tail, and in reading it we should keep in mind that, from its very beginnings, the American nation, following the Sermon on the Mount, indulged in the dream of building a city upon a hill:

> Well, my plan is t' help people. ... And, and, whatever ... it is I do t' help, for it, these people may someday jus' possibly name streets after me. Cities. Counties. States! I'll ... be as famous as Dan'l Boone! ... An' somewhere, on top of a beautiful mountain that overlooks more plains 'n rivers than any other mountain, there might even be a statute of me sittin' on a great white horse, a-wavin' my hat t' everyone down below. ...

For Cody, helping others means helping himself. He dreams of a mythic elevation and a striking pose such as that he assumes in the first scene when he enters his show. In part, his dream comes true; however, not as recompense for extraordinary deeds, as he supposes, but solely as the consequence of the lies Buntline has published about him. Following his own advice to Spotted Tail, "you've got to adjust," he sells his soul and complies with the expectations of the people around him in order to realize his dream. He is, e.g., not supposed to acknowledge publicly his friendship with the Indians, since the myth of the western hero defines him as the conqueror of an uncivilized and inferior culture. Cody surrenders to the power the legend has over him and is completely helpless; once he has adopted his role, he cannot but maintain it, although sometimes he would like to be himself again. In each scene he starts the ball rolling, but then loses control and is stunned; this underlines the vanity of his heroism. A lucid example is the command performance in the White House, which takes an unintended turn when Hickok disapproves of Buntline's unrealistic, escapist melodrama and presents a genuine rape and a genuine murder.

He protests against the "humiliation o' havin' to impersonate my own personal self" (Scene 7), against the demolition of his identity. Cody has already given up his personality and expects everyone in his show to do the same. Hickok defends his identity by juxtaposing the superficial sensationalism of the melodrama with the brutal reality of the Wild West; Chief Joseph (Scene 9) uses "exaggerated and inappropriate", i.e. unauthentic gestures to give his capitulation speech a tone of alienation; and John Grass (Scene 9) opposes the commercialization of Indian rites in the show by sacrificing himself and revealing the falseness of Buffalo Bill's world. Whatever Cody did, he always falsified reality and helped design the fiction of the Wild West. The climax in his identity crisis is reached in scene 12, where the hero, who in his dream is "effortlessly in control of the whole world", enters Hickok's saloon as a "dead man" who has "just found hell", to use the words of Jesse James' song. Cody here returns from the Wounded Knee massacre, where he stared into the abyss of his existence, the gulf between his original identity as William Cody and his role as Buffalo Bill, and where he recognized his responsibility and utter helplessness. Now he seeks a way out of his identity crisis and asks Hickok's advice. However, Hickok himself has in the meantime yielded to the financial temptations of commercializing the Wild West legend, profitably multiplying Western heroes, making Cody realize how separate and independent his role has become. Shooting at the replicas of himself, Cody tries to destroy the false, mythic part of his split soul; of course, he hurts only himself, or the residue that is left of him, so that "he screams as he shoots". But the legendary Buffalo Bill now leads his own life. Cody has lost all power over him.

The final scene dramatizes Cody's last and most desperate attempt to end the nightmare of split identity and to reintegrate his personality. As Cody, the former friend of the Indians, he is now a mere corpse and therefore able to talk with the dead Sitting Bull. He lives on only as Buffalo Bill, impersonating the dream of the nation and propagating the official version of the massacre. Although the justification for slaughtering the Indians is flimsy and hypocritical, it offers him a way out of his crisis of identity by complete identification with the collective voice, its ideals and reasoning. So it is no longer he who has to create a fantasy the nation can indulge in. He seeks shelter in the hypocrisy of the collective and finds the justification for his behavior in the dream, nightmare and escapism of the nation. He need no longer defend himself individually as he did in the first scene ("I am a fine man. And anyone who says otherwise is WRONG!"), but can now hide behind the collective statement: "anyone who thinks we have done something wrong is wrong!" This also indicates that he has given himself up; William Cody is a living corpse and only survives as Buffalo Bill in the false world of the show and as the grossly distorted effigy in the museum show case. Thus he has the same fate as the buffalo, exterminated as a species and of which only a false artifact in the exhibition remains, and as the Indians, who have been annihilated as a race and who live on only as "handsome replicas" made of "genuine wood". In each case only false effigies remain; the genuine thing is annihilated and survives as a mere imitation for show business or the tourist industry.

Indians is not only a commentary on the Vietnam War, as has frequently been pointed out, but it demonstrates how a group with a false conception of its superiority will destroy its outsiders either by suppression or assimilation. It is a disillusioning comment on the attitude of the American nation towards its minorities and questions the myth of its national greatness. It wants to replace the dream by nightmare and open America's eyes to its historical guilt. Just as he has Cody feel dizzy whenever his dream turns stale, so Kopit wants the spectator to be bewildered and shocked when he sees through the legend of his nation's past. Not only the very first scenic unit (the glass cases), but indeed the whole play is intended to evoke a "sense of dislocation" in the audience through its theme and structure and to initiate a process of disillusionment and self-knowledge, so that at the end the audience will look with different eyes on the now recurring museum tableau and, symbolized by it, the foundations of the American nation.

With *Wings* (1978) Kopit has probably reached the theatrical limits of dramatizing a split consciousness. It treats the first two years of Emily Stilson's recovery from a stroke and, in particular, describes her attempts to reassemble her completely disintegrated world. Well into her seventies, she is like a baby again and has to start from scratch. Kopit is not interested in a medical or linguistic problem, but rather in an issue of human existence, which he defines in the preface: "It is a very scary business, this job of exploring who we are." *Wings* demonstrates how a human being, at the zero point of his identity and his relation to life, starts out on his quest for a meaning to his existence. As in all his other plays, Kopit is here concerned with the depiction of the interior landscape of a human being who lives in a dreamlike haze which, at the moment of its recognition, turns into nightmare. But in *Wings* the look into a man's soul is much more consistent and radical than ever before. Undoubtedly, it was a major problem for Kopit to dramatize such a perusal of an individual psyche within the concrete dimensions of the stage. Perhaps appropriately, therefore, *Wings* was originally a radio play; its history is outlined in the preface to the published stage version. Thematically, *Wings* was more appropriate for radio than theater and the problems Kopit had with the stage adaptation are reflected in the extensive explanatory notes and stage directions which are necessary for a better understanding of what must be a unique combination of unusual theme and pioneering technique. The "Notes on the production of this play" elucidate these problems.

> The stage as a void.
> System of black scrim panels that can move silently and easily, creating the impression of featureless, labyrinthine corridors. Some panels mirrored so they can fracture light, create the impression of endlessness, even airiness, multiply and confuse images, confound one's sense of space. . . .
> The scenes should blend. No clear boundaries or domains in time or space for Mrs. Stilson any more.
> It is posited by this play that the woman we see in the center of the void is the intact inner self of Mrs. Stilson. This inner self does not need to move physically when her external body (which we cannot see) moves. Thus, we infer movement from the context; from whatever clues we can obtain. It is the same for her, of course. She learns as best she can.
> And yet, sometimes, the conditions change; then the woman we observe is Mrs. Stilson as others see her. We thus infer who it is we are seeing from the context, too. Sometimes we see both the inner and outer self at once.
> Nothing about her world is predictable or consistent. This fact is its essence.
> The progression of the play is from fragmentation to integration.

In four scenes the play follows this progression. Mrs. Stilson's recovery is reflected in her increasing ability to comprehend the world around her and react properly, i.e. with syntactically right and semantically meaningful sentences. Right after the stroke she is utterly unable to communicate; one of her first sentences, for example, is the following answer to the doctor's question "Where were you born?" (p. 35)[8]: "Never. Not at all. Here the match wundles up you know and drats flames fires I keep careful always —". And this already is a great advance from her starting point. Her ability to comprehend the talk of others also improves considerably. But we seldom hear the words in the play when they are actually pronounced; we get them filtered instead through her consciousness. Very often there is a striking discrepancy both between her thoughts and actual utterances and between the doctor's words and what she eventually understands; consider for example the following conversation:

FIRST DOCTOR:	Mrs. Stilson, who was the first President of the United States?
MRS. STILSON:	*Washington.*

SECOND DOCTOR:	Mrs. Stilson, who was the first President of the United States?
MRS. STILSON:	*Washington!*
SECOND DOCTOR TO FIRST:	I don't think she hears herself.
FIRST DOCTOR:	No, I don't think she hears herself.

THE TWO DOCTORS EMERGE FROM THE SHADOWS, APPROACH MRS. STILSON. SHE LOOKS UP IN TERROR. THIS SHOULD BE THE FIRST TIME THAT THE WOMAN ON STAGE HAS BEEN DIRECTLY FACED OR CONFRONTED BY THE HOSPITAL STAFF. HER INNER AND OUTER WORLDS ARE BEGINNING TO COME TOGETHER.

FIRST DOCTOR:	Mrs. Stilson, makey your naming powers?
MRS. STILSON:	What?
SECOND DOCTOR:	Canju spokeme?
MRS. STILSON:	Can I what?
FIRST DOCTOR:	Can do peeperear?
MRS. STILSON:	*Don't believe what's going on!*
	(pp. 30/31)

The camera taking the pictures of Mrs. Stilson's interior landscape is never static but shifts constantly between an outer and inner perspective. The focus for Mrs. Stilson as well as for the spectator is in a continuous state of flux, and this makes it very difficult both for her to find a meaningful order in the world she perceives and for us to follow the ramblings of her mind. By this technique our images of the depicted world are also disintegrated and distorted. Only very gradually do the inner thoughts and outer images begin to overlap and constitute a meaningful complexity. But at first this does not make her life any easier; on the contrary, the process of recovery is a process of comprehending her situation, so that her return to mental normality initially causes several severe crises to which she reacts with terror and horror.

The main reasons for Mrs. Stilson's intellectual aphasia is her amnesia. She cannot remember and pronounce properly the words for the objects she sees or the ideas she wants to express. Only very slowly does her memory come back, starting with random and scattered recollections of her distant past when she performed extraordinary barnstorming feats as an aviatrix and wing-walker. In her desperate attempt to explain her situation she comes to the conclusion that she must have landed in a desert and is now imprisoned in Romania for espionage. Although in the end she is able to explore her world physically and verbally and sees much more clearly the relations between the fragments of the mosaic of life, her mind remains vagrant, as if carried away on wings. She never regains complete control over her consciousness. So the title is not only an allusion to her past as an aviatrix, although this previous occupation is a concretized metaphor of her state of mind after the stroke. Through her illness Mrs. Stilson has lost her wings of life, which carry us up to some distant point from where we can see the pieces of the mosaic in perspective and recognize the ordering pattern, the structures, systems and categories that alone give sense to our world. At the same time, through the stroke she has grown new wings, which carry her away from our world into a realm of her own, where the categories of space and time no longer exist. And finally, in the course of the play she again grows her old wings, through mastery of the language.

WINGS does not claim to be a case study, but Kopit's description of the symptoms of a stroke patient is confirmed by clinical accounts of aphasics, e.g. by Zasetsky's memoirs[9], which influenced *Wings*, as Kopit admits in the preface. Zasetsky wrote: "I always feel as if I'm living out a dream — a hideous, fiendish nightmare — that I'm not a man but a shadow, some creature that's fit for nothing... [10]. To lose one's life through a stroke is certainly a nightmarish experience; but even to read the accounts of Zasetsky's and Mrs. Stilson's illnesses is a nightmare, especially when through them our dream of living in safe and predictable patterns is destroyed. They remind us of the essence of life, suffering and death, and through them we experience something which can easily happen to us all, and in a very near future. Thus, *Wings* is both an excellent and deeply moving vision and a fascinating experiment about a dream world which we cannot vision and a fascinating experiment about a dream world which we cannot fully understand, because we deem ourselves so far away from it, but of which we are very frightened.

The plays Kopit has published to date form an integrated whole. They are variations on the theme of dream and nightmare resulting from identity crises and they all show his hand very clearly. Their thematic relationship is not an indication of weakness, or even of lack of imagination on the part of the author, but is all the more proof of the extraordinary quality of his art. For, in contrast to many authors, Kopit does not quote himself, and he succeeds in introducing a diversity which never leaves the audience bored. Furthermore, it is just this thematic relatedness of the plays which draws our attention to Kopit's virtuosity as a stage technician. His experimenting with the formal possibilities of the theater is one of the most fascinating parts of his work. Sometimes he is even willing to exceed the audience's comprehension in order to involve them in the crisis taking place on the stage. The central experience of most of his protagonists — and spectators — is that of Mrs. Stilson: "Then ... I left my body."

NOTES

1. For a list of Kopit's plays and for biographical data cf. *Contemporary Dramatists*, 2nd ed., ed. James Vinson (London, 1977), and H. W. Wilz, "Arthur Kopit: *Indians*," in *Das amerikanische Drama der Gegenwart*, ed. H. Grabes (Kronberg: Athenäum, 1976), pp. 44–64. Further articles on Kopit: U. Denecke, "Mythos und Rollenkonflikt in Arthur Kopit's *Indians*," in *Theater und Drama in Amerika*, ed. E. Lohner and R. Haas (Berlin: Schmidt, 1978), pp. 375–387; Th. Grant, "American History in Drama: The Commemorative Tradition and Some Recent Revisions," *Modern Drama*, 19 (1976), 327–339; V. M. Jiji," 'Indians': A Mosaic of Memories and Methodologies," *Players*, 47 (1972), 230–236; J. B. Jones, "Impersonation and Authenticity: The Theater as Metaphor in Kopit's *Indians*," *Quarterly Journal of Speech*, 59 (1973), 443–451; J. Lahr, "Arthur Kopit's *Indians*: Dramatizing National Amnesia," in *Acting Out America* (Harmondsworth: Penguin, 1972), pp. 55–72; A. C. Murch, "Genet — Triana — Kopit: Ritual as 'Danse Macabre'," *Modern Drama*, 15 (1972), 369–381; D. L. Rinear, "*The Day the Whores Came Out to Play Tennis*: Kopit's Debt to Chekhov," *Today's Speech*, 22 (1974), 19–23.

2. References to *The Questioning of Nick, Sing to Me Through Open Windows, Chamber Music, The Conquest of Everest, The Hero*, and *The Day the Whores Came Out to Play Tennis* are to Kopit, *The Day the Whores Came Out to Play Tennis and Other Plays* (New York: Hill and Wang, 1965).

3. References to *Oh Dad* are to *Off Broadway Plays 1* (Harmondsworth: Penguin, 1970), pp. 19–70.

4. Kopit, *Oh Dad* (New York: Hill and Wang, 1960), p. 11.

5. The interview is included in Kopit, *Indians* (New York: Bantam, 1971), n. pag.

6. Cf. *The American Indian and the United States, A Documentary History*, ed. W. E. Washburn (New York: Random House, 1973), p. 203.

7. Kopit in his introduction to *Indians* (London: Methuen, 1970), n. pag.

8. References are to Kopit, *Wings* (New York: Hill and Wang, 1978).

9. In A. R. Luria, *The Man With a Shattered World* (London: Cape, 1973). For clinical case studies of aphasia cf. the series *Neurolinguistics*, ed. R. Hoops and Y. Lebrun (Amsterdam: Swets and Zeitlinger, 1977 ff.).

10. Luria, *Man With a Shattered World*, p. 12.

Ronald Ribman:
The Artist of the Failure Clowns

GERALD WEALES

In *Harry, Noon and Night* (1965), Ronald Ribman's first play,[1] Harry describes Moko, "a failure clown," whom he saw perform when he was a boy back in Ohio. "The kind that everything goes wrong for," Harry says, and provides a list of devices (the exploding cannon, the door that will not open, the kick in the pants) designed to provoke laughter. Harry goes beyond the professional image as he remembers how his brother Archer, who insisted "that the clowns were clowns even when they weren't wearing clown suits," took him behind the scenes where he saw an "old, old man bent over. ... silver lines of tears running" down his face. Harry's identification with Moko is clear not only in his unhappy boy's tears, but in the generalizations he makes about clowns who always think at first that "they can make it." Shifting from third to second person, Harry lists disasters that have not yet happened, one of which ("You haven't vomited in the plane yet") is a direct reference to his having been washed out of the air force in which Archer was a hero, a medal winner.

At one level, *Harry, Noon and Night* is a play about a young man, a failed artist, a victim of his older brother's assurance and success, who wants to get away from occupied Germany and from Immanuel, the man with whom he lives, to return to a mythical home ("It's summer all the time in Ohio"), but who contrives not to let his brother rescue him. "God, let me escape; God, let me escape," he remembers Moko's saying, but when he rolls Immanuel in a mattress in the third scene to prove that his friend is a clown too and that "Once you're in, you're in," he is closing the trap on himself. Ribman is not writing a conventional psychological play, however; *Harry* is awash with clowns. In each of the three scenes (that designation is used although the divisions are as long as acts usually are), one character

75

makes a fool (a clown) of another. In the first, Harry, pretending to be a correspondent for *American Farm and Garden*, conducts a demented (and very funny) interview with a soldier, punctuated with lines like "Don't be a clown" and "don't clown around with me." In the second, in which the word clown is not used, Immanuel, always plausible in his irrationality, reduces the practical Archer ("Everything can be fixed but you have to have the right attitude") to incoherence and sends him running into the street. The last scene not only allows Harry to humiliate Immanuel, but sets up the quarrel with the neighbors downstairs which brings Harry's arrest and keeps him from meeting his brother whose name he is calling as the play ends.

The German setting allows Ribman to extend his clown image in ways that some members of the audience might find distasteful. In the first scene Harry tells the soldier he is going to see "the Dachau circus. . . . and Moko . . . Moko, the crying clown." In the final one, denouncing his German neighbors as Nazis, he goosesteps to the title song from *Der Fuehrer's Face* (1942), Donald Duck's contribution to the American war effort; he later calls out, "This is the Fuehrer speaking. Tomorrow we will put on the clown mustaches." Victim and victimizer alike share the failure clown image. Harry, who knocks down the prostitute at the end of the first scene, who crowns his neighbor with a flowerpot, who is relentless in his treatment of Immanuel, is a violent character as well as a pathetic one, inept in both roles. "I'm not a clown," Immanuel says in the last scene. "I'm a human being." In *Harry, Noon and Night* those labels become interchangeable.

In *The Journey of the Fifth Horse* (1966), Ribman's next play, the focus is narrower although there are a great many more characters. It might be possible—listen to the incredible argument between Kirilla and Bizmionkov on government responsibility, watch Sergey writhe in the dead man's suit ("It hates me"), hear Gregory's cry for help at the end of the first act—to see all of them sharing the necessary limitations of the "human being," as the phrase takes on resonance from its use by Immanuel. Yet, the play, based "in part" on Turgenev's *Diary of a Superfluous Man*, concentrates on two failure clowns, two fifth horses. Ribman gets his titular image from Turgenev. A fifth horse is an extra one attached to a four-in-hand by a short rope which not only renders it useless, but cuts it painfully. Chulkaturin, Turgenev's superfluous man, and Zoditch, Ribman's remarkable creation out of a single line of the Russian novelist ("This manuscript was read/And Its Contents were not Approved/by Piotr Zudoteshin"), are unwilling brothers in pain and pointlessness.

The story of Chulkaturin's courtship of Liza—if so blatant a misunderstanding can be called a courtship—is essentially Turgenev's plot. The young man's desire to escape his own isolation ("I have never known anybody" "There has been no one") allows him to read in Liza's playfulness and her sudden tears — both of which presumably stem from her youth and the air of expectation that hangs over her — a love that she does not feel for him. When the dashing captain arrives on the scene and conquers her in an instant, Chulkaturin is provoked into a duel which, emphasizing his brave clownishness, isolates him still further from Liza, from society. Zoditch, the publisher's reader unwillingly stuck with the manuscript, invents a nonexistent Chulkaturin he can hate ("your Mediterranean villas, your ladies"), a mask that he hopes will keep him from recognizing himself in the dead diarist. "You cannot make weddings out of tears!" he says, reacting angrily to Chulkaturin's exuberance after the scene with Liza. "There is nothing written down here to make weddings from!" Yet, he fantasizes a romance with Miss Grubov, his dead employer's daughter, and allows himself to believe his landlady wants to marry him. "I do not live on fairy tales," he tells the servant when she brings him extra coal, but within a few speeches he has begun to find the wrong significance in the gesture (in fact, the landlady is planning to raise his rent) and to examine the barest nuance in her simple remarks ("Oh, Mr. Zoditch, your gloves.... Ah, Mr. Zoditch, your rent"): "Ahs and ohs have meanings.... One does not say 'ah'...'oh' just for the pleasure of opening a mouth." At the end, having been rejected by the landlady and humiliated in the process ("You are too old, too ... short"), he reads (watches) Chulkaturin's discovery that Liza will marry Bizmionkov, the family friend, and cries out, "This is a story of lies!...I reject this manuscript! I reject you!" The imaginary Chulkaturin and the real Zoditch stare at each other and, as Chulkaturin's outstretched arm falls, like that of the caged monkey whose description the disembodied voice uses to open and close the play, Zoditch asks, "What do you want of me?" In rage (both he and Chulkaturin have parallel moments of irrational anger), he throws the manuscript away. "I am the one that is loved. There is no other ending." At the beginning of the play, Zoditch is standing on a ladder, hanging crepe on the portrait of Mr. Grubov, and the cheeky Rubin, assuming that Miss Grubov has no interest in Zoditch, says, "Well, it's all a ladder, Mr. Zoditch. It's up or it's down. We can't be keeping our feet on the same rung." By the end of the play, Zoditch has come down with a vengeance.

Both the failure clown and the fifth horse are images, like Tennessee Williams's fugitive kind and Edward Albee's separate cages, which with a little discreet doctoring can be made to represent the recurrent thematic concerns of the playwright. They are applicable for Ribman's work as a whole only if all men are clowns, all horses — given the correct angle of vision — turn out to be fifth ones. It becomes clear, as the Ribman plays accumulate, that the playwright's world is one in which men are inevitably trapped between aspiration and possibility, limited by psychology, society, mortality. In an early poem, "Creation: Morning and Afternoon,"[2] Ribman brings lions, zebras, "hot swarms of gathering flies" to a scene that moves from celebration to uneasiness to "witness to the first gigantic lie." Death is implicit in life, failure in the promise of success, Harry's night in his noon. Whether man is a victim of forces from within or without, whether the destructive other is malevolent or purely gratuitous, man is limited by the situation, mundane or metaphysical, in which he finds himself and which, as likely as not, he helped to create. In *The Poison Tree* (1976), Hurspool, forced to plant a knife on a fellow prisoner, asks, "Why Jefferson?" Di Santis, the guard who insists on the setup, answers, "Oh, I don't know. Why not Jefferson?"

In the two Ribman plays of 1967—*The Final War of Olly Winter,* a television drama written for CBS Playhouse, and *The Ceremony of Innocence*—the sense of the human condition described above becomes central to the work, both dramatically and ideationally. Not that that was immediately apparent when the plays were first performed. Given the antiwar sentiments abroad in the land, the plays looked like straightforward pacifist statements. And they are pacifist statements, at least at one level. The killing sequences of *Olly Winter* have not the slightest hint of heroism about them, and Ribman's comment in the stage directions about Olly's anger at "war that makes people do such things" confirms what is implicit in the visual sequences. Speaking of *Ceremony* a few years after its initial production, when a revised version was about to be broadcast, over NET, Ribman told John Gruen (New York *Times,* June 7, 1970) that "it's not about hawks and doves, or the Vietnam war." Yet, the jingoism of Sussex and the bloody-minded nastiness of Emma are almost cartoon-like in their excess; Ribman could argue that such people do exist, that they surface noisily in times of crisis, but characters do not become realistic simply by having real-life counterparts. Overstatement, whatever aesthetic uses a playwright has for it, can—if the circumstances are right— seem like the manipulations of propaganda.

Looking back on the two plays today is a little like re-reading Arthur Miller's *The Crucible* outside of the immediate political context that produced it. They seem to have much more to do with Ribman's work as a whole than with the antiwar sentiments of the late 1960s. For a professional soldier, Olly Winter, an American black, is a remarkably gentle man, a competent killer with no instinct for his trade. The play is a distant relative of the kind of fantasy in which a community of sweetness is built in a setting of horror. As Olly picks up the Vietnamese girl, the dog, the baby, even the Vietcong prisoner, he accumulates his own motley army, one that might almost make beneficent sense of the phrase "final war." The jungles of Vietnam are not the forest of Arden, however. Circumstances prescribe his death, just as — so the flashbacks show us — they have dictated his life, stifling his best impulses (the smile exchanged with the little boy on the subway, the moment of affection with the cat) by teaching him to survive not live (his defending himself in the schoolyard), by showing him, through the deaths of his mother and sister, that the world builds fences around human possibility.

The theme of *The Ceremony of Innocence,* Ribman told Gruen, is "man's irrationality." The play is an historical drama, set in the eleventh century, with a protagonist (King Ethelred) who tries and fails to bring peace and an enriching civilization to England. The action is double. In the dramatic present, Ethelred is faced with a typical Ribman choice which is no choice at all. Three men (Kent, the disappointed idealist; Sussex, the mindless patriot; Aelfhun, the self-serving Bishop) come to persuade Ethelred to leave the monastery in which he has taken refuge and to lead the English forces against the invading Danes. Whether he agrees or not, the England he envisioned is already destroyed. Within the frame of this plot lie the events of the preceding year, of which the murder of the Danish princess is both culmination and defining image, which have sent Ethelred into his retreat. Over the protests of his mother, his wife, his son and Sussex, Ethelred buys peace with the Danes, hoping that, without the preoccupations of constant war, he can bring learning, science, art, well-being to his people. "I sought to find a dozen men to plant an orchard," he says at the end of the play, "while all about me nature bloomed a thousand lunatics ready to chop it down." The chief of these lunatics is Ethelred's own son, Edmund. "Are you a madman?" Ethelred asks when he discovers Edmund ripping up the Danish princess's clothing, as though in destroying Thulja's belongings he were tearing the peace treaty to shreds. It is Edmund's perverted sense of English dignity that leads to the killing of the Danish farmers, to his own death, to the murder of Thulja, to a new Danish invasion.

The play is after more complex causes. Irrationality lies closer to the throne than the king's son. When Emma, who is preoccupied with sex in most of her speeches, begins her hysterical denunciation of Thulja as a copulating beast, Ethelred "Loses control," as the stage direction says, begins to beat her and "absorbed in his own violence, fails to hear THUL-JA's cry" when she is stabbed by his mother. This is only the most graphic presentation of Ethelred as a believer in human reason who cannot control even himself. A more important instance comes at the end of the first act. Angry at Edmund's refusal to understand what he hopes to gain for England from the Danish peace, Ethelred starts to strike him, but backs off when he sees that such violence is what Edmund wants. Instead he gives him a lecture on kingship which degenerates as it goes on, ending with his shouting after his departing son, "You will help me hold this truce! Edmund! Edmund!" At the end of the play, Ethelred asks Kent, "Are we in a dungeon? Is this world a dungeon wherein men in their chains strike one another?" Kent answers, "Yes! Though you would not have it. Yes!" and then gives a long, ugly speech on the meaninglessness of human action, the more moving for coming from a man who has earlier assured a doubting king, "Men are reasonable, my liege; they will choose the path of reason." The king, whose last words are for the dead girl, decides not to fight, but he has already had his part in the drowning of innocence, if Thulja is the "innocence" of the title. It is possible—although I hesitate to push this reading too far—that she too is a contributor to the final catastrophe, that her extreme goodness is a kind of excess, a form of irrationality. Simple victim or participating victim, Thulja is the unredeeming sacrifice in a world in which, as the Yeats epigraph says, "The best lack all conviction, while the worst/Are full of passionate intensity."

It was not until 1976 and *The Poison Tree*[3] that Ribman produced another major play. In the years between, there were the three one-act plays that constituted *Passing Through from Exotic Places* (1969); "The Most Beautiful Fish," the sketch that Ribman contributed to *Foul!* (1969), the educational television program in which ten off-Broadway playwrights were asked to deal with the problem of pollution; *The Angel Levine* (1970), the film version of Bernard Malamud's story, for which Ribman shared screenplay credit with Bill Gunn; the fascinating one-act *Fingernails Blue As Flowers* (1971); and *A Break in the Skin*, a play which Ribman kept rewriting (1970–1973) without achieving a finished form that suited him, as its absence from the Ribman collection (*Five Plays*, 1978) indicates. It would be possible to consider any of these works in the thematic context I have been developing—for instance, to contemplate the negative ambiguity that director Jan Kadar imposed on *The Angel Levine* to replace the positive ambiguity of the original Malamud ending—but limitations of space make impractical so detailed an examination of Ribman's work.

The Poison Tree, despite its failure in the commercial theater, is one of Ribman's most intriguing plays. If Ethelred's England is a place made impossible by the men who inhabit it, the prison in *The Poison Tree* is a place which dictates impossibility for the men who are forced to live there. The titular image comes from one of Willy Stepp's speeches: "We are a tall black tree full of poison from which they ain't about to recover no way." The "they" are the white world and the "we" are the black prisoners who have learned to hate "the man and that is precept number one of revolutionary progress." Willy is a criminal whose jailhouse reading has turned him into a jargon-spouting revolutionary. Despite the parodic overtones of his speeches about "the over-pig" and his "pig hirelings," he is the one who best understands the prison: "You think white milk ain't gonna turn sour same as chocolate milk you keep it in here long enough?" His recognition of what the prison does finally robs him of the poison-tree image in the narrow sense in which he uses it. The prison itself is a poison tree, metallic rather than natural, which infects its own branches, black or white, prisoner or guard. "I dunno, after a while everything around here goes blah," Friezer explains to a new guard. "I guess it's just the place, you know. It does things to you, you don't even think about." A few speeches earlier he mentions "these migraine headaches" he gets.

After an opening in which a prisoner in the Adjustment Center breaks the neck of a guard, the play divides its time between two groups—a handful of guards and the prisoners, all black, who share a cell. These include Willy Stepp; Jefferson, who wants a parole, imagining that he can return to the reform school which was the only home he has known, and who commits suicide after the discovery of the knife in his bunk; Hurspool, the longterm prisoner, broken in spirit, who plants the knife on Jefferson; and Bobby Foster, at once the most sensitive and the most helpless man in the cell. "He was my friend," Foster says of Jefferson, "and I gave him what he always got outa his life — nothin'." All that he can give the dead Jefferson is Hurspool's life, but the old man is already dead as his long speech on what the prison has done to him shows. The only response that Bobby can give to the situation in which he finds himself—as his impulse to hit Di Santis indicates—is the violence that the prison and his whole life have taught him. In the last scene, in which he rejects Willy's rational reason for not killing Hurspool—that his death will not help the "cause"—Bobby's espousal of "feeling" exposes Willy as one with Hurspool, another victim of the system. "Pretty soon there ain't no names," Hurspool says, explaining why he could spy on his fellow prisoners, why he could let Di Santis force him to set Jefferson up. "They just uniforms they put in the cell with me." Willy says, "You wanna survive in here you gotta believe in somethin' beside people," and he follows the sentence with a litany of "People ... " lines which elicits Bobby's "No names, no faces, just uniforms, huh Willy?"[4]

Outside the cell, the guards are undergoing a similar disintegrative process. Like the prisoners, most of them began as losers—a failed chicken farmer, a failed hamburger stand operator, a failed insurance adjuster. Inside they become pushers, grow callous, develop headaches. Sergeant Coyne, who imagines that he goes by the rules, can keep that illusion only by shutting his eyes to much that goes on around him. It is Di Santis who is the most interesting of the lot. In production he can easily become a caricature of the villainous prison guard, a creature defined by his oily malevolence, his racist jokes, his scarcely masked threats. In fact, he is the Kent of this play, the disillusioned idealist implied by Willy's "That mother was good he first come here, you know that." The murdered guard of the play's opening was his friend, as both Sergeant Coyne and the stage directions say, and his behavior can be understood only in terms of that death. In the long, disjointed speech he makes at the end of the play, he says, "You got a friend, and that friend means something to you because maybe for the first time in your life you run into someone who gives a shit about you, sees something in you," and he stumbles across his loss to make an apology of sorts, one which no one wants or can accept. His death at Hurspool's hands may not be quite as inevitable as Ribman thought when he called the line of the play "the classic Greek kind of thing,"[5] but it makes a neat ending, a strangling to match the opening murder, the fruit of the poison tree.

With his most recent play, *Cold Storage* (1977), Ribman lets his characters face mortality, an antagonist more relentless than man's irrationality or his prison system. The playwright had already approached the subject in *Fingernails Blue As Flowers,* in which, in one of those speeches that the other characters hear only as inarticulate muttering, Naville comments on "that untouchable cold spot" within all of us, "that small glacier of chilling ice that year by year pushes deeper against our heart. . . . until quite suddenly we have grown much older and find ice crystals forming in the mouth, closing down our speech, paralyzing our tongue, fingernails blue as flowers." Naville, to be played by an actor in his early thirties, is a once powerful figure who devoured those around him (the play is full of references to hunger, to eating), reduced now to an old man trapped in a beach chair and in his past. The play is an image of inevitable disintegration, ending as his mouth freezes *"into a zero."*

The characters in *Cold Storage* are not inarticulate—certainly not Parmigian, the dying fruit peddler for whom Ribman has written some of the most flamboyant speeches of his career. The play, which takes place on the roof garden of a hospital, is a confrontation between Parmigian and Richard Landau, "an investment adviser in fine art," who has come in for exploratory tests. From his first long speech, an outrageous and very funny denunciation of nurses who refuse to say they are Puerto Rican—made acceptable by the unruffled presence of Miss Madurga, its ostensible subject—Parmigian assaults Landau, trying to penetrate the wall that the art dealer has built around himself. His weapons are fantasy, hyperbole, rampant metaphor, cross examination, prophecy, instant philosophy, practical advice and, always, the incessant flow of words that keeps him from the inevitable silence. Whenever, usually in a moment of anger, Landau lets slip a personal reference, Parmigian is on it in an instant, like a detective after a clue to Landau's "filthy dreams," like a dog after a bone because "Dreams other people throw out with the garbage I can spend a whole day living on." The "real pornography" of the brain, Parmigian explains, rejecting Landau's assumption that he expects to hear about sexual perversions, is "the will-o'-the-wisp you've been pursuing all your life, the lodestone, the magnetic star that pulls you and all of us through all the years of our life." When Landau finally begins to speak, broken open by Parmigian's vulnerability not by his agression, we discover that the pull on him has been the past. A survivor of the Holocaust, Landau has spent his life trying to rediscover the family who died for him. "You're not waiting for a death sentence here," Parmigian says, "because you're still waiting for a death sentence from the time you were eight years old!" Having invented an elaborate explanation of suffering as absurdity, one that might have become the ideational point of a more conventional play, Parmigian dismisses instant solutions by answering Landau's questioning request for help with "I'm not a psychiatrist. This analysis is from a movie I once saw with Ingrid Bergman and Gregory Peck." Landau begins to laugh, awkwardly at first, and even makes a pathetic joke.

The play's affirmation is dramatic not pedagogic. It lies in the two characters' coming together, the one having learned a little about how to live, the other about how to die. At the end of the play, as Landau starts to leave the roof, Parmigian asks, "Will you take me inside with you?" When Landau agrees, he says, "Look, off with the brake, off with everything, and I'm ready to roll." It is the line that he uses early in the play when he asks Landau to push his wheelchair off the roof. A suicidal line, however playfully delivered, has become an acceptance of the hospital and all that it implies. There is a similar statement in the way the last line of the play echoes the final line of the first act. The ending of that act is somewhat misleading because it seems at first glance to reflect a taste for sentimental irony which occasionally emerges in Ribman's work. In *The Poison Tree,* for instance, when the guards collect the dead Jefferson's belongings, checking off the items as they go, the scene ends with "One pair of shoes," and they sack up the shoes that the prisoner has polished with such high expectations all through his first scene. Here, as the much maligned Miss Madurga wheels Landau offstage, she stops to give Parmigian an ice-cream bar, pretending that it is left over from her lunch. Concentrating on that stagey gesture, an audience might forget to listen to Parmigian. As Landau disappears, Parmigian shouts, "Remember what I said to you! Be interesting!" Along, speaking *"softly to himself,"* he repeats "Be interesting," as though he were admitting that for him it is a survival device. At the end of the play, as the two men agree to meet again, he says, "I promise you a very interesting day," but now the awful urgency has gone out of the line.

With *Cold Storage* Ribman has returned to the exuberance, the outrageous inventiveness of *Harry, Noon and Night,* but the later play is different in tone from all the Ribman plays that have gone before. The playwright is as relentless as ever in what he expects for man, but the play accepts inevitability with warmth, with humor, almost with gaiety. "Well, all my characters are crying out against the universe they can't alter," Ribman told Anne Roiphe (New York *Times,* December 25, 1977). "They are battling against an unseen and always victorious enemy and they go on battling. All of my characters suffer, as Keats did, from a sense of beauty that deteriorates with the inevitable passage of time. I can't stand to see how beautiful things are destroyed ... but that's the human condition." There is a neat ideational line from the failure clown to the battler who cannot win, but there are no "silver lines of tears" on Parmigian's cheek.

In following a thematic track from Harry to Parmigian, I have emphasized the shared ideational concerns of the Ribman plays. By concentrating on matter rather than method, however, I have necessarily left much in the plays untouched. I would like to return to them now, but — oddly enough—the path to method takes me once again to theme.

A secondary theme in *Harry, Noon and Night* —one important enough to command the Wallace Stevens epigraph—has to do with ways of seeing. "Man, you see everything all wrong," the soldier says to Harry in the first scene of the play when (in a sequence that balances Immanuel's attempt to make Archer see his balloon-selling father in the second scene) Harry keeps pointing to the nose-picking man in the other room, an Archer fantasy figure whom the soldier never does discern through the smoke. "You do not see things as they are," Immanuel tells Archer, after having offered his toe clippings as relics, "holy water" from an ordinary milk bottle. "I got a blue guitar, you know," Harry says in the last scene. "I see things as they are." No one sees things as they are, of course, because things in this play have no verifiable reality. The grotesquerie of Harry and Immanuel shares with the presumed practicality of Archer and the soldier a tendency to alter the environment to fit some preconception of it. Immanuel, having tried to show Archer lubricious hunchbacks and a little girl in one of Harry's abstract paintings, has to have a Norman Rockwell Thanksgiving cover explained to him. "That's the turkey," Archer says in exasperation. "You better get yourself a pair of glasses." A pair of glasses like the ones worn by the boy and girl in "The Most Beautiful Fish," perhaps. Fishing in the Hudson River, they pull in "a large gelatinous shapeless mass" over which they exclaim happily. "You know what your trouble is, old man?" the boy says to the bum who insists it is not a salmon. "You don't have sunglasses." Ribman's plays are full of characters whose powers of perception are altered by choice or by necessity. Sussex, looking through the glasses of English complacency, is convinced in *The Ceremony of Innocence* that the Danes will not keep the peace simply because the king's daughter is hostage because "The Danes do not love as we love."

I could go on citing examples to indicate Ribman's fascination with this subject, but his use of an epigraph from Wallace Stevens's "The Man with the Blue Guitar" suggests that he is primarily interested in the artist's way of seeing. Perhaps it is not Harry, but the playwright, who has the blue guitar. If so, the tune alters from play to play, for no one among the practicing American dramatists has so large a body of work in which the plays so little resemble one another, at least on the surface. The dissimilarity among the Ribman plays has made it difficult for commentators to fit him neatly into a single genre, a definite style. In some cases they seem to have donned distorting glasses of their own. John Gruen, in the interview quoted earlier in this essay, speaks of Ribman's "stark and turgid realism," a phrase that makes no sense at all except as a reflection of a distaste for Ribman which the article makes no attempt to mask. The only Ribman play that approximates realism as the word is customarily used is *The Poison Tree,* which had not been written at the time of the Gruen interview, and even it fits uncomfortably under the label. Turner's wild dance to music which only he hears, an ecstatic outpouring which culminates in the killing of the guard, and the almost catatonic behavior of Heisenman in the neighbor cell might be seen as realistic responses to the Adjustment Center. Still, coming as they do at the beginning of the play, they serve as visual metaphors for the poisoning effect of the prison. When the dead Jefferson turns up in the last scene, comparing the homemade rope with which he hanged himself to the playground swing he knew as a boy, while his body bag swings in the prison yard, it is not apparent whether he is Bobby's conjuration or Ribman's device. In either case he is not quite the stuff of which realistic plays are made.

For the rest, Ribman's plays touch a variety of genres and casually use antirealistic devices. *Harry, Noon and Night* was originally seen as a kind of black comedy (*v.* my remarks in *The Jumping-Off Place*), presumably because the phrase was so much in the air in the 1960s. No such encompassing label is necessary, however, to recognize that each of the scenes is an artificially designed confrontation, controlled by the stronger of the pair in each instance (Harry in 1 and 3, Immanuel in 2), and that the barest plot line ties them together. In *The Journey of the Fifth Horse,* scenes from Zoditch's real world, from his fantasy world and from Chulkaturin's diary share the same space and the same actors since Zoditch, while denying his likeness to Chulkaturin, peoples his reading with the faces he knows. The realism of *The Final War of Olly Winter,* that the Vietnamese characters speak Vietnamese for the most part, is in fact a kind of antirealism since it creates community through cross-lingual, gestural communication, a usage that conventional realism might aspire to but would scarcely attempt. *The Ceremony of Innocence* is a play within a play—unusual in an historical drama—and inventive within its chosen form; Edmund's killing of the Danish farmers is enacted in slow motion in a red light as he describes what happens, almost laconically, against the rhythmic beat of a drum, and the comments that follow are from speakers isolated in individual spotlights. The short plays that make up *Passing Through from Exotic Places,* whether satiric *(Sunstroke),* sentimental *(The Burial of Esposito)* or incipiently ironic *(The Son Who Hunted Tigers in Jakarta),* are conceived broadly—the play as cartoon—although, in this case, I do not know—except for *Sunstroke* —whether aesthetic decision or artistic uncertainty is at work. *Cold Storage* is a debate, a duet, a game of verbal handball, one of the funniest serious plays in the American theater. When one remembers that *Harry, Noon and Night* was the result of Ribman's attempt to write a one-act play to be performed with the still unproduced *Day of the Games* and when one looks at this disparate group of plays side by side, it is easy to imagine that Ribman begins with an image, an idea or the sound of a voice and follows it, the blue guitar ringing changes on the playwright's perceived reality and the immediate occasion of that reality constantly retuning the blue guitar.

If my improvisation on Stevens's guitar suggests that there is an accidental quality to Ribman's work, the metaphor is misleading. The plays as they stand are wonderfully complex works in which ideas, images, particular lines surface, disappear, return, sometimes simply as echoes, sometimes enriched with new dramatic or thematic significance, as the description above of the end of *Cold Storage* indicates. Or take an example from *Harry, Noon and Night.* In his account of his job in the first scene, Harry harps on his fear of being fired: "I got a kid that's stone-blind depending on me." He mentions the "stone-blind kid" three times, so when Immanuel unveils the statue in the second scene, alert members of the audience will recognize the figure even without the label that Ribman puts in the stage directions. "What's the matter with its eyes?" asks Archer. "It's blind," Immanuel answers, and Archer counters, "It's unfinished, that's all." In the last scene, Harry contemplates giving the statue "eyes to see with. Big granite eyes," which I suppose would make him a stone-sighted kid. It is funny when the blind cupid is unveiled—an intellectual smile if not a belly laugh—but the repeated image is more than a running gag. It ties in with

Immanuel's need for glasses from Archer's point of view and with Archer's inability to see through Immanuel's eyes. When the latter offers to come into the toilet to verify the absence of toilet paper, Archer says, "I'm not blind. I can see what's here." He has spent the scene trying to see what may not have been there (the figures in Harry's painting, the old man selling balloons on the corner). "I can't see any difference," he says when Immanuel offers him two identical strings of beads, one for fifty cents, the other for nine dollars. "There is a difference," Immanuel insists—of eight dollars and a half, but he never says that. In this scene, in the whole play, the stone-blind kid is one of a host of references, lines, actions that contribute to the secondary theme discussed in the paragraph on the blue guitar with which this section of the essay opens.

The juxtaposition of line and prop in the example above, Harry's speech in 1 solidifying into a statue in 2, somewhat belies Ribman's insistence in the Gruen interview, "My plays are about words.... The words are what matter." He is a marvelously verbal playwright, but often the intricacy of his language is set off by a presentational device that is purely visual. Much of what Immanuel has to say at the beginning of his scene is underscored by the fact that he is cleaning a fish at the time, using the aggressive chopping movements as emphasis or counterpoint. It is a device that Ribman so liked that he used it in the unproduced television play *If My Father's House Be Evil* (1948) and, in a variation, in the meat-grinding scene in *The Journey of the Fifth Horse*. Ribman followed his remarks on "words" with the complaint that audiences go to see plays where once they went to hear them. It is true that audiences—American audiences, at least—do not listen as carefully as they should if they want to get the full effect of plays like those of Ribman, but it is not a matter of the eye upstaging the ear. Playwrights who work with any subtlety have always been faced with audiences who stay on the surface of plays, visually as well as verbally, and who experience new plays as variations on old ones. In Ribman's case this could be unfortunate if *The Ceremony of Innocence*, for instance, were dismissed as a pacifist play about some old king, or *The Poison Tree* as a prison play about racism. Or if the density of his work came across as "stark and turgid realism." Whatever Ribman may have said in the 1970 interview,[6] it is not a case of his playing only to the ears of audiences that come to look. His visual sense is obvious in the script for *The Final War of Olly Winter*, and some of the suggested juxtapositions— the boy's hands stroking the cat, the man's hands cleaning the weapon— work on the screen as he wants them to, as more than information-giving images. I have already mentioned scenes—the dialogueless opening of *The Poison Tree*, the killing of the Danish farmers in *Ceremony*—which illustrate Ribman's understanding of the impact of visual effects in the theater and their use in the service of metaphor and theme. From the prostitute in the first scene of *Harry* to Miss Madurga at the opening of *Cold Storage,* Ribman has provided characters who silently insist, "Listen to what the talkers have to say, but keep an eye on me at the same time."

This emphasis on the non-verbal elements in Ribman's work is simply a way of saying that Ribman, who started out to be a poet, is a playwright in the complete sense of that word. It is certainly not an attempt to diminish his talent for words. Whether he is writing idiomatically *(Harry, Noon and Night)* or more formally *(The Journey of the Fifth Horse),* whether he catches a street rhythm which is not his own *(The Poison Tree)* or invents a rhythm to suggest the past *(The Ceremony of Innocence),* he creates highly articulate characters who illustrate both the precision and the ambiguity of language. As a character argues his case—Sussex in *Ceremony,* say, or Willy in *The Poison Tree*—Ribman uses the words to define the man, to separate the kernel from the ideological shell. When the character shares Ribman's sense of the wonder of words, as Parmigian does in *Cold Storage,* the play conveys sheer delight in language. Let me take two examples from that play—Ribman's richest to date—to indicate the ways in which he works with words. "You not only survived, Landau, you triumphed!" Parmigian says. "A boy with no education turns himself into a man who can almost tell the difference between a Van der Heyden, whatever that is, and a Pieter Brueghel." Parmigian is not trying to convince Landau that what he says is true; he is trying to exasperate him into a state of mind that will pull him past the guilt he feels for having survived. The glory of the line is the adverb, that "almost," for it carries us back to the exchange early in the scene in which, under Parmigian's needling, Landau says that his "biggest mistake" was once buying a Brueghel engraving that turned out to be by Van der Heyden. Parmigian belittles the confession with his own mistake involving pomegranates, which turn into plantains a few speeches later, and in the process mockingly questions the limiting terminology he uses to trap Landau into speech.

The other example is more complex and, since it involves two metaphors expressed in different acts, more difficult to grasp in the theater. Responding to Parmigian's remark about his "marvelous quality of surface veneer," Landau says:

> If you're interested in surface veneer, perhaps I might show you something in a nineteenth-century Chinese lacquer box. You might find it interesting to see how coat upon coat of lacquer can be laid down until the box itself may be removed leaving nothing behind but the form and the lacquer—the black, brilliant, slightly poisonous lacquer.

At the end of the play, Landau's rumination on the "bits and pieces" which are all he has of his past sets Parmigian to thinking of tire patches:

> You know, it would amaze you what you could do with a good patch. The patches on this 1933 Buick were so good that when the tires disintegrated the patches kept rolling for another hundred and seventy-two miles. They ran over a state trooper who was giving a speeding ticket to a nun that looked like a penguin.

The speeches are characteristic of the speakers. the primness of the "perhaps," of the "You might," even of the adjectival build at the end of the speech suggests the care with which Landau carries himself, his tendency to avoid directness. Or to use it like a stiletto. The exuberance in the other quotation, the false exactitude (the year of the car, the precise mileage) and the plausibility modulating into nonsense are pure Parmigian. Beyond style, content. Each of the speeches is a metaphor for the speaker. Landau has so coated himself with the lacquer of guilt and loss that the box of self has been removed. Parmigian, who is all patches (*v.* his description of his body at the beginning of the play), is still rolling with enough force to run down a Landau if not a state trooper. Yet the two metaphors are the same, each an image of an intact surface with nothing inside. One is an emptiness metaphor, however; the other about survival. In effect, Parmigian is making Landau an offer—replace your poisonous lacquer with my still running patches. Landau laughs again, presumably at the old joke about the nun-penguin lookalikes, and the two men exit together. The metaphors, which have seemed so true, are suddenly insufficient. Men are not metaphors, after all—not even dying men.

Ribman uses words, but writes about men. It takes more than articulated images to produce a playwright of substance.

NOTES

These are the editions of Ribman's plays used in the essay.

The Final War of Olly Winter, in *Great Television Plays,* ed. William I. Kaufman. New York, Dell, 1969, pp. 259–301. (Laurel Edition)

Fingernails Blue As Flowers, in *The American Place Theatre: Plays,* ed. Richard Schotter. New York, Dell, 1973, pp. 1–30. (A Delta Original)

Five Plays, New York, Avon, 1978. (A Bard Book) (Contains *Harry, Noon and Night, The Journey of the Fifth Horse, The Ceremony of Innocence, The Poison Tree* and *Cold Storage*)

"The Most Beautiful Fish," *The New York Times,* November 23, 1969, Section 2, p. 21.

Passing Through from Exotic Places, New York, Dramatists Play Service, 1970. (Contains *The Son Who Hunted Tigers in Jakarta, Sunstroke* and *The Burial of Esposito*)

1. First play to be produced. *Day of the Games,* written when Ribman was a graduate student at the University of Pittsburgh, was published in the university literary magazine, *Ideas and Figures,* 13 (Spring 1959), 34–53. It was revised as a one-act play in 1963, the year in which the first version of *If My Father's House Be Evil* was written. The revised *Day* and an unproduced television version of *Father's House* (1968) exist only in typescript, as do the various versions of *A Break in the Skin* (1970–1973).

2. Susan H. Dietz. *The Work of Ronald Ribman: The Poet as Playwright,* unpublished dissertation, University of Pennsylvania, 1974, p. 253. The appendix of this work, pp. 251–282, contains a selection of Ribman's poetry, much of it never published elsewhere.

3. An earlier version of this play was performed in Philadelphia and Westport, Connecticut, in the summer of 1973. When the revised version, Broadway bound, played Philadelphia in November 1975, it still had a scene in which Sergeant Coyne's wife appeared. The Property List in the acting edition (New York: Samuel French, 1977) still provides for the missing actress.

4. The name is spelled "Willie" in this speech (*Five Plays,* New York: Avon, 1978, p. 280), but I assume it is a typographical error taken from the acting edition (New York: Samuel French, 1977, p. 73) and kept alive by sloppy copy editors.

5. In an unpublished interview with Susan Dietz, July 23, 1973.

6. "But a writer's remarks can never be taken as serious evidence." Joyce Carol Oates, "The Tragic Vision of *The Possessed,*" *The Georgia Review,* 32 (Winter 1978), 882.

The Sighted Eyes and Feeling Heart of Lorraine Hansberry

MARGARET B. WILKERSON

The Black Arts Movement of the 1960's seemed to burst on the American theatrical scene with no warning. The plays of LeRoi Jones (now Amiri Baraka), Ed Bullins and others appeared, it seemed, from nowhere, called forth from hidden reserves of anger deep within the black community. Few had recognized the strains of militance in the earlier voice of Lorraine Hansberry. Only in hindsight do we now realize that Hansberry heralded the new movement and, in fact, became one of its major literary catalysts. The commercial success and popularity of her first play blinded some to her vision of light; suppression of her other works robbed the public of her insights and her warnings of the cataclysmic civic revolts to come. Only now, in retrospect, do we begin to comprehend her significance as an American and a black writer.

She was born in 1930 and died of cancer in 1965. Yet during her scant 34 years of life, she made an indelible mark on American theatre. She was the first black playwright and the youngest of any color to win the New York Drama Critics Circle Award for the Best Play of the Year, earning it for her first play, *A Raisin in the Sun*. The drama, which opened on Broadway in 1959, was a landmark success and was subsequently translated into over 30 languages on all continents, including the language of East Germany's Sorbische minority, and produced in such diverse countries as Czechoslovakia, England, France and the Soviet Union. The play became a popular film in 1964 and a Tony Award-winning musical in 1973.

Her brief life yielded five plays, (one of which was completed by her former husband and literary executor, Robert Nemiroff), and more than sixty magazine and newspaper articles, plays, poems and speeches. She also wrote the text for *The Movement*, a photographic essay on the Civil Rights Movement. *To Be Young, Gifted and Black*, her autobiographical play, toured the country after her death, playing to thousands on campuses and in communities, and adding a new and vital phrase to the American idiom. An activist artist, she spoke at Civil Rights rallies, writers' conferences and confronted then-U.S. Attorney General Robert Kennedy in a controversial meeting with black leaders about the role of the FBI in the Deep South. Her significance, however, does not rest solely on these activities nor even on her record of productivity. Hansberry is important because of her incisive, articulate and sensitive exposure of the dynamic, troubled American culture. That she, a black artist, could tell painful truths to a society unaccustomed to rigorous self-criticism and still receive its praise is testimony to her artistry.

There has been much mention of the fact that Lorraine Hansberry was born into material comfort on the Southside of Chicago, that she grew up as part of the middle-class and was therefore privy to opportunities denied others. While that may be true, there is another side to her background which must be acknowledged. In order for her family to purchase a home in a previously all-white neighborhood, her father had to wage a legal battle all the way to the U.S. Supreme Court. When the family finally moved in, the home was attacked by a racist mob—a brick hurled through the window narrowly missed the 8 year-old Lorraine. Earlier she had lived in a ghetto, the product of rigid housing segregation which kept all blacks, regardless of income, confined to the same neighborhood. She went to school and made friends with other black children whose families were not as well off as hers, and never forgot the lessons she learned from them. There are no easy generalizations about her early life, except those intended to justify simplistic views. The comfort to which she was born is only relative when one looks at the whole of American life; it did not isolate her from the struggles and the anger of poor people.

Although her plays are not autobiographical (except *To Be Young, Gifted and Black),* the origins of their themes can be found in several important facts from her childhood and youth. According to Hansberry, the truth of her life and essence begins in the Chicago ghetto where she was born:

> I think you could find the tempo of my people on their back porches. The honesty of their living is there in the shabbiness. Scrubbed porches that sag and look their danger. Dirty gray wood steps. And always a line of white and pink clothes scrubbed so well, waving in the dirty wind of city.
>
> My people are poor. And they are tired. And they are determined to live.
>
> Our Southside is a place apart: each piece of our living is a protest.[1]

From her parents she learned to have pride in the family and never to betray the race. But she also learned that freedom and equality for her people were not likely to come through the American democratic way. She had seen her father spend a small fortune fighting the restrictive covenants of Chicago, then die a permanently embittered exile in a foreign country, having seen few results from his efforts. She had little desire for the materialism characteristic of her class since her kindergarten days when she was beaten up by classmates: her mother had dressed her in white fur — in the middle of the depression. She came to respect the pugnacity of her peers, children from the ghetto who were not afraid to fight and to defend themselves. From these and other early experiences she developed a deep empathy for the desires and frustrations of her people, and a respect for their beauty and vigor.

She attended the University of Wisconsin, but left shortly to find an education of a different kind. Moving to New York City, she took a job as a journalist on the Negro paper, *FREEDOM*. Here she began to refine her writing skills and came to know some of the greatest black literary and political figures of her time, among them W. E. B. DuBois, Paul Robeson and Langston Hughes. They became the artistic and philosophical reference points for her later works. The *FREEDOM* editor, Louis Burnham, she would credit with teaching her: "That all racism was rotten, white or black, that *everything* is political; that people tend to be indescribably beautiful and uproariously funny. He also taught me that they have enemies who are grotesque and that freedom lies in the recognition of all of that and other things."[2] It was at this point in her life that she consciously decided to be a writer.

As a black writer, Hansberry was caught in a paradox of expectations. She was expected to write about that which she "knew best," the black experience, and yet that expression was doomed to be called parochial and narrow. Hansberry, however, challenged these facile categories and forced a redefinition of the term "universality," one which would include the dissonant voice of an oppressed American minority. As a young college student, she had wandered into a rehearsal of Sean O'Casey's *Juno and the Paycock*. Hearing in the wails and moans of the Irish characters a universal cry of human misery, she determined to capture that sound in the idiom of her own people — so that it could be heard by all. "One of the most sound ideas in dramatic writing," she would later conclude, "is that in order to create the universal, you must pay very great attention to the specific. Universality, I think, emerges from truthful identity of what is.... In other words, I think people, to the extent we accept them and believe them as who they're supposed to be, to that extent they can become everybody."[3]

Such a choice by a black writer posed an unusual challenge to the literary establishment and a divided society ill-prepared to comprehend its meaning.

"All art is ultimately social: that which agitates and that which prepares the mind for slumber," Hansberry argued, attacking another basic tenet held by traditional critics. One of the most fundamental illusions of her time and culture, she believed, is the idea that art is not and should not make a social statement. The belief in "l'art pour l'art" permeates literary and theatrical criticism, denying the integral relationship between society and art. "The writer is deceived who thinks he has some other choice. The question is not whether one will make a social statement in one's work — but only *what* the statement will say, for if it says anything at all, it will be social."[4]

It would have been impossible for a person of her background and sensitivity to divorce herself from the momentous social events of the 1950's and 1960's. This period witnessed the beginning of a Cold War between the U.S. and Russian superpowers, a rising demand by blacks for civil rights at home, and a growing intransigence by colonized peoples throughout the world. Isolation is the enemy of black writers, Hansberry believed; they are obligated to participate in the intellectual and social affairs of humankind everywhere.

In a 1959 speech to young writers, she explained the impact of social and political events on her world view.

> I was born on the South Side of Chicago. I was born black and a female. I was born in a depression after one world war, and came into my adolescence during another. While I was still in my teens the first atom bombs were dropped on human beings at Nagasaki and Hiroshima. And by the time I was twenty-three years old, my government and that of the Soviet Union had entered actively into the worst conflict of nerves in human history — the Cold War.
>
> I have lost friends and relatives through cancer, lynching and war. I have been personally the victim of physical attack which was the offspring of racial and political hysteria. I have worked with the handicapped and seen the ravages of congenital diseases that we have not yet conquered, because we spend our time and ingenuity in far less purposeful wars; I have known persons afflicted with drug addiction and alcoholism and mental illness. I see daily on the streets of New York, street gangs and prostitutes and beggars. I have, like all of you, on a thousand occasions seen indescribable displays of man's very real inhumanity to man, and I have come to maturity, as we all must, knowing that greed and malice and indifference to human mis-

ery and bigotry and corruption, brutality, and perhaps above all else, ignorance—the prime ancient and persistent enemy of man—abound in this world. I say all of this to say that one cannot live with sighted eyes and feeling heart and not know and react to the miseries which afflict this world.[5]

Hansberry's "sighted eyes" forced her to confront fully the depravity, cruelty and utter foolishness of men's actions, but her "feeling heart" would not allow her to lose faith in humanity's potential for overcoming its own barbarity. This strong and uncompromising belief in the future of humankind informed her plays and sometimes infuriated her critics.

Her best-known play, *A Raisin in the Sun,* dramatizes the seductiveness of American materialistic values. The title and theme are taken from a Langston Hughes poem, "Harlem," which asks: "What happens to a dream deferred?"[6] The dreams of the Youngers, a black family living in Southside Chicago, have gone unfulfilled too long. Their hopes of enjoying the fruits of freedom and equality have been postponed as they struggled merely to survive economically. Into this setting comes $10,000 insurance money paid upon the death of Walter Younger, Sr. Lena Younger (Mama) and her adult son, Walter, clash over the money's use. Mama wants to save some for her daughter Beneatha's college education and make a down payment on a new house in order to get the family out of the cramped quarters and shared bathroom of their tiny apartment. Walter wants to invest in a liquor store. They share the dream of improving the family's situation, but Walter, consumed with the frustrations of his dead-end chauffeur's job, believes that the money itself is synonymous with life. The possession of money and the things it can buy will make him a man in the eyes of his family and society, he asserts.

The intrusion of American cultural values is evident both in this tug of war and in the character of Lena. Mama, who initially fits the popular stereotype of the Black Mammy, seems to be the domineering head of household. She rules everyone's life, even making a down payment on a house in an all-white neighborhood without consulting her son. However, as she begins to comprehend the destructive effect of her actions on Walter, she relinquishes her authority and gives him the balance of the money to invest as he wishes. Walter's elation is short-lived, however, because he loses the money by entrusting it to his "partner," a slick con man who disappears. In an effort to recover his loss, Walter tells his family that he will accept money from his prospective neighbors who would rather buy him off than live next door to him. The decision is a personal test for Walter, for he is sorely tempted to sacrifice his pride and integrity for mercenary values: "There ain't no causes—there ain't nothing but taking in this world and he who takes most is smartest—and it don't make a damn bit of difference *how*."[7] In a highly dramatic moment, Walter gets down on his knees and shows his mother how he will beg, if necessary, for the white man's money—scratching his head and laughing in the style of the old Uncle Tom. Even with this display, Mama does not berate him, but rather surrounds him with her circle of love and compassion, saying to the others who have witnessed this scene:

> Have you cried for that boy today? I don't mean for your-self and for the family 'cause we lost the money. I mean for him; what he been through and what it done to him. Child, when do you think is the time to love somebody the most; when they done good and made things easy for everybody? That ain't the time at all. It's when he's at his lowest and can't believe in hisself 'cause the world done whipped him so.
>
> When you starts measuring somebody—measure him right, child. Measure him right. Make sure you done taken into account what hills and valleys he come through before he got to wherever he is.[8]

Just as the stereotyped image of the Mammy gives way to the caring, understanding mother, historic cornerstone of the black family, so the materialism of Walter crumbles before his reaffirmation of traditional values of pride and selfhood. He tells the baffled representative of the hostile white community that he and his family will move into their house because his father and the generations before him earned that right. Walter speaks the words and takes the action, but Mama provides the context. She, who embodies the race's will to transcend and who forms that critical link between the past and the future, articulates and transmits the traditions of the race to the next generation. Her wisdom and compassion provide the context for him to attain true manhood, to advance materially without becoming materialistic.

The story of the Younger family is the story of a struggle to retain human values and integrity while forcing change in a society where human worth is measured by the dollar. Through the supporting character, Asagai, an African intellectual, the personal dynamics of that struggle become a microcosm of the struggle for liberation throughout the world and especially in Africa. Hansberry achieves this connection through Asagai's response to Walter's foolish mistake. He warns the disappointed Beneatha that she is using her brother's error as an excuse to give up on "the ailing human race" and her own participation in it. Beneatha argues that Walter's action is no different from the pettiness, ignorance and foolishness of other men who turn idealistic notions of freedom and independence into absurd dreams. But Asagai reacts vehemently, proclaiming that one mistake does not stop a movement. Others will correct that mistake and go on, probably to make errors of their own — but the result, however halting, is movement, change and advancement forward.[9] Thus, in a parallel action, Asagai affirms Mama's loving support of Walter by restating her position in the sociopolitical terms of African freedom struggles. While Mama may seem to be merely conservative, clinging to an older generation, it is she who, in fact, is the mother of revolutionaries; it is she who makes possible the change and movement of the new generation.

Despite Mama's importance to the theme, Walter remains a worthy and unique counterpoint. In his own way, Walter signals the wave of the future. He is restless, hungry, angry — a victim of his circumstance but at the same time the descendant of his proud forebears, struggling to transcend his victimhood. When he, in a drunken flare, leaps onto a table and assumes the stance of an African chieftain, he unconsciously embodies that proud and revolutionary spirit which is his heritage. When he quietly refuses the white citizens' pay-off at the end of the play, he becomes the symbolic father of the aggressive, articulate black characters who will stride the boards in the 1960's. Indeed, Walter, who has begun to shed the materialism of the majority culture, leads the march to a different drum.

Testimony to Hansberry's craftsmanship is the fact that these complex themes and perceptions are presented unobtrusively, emerging naturally as a result of action and dialogue. A master of heightened realism, she carefully orchestrates the moods of the play, using highly symbolic, non-realistic actions when needed and guiding both performer and audience through a maze of emotional and humorous moments. The play makes a social statement, but not at the expense of its ability to engage. In fact, the miracle of this popular play is that Hansberry successfully involves her audience, whether white or black, in a complete identification and support for the struggles of this family.

The Drinking Gourd, the next play completed by Hansberry, was never produced. Commissioned in 1960 for the National Broadcasting Company, it was to be first in a series of ninety-minute television dramas commemorating the Centennial of the Civil War. Deemed too controversial for the American television-viewing public, it was put on the shelf with notations commending its excellence and was later published posthumously by Robert Nemiroff.

Named for the Negro slave song which contained a coded message of escape, *The Drinking Gourd* is an incisive analysis and indictment of American slavery as a self-perpetuating system based on the exploitation of cheap labor. More than an historical piece, this provocative work identifies the slave system as the basis for the country's economic philosophy and later capitalistic development; it dramatizes the devastating psychological and physical impact of the slave institution on both master and slave. As in *A Raisin in the Sun,* the message is not delivered in a heavy-handed manner, but is derived from the characters and actions of the drama.

Three distinct classes of people are a part of this world of slavery: the master, the slave and the poor white. During the course of the play, set at the beginning of the Civil War, the impact of the slave system on each class is starkly portrayed, with each becoming a victim of its economic realities. Hiram Sweet is the ailing master of a slave plantation which is losing money, in part because Hiram's relatively humane policies do not produce enough to compete favorably with larger, less liberal plantations. The slave Hannibal, son of Rissa, Hiram's confidant, is contemptuous of his situation and is preparing to escape. Zeb, a poor white farmer, finds that he is being squeezed out by the larger plantations and so agrees to become an overseer on Hiram's land—against the advice of his friend.

Although Hiram is sensitive enough to be uneasy about the morality of slavery, he is not perceptive enough to recognize his ultimate powerlessness as a master. In an angry speech justifying a special favor he is granting to Rissa's son, Hiram says to his wife: "I am master of this plantation and every soul on it. I am master of this house as well...There are some men born into this world who make their own destiny. Men who do not tolerate the rules of other men or other forces."[10]

However, as Hiram's health fails, the control of the plantation is taken over by his immature, simple-minded son, Everett. The opposite of his father, Everett runs the plantation with a harsh hand, hiring Zeb to enforce his new policies. When Everett discovers that Hannibal has learned to read, he orders Zeb to carry out a brutal punishment — to put out Hannibal's eyes. The blinding of Hannibal shatters the illusion that slavery can be redeemed from its moral bankruptcy. The master cannot protect the son of a woman for whom he cares; the slave's friendship with the master cannot prevent a human catastrophe; and the poor white farmer cannot maintain any semblance of self-respect and humanity while being an overseer. The disease of the slave institution infects them all.

Each character succumbs to the economic realities of an exploitative system gone wild. Hansberry drives her point home in a climactic moment near the end of the play. The dying Hiram goes to Rissa's cabin in the slave quarters where she is caring for her blinded son, and says:

> I—I wanted to tell you, Rissa—I wanted to tell you and ask you
> to believe me, that I had nothing to do with this. I—some things
> do seem to be out of the power of my hands after all ... Other
> men's rules are a part of my life ...

Rissa, angry and embittered, looks up at him and says: "Why, ain't you Marster? How can a man be marster of some men and not at all of others...."[11] She turns away from him and continues tending to her son. A dejected, defeated man, Hiram leaves the cabin. Weak from his illness, he falls in the dirt outside of the cabin. Rissa, ignoring his cries for help, closes the door on him as he dies near her doorstep.

Hiram's death marks the demise of this world, but Hansberry intimates that the insidious effects of slavery will be far-reaching. In the final words of the play, the Soldier/Narrator says:

> Slavery is beginning to cost this nation a lot. It has become a drag on the great industrial nation we are determined to become; it lags a full century behind the great American notion of one strong federal union which our eighteenth century founders knew was the only way we could eventually become one of the most powerful nations in the world. And, now, in the nineteenth century, we are determined to hold on to that dream. ...And so...we must fight. There is no alternative. It is possible that slavery might destroy itself—but it is more possible that it would destroy these United States first. That it would cost our political and economic future.... It has already cost us, as a nation, too much of our soul.[12]

Although Hansberry remains faithful to the parameters of the historical period, she argues that America will continue to pay a high price for its adoption of a slave economy.

The controversy which this drama sparked in the executive chambers of NBC can be attributed to the myths which Hansberry attacks in this play. She dares to place in the mouth of a black woman slave the words which destroy the genteel illusion of a humane and necessary, though peculiar, institution. She also permits this woman to choose, consciously and without ambivalence, the well-being of her son over the needs of her dying master—an act which belies the dearly-held stereotype of the faithful, self-deprecating servant. Hansberry also uses the play as an occasion to debate basic notions that slaves were happy, compliant and loyal, and that the institution of slavery was not a primary issue in the Civil War.

Although the play has never stood the test of performance, the script is tight and utilizes the short, intimate scenes characteristic of effective television drama. Hansberry had a sure sense for this medium and, had the play been produced, she would have moved the electronic medium closer to maturity.

The next Hansberry play which the public would see was *The Sign in Sidney Brustein's Window*. By the time it opened on Broadway in 1964,

Hansberry's cancer had already been diagnosed, and she was in and out of hospitals, often needing a wheelchair to get to and from rehearsals. Opening to mixed critical reviews, *Sign* played for 101 performances and closed the night of her death, January 12, 1965. It was destined to go down in theatrical history books as a triumph, however, because a loving public fought to keep it open, raising money and donating time to help it to survive.[13]

A play of ideas, *Sign* angered and confused critics for two basic reasons. First, it was not about the black experience; in fact, it had only one black character in it. Lorraine Hansberry, hailed by the establishment as a new black voice, had written about white artists and intellectuals who lived in Greenwich Village. Second, the play firmly opposed the vogue of urbane, sophisticated ennui and the glorification of intellectual impotence so typical of the period. It dared to challenge the apathy of the American intellectual and his indifference to the serious problems overtaking the world.

In this play, plot is secondary to character and serves only as a vehicle for Sidney Brustein's personal odyssey towards self-discovery. Sidney has agreed to work on the campaign of a local politician who has promised to bring social reform to his New York neighborhood. Through a series of confrontations with family and friends, Sidney is given an intimate look at the human frailties which lie behind the mask of each character. The most startling revelations center on his wife and sisters-in-law: Iris, his beautiful, long-haired protegee who no longer wishes to play the ingenue role and desires rather the tinsel of stardom; Gloria, the sensitive callgirl who commits suicide because she cannot bear her burden of guilt and loneliness; and Mavis, the bourgeois Philistine whose image belies the painful compromise and courage of her personal life. Sidney, the symbol of modern man, stares human ugliness full in the face and seems powerless against it: "Wrath has become a poisoned gastric juice in the intestine. One does not *smite* evil any more: one holds one's gut, thus—and takes a pill."[14]

When he discovers the duplicity and corruption of his politician friend, he has every reason to return to his posture of intellectual apathy, condemning in colorful prose the world around him. But his odyssey through the maze of human suffering has changed him; Gloria's death has changed him:

> That which warped and distorted all of us is. . . all around; it
> is in this very air! *This world* — this swirling, seething madness
> —which you ask us to accept, to help maintain—has done this—
> maimed my friends — emptied these rooms and my very bed.
> And now it has taken my sister. *This* world! Therefore, to live,
> to breathe—I shall *have* to fight it!
> . . .

> [I am] A fool who believes that death is waste and love is
> sweet and that the earth turns and men change every day and
> that rivers run and that people wanna be better than they are and
> that flowers smell good and that I hurt terribly today, and that
> hurt is desperation and desperation is — energy and energy can
> *move* things.... [15]

This strong affirmation of life in the face of human frailty and cosmic
absurdity was unusual in the world of professional theatre, but very consistent with the beliefs of Lorraine Hansberry.

Upon the author's death in 1965, *What Use Are Flowers?*[16] and *Les
Blancs* remained essentially unfinished works. In late 1961, *What Use Are
Flowers?* was conceived as a fantasy for television, in response to contemporary debates about the destruction or survival of the human race. After
her experience with *The Drinking Gourd,* Hansberry began to reconcep-
tualize the play for the stage, but never lived to complete the idea. What
survives is the draft of a short play about a hermit who returns from a
self-imposed exile only to find wild children orphaned by a nuclear
holocaust. As he decides to civilize the children and chooses those aspects
of civilization worthy of repeating and necessary to their spiritual and
intellectual growth, the audience gains a fascinating insight into the
priorities of our western culture.

Hansberry has a talent for asking the evocative question which goes to
the heart of the matter. After teaching the children the meaning of such
words as clay, pot and sun, the Hermit attempts to explain the importance
of beauty, using a bouquet of flowers as an example. One of the children
asks, "What use are flowers?" And the Hermit is momentarily stymied in
his effort to explain this intangible but crucial aspect of a civilized and
humanistic view. He finally answers that the uses of flowers are infinite. In
that exchange is the crux of the play: the Hermit's real challenge is to teach
these pre-literates to control and overcome their habit of violence so that
they can learn the uses of love and compassion, cornerstones of
civilization.

Fantasy is an apt term for this play because it lacks the specificity of
cultural reference points which is a hallmark of Hansberry's work. However one misses this richness which is typical of her plays, the dramatic
situation warrants the treatment of human actions in a more or less
abstracted form. Scenes from this play have been performed, but the work
in full has yet to be produced.

Les Blancs was a consuming labor of love for Hansberry. Throughout
her last year and a half of life, even while *Sign* struggled towards production, she worked at *Les Blancs,* carrying it in and out of hospitals, writing

and rewriting , polishing and refining. Two years earlier, a scene from the draft work had been staged for the Actors Studio Writers' Workshop and Hansberry had been encouraged by its reception. Robert Nemiroff acted as her sounding-board-advocate-critic as she sought a structure "flexible enough to contain and focus the complexity of personalities, social forces and ideas in this world she had created."[17] After many discussions with him, she broke through and outlined the major structural and character developments she wanted. After her death, Nemiroff continued the work, "synthesizing the scenes already completed throughout the play with those in progress, drawing upon relevant fragments from earlier drafts and creating, as needed, dialogue of my own to bridge gaps, deepen relationships or tighten the drama along the lines we had explored together."[18]

The result of this collaborative effort is a remarkable play which asks an urgent question of the Twentieth Century: Can the liberation of oppressed peoples be achieved without violent revolution? *Les Blancs* is the first major work by a black American playwright to focus on Africa and to pose this question in the context of an African liberation struggle.

Tshembe Matoseh, a black African, has returned to his homeland for his father's funeral. During his visit, he is caught up in his country's struggle to oust the white colonialists after many years of peaceful efforts to negotiate their freedom. His family's tribe urges him to lead the violent struggle, while his brother, Abioseh, who has converted to the Catholic priesthood, abhors the native effort and in fact betrays one of the leaders to the local police. Tshembe's dilemma is classic; the parallels to Hamlet are obvious. But Hansberry, instinctively recognizing the inappropriateness of relying only on a western literary reference point, provides Tshembe with another metaphor—from African lore—Modingo, the wise hyena who lived between the lands of the elephants and the hyenas. Ntali, one of the African insurgents, explains to Tshembe in an effort to engage him in their struggle. Modingo was asked by the hyenas, the earliest inhabitants of the jungle, to settle their territorial quarrel with the elephants who want more space because of their size. Modingo, whose name means "One Who Thinks Carefully Before He Acts," understands the arguments offered by both and refuses to join either side until he has thought on the matter. While he thinks, the hyenas wait—too long, because the elephants move in and drive the hyenas from the jungle altogether. "That is why the hyena laughs until this day and why it is such terrible laughter: because it was such a bitter joke that was played upon them while they 'reasoned.' "[19]

Hansberry does not shrink from the controversy and desperation implicit in this theme. The question, which is debated from all sides, is complicated by the presence of white characters of good will, kind intent and proven loyalty. But the wheels of violent revolution have already been set in motion by the very first contact between colonizer and native. One mistake is compounded by another, leading inevitably to a bloody holocaust. Like the inevitability of change predicted by Asagai in *A Raisin in the Sun,* the moment comes when Tshembe must embrace his destiny and fight the historical intruders. The decision is fraught with pain because he must begin by murdering his own brother and setting off the attack which kills the gentle white woman, his surrogate mother, who had nurtured him from birth. As the play ends, a hyena-like, sobbing laughter breaks forth from Tshembe.

Throughout the play, Tshembe's understanding of the complexities, his ability to see both sides and to love genuinely across color lines is at war with his native history. His psyche, which is tied to the spirit of Africa, is personified by a woman dancer who constantly calls him to action, back to the struggle of his people.

The play was first performed at the Longacre Theatre in New York City in 1970, and evoked very strong reactions from its reviewers. Just as the audience divided into two camps, cheering for different sides, so the critics seemed unable to avoid such partisanship and criticized the play according to their feelings about the central question of the play. *Les Blancs* is a courageous, well-crafted work, but a challenge to perform for an audience unaccustomed to encountering complex and disturbing questions in the theatre. Its existence marks Hansberry as a visionary who accurately read the signs of her times and foreshadowed the impending African struggle for liberation. The play also forces a reassessment of the term "terrorist" which has become a meaningless label which masks the desperation and sometimes the inevitability of violence.

Hansberry defined realism as "not only what *is* but what is *possible*."[20] *Les Blancs* in particular fits this definition, for Hansberry did not advocate violent revolution, but used the theatre as a medium for a passionate encounter with the consequences of our heroic as well as our foolish actions. Her work has yet to receive the critical attention due her immense talent.[21]

Behind the vibrant theatre of the 1960's and 1970's stand the pioneering figures and themes crafted by Hansberry, who forced the American stage to a new level of excellence and human relevance. In play after play, she sensed the mood of her times and anticipated the future — the importance that African politics and styles would assume, the regeneration of commitment among American intellectuals, the seductiveness of mercenary values for black-Americans, and the proliferation of liberation struggles throughout the world. The theatre was a working laboratory for this brilliant woman whose sighted eyes and feeling heart caused her to reach out to a world at once cruel and beautiful.

NOTES

1. Lorraine Hansberry, *To Be Young, Gifted and Black: Lorraine Hansberry in Her Own Words*. Adapted by Robert Nemiroff. New York: New American Library, 1970, p. 45.

2. *Ibid.*, pp. 99–100.

3. *Ibid.*, p. 128.

4. Lorraine Hansberry, "The Negro Writer and His Roots: Toward A New Romanticism," in a speech delivered to Black Writers' Conference, Henry Hudson Hotel, New York City, March 1, 1959, pp. 5–6.

5. *Ibid.*, p. 41.

6. Langston Hughes, *Selected Poems*. New York: Alfred A. Knopf, 1971, p. 268.

7. Lorraine Hansberry, *A Raisin in the Sun/The Sign in Sidney Brustein's Window*. New York: New American Library, 1958, p. 122.

8. *Ibid.*, p. 125.

9. *Ibid.*, pp. 114–116.

10. Lorraine Hansberry, *The Drinking Gourd* in *Les Blancs: The Collected Last Plays of Lorraine Hansberry,* ed. by Robert Nemiroff. New York: Random House, 1972, pp. 259–260.

11. *Ibid.*, p. 306.

12. *Ibid.*, pp. 309–310.

13. Robert Nemiroff describes this history in "The 'Final' 101 Performances of Sidney Brustein: Portrait of A Play and Its Author" in Hansberry, *A Raisin in the Sun/The Sign in Sidney Brustein's Window*, pp. 138–183.

14. *Ibid.*, pp. 274–275.

15. *Ibid.*, pp. 317–318.

16. *What Use Are Flowers?* is in *Les Blancs: The Collected Last Plays of Lorraine Hansberry.*

17. Lorraine Hansberry, *Les Blancs* in *Les Blancs: The Collected Last Plays of Lorraine Hansberry*, pp. 44–45.

18. *Ibid.*, p. 45.

19. *Ibid.*, p. 126.

20. *To Be Young, Gifted and Black.* New York: New American Library, 1970, p. 236.

21. *Freedomways*, Vol. 19, No. 4, 1979, is a special issue on Lorraine Hansberry and offers the most recent, significant reassessment of her life and works. This issue also contains a discussion of the author's feminism (pp. 235–245) and the most comprehensive bibliography to date on Hansberry, pp. 285–304.

Amiri Baraka (LeRoi Jones)*

WERNER SOLLORS

*This essay is in part reprinted from *Amiri Baraka/LeRoi Jones: The Quest for a "Populist Modernism"* (New York, 1978) with the permission of Columbia University Press. This book also contains a fuller documentation of all sources used and a comprehensive Baraka bibliography. Parts of this essay were first presented at the College Language Association Convention in Savannah, 1976.
© Columbia University Press 1978.

The plays by Afro-American writer LeRoi Jones (born in Newark, N.J. in 1934), who has used the African name Amiri Baraka ("blessed prince") in his civil and literary life since 1968, illustrate the political and artistic changes Baraka's writing underwent in the past 20 years. Among the twelve plays discussed on the following pages, the early works reflect, and in some ways herald, the gradual change in mood from the Bohemian life of the Beat Generation in the 1950's to the new race consciousness and political flamboyance of the 1960's, the later plays show Baraka's commitment, first to Black cultural nationalism and, in the case of the last play, to Maoism.

Baraka's first drama, "The Eighth Ditch (Is Drama," published and performed in 1961, is indicative of the interference of the "social" with the lyrical world of a poet's imagination who is obsessed with a narcissistic self-division into two personae, one "46," a young middle-class Negro boy scout, and his counterpart, guide, and seducer, "64," an older under-privileged Black boy scout who introduces himself with the Melvillean salute "Call me Herman," and who is full of blues and allusions. The pure physical expression of which 64 and 46 seem capable in isolation is threatened and debased when other boy scouts in the camp find out about their homosexual affair.

This brief lyrical drama anticipates central structural elements of Baraka's later drama. Viewed on the literal level, the drama represents the two protagonists' inability to maintain a truly intimate sexual relationship, since they are confronted with the threatening presence of "others." At the end of the play, "46" is no longer a lover; for the benefit of the other boy scouts, he has been reduced to a commodity, an object. As in the later plays, *The Toilet* and *Dutchman,* the dramatic conflict originates with the assumed hostility of the not very well characterized "others" (boy scouts, classmates, or subway riders) toward the sensitive protagonists, a hostility which perverts love into abuse, into violence, or into the very act of killing.

In *The Eighth Ditch,* as in *Dutchman,* a division separates a more intimate scene in which only the protagonists are on stage from a more hostile scene in which the infringement of "others" changes the private interaction into a public performance. This transformation is only possible, however, because the original interaction of the protagonists already contained the latent possibility of aggressiveness: 64's seductiveness, as well as Lula's flirting, are suggestive of aggression. Still, only the presence of "others" brings about the actual change. In Baraka's terms, these others reify the verb-process of intimate communication into a "noun," a defining power associated with hell. At this point, even the "social" reading of the play refers us to the Beat poetic, which compares the act of creation with orgasm and views others, critics, readers, or listeners, with hostility. Whether we focus on the division of the self into a 64 and a 46, or on the confrontation between 46/64 and the "others," *The Eighth Ditch* remains a drama of the lyrical self.

The play is suggestive of a reaching out for the "social," while assigning the source of "drama" to a divided self. *The Eighth Ditch* also reflects the private fears of an expressive artist whose self-revelations are leading him to an increasingly "public" career. Baraka's next plays, which continued the theme of a confrontation between sensitive protagonists and a hostile world of "others," made Baraka a public figure.

The Toilet, first performed in 1962, is set in an urban high school and deals again with loving self-expression in terms of homosexuality. The one-act play contrasts the homosexual relationship of two protagonists with the hostile and threatening, all-male outside world. Again, homosexuality is viewed positively by Baraka both as an outsider-situation analogous to, though now also in conflict with, that of Blackness, and as a possibility for the realization of "love" and "beauty" against the racial gang code of a hostile society. But there is also a new element of race consciousness in the play.

In the course of the one-act play, Black student Ray Foots has to deny and denounce his love for white student James Karolis. Although Ray had written him a love note, he feels compelled in the presence of other students to deny his own feelings, to act tough, and to let the other students rough up his beloved. Only after the others leave the latrine can Foots express his feelings by cradling the beaten Karolis. In *The Toilet,* the Black protagonist has to choose between his generic identity as "Foots" and his individual peculiarity as "Ray." While Foots denotes a "lower" kind of "plebeian" existence, that is closer to the ethnic roots and the soil, "Ray" suggests a more spiritual personality with a cosmic genealogy.

On one level, *The Toilet* is the affirmation of Ray's individual self-expression—of a person different from that majority which defines his reality negatively. *The Toilet* contrasts the possibility of the free expression of homosexual love, as admission of "any man's beauty," not only with the repression of this freedom of the protagonists through a "social order," but, more than that, with a total inversion of the positive metaphor of homosexuality into the perversion of sadism.

The Toilet is undoubtedly an indictment of a brutal social order, depicted fittingly against the background of a filthy latrine. This time, however, in Baraka's familiar confrontation of outsiders with the group, the representatives of the "social order" are young Black males; they are the kind of group Baraka increasingly attempted to speak for, and with whom he tried to identify, in opposition to "Liberals."

The approach to the play as a perverted "love story" is thus challenged by an interpretation of the majority-minority relations that inform *The Toilet.* With this focus, the function of homosexuality and the roles of Ray Foots and James Karolis appear in a different light. Instead of representing love and the situation of the outsider, homosexuality now becomes a metaphor for acceptance in the white world. In other words, homosexuality becomes the gesture of individual assimilation, of trying to rise above the peer group, of "liberal" betrayal. As a consequence, the identity of a down-to-earth "Foots" would now seem somewhat more desirable than that of the lofty "Ray," who has removed himself from his ethnic reality. For, if the "love story" is a sentimentalization of "Ray," the "black-and-white story" is a bitter acceptance of Foots. And this acceptance, which implies a painful exorcism of interracial and homosexual love, was increasingly felt to be necessary by Baraka.

Baraka's most famous play, *Dutchman,* leaves the homosexual theme behind and focuses with full power on the theme of a heterosexual, interracial encounter, which, however, still bears traces of the divided self.

In *Dutchman,* first performed in 1964, the dramatic encounter of a twenty-year-old middle-class Negro and a thirty-year-old white Bohemian woman takes place as an absurdist ritual on the New York subway. The woman, Lula, flirts with the young man, Clay; her aggressive hipness makes Lula the dominant partner. In the presence of other subway passengers, her attacks become harsher and more provocative; when Clay explodes with anger, he is stabbed to death by the aggressive white woman who, at the end of the play, approaches her next victim, another young Black man.

Clay and Lula, who are individuals and allegorical types, desired "invisibility" as an escape from history into a transracial sexual encounter in a Bohemian "groove." The hostility between them is at its lowest point in the play when the other passengers appear. The presence of these "citizens" increases Lula's aggressiveness and helps to reveal that her idyllic description was an illusion, that her and Clay's *situation* does not leave them this "liberated" alternative. Lula acts as if obsessed, and Clay responds "almost involuntarily." As more and more people board the train and move closer and closer to the two main figures, the private dialogue between Clay and Lula assumes, increasingly, the character of public address expressed in more and more aggressively obscene language. Only when the "others" laugh with Lula at Clay does Clay raise his voice and address the passengers directly; and only after Lula has reached an agreement with the "citizens" does she stab Clay (whose body is, fittingly, disposed of collectively by the group of train riders).

The absurdist situation of *Dutchman* is a two-fold inversion of that of *The Toilet*. On the one hand, the physical victims have changed: instead of the white Karolis, who could be comforted by Ray Foots in the end, the Black Clay has become the victim of Lula's (and America's) violent racism. On the other hand, the sequence of action elements has been inverted, and thereby the statement of *Dutchman* has become much less ambiguous: the conciliatory ending of *The Toilet* corresponds to the ostensibly harmless idyll at the end of scene I in *Dutchman,* and the violence in the course of *The Toilet* is paralleled by the murder at the end of *Dutchman*. These changes allow no hope for a solution to the race problem through "love," as at least one reading of *The Toilet* suggested.

Like *The Eighth Ditch, Dutchman* is a drama of the divided self. Like "64" and "46," Lula and Clay represent different aspects of an artistic consciousness which has divided itself into opposing forces. Lula first becomes visible to Clay as he looks "blankly toward the window" of the train; this suggests the genesis of the woman out of the Adam's rib of Clay's mirror image. Clay, like "46," is the "buttoned down" Negro par excellence, the incorporation of Baraka's own rejected New Jersey Black middle-class background. Clay is a "type" from the "dead" world of unconditional assimilationism, of "lukewarm sugarless tea" and tall skinny black boys with phoney English accents, of "hopeless colored names," of "three-button suits," social-worker mothers and would-be Christians.

In her taunting of this "Black Baudelaire" (pp. 19–20), Lula resembles "64." Ten years older than Clay, she is perceptive to the point of omniscience. She knows everything about Clay's life, his origins, his destination on the train, and his friends' names; she is even aware of Clay's most intimate incestuous memories or fantasies (p. 9), and, she knows all about Black manhood, which Clay so energetically represses. Lula is perhaps everything Clay does not at first permit himself to become. She proceeds to confront him with increasingly harsh racial insults:

> LULA.   Clay, you liver-lipped white man. You would-be Christian. You ain't no nigger, you're just a dirty white man. Get up, Clay, Dance with me, Clay.
> CLAY.   Lula! Sit down, now. Be cool.
> LULA.   *(Mocking him, in wild dance)* Be cool. Be cool. That's all you know ... shaking that wildroot cream-oil on your knotty head, jackets buttoning up to your chin, so full of white man's words. Christ. God. Get up and scream at these people. (p. 31)

This gesture changes the characters' interaction abruptly. Virtually without any "development," the protagonists change their functions to themselves, to each other, to the other train riders, and as artistic self-projections. The other sides of their Janus-faces suddenly emerge. If until this point Lula was the protagonist of the play, Clay now becomes the hero. As he drops the bourgeois masquerade, he (in the most famous section of *Dutchman*) vents his aggression and pent-up violence and posits a Black mystique, an inner identity of repressed murderous instincts held back forcefully by masks and sublimated by artistic expression:

> The belly rub? You wanted to do the belly rub? ... Belly rub is not Queens. Belly rub is dark places, with big hats and overcoats held up with one arm. Belly rub hates you. Old bald-headed four-eyed ofays popping their fingers ... and don't know yet what they're doing. They say, "I love Bessie Smith." And don't even understand that Bessie Smith is saying, "Kiss my ass, kiss my black unruly ass." Before love, suffering, desire, anything you can explain, she's saying, and very plainly, "Kiss my black ass." And if you don't know that, it's you that's doing the kissing.

> Charlie Parker? Charlie Parker. All the hip white boys scream for Bird. And Bird, saying, "Up your ass, feeble-minded ofay! Up your ass." And they sit there talking about the tortured genius of Charlie Parker. Bird would've played not a note of music if he just walked up to East Sixty-seventh Street and killed the first ten white people he saw. Not a note! And I'm the great would-be poet. Some kind of bastard literature ... all you need is a simple knife thrust. Just let me bleed you, you loud

whore, and one poem vanished. A whole people of neurotics, struggling to keep from being sane. And the only thing that would cure the neurosis would be your murder. Simple as that. I mean if I murdered you, the other white people would begin to understand me. You understand? (pp. 34–35)

Clay's address is often cited as the pumping Black heart of the New Black Aesthetic and of the Black Arts Movement of the 1960's. Clay becomes, at this point in *Dutchman,* a Black nationalist spokesman who rejects his middle-class background to affirm a restoration of sanity for the wretched of the earth; yet he articulates, at the same time, what Lula asked of him. At the same time, however, Clay hopes to escape into the shelter of artistic sublimations: "Safe with my words, and no deaths, and clean, hard thoughts, urging me to new conquests" (p. 35). At the end of his speech, Clay the artist reaches for his books; Lula quietly takes out her knife.

For Lula, too, has been transformed, from the omniscient Bohemian into an incorporation of everything that is murderous in white Western society. An agent of repression, Lula must silence Clay in order to bring the *Dutchman* ritual to an end. Before Clay's speech, Lula represented a positive challenge to Clay's middle class mask; now, Lula is a bookkeeper of murder, who keeps a notebook of the "contracts" she fulfilled. The play is Lula's and aesthetic protest's last stand. She is only the physical victor of the play; spiritually, she has been exorcised. *Dutchman* indicates the direction Baraka's art would take: toward Clay's speech, into the contradictions of surealism, artistic sublimation and "real" action, and away from whiteness, femininity and absurdism, which would become the unambivalent stigmata of decadence in his later work.

In 1965, the year of the assassination of Malcolm X and the ghetto revolt of Watts, Baraka withdrew from the literary avantgarde that had been his cultural home, and moved to Harlem. There he started the Black Arts Repertory Theatre/School, employing only Black actors and catering exclusively to Black audiences. The Harlem theatre project, although short-lived, was an innovation that revolutionized Black theatre in America: it provided a model that was quickly followed throughout urban Black America. Among Baraka's own plays performed at the Black Arts Repertory Theatre/School was *Experimental Death Unit No. 1*. This play was first performed at St. Mark's Playhouse and first published in the Bohemian *East Side Review,* but it is still characteristic of the new, post-*Dutchman,* Black Arts Repertory style. The play is a short "Black" continuation of *Waiting for Godot.* Two white bums from the Theater of the Absurd, Duff and Loco philosophize in Barakian lyricisms about life and art, beauty and intelligence, when a Black prostitute appears on the Third

Avenue scene. Duff and Loco make perverse propositions to the woman who is in need of money and entices the two men. The two men begin to make love to the woman in a hallway, when the Black group for which the play is named comes marching in, behind a "pike on the top of which is a white man's head still dripping blood" (p. 13). The group leader orders Loco, Duff, and the Black woman killed; the white men's heads are cut off and fitted on two poles. The bodies are pushed into a heap, and the experimental death unit marches off.

The play contrasts the Black soldiers with the world of white decadence of which the Black prostitute has become a part. The punishment, execution by shooting, is very clear, but the crime, decadence, is vague; a possible definition of the crime would come very close to the old absurd idols of the Beat Generation: homosexuality, interracial sex, and blasphemy. "Death Unit" seems more concerned with exorcising old Bohemian idols than with presenting a well-defined Black nationalist cause; but it is noteworthy that in Baraka's first anti-absurdist play, the Black military avantgarde kills off what used to be the literary avantgarde, as the bloody message attempts to do away with the absurd form of Baraka's previous plays.

The difference between the play's decadent victims and their Black executioners is further developed in the later play, *Home on the Range*. This short sketch was first performed at Baraka's Spirit House in Newark and subsequently presented at a benefit for the Black Panther Party in 1968. A BLACK CRIMINAL climbs through the window into a house of a white middle-class family. After threatening everybody by shooting at a loudspeaker, the criminal directs the family members as they sing "America the Beautiful" and the Negro National Athem, "Lift Every Voice and Sing" (p. 110). At this moment, a CROWD OF BLACK PEOPLE enters the house, and a party begins. The daughter of the family dances with a middle-class Black, the mother does the jerk with two big Negroes, the son crawls after a "black red-eyed girl with blonde hair and round sunglasses" (a Lula-image), and the father dances around "nude with a young negro in leather jacket who waves his knife in front of him to make the father keep his manly distance" (p. 110).

The whites in the play fall asleep after an orgiastic Black-white party and become a pile of "weird talking grays" (p. 111). Like in "Death Unit," white conduct is decadent; furthermore, white speech is reduced to unintelligible gibberish:

SON.   Gash. Lurch. Crud. Daddoon.
FATHER,   *turns to son.* Yiip. Vachtung. Credool. Conch-
               mack. Vouty.

MOTHER,	*screams suddenly at scene.* Ahhhhyyyyyyy... Grenchnool crud lurch. *Rushes forward. SON restrains her.*
CRIMINAL.	What kind of shit is this? What the fuck is wrong with you people? (p. 107)

As a negation of the "native languages" spoken by Blacks in *Tarzan* and *King Kong* movies, the language of the whites in "Home on the Range" is reduced to meaningless word fragments reminiscent of some Ionesco dialogues. As Baraka exercises cultural inversion, all white characters become bald sopranoes, whereas Black people speak a realistic and intelligible English. In *Death Unit,* Baraka could resolve the cultural confrontation of white and Black, of literary and political avantgardism, only with an execution squad; in *Home on the Range,* the Black party alone works its voodoo on the decadent whites who merely fall asleep in exhaustion. A BLACK GIRL prophesies a rhetorically traditional new beginning as the play ends:"Hey look, the sun's coming up. *Turns around, greeting the three brothers.* Good Morning, Men. Good Morning" (p. 111).

Death Unit and *Home on the Range* are attempts at de-brainwashing a Black audience, and at exorcising Baraka's literary past, by ridiculing absurdist drama as an expression of white degeneracy. Against this degenerate white world, Baraka poses the orderly military violence of the Black execution squad and the power of Black music and dance. The references to Robin Hood movies and to Frankenstein as well as the very title of *Home on the Range,* are indicative of another familiar technique, which Baraka now uses to reach Black audiences: he continues his adaptations of American popular culture, even in the process of inverting its mythology.

The most famous example of a Black nationalist popular culture play is *Jello,* a drama written for, and performed at, the Black Arts Repertory Theatre/School. *Jello* is a parody of the Jack Benny radio and television show; in the course of *Jello,* Eddie "Rochester" Anderson, Benny's chauffeur-servant, appears in a new, revolutionary role. Rochester lets his hair grow long, is "postuncletom" in appearance, and demands his "back pay" from Jack Benny. Although the miserly Benny does, eventually and reluctantly, part with his $300 in petty cash, Rochester still wants more: "I want everything you got except the nasty parts" (p. 19). Perhaps as an elaboration of these "nasty parts," Benny is later accused of advocating "art for art's sake" (p. 37). While Rochester knows everything about Benny, Benny knows nothing about his chauffeur and "friend." In the key speech of the play, Rochester almost becomes another Clay; he voices his moral grievance, which, of course, exceeds the demand for back pay, and criticizes the medium which the play parodies, that "evil tube."

And you talking about my shitty li'l life, man I tol' you you don't know nothin' about my life. (*Quick jerk*) What I do, or think. Except you might know a little something about what I really think of you ... ha ha, now. ... I know all about your life, my man, and if I was you, or any of them people like you, I'd stick a shot gun in my mouth. (pp. 25–26)

When the other characters enter the studio to sing and act their parts in the comedy hour, Rochester stops talking like Baraka's mouthpiece and resumes his servile mask. He is so convincing that, although Benny tries to warn the others about Rochester, "highvoiced fag" Dennis Day and "TV/radio-dikey" Mary Livingston fall for Rochester's clowning and do not think that Benny is serious. When Dennis realizes the truth, he screeches like an old lady, but Rochester takes his wallet anyway. Rochester now approaches Mary, who hides her money under her skirt, and the play becomes a satire of Black-white sexual relations. After Mary faints on top of Dennis, Don Wilson enters the scene. At first, he is puzzled by the deviation from the script of the show, but finally he does his routine and conveys the word from the sponsor, which gives the play its title:

Ladies and Gentlemen, The Benny Show has been brought to you by J-E-L-L-O, Jello, America's favorite dessert. Remember, it comes in five delicious flavors, Raspberry, Orange, Cherry, Lemon and Lime. Kids adore it. Remember J-E-L-L-O. (Big dripping voice) America's FAVORITE DESSERT. YOU'LL LOVE IT! (p. 37)

Baraka gives the ritual of the commercial an alternate ending. Rochester knocks out Don Wilson, searches his Jello-filled pockets for money, finds Don's wallet tied in a Jello bag and declaims: "Goodbye Mr. Benny. The program's over. I leave you to your horrible lives!" (p. 38).

A Black Mass continues the technique of inverting elements of American popular culture; it parodies *Frankenstein* as one-dimensionally as *Jello* parodied the Jack Benny show. *A Black Mass,* however, is also a Black ritual which incorporates the mythology of the Nation of Islam into a Black nationalist play which questions the functions of art and creativity. The play was written in 1965 and first performed at Proctor's Theater in Newark, in May 1966.

The plot of the play is based on Elijah Muhammad's description of the origins of the white "devil" race, a part of the doctrine the Nation of Islam discarded after Elijah Muhammad's death. Muhammad narrated this "manifest truth" in what appear to be very American terms. Only Blacks were living on earth when,

> 6,600 years ago, as Allah taught me, our nation gave birth to
> another God whose name was Yacub. He started studying the
> life germ of man to try to make a new creation.

The mutant "devils" created by Yacub on Patmos were "really pale white,
with really blue eyes," aboriginal Caucasians, intent on ruling the black
nation. Not surprisingly, "all of the monkey family are from this 2,000 year
history of the white race in Europe."

In *A Black Mass,* Baraka takes this obvious inversion of white racist
folklore, designed to extend a Black race consciousness into a mythological pre-history, and adapts the story to his aesthetic perceptions in order to
transform it into a popular culture parody, a ritual, and a play about art. The
scene is a "fantastic chemical laboratory" (p. 21) of Faust, Frankenstein,
alchemists, and Hermes Trismegistos, the perfect setting for "Black
Magic." Baraka's Jacoub is a restless Faustian spirit who brings change
into the static world of his Black fellow magicians, Nasafi and Tanzil. At the
beginning of the play, they are busily searching for a potion to countereffect
Jacoub's last invention, "time, white madness" (p. 22) and try to teach him
that "Everything already exists. You cannot really create" (p. 25). Jacoub,
however, is deaf to their pleas, and works with dedication on his magnum
opus, the making of a "man like ourselves, yet separate from us. A neutral
being" (p. 25)—an allusion to Dante—a homunculus, a monster, a beast.
His experiment is an act of defiance against nature, and as he outlines his
project, the earth trembles, the sea shudders, and the elements are in
rebellion. The women Eulalie, Olabumi, and Tiila seek shelter in the
laboratory, as Jacoub is mixing his "final solution" (p. 28). The experiment
is successful, and the theatrical moment of the "birth" of the monster is
also the transsubstantiation of the Black Mass; underlined by unusually
shrill Sun Ra-laboratory background music, this scene is in the best tradition of popular Gothic:

> A crouched figure is seen covered in red flowing skins like
> capes. He shoots up, leaping straight off the stage screaming....
> The figure is absolutely cold white with red lizard-devil mask
> which covers whole head, and ends up as a lizard spine cape.
> (p. 30)

This comic-book monster of the leaping lizards variety yells "I White.
White. White", the women scream, and Nasafi and Tanzil warn Jacoub that
"THIS THING WILL KILL" (p. 31), but Jacoub is not horrified by his
creation; he attempts to teach the white beast how to speak—a satirical
inversion of the Black-white relationship of Robinson Crusoe and Friday.

Jacoub's beast, however, will not be educated and soon attacks the
women and makes Tiila the second monster in the play. Whiteness appar-

ently spreads like vampirism. Jacoub's mistake is the flaw of countless scientists in science fiction.

Jacoub, the cold, rational scientist, interfered with nature, and trusted "the voids of reason" (p. 35). Even when the danger emanating from the beast becomes quite obvious, Jacoub wants to "teach" the monster and restore Tiila to her original identity; and so he ignores Tanzil's suggestion to "set these things loose in the cold north" (p. 36). Eulalie and Olabumi start singing, and as their song changes from purring to screams of horror, Jacoub remains optimistic:

> "I will begin to teach them. I will have Tiila back....(*Gesturing*)
> I will prove the power of knowledge. The wisdom locked be-
> yond the stars (p. 38)."

His gesturing is a signal for the monsters to "spring into animation, attack-ing the magicians and women, killing them with fangs and claws" (p. 38). Jacoub, who dies last, condemns the beast, with his final breath, to the caves of the north: "May you vanish forever into the evil diseased caves of the cold" (p. 38).

The play ends in turmoil, as the white beasts move out into the audience, "kissing and licking people" and screaming "Me!" and "White!" The Black Mass is over, except for the sermon, which is deliv-ered through a loudspeaker:

> *NARRATOR:* And so Brothers and Sisters, these beasts are
> still loose in the world ... Let us find them and
> slay them. Let us lock them in their caves. Let
> us declare the Holy War. The Jihad. Or we
> cannot deserve to live. Izm-el-Azam. (p. 39)

The play's "anti-white" message is subverted by the utilization of the *Frankenstein* tradition. Monsters, be they King Kong, Dracula, corpses revivified by Dr. Frankenstein or beasts concocted in Jacoub's laboratory, evoke not only horror and fear, but also pity; and the beast in "Black Mass" is "evil" only when evaluated with a set of rules outside of the play. Within the context of the "mass," however, the beast is as pitiable as Franken-stein's creature—who was left companionless by his creator and resorted to sublimatory violence by mistake, by justifiable anger, or by commands from the wrong brain. The shadow of evil ultimately lurks over the creators, and not their creatures; and Dr. Frankenstein, King Kong's promoter, the Mummy's extomber, or Jacoub will receive less sympathy and emotional identification from an audience than the "horrible" monsters they create. *A Black Mass* is, to be sure, a play against white devils; but it is at least as much an indictment of Blacks who create them.

Baraka faced this problem again in the criticism of white-oriented Blacks in *Madheart*. The "beast" of this "morality play" is a "zombie" from the "caves" (p. 71), called "Devil Lady"—a Black nationalist extension of Lula. With the help of "White Magic" (p. 77), this paradigm of American popular culture has "brainwashed" two Black women ("mother" and "sister") into following the white ego-ideal, whereas "Black Man" and "Black Woman" are idealized as active representatives of the Black value system. They interrupt the white fantasies of "mother" and "sister"—" ... a white boy's better, daughter ... (p. 77)—with the diagnosis of the sickness and the Barakian suggestion for a cure:

BLACK MAN: I should turn them over to the Black Arts and get their heads relined.

BLACK WOMAN: They've been tricked and gestured over. They hypnotized, that's all. White Magic. (p. 77)

The play itself is just such an endeavor on behalf of the Black intellectual to "reline" the heads of Black audiences.

In an inversion of *Dutchman*, Black Man kills the white devil lady. The Black sister in "Madheart" almost dies with her, thinking that "she has to die because that white woman died" (p. 78). Mother, too, demonstrates her white-orientation in ridiculous invocations of white culture:

MOTHER: Tony Bennett, help us please. Beethoven, Peter Gunn ... deliver us in our sterling silver headdress.... Batman won't love me without my yellowhead daughter. I'm too old for him or Robin (p. 83).

The interaction of Black man and Black woman, on the other hand, is exemplary of Baraka's narrow vision of an ideal Black consciousness, liberated by the espousal of the Black value system:

BLACK WOMAN: I ... oh love, please stay with me ...

BLACK MAN: Submit, for love.

BLACK WOMAN: I ... I submit. (*She goes down, weeping.*) I submit ... for love ... please love. (*The MAN sinks to his knees and embraces her, draws her with him up again ...*)

BLACK MAN: You are my woman, now forever. Black woman.

BLACK WOMAN: I am your woman, and you are the strongest of God. Fill me with your seed. (*They embrace ...*) (pp. 82–83)

This scene illustrates one limitation of Baraka's concept of a Black nationalist consciousness. Perhaps because the devil is portrayed as a white lady, there is agitation against the devil as a woman; and this misogynous sentiment also affects the few "positive" portrayals of Black women in Baraka's works. Like "Black woman" in *Madheart*, these women are characterless, passive, submissive projections of the same male chauvinist imagination that created the image of the white witch.

Slave Ship: A Historical Pageant, one of Baraka's most interesting plays of the Black nationalist period, attempts to raise the political consciousness of Black audiences by first showing historical models of Black oppression and then breaking them on stage and inviting the audience to join in the ritual. Baraka's only endeavor to write a historical play — beyond the mythmaking of *A Black Mass* — interprets Black history somewhat statically, as a chain of similar oppressive situations, in each of which Blacks are the victimized group. On stage, the lower boat deck of the middle passage is transformed, first into slave market and "quarters," and finally into a contemporary Black ghetto. At the same time, the whites on the upper tier change their functions — from captain and sailors to slave dealers and plantation owners, and finally, to white business men. Between the two groups of white oppressors and Black people is the middleclass Uncle Tom, who is at first a shuffling "knee-grow" aboard ship, later betrays Nat Turner's rebellion to his slave-master, and finally appears in a reverend's suit as a parody of Martin Luther King:

> I have a trauma that the gold sewers won't integrate. Present fink. I have an enema...a trauma, on the coaster with your wife bird-crap. (p. 12)

The Afro-American history survey provides political dynamite for the contemporary audience: the Black actors demonstrate that breaking the chain of oppression requires violence against white oppressors and Black traitors. As in *Home on the Range*, Black music is essential for the coming of the revolution; and at the end of the play, actors and audience are united in a chant, dancing to Archie Shepp's music around the traitor's head.

The play is still very much concerned with relining heads and equates, much too easily, the decapitation of the Black "traitor" with final victory in the struggle for liberation; still, *Slave Ship* demonstrates the vitality of Baraka's ritualized Black theater, as he transcends the narrow interpretation of Black nationalist family conduct and utilizes Black music, African words, and dance in order to include the audience in an aesthetic spectacle.

While most of Baraka's Black nationalist plays contain elements of agitation, many of them concentrate on attitudes and cultural values, and only a few express immediate political propaganda. Among these committed plays, *Arm Yourself, or Harm Yourself* is a prominent, though largely unknown example. Published in an edition of 500 copies by Jihad Productions in 1967, this ten-page "message of self-defense to Black men" is a one-dimensional effort at "pure commitment," and its dramatic form is merely a vehicle.

The New Left conviction that the police force in a capitalist society represented not only the violent arm of an exploitative system, but was, in itself, the enemy of the people par excellence, was embraced by various groups, ranging from Weathermen to factions in the Black Panther Party. Policemen were frequently depicted and — in confrontations — addressed as "pigs." It is exactly this interpretation of the policeman as a murderous pig that *Arm Yourself* propounds.

In the prelude ("in dark"), policemen knock and kick at the door of a ghetto apartment and finally shoot through the door. When the lights come up, two Black men are arguing; the "First Brother" is in awe of whites and pessimistic about his own chances, while the "Second Brother" displays a spirit of optimism that seems based on the fact that he has a gun. After a renewed round of gunshots, a Black man, Paul, "staggers onto stage" (p. 4) and dies. In tears, his wife tells the Brothers that the police shot Paul as he tried to defend her against a policeman who "put his hands ... on me ... asked me for identification" (p. 5). The two Brothers continue to argue in the following vein:

> SECOND BROTHER: You don't deserve no woman ... if you can't protect them.
>
> FIRST BROTHER: *(Helping Sister up)* How we gonna protect the women...we don't have no power ...
>
> SECOND BROTHER: And you never will ... (p. 7)

Arguing about the protection of the object sister, the brothers begin to insult each other. Reminiscent of Lula's invective against Clay, the Second Brother calls his opponent "the true negro of negroes...the king of negroes ... old raghead, sugarlip, heself" (p. 8); and soon the brothers fight each other. A "copvoice" discovers them, and the police fire guns. The armed brother is struck first, the first brother next and the woman is hit last. The play ends with a reminder of the Nazi genocide:

> COPS: Dumb niggers ... we oughtta send 'em all to the goddam gas chamber.
>
> COPS: Don't worry mac. we will we definitely will. (they laff, kick bodies, go off) (p. 10)

Arm Yourself or Harm Yourself shows Baraka's idiom in several ways.

There is the combination of sex and racism that shaped so many of his dramatic creations: the lecherous policemen provoke the Black man to defend his woman (the passive role assigned to the female is also typical) and the Black man who understands the message of self-defense embraces the gun as a penis symbol of his manhood. There are verbal echoes from *Dutchman, A Black Mass,* and *Madheart* in *Arm Yourself.* And Baraka works with his familiar method of showing victims rather than heroes: *Arm Yourself* has no Black survivors.

Baraka's unpublished play, *The New Ark's a moverin,* first performed in Newark in 1974, is meant to be a "political statement about the city." With a mixture of ritual, agitprop, and Baraka quotations, it caricatures white and Black political figures in Newark, and contrasts scenes in which their follies and treacheries are exposed, with texts which envision a better world—one of "progressive perfection," of "Nationalism, PanAfrikanism, Ujamaa Socialism." The characters introduce themselves in short street verses which sound like introverted signifying, and expose their own shortcomings:

> IMPERIALE: (Enters in Roman Toga with olive branch
> around his head) (To tune of "God Bless
> America") I'm jelly belly ANT-Knee
> jelly belly ANT-Knee
> AntKnee Ant Knee
> AntKnee Captain Spaghetti
> to you—AntKnee Antknee
> AntKnee Imperiale
> Imperiale-ism
> Imperiale-is my
> name—Imperialism is (my)
> Game.

More sketches, pantomimes, and invectives against white "liberals" are backed up by slides of "famous white folk—liberals that niggers dig" including ... Roosevelt, Kennedy, ... Beatles ... Lincoln, ... LBJ, Jesus, Stalin, Marx." Then a city council "meeting" (consisting of introductions by members in the style of the Imperiale introduction) is juxtaposed to Touré's reflections on the political leader as a representative: "True political leaders of Africa ... can only be committed men, fundamentally committed against all the forms and forces of depersonalization of African culture (pp. 8–9). When Newark's Black Mayor Kenneth Gibson appears to the sound of "Hail the Conquering Hero" he is questioned first by a "crowd" of people, and then by a community leader, called "advocate" in the play. The play ends with the advocate's plea that "all power should flow from the will of the people" and the chorus' demand for a change.

In *The New Ark's a moverin,* the caricatures expose political vices, but the solutions offered are politically vague. Written in the year of Gibson's reelection, the play neither endorses nor completely rejects him as a candidate. One of Baraka's more recent plays, *The Motion of History* goes much further than the Newark agitprop play.

The Motion of History was written in 1975/76 and first performed at the New York Theater Ensemble in 1977. In the tradition of *Slave Ship,* it is an attempt at creating a largescale picture of historic situations of oppression and rebellion in America. The play, which has an appendix of historical sources, is an inventory of sketches of revolutionary activities in America, from Nat Turner to Malcolm X, from Denmark Vesey to Robert Williams. At times, the scenes are based on sources (for example, Walker's Appeal), in other instances they represent imaginative re-interpretations of American history (as in the creation of Bacon's rebellion as an interracial revolt against slavery and servitude). The reader who remembers Baraka's invectives against Martin Luther King and the civil rights movement in *Slave Ship,* will be especially surprised to find a strong and positive sketch of Chaney, Schwerner, and Goodman and an homage to King. This wide range of historical material culminates in a contemporary plot which centers on the development of two ex-Bohemians who decide to go back home and to become revolutionaries in their own communities. At first, they are shown as de-ethnicized and alienated men who communicate in a language evocative of Baraka's early lyrical prose:

> *BLACK DUDE:* ... You see I grew up in this country, was a child here, went through school, exposed to some of it the bitterest agony of it like a halfmoon, half lit, half smart, half slick, half integrated. Where I'm at. Because for everything I carry there is another half to me. My fullest memory from a fullest self. Why? I'm here with you ... but no there's something more, I know —
>
> *WHITE DUDE:* A half moon. You asked me my name, its Moriarty. I'm Irish-Italian on my fathers side, a Polish-Hungarian Jew on my mothers side. You slept with my sister, my wife and my father's colored friend's daughter. I'm a half moon too, in a way, though I don't know what you're talking about. Except there's a side a me didn't come in the hard steamers, a side of me aint a dirty immigrant, spit on ... no Irish or dogs, no wops, no Polacks, no hunkies —
>
> *BLACK:* You're a hunkie? (pp. 80–81)

This interchange reminds one of Baraka's early drama of the divided self; the "Black dude" is struggling for a Black identity under his bourgeois façade, like Clay once did; and the "white dude" gropes for his own legacy of political-ethnic opposition to "America," echoing, perhaps, Lula, who claimed that her mother was a communist.

The Black and white "half moons" share an ambivalence toward ethnic roles; in Baraka's sense, their "verb force" has been usurped by "nouns," but they try to resist the results of their Americanization. While the White Bohemian hesitatingly suggests "hedonism" as a way to "feel" a new identity, the Black dude—like "64" in *The Eighth Ditch*—takes Bebop as a point of departure:

> Religion died when Bebop was born. And when I put on those windowshade glasses, tho I aimed to put on a good suit and get me a briefcase and ride the elevator to the top floor of the new negro building, still they'll be some trouble out of me. (p. 82)

As Black and white halfmoon search for their identities, the scene changes to the march on Washington on a movie screen, through which white and Black dude stick their heads in order to hear the end of Martin Luther King's speech, "his shadow across them."

> I have a dream that one day little black children and little white children will walk together and play together, I have a dream that one day my children will be judged by the content of the character rather than the color of their skins, I have a dream...
>
> *BLACK & WHITE:* (lights up) We're playing together now.
> *BLACK:*   But what's it mean? (p. 83)

The 1963 bombing of the children in Birmingham and Malcolm X's speech in response to those murders add a tone of confusion to the Bohemian life, which now appears as a hedonistic dance on the volcano.

After Malcolm X's assassination, Elijah Muhammad is seen usurping Malcom's political message by a white-devil-demonology, which Baraka now sees with more distance than he did in *Black Mass*. The message of the Black Panther Party is equally garbled and "comes out of the two radios different," because of the interference of white voices.

Karenga and Carmichael, Suni Muslims and Hippies round off the panorama of a confused and rebellious decade, in which King's last speech appears to be a true voice in the wilderness.

As in *The New Ark's a moverin,* newly elected and appointed Black officials prove to be part of the old corruption, as a scene with a Black police chief indicates. After an elaborate black handshake and a Swahili welcome, this police chief is unwilling to investigate the death of a Black man at the hands of the police. As Richie Moriarty and Lennie (the white and Black dudes) come back to their homes, they begin to ask questions which illustrate the many concrete contradictions of capitalism. Independently, they attack racist and chauvinist notions which separate whites from Blacks, in conversations with their own peer groups, at their jobs and at parents' meetings. In the last scene, Lennie and Richie meet again at a political congress and listen to a speech by the representative of the Puerto Rican Revolutionary Alliance, who demands the founding of a Leninist "revolutionary vanguard party." The play ends as "the delegates begin cheering and surging forward...Richie and Lennie among them." In Baraka's new vision of the world, the motion of history is about to be fulfilled.

From introspective Bohemian to Maoist agitator, Baraka has traversed American culture of the 1960's and 1970's, incorporating radical changes yet maintaining at least some dramatic continuity. *Dutchman* remains the center of his dramatic curve, prefigured by the focus on self-division and separation of lovers and others in *The Eighth Ditch* and *The Toilet,* and echoed in many passages of the Black nationalist plays of the 1960's. As *The Motion of History* suggests, Baraka has returned to the theme of a male Black-white self-division even after his most recent political transformation.

Ed Bullins:
The Quest and Failure
of an Ethnic
Community Theatre

PETER BRUCK

I learned how to survive. I'm a street nigger.

Ed Bullins, in an interview, *The New Yorker*, June 16, 1973

Revolution is gone out of currency. We are not protesting to whites. We are having a discourse, a discussion, a dialogue between black and black — writers and the audience.

Statement by Ed Bullins, *ibid*.

My poor brother, language is more than words...it is deeds and gestures... and silence.

Ed Bullins, *The Duplex*, 1971

Perhaps more than any other black literary genre the history of drama reflects both the socio-cultural intricacies of creating an authentic black outlet as well as the political aspirations that came to be associated with the creation of such an outlet. After the destruction of the African Grove Theater in 1823 where, as James Weldon Johnson reports in his *Black Manhattan*, "the gentlemen of color...have graciously made a partition at the back of the house, for the accommodation of the whites,"[1] black playwrights and actors had not only lost their first ethnic stage but, moreover, had also been deprived of the opportunity to develop productions of their own. The ensuing consequences of this cannot be over-stressed, and the history of the black theater since 1823 to the opening of Harlem's New Lafayette in 1968 may well be read as the painstaking attempt to regain the former cultural independence.

After the loss of their initial theatrical outlet, Afro-American playwrights and actors became increasingly the victims of the socio-literary exigencies of their time and were forced to succumb to the pre-conceived notions of their white audience. The emergence of such stereotypes as the buffoon, the tragic mulatto and others[2] as well as the various minstrel and vaudeville shows dominated the nineteenth-century stage and came to exert such a pervasive influence on the white audience that by the 1920s it "had ingrained in its imagination a view of the Negro that was comic and pathetic. The theatrical darky was childlike; he could be duped into the most idiotic and foolish schemes."[3]

The first playwright who attempted to counteract such stereotyped habits with some success was Langston Hughes whose *Mulatto* was staged on Broadway in 1935 and enjoyed the longest run of any black play prior to Lorraine Hansberry's *A Raisin in the Sun* (1959). It is important to realize, however, that the Broadway performance distorted the original text in many ways. Thus several melodramatic effects were introduced for, as Hughes recalls in his autobiography *I Wonder As I Wander*, the producer insisted that "you have to have sex in a Broadway show."[4]

This script revision throws a significant light on the limiting conventions that the playwright had to face if he wanted to reach a white audience. What is more, it succinctly demonstrates the crucial impact of 'white' theater institutions and managers upon the evolution of black drama. Forced to maneuvre within the narrow confines of decorum, the dramatist had to evolve a series of strategies. Foremost, of course, this meant evading the portrayal of angry blacks or showing an open race conflict on stage. Translated into terms of content, the writer had to subscribe to the white cultural code by depicting exemplary blacks who would aspire to the values of the white society. Hansberry's *A Raisin in the Sun* is here the case in point. As a black version of the American Dream, *A Raisin* is stylistically traditional and clearly echoes a popular white set of cultural values. In Hansberry's own words: "This wasn't a 'Negro play'. It was a play about honest-to-God, believable, manysided people who happened to be Negroes."[5] Only five years later, this stance proved to be dated as a new generation of playwrights captured the attention of the critics. Hansberry thus marks the end of the "old black drama"[6] which chiefly catered to the literary and political tastes of a predominantly white middle-class public.

The political and literary aesthetics that began to evolve in the 1960s broke with the conventions of the traditional black drama in nearly every respect. Playwrights such as Amiri Baraka (LeRoi Jones) and, in particular, Ed Bullins, no longer sought a white audience. Instead, they set out to realize the programmatic outline of black theater which W. E. B. DuBois had formulated in 1926: "Negro theater must be:

I. *About us*. That is, they must have plots which reveal Negro life as it is.

II. *By us*. That is, they must be written by Negro authors who understand from birth and continual associations just what it means to be a Negro today.

III. *For us*. That is, the theater must cater primarily to Negro audiences and be supported and sustained by their entertainment and approval.

IV. *Near us*. The theater must be in a neighborhood near the mass of ordinary Negro people.[7]

An analysis of the political leanings of Baraka and Bullins, their respective rhetoric and political stances, will show not only a great deal of similarity but also significant differences which are important for an understanding and appreciation of Bullins both as playwright and as cultural activist.

I

In an interview with Marvin X, Bullins characterized his relationship to Baraka as follows: "I didn't really find myself until I saw *Dutchman*. That was the great influence on my life."[8] This frank confession suggests that Bullins regards himself as Baraka's disciple, which, indeed, many of his cultural activities would seem to indicate. Following the example set by Baraka, Bullins founded an all black theater in San Francisco in 1966 and from 1967 until 1973 worked as writer-in-residence at the all black New Lafayette theater in Harlem. He thus not only shared Baraka's concern for the foundation of an exclusively ethnocentric stage but also became a very influential editor. In 1968 Bullins edited a special number of *Drama Review*, which was solely devoted to Black Theater, and from 1968 to 1973 he was the editor-in-chief of *Black Theatre*.

Another common denominator consists in their stress on the exclusivism of a Black Aesthetic. Both ascribe a distinctly *ontological* status to the black experience, insisting that it is intelligible only to other blacks. Hence the attempt to formulate a black conceptualization of drama in opposition to the standard theater vocabulary; hence also the dismissal of contemporary art forms as "western."[9] Bullins, for example, charges 'western' drama with sterility and a lack of innovation ("for the white man there are no new stories, or plots, or characters; and somehow, by the time they filter down to present day theater, there are *no* really new ideas in this culture"[10]) and calls for a new "alphabet [of] black stylistic, symbolic and literal image/renditions."[11]

The underlying premise of this ethnocentric philosophy of theater, is, of course, a functional view of art. In Bullins' own words:

> The purpose is that it [the black theater] would be a medium for communication to raise the consciousness throughout the nation, for black artistic, political, and cultural consciousness....It would be an institutional base to lay the foundation of our society and our culture and our nation.[12]

The populist, utopian slant of this statement is clear. Yet, how is the black theater to contribute to the creation of a black nation? Whilst Baraka clearly adopted Ron Karenga's classic assertion that "all Black art...must be functional, collective and committing"[13] Bullins has shied away from such an unequivocal commitment. For if we discard such statements as "when it's time to show a gun...a gun should appear on the poster, on the stage, in the film, or in your hands"[14] as mere radical verbiage, we will find that Bullins does not aspire to a revolutionary, neo-marxist approach. Unlike Baraka, who in his early years as a dramatist demanded a "revolutionary theatre [which] must *expose* ... accuse and attack"[15] and who currently seems to be taking up a Maoist stance,[16] Bullins' theatrical concept has always been somewhat vague, or at least ambivalent. Consider the following two statements:

> I hope that all of us will ... produce, create that is, for we are creators, revolution. And that, I think, is the true role of the revolutionary artist.[17]
>
> Black Art is to express what is best in us and for us Black people. Black theater is ... a people's theater, dedicated to the continuing survival of Black people.[18]

How does one, aesthetically speaking, reconcile the hope for revolution with the wish for survival? In other words, how are the two aspirations to be combined in theater politics? Bullins' seemingly contradictory position lends itself, however, to a dialectical-historical explanation. In the 1920s Alain Locke, one of the leading figures of the Harlem Renaissance, had this to say about the politics of black drama: "The creative impulse is, for the moment, caught in this dilemma of choice between the drama of discussion and social analysis and the drama of expression ... of folk life."[19] Whilst Locke's first conceptual label would seem to suggest a *théâtre engagé,* his second rubric refers to the tradition of folklore as an important cultural source which the playwright should attempt to convey to his black audience. Dialectically speaking, Locke's antagonism finds an initial solution in Bullins' theater, which clearly represents a new stage in the evolution of black drama. As his plays are beset with urban *lumpen* blacks and their subcultural life-style of hustling, he transcends both the realm of mere social analysis and of a mere portrayal of folk life by seeking to fuse these realms in the minute depiction of various facets of black existence.

The dramatic rendering of these facets entails almost photographic snapshots of characters and situations. Whereas Bullins, at least in his thus far uncompleted *Twentieth Century Cycle*, seems to be working toward a totality of black experience, his individual plays only *spotlight* events without providing a consistent and causally linked plot. Unlike the conventions of the absurd theater, however, where the spectator/reader is confronted with meta-linguistic reflexions and the search for adequate expression, and unlike post-modernist fiction where the reader has to act as the semantic co-author, Bullins does seem to intend to provide his audience with a meaningful point of orientation. For the apparent plotlessness and stasis of his plays dissolve if one views the plays as a continuing kaleidescope of black life. Since, however, Bullins uses recurrent figures and themes in several of his plays — which are to reappear in his forthcoming dramas — and since, moreover, his programmatic theatrical cycle is still unfinished, any critical reading must necessarily be tentative.

It will thus come as no surprise that critics have thus far interpreted Bullins most diversely. Although terms such as "theater of confrontation"[20], "drama of self-celebration"[21], "theater of black experience"[22], or "theater of reality"[23] have tended to limit the critical discussion, they also denote important single aspects of Bullins' dramatic universe. Instead of adding another label to this impressive list, it seems to me to be more promising, if only for heuristic reasons, to approach Bullins on his own terms. This will include an analysis of the political implications of the theme of hustling, an examination of his major dramaturgical devices as well as the attempt to relate the style and voice of his plays to his political and cultural stance.

II

In his *Autobiography*, the late Malcolm X described the politics of hustling as follows:

> The ghetto hustler is internally restrained by nothing. He has no religion, no concept of morality, no civic responsibility, no fear — nothing. To survive, he is out there constantly preying upon

others, probing for any human weakness like a ferret. The ghetto hustler is forever frustrated, restless, and anxious for some 'action'.[24]

The black urban world of dope, prostitution, thievery and general immorality is a dominant feature in many of Bullins' plays, notably in *Goin' a Buffalo*. The play is set in Los Angeles in the early sixties and centers on the dream of Curt and his wife Pandora "to get out of this hole" (p. 31)[25] and make it to Buffalo. Bearing in mind that Buffalo was one of the most deserted and run down cities of the late 1960s, we see how Bullins ironically undercuts the aspirations of his characters from the very beginning; indeed, the play exposes the futility of such a dream.

Goin' a Buffalo opens with a chess game between Curt and his friend Rich. The first and last lines of scene 1 — "I just about have you up tight, Rich" (p. 4)/"Checkmate, man" (p. 18) — symbolically introduce the notion of conflict which pervades the dramatic action. In point of fact, the whole action may be viewed as a series of attempts on the part of the characters to move each other into a position of 'checkmate'. After Art Garrison, a friend of Curt's from former days in prison, appears on the stage we witness an increasing amount of violent confrontations. Art, the archetypal hustler, who also appears in *The Fabulous Miss Marie* and *The House Party*, finally outsmarts Curt and takes possession of the two prostitutes Pandora and Mamma Too Tight.

As in most of Bullins' plays, a rather trite plot initially blurs an adequate understanding of the text. If set against the politics of hustling, however, an interesting stratification of meaning evolves. Thus the dream of the hustling couple Curt and Pandora —

> Well, I ain't no whore.... I'm just makin' this money so Curt and me can get on our feet. One day we gonna own property and maybe some business when we get straight ... and out of this town. ... [Curt's] a good hustler but he's givin' that up after a while. He can be anything he wants (p. 60) —

is unmasked as false, i.e. 'white', during the course of the action. The drive of the hustler to become wealthy and to attain a higher social goal is viewed here as a perverted attempt to gain a white middle-class respectability. In Bullins' dramatic universe such a dream always paves the way to self-destruction. This becomes particularly clear, if we consider the circular shape of the action. For when Art, having betrayed Curt to the police, finally takes over both Pandora and Mamma and physically abuses Pandora in the last scene, he reenacts the brutality that Curt displayed in Act I. In the parasitic world of hustling where, as Art puts it, "you look for any break you can make" (p. 92), nothing is ultimately changed; instead we come to realize that Art will also become the prey of others some day — which, indeed, turns out to be his fate in *The House Party.*

Goin' a Buffalo dramatizes one central aspect of black urban life under the impact of an all-engulfing white world. Such a reading becomes more obvious if we take into account the minute description of the expressionistic scene design of Act I and III where whiteness dominates. The explicit use of this color suggests that all figures are symbolically caught in the dreams of the white man's world where they can no longer perceive, much less aspire, to a genuine black existence.

In many of Bullins' plays such an existence is often tentatively expressed by the dramaturgical device of music which serves as a contrast to the false hopes of the characters. Almost from the very beginning the onstage action is accompanied by bebop music. From a socio-historical point of view this form of jazz has been interpreted as a reaction against the commercialisation of black music in the 1940s and, in keeping with LeRoi Jones' dictum, as basically "anti-assimilationist."[26] Significantly, the ethnic message of the bebop remains unnoticed by the dramatic figures who appear to be completely brainwashed by 'white' cultural values. The name of the white prostitute Mamma Too Tight is here the case in point. If we consider that *Mama Too Tight* is also the title of a well-known piece of jazz which was modernized and recorded by the free jazz musician Archie Sheep in 1966, the name given to this white character takes on the function of an allusive sign which symbolically refers to the colonisation of original black culture.

The pattern of a cultural de-brainwashing is at the center of almost all of Bullins' plays. Its dramatic rendering shows Bullins to be highly flexible both in terms of form and style. *The Pig Pen*, for example, explores the exploitation of the teachings of Malcolm X at a neo-bohemian black/white sex and drug party. Here as elsewhere the level of speech is an indicator of the degree of authentic black consciousness. Thus the pseudo-intellectual Len Stover, commenting on the latest poetry of his friend Ray, employs what may be called standard white critical terminology: "Yes ... such progress ... amazing control ... and how you've overcome those first rudimentary handicaps." (p. 57)[27] *The Electronic Nigger*, on the other hand, makes use of the linguistic device of the elaborate code in order to expose the hollowness of this level of speech when used by a black man. Similarly, *Clara's Ole Man* denounces the rhetoric of the college prep student Jack as white by contrasting it with the "language of soul"[28] spoken by both Big Girl, a psychiatric warden, and by the four hustlers Stoogie, Bama, Hoss and C.C. While these two different levels of speech aptly link the linguistic code to what Bullins would term 'white' and 'black' consciousness, respectively, they reveal at the same time a strange inconsistency on the author's part; for Clara, lesbian lover of Big Girl, constantly mingles the two codes. Even though this may be read as an expression of her emotional confusion, no meaningful pattern is discernible, since the development of the dramatic action does not support these linguistic shifts.

A more feasible use of such speech levels and the ethnic values attached to them can be found in the play *In New England Winter*. The story of *In New England Winter* is simple but full of point. The present action which spans several hours of one day in 1960 shows Cliff Dawson, his half brother Steve Benson, Chuckie and Bummie as they plan a hold-up in a supermarket. This period of time is marked by a series of violent, personal confrontations between the gang members, and covers scenes 1, 4, and 7. Scenes 2, 3, 5, and 6 take place at the apartment of Steve's girlfriend Liz in 1955 and are also characterized by violent conflicts. By using a simultaneous stage set Bullins contrasts the present and the past in such a way that the present action, which is motivated on Steve's part by his desire to renew his former love affair with Liz, exposes the futility of such a longing from the beginning. Here, as in *Goin' a Buffalo* and in *The Duplex*, the search theme ultimately portrays a false, i.e. 'white' consciousness. Hence Bullins' characters never achieve their quest; hence also the structural stasis[29] of his plays, which seems to be a necessary result of his aim of de-brainwashing the minds of his black spectators.

In New England Winter links the theme of search to the quest for order which, significantly, is again depicted as a white quest. In the first scene, for example, Steve fanatically insists on rehearsing the planned hold-up in minute detail, declaring that he wants "a sense of realism brought into this room." (p. 135)[30] The rehearsal, however, only leads to violent encounters among the group members and underlines the uselessness of planning the future. Steve's time perspective thus differs markedly from that of his fellow gang members and, most notably, from that of his half brother Cliff:

STEVE.   I got to get myself ready to meet the future, Cliff. Don't you see?
CLIFF.   The future is with us right now, brother. We drown in our future each breath we take. It's phoney promises leak into our brains and turns them to shit!
STEVE.   Come off it, Cliff. It's because of not planning that our futures are always so bleak. (p. 160)

This difference of time perspectives is, sociologically speaking, a pointer towards two distinctive philosophies of life.[31] While Steve is future oriented, thus following a rational and impersonal concept of time, Cliff, by contrast, views time as irrational and personal. What is more, Cliff associates a rational orientation toward the future with a loss of emotion. Thus he sarcastically remarks: "Yea...there's somethin' wrong with me. I feel. Mostly I feel good. Mostly I'm so emotional that I have to drink myself to sleep after I become exhausted by a woman (p. 162). By implication, then, Steve's rationality not only deprives him of his feelings but also shows him to be infected by a white middle-class consciousness. This is made further apparent by the use of color symbolism in the second scene:

> LIZ. Steve's lived in snow all his life. All his life. I guess that's why he's so cold most of the time. A cold, hard northern black bastard....Oh, we must love quick... for they might come for him ... they might come to steal him away. Steal his blackness...steal his spirit and soul ... steal his manhood and make him not mine (pp. 149/150).

If set against the present action, Liz's soliloquy makes it clear that Steve already lost an authentic black identity in the past. This becomes even more obvious when we consider the various communicative habits displayed by the different characters. Unlike Steve, the verbal behavior of Chuckie and Bummie as well as that of the hustlers Oscar, Crook and Liz's sister Carrie have as their common denominator a specific black ghetto street language. Note the following verbal interplay between Crook, Carrie, Oscar and Liz:

> CROOK. Oh, I know a lot about Liz, I know a lot, Oscar.
> CARRIE. What do you know? You don't know shit about my sister, man.
> CROOK. Relax... relax, Oscar's woman.
> OSCAR. Ha ha ha...look at little Crook Crook. The dwarf slickster, that's him. Havin' kitchen debates with the ladies. That's your speed, ain't it, short and sly?
> CROOK. If you know then you know, friend of mine.
> OSCAR. He got his style from old John Garfield movies... ha ha...and hasn't changed it in fifteen years...
> LIZ. Oscar...leave Crook alone.
> CARRIE. Nawh, he shouldn't...that sawed off little nigger ain't no good.
> CROOK. I went and got the wine, didn't I?
> CARRIE. Fuck that.
> CROOK. Drunk already and only after half a glass.
> CARRIE. Fuck you!
> CROOK. Sure sign of a drunk.
> LIZ. Stop it, Carrie.

OSCAR.	You know, short and square ... there might be something in what she's saying.
CROOK.	Poor Crook.
LIZ.	Leave him alone.
OSCAR.	Awww, he's a good nigger...me and him done did a lot of good jail time together.
CROOK.	Good Crook.
CARRIE.	He ain't shit.
LIZ.	Crook and Carrie and me grew up together, Oscar.
CROOK.	Ole, faithful Crook.
CARRIE.	He still ain't shit...nigger tried to rape me when I was eleven.
CROOK.	This young lady has a fine memory. Would have gotten it too 'cept for Liz seein' me playin' with her baby sister and runnin' up and down the street screamin' for her mamma.
OSCAR.	But that nigger can steal...whewww. Steal your eyeballs out while you lookin' at him with them... if you let him. (p. 153)

The type of language employed here is not meant to denote any social pathology nor is it only a manifestation of Black English as some critics would have it.[32] Rather, the aggressive joking activity is in the tradition of that form of verbal contest known as *rapping*.[33] This particular communicative habit is a highly stylized, competitive maneuver in which, as Thomas Kochman has pointed out, "one raps *to* rather than *with* a person." Rapping is hence "to be regarded more as a performance than a verbal exchange."[34] This aspect also helps to explain the discontinuity of the dialogue which is not to be confused with the speech conventions of modernist theater. For the apparent disconnectedness of the speech events in Bullins' plays refer not so much to a Chekhovian tradition[35]; rather they ultimately express a fundamentally black perspective of a distinct set of urban language. Consequently, such verbal strategies as rapping, signifying and others[36] always serve as ethnographic indicators in Bullins' dramatic universe which distinguish a genuine black consciousness from a 'false' white consciousness.

Another important linguistic aspect of the above passage reveals itself in the use of what Claude Brown has called "the language of soul." Consider, for instance, the use of the word "nigger" by the black characters in this context. If the term were employed by whites, it would carry the standard depreciatory connotation and would have to be classified as a vulgar expression. Here, however, the term is neither a derogatory synonym for Negro nor an obscene expression. Following Claude Brown who has described the term as "the most soulful word"[37] we come to realize that "nigger", when used by Carrie denotes a kind of hostility toward Crook, whereas Oscar uses it to express fondness. Together with rapping, the use of soul language best demonstrates Bullins' search for an innovative, authentic black vocabulary.

III

Even though critics have maintained that Bullins' "plays are almost totally devoid of political or ideological content"[38] and that he shies away from an open political attack[39], it seems to me that both his conventional theater and, in particular, his ritual and agitprop drama display an overt political message. The intentions underlying the use of these forms show at the same time different cultural aims on Bullins' part which to my mind expose a fundamental discrepancy in his thinking.

The stage directions of *It Bees Dat Way*, which was first presented at a London theater in 1970, demand for example that "this ritual is to be given in a location that is frequented by a white audience"[40] (p. 5). Five of the six black actors are hustlers and only Corny acts as a political agitator. *It Bees Dat Way* has done away with the traditional separation between stage and audience. The play opens with both the actors, who are not distinguished as such, and the audience entering the room. Immediately the black actors attack the "predominantly white audience" (p. 5) verbally and physically. The series of verbal assaults is obviously meant to present various facets of the ghetto psychology, as it discloses a pattern of behavior ranging from hustling, open aggression to mere uncle-tomism. It is only the zombie-like Corny, survivor of previous riots, who explicitly calls for revolutionary action:

> GET YO GUN ... IS DEATH ANY WORSE THAN THIS, BROTHERS ... CAN THEY KILL US ANY MORE THAN THEY HAVE ALREADY? (p. 16)

Corny's exhortation remains unheard, however. Instead, Sister replies: "For nex' to nothin' I can get me a fix, baby. So what if someone does have a little fun?" (p. 16) *It Bees Dat Way*, which clearly alludes to the ghetto riots of the 1960s, presents a psychological explanation of the failure of black revolutions for, so Bullins seems to say, as long as the ghetto dwellers indulge in their parasitic hustling, unified, collective actions cannot be brought about. While the validity of this explanation is certainly not to be disputed, one might nonetheless inquire into the appropriateness of both the dramatic form and the surroundings selected to demonstrate this thesis.

Kenneth Burke once described the underlying idea of the ritual as the "sense of the group's consubstantiality"[41] and Robert Macbeth, director of the now defunct New Lafayette Theater, had this to say about the ritual:

> It can clarify for Black people their ultimate strengths and powers. ... It is a releasing kind of experience. ... People use their spiritual forces toward one kind of object, which is the togetherness, the nation, the nationhood, the Being, the realization, the recognition of self.[42]

Viewing *It Bees Dat Way* in the light of these observations, one cannot help wondering if Bullins may not have used the wrong means to achieve his political ends. For why explain the failure of a black revolution to a white audience? In point of fact, the insistence on a white public could very well evoke a two-sided, racial sense of consubstantiality which, one would presume, must be detrimental to Bullins' idea of a theater in which "we are having ... a dialogue between black and black — writers and the audience."[43]

An equally puzzling discrepancy is to be found in the street play *Death List* which is dedicated to the Palestine National Liberation Movement. Here the militant Blackman reads to the audience a list of 64 blacks to be killed as traitors while his antagonist, Blackwoman, pleads for non-violence. Throughout this dialectical arrangement of statements Blackwoman clearly has the better side of the argument, since Blackman basically only gives a rather trite, monotonous account of the peoples' enemies. *Death List* thus falls short of Bullins' own "Short Statement on Street Theatre", as it is neither a "satirical piece on current counter-revolutionary figures" nor does it "give the masses identifying images, symbols and challenging situations."[44]

One may regard the apparent shortcomings of *It Bees Dat Way, Death List* and other rituals and agitprop plays as a confusion of a writer's purpose. This is not to dismiss Bullins as a second-rate propaganda writer or to disparage the black writer's legitimate attempt to present art that is committed. This is simply to point out that despite the repeated invocations of the black community, there remains the unresolved struggle between the artist and the people who are yet to learn the 'right' black consciousness from him. It seems to the present writer that Bullins is at his best when he conveys this consciousness in the realistic plays of his *Twentieth Century Cycle*.

IV

In his role as cultural activist, Bullins has come close to realizing DuBois' call for an ethnic theater. Yet when the New Lafayette, where many of his realistic plays were initially staged, had to close in 1973 through lack of funds, Bullins lost his most important theatrical outlet. As irony would have it, even the cultural nationalists were unable to run a theater of their own without the financial aid of such foundations as Ford and Rockefeller. More important than this, however, is perhaps the fact that the New Lafayette also failed as a community theater since it could not nearly achieve economic self-reliance. Whilst this failure clearly deserves some sociological scrutiny, which for the want of precise data is beyond the scope of this essay, it seems to me to be equally fruitful to view the decline of the New Lafayette against the political aims associated with it.

In 1973 Robert Macbeth described these aims as follows:

> Our job has always been to show black people who they are, where they are, and what condition they are in. We take the view that a community heals itself from within. There are many sources of healing within the community, and theater is one of them. But our function, the *healing function of theater* and art, is absolutely vital. [45]

Most of Bullins' plays obviously follow this pattern as he confronts his audience with the misery, despair and violence of urban *lumpen* blacks, thereby trying to make "the members of [the] community see themselves in all their terrible ugliness — in hopes that from this profound glimpse, they will be cleansed." [46] The belief in a cathartic function of black theater which would "psychically redirect the energy of the oppressed" [47] and hence work toward a black cultural nationhood has not yet met with the necessary response of just that community. In his attempt to debrainwash the minds of his spectators Bullins may have overlooked precisely that point of orientation which Steve Benson indicated in *The Duplex:* "What I'm due for now ... is only to be a nigger ... or be black ... nothing short of those two absolutes. To work in this whiteman's land ... or build one of my own ... to give a last ditch try to save my balls." [48] As Bullins leaves out any specific delineation of how to survive in "this whiteman's land", there remains a great deal of political helplessness, if not pessimism at the core of his work.

This dour, pessimistic outlook also dominates the one act play *The Taking of Miss Janie*, which was first produced at Woodie King's New Federal Theater and was then shown at Joseph Papp's off-Broadway Newhouse Theater in Lincoln Center. The play, which won Bullins the New York Drama Critics' Circle award as best play of 1975, is a sequel to the interracial, neo-bohemian world of *The Pig Pen*. The time period of *The Taking of Miss Janie* is the 1960s. Unlike the previous plays, however, the cast of characters is no longer caught in time, rather they review the sixties from the perspective of the mid-seventies. The dramatic action centers around the troubled relationship between the white college student Janie and her black lover Monty who finally rapes her at a party. The action is interspersed with numerous segments of dialogue between the black and white party guests as well as short soliloquies, all of which allude to the politics of the 1960s. Len Stover, for example, who first appeared in *The Pig Pen* and who has now become a "working capitalist" (p. 253)[49] addresses the audience like this: "Tonight you are looking into some of the makings of the sixties... which, of course, went to make the seventies. Just think... at this moment in our story, the Kennedys have still to be disposed of, Malcolm X hasn't passed from the scene, Watts has to happen, Martin Luther King Jr. must go to the mountain... never to return..." (pp. 252–53). This interracial sequence of names points to the shattered hopes and apsirations that were once associated with each individual figure and event. What is more, it seems to suggest that Bullins has abandoned the all-black perspective that characterized his previous work. Consider the following verbal interplay between the two blacks Rick and Peggy which might equally well have been uttered by any white SDS member:

> PEGGY: We all failed. Failed ourselves in that serious time known as the sixties. And by failing ourselves we failed in the test of the times. We had so much going for us ... so much potential ... Do you realize it man? We had the youth of our times ... And we blew it. Blew it completely. Look where it all ended. Look at what happened! We just turned out lookin' like a bunch of punks and freaks and fuck-offs. ...
>
> RICK: But I am not allowing myself to be held to blame. ... History will vindicate me.
>
> PEGGY: Hey, man... you know, you never left yesterday. You're confused like all of us ... (pp. 254/55)

Even though Bullins has maintained that the rape is the predominant feature in *The Taking of Miss Janie* and that it represents "a symbol of race relations and conditions" (p. 365), the play itself does not support this assertion. Instead, it seems to echo the doom of the black American, for when Mort, the white junkie, and Monty, the black student of poetry, shout their political catchwords at each other, Monty, as the stage direction makes clear, is deeply perturbed by the following remark by Mort: "You can't kill me any more than you can kill the last century. I'm in your head, nigger, like your nightmares" (p. 255).

    The Taking of Miss Janie signals the breakdown of a cultural and political utopia. Moreover, it suggests that Bullins, who once set out "to revolutionize the consciousness of the Black people in Harlem through theatre"[50] finally came to realize that it is both culturally and aesthetically impossible to overcome the much deplored "entrenchment of Western ideals."[52] Notwithstanding the fact that his plays have so far not "inspired creation of the nation"[53] they must be credited with having perceptibly revitalized the black stage. And as they continue to be produced at various off-Broadway theaters[54] they may very well lead Bullins, if not into the mainstream of contemporary drama, at least away from the exclusivism of an all-black aesthetic. This might not be Bullins' intention at all, but then, as he succinctly observed, "a political, social or militant type of solidarity within the black community in this country at this moment does not exist."[55] If the failure of his own theater politics is viewed against this statement, it helps us not only to understand some of the problems facing the black as committed artist but also argues the need for a reappraisal of these activities in the light of the black political and cultural hopes of the sixties.

NOTES

1. James Weldon Johnson, *Black Manhattan*. New York: Atheneum, 1972, p. 78
2. For the use of these and other stereotypes cf. Sterling Brown, "Negro Characters as Seen by White Authors," *Journal of Negro Education*, 2 (1933), 179–203
3. Nathan I. Huggins, *Harlem Renaissance*. London — New York: Oxford UP, 1973, p. 251
4. Langston Hughes, *I Wonder As I Wander: An Autobiographical Journey*. New York: Hill & Wang, 1964, p. 311
5. Lorraine Hansberry as quoted by Nan Robertson, "Dramatist Against Odds," *New York Times*, March 8, 1959, Sec. 2, p. 3
6. Herbert Grabes, "Schwarzes Drama auf dem Weg zur 'Black Aesthetic'," in H. Grabes, ed., *Das amerikanische Drama der Gegenwart*. Kronberg: Athenäum, 1976, p. 149; cf. also Werner Sollors, "The New Black Theatre," in Edgar Lohner/Rudolf Haas, ed., *Theater und Drama in Amerika: Aspekte und Interpretationen*. Berlin: Erich Schmidt, 1978, p. 137
7. W. E. B. DuBois, *Crisis*, 32, July 1926; the quote is taken from Nathan I. Huggins, *Harlem Renaissance*, op. cit., p. 292
8. Marvin X, "An Interview with Ed Bullins: Black Theater," *Negro Digest*, 18, April 1969, p. 16. This interview is also reprinted in Ed Bullins, ed., *New Plays From The Black Theatre*. New York: Bantam, 1969. Interestingly enough, the quote above is left out in this version.

9. Ed Bullins, "The So-called Western Avant-garde Drama," in Addison Gayle, ed., *Black Expression: Essays by and About Black Americans in the Creative Arts*. New York: Weybright & Talley, 1969, pp. 143–146

10. *Ibid.*, p. 145.

11. Ed Bullins, "Black Theater: The '70s — Evolutionary Changes," *The Theme Is Blackness*. New York: William Morrow, 1973, p. 8

12. Marvin X, "An Interview with Ed Bullins," op. cit., pp. 12–13

13. Ron Karenga, "Black Cultural Nationalism," in Addison Gayle, ed., *The Black Aesthetic*. Garden City: Anchor, 1972, p. 32

14. Statement by Ed Bullins as quoted in "Talking of Black Art, Theatre, Revolution and Nationhood," *Black Theatre*, 5 (1971), 24

15. LeRoi Jones, "The Revolutionary Theatre," *Home: Social Essays*. New York: Morrow, 1966, p. 210

16. Cf. Werner Sollors, *Amiri Baraka/LeRoi Jones: The Quest For A 'Populist Modernism'*. New York: Columbia UP, 1978, p. 254 f.

17. Statement by Ed Bullins as quoted in "Talking of Black Art, Theatre, Revolution and Nationhood," op. cit., p. 19

18. Ed Bullins, "Black Theater: The '70's — Evolutionary Changes," *The Theme Is Blackness*. op. cit., p. 15

19. Alain Locke, "The Drama of Negro Life," in Gayle, ed., *Black Expression*, op. cit., p. 125

20. Cf. Don Evans, "The 'Theater of Confrontation': Ed Bullins Up Against The Wall," *Black World*, 23, April 1974, 14–19

21. Samuel A. Hay, "African-American Drama 1950–1970," *Negro History Bulletin*, 36, January 1973, 6

22. Geneva Smitherman, "Ed Bullins/Stage One: Everybody Wants To Know Why I Sing The Blues," *Black World*, 23, April 1974, 5

23. Werner Sollors, "Ed Bullins," in H. Grabes, ed., *Das amerikanische Drama der Gegenwart*, op. cit., p. 218

24. *The Autobiography of Malcolm X*. Harmondsworth: Penguin, 1968, p. 422

25. Page numbers in parentheses refer to the following edition: Ed Bullins, *The Electronic Nigger And Other Plays*. London: Faber & Faber, 1970

26. LeRoi Jones, *Blues People: Negro Music in White America*. New York: William Morrow, 1963, p. 181. Cf. also Philippe Carles/Jean-Louis Comolli, *Free Jazz, Black Power*. Translated from the French, Frankfurt: Fischer Taschenbuch, 1974, p. 177 f.

27. The page number in parentheses refers to the following edition: Ed Bullins, *Four Dynamite Plays*. New York: William Morrow, 1972

28. See Claude Brown, "The language of soul," in Thomas Kochman, ed., *Rappin' and Stylin' out: Communication in urban black America*. Urbana — Chicago: Illinois UP, 1972, pp. 134–139

29. Critics, of course, have not failed to detect this. Warren True in this context develops a parallel to Chekhov which is not very convincing because he chooses to disregard the political implications of this structural element. See

Warren R. True, "Ed Bullins, Anton Chekhov, And The 'Drama of Mood'," *CLA Journal*, 20 (1977), 521–532

30. Page numbers in parentheses refer to the following edition: Ed Bullins, ed., *New Plays From The Black Theatre*. New York: Bantam, 1969

31. Cf. John Horton, "Time and cool people," in Kochman, ed., *Rappin' and Stylin' out*, op. cit., p. 19 f.

32. Cf. for example Werner Sollors, "Ed Bullins," in Grabes, ed., op. cit., p. 217

33. For a detailed discussion of this device see Thomas Kochman, "Toward an ethnography of black American speech behavior," in Kochman, ed., op. cit., pp. 214–264

34. *Ibid.*, p. 245

35. Cf. Warren R. True, "Ed Bullins, Anton Chekhov, And The 'Drama of Mood'," op. cit., p. 529

36. Cf. the article by Claudia Mitchell-Kernan, "Signifying, loud-talking, and marking," in Kochman, ed., op. cit., pp. 315–335

37. Claude Brown, "The language of soul," in Kochman, ed., op. cit., p. 134

38. Jervis Anderson, "Profiles: Dramatist," *The New Yorker,* June 16, 1973, 55

39. Werner Sollors, "Ed Bullins," in Grabes, ed., op. cit., p. 202

40. Page numbers in parentheses refer to the following edition: *Four Dynamite Plays*, op. cit.

41. Kenneth Burke, *The Philosophy of Literary Form: Studies in Symbolic Action*. New York: Vintage, 1957, p. 93

42. Marvin X, "The Black Ritual Theatre: an interview with Robert Macbeth," *Black Theatre*, 3 (1969), 24

43. Statement by Bullins as quoted by Jervis Anderson, "Profiles: Dramatist," op. cit., p. 57

44. Ed Bullins, "A Short Statement on Street Theatre," *The Drama Review*, 12 (1968), 93

45. Statement by Robert Macbeth as quoted by Jervis Anderson, op. cit., p. 52 (My Italics)

46. Geneva Smitherman, "Ed Bullins/Stage One," *Black World*, op. cit., p. 5–6

47. Larry Neal, "The Black Arts Movement," in Gayle, ed., *The Black Aesthetic*, op. cit., p. 272

48. Ed Bullins, *The Duplex: A Black Love Fable in Four Movements*. New York: William Morrow, 1971, p. 121

49. Page numbers in parentheses refer to the following edition: Otis L. Guernsey Jr., ed., *The Best Plays Of 1974–1975*. New York: Dodd, Mead & Company, 1975

50. Ed Bullins as quoted in "Talking of Black Art, Theatre, Revolution and Nationhood," *Black Theatre*, op. cit., p. 23

51. Ed Bullins, "The So-called Western Avant-garde Drama," in Gayle, ed., *Black Expression*, op. cit., pp. 145–46

52. Statement by Ed Bullins as quoted by Brandon R. Blackman, "Black Hope of Broadway," *Sepia,* 24, December 1975, 67

53. Ed Bullins, "Black Theater: The '70's — Evolutionary Changes," *The Theme Is Blackness*, op. cit., p. 12

54. This information is borrowed from the last four editions of Guernsey's annual *Theater Yearbook*.

55. Statement by Ed Bullins as quoted by Brandon Blackman, op. cit., p. 67

Consider the Possibilities: An Overview of Black Drama in the 1970's

WINONA L. FLETCHER

Writing an overview of black drama in the 1970's is like loading your car in New York with good friends and driving across country to Los Angeles in ten days. You know your starting point, your destination, and how long you have to get there, but then you are faced with all the choices to be made in between. What route is the best — via the widely publicized points of interest or over a relatively obscure pathway that promises intriguing new insights? How many stops do you dare make along the way and yet manage to arrive on schedule? How do you resist the temptation to detour down beckoning side roads filled with suspense — and sometimes with ruts and deadends? How many sign posts must you see along the way to assure your passengers that you are on the right road and can read the map? How long should you hesitate at the forks of the roads when disparate views pull you in several directions? Consider all the possibilities!

When one looks at the long list of black plays produced solely on Off-Broadway and Off Off-Broadway; read that over 200 black playwrights were known to have been writing in 1970 and that one black workshop alone discovered 40 new black women writers between '73 and '76; receive responses from over 180 active black theatres to an inquiry on new playwrights in 1977; receive daily in the mail unsolicited scripts to be read from unknown playwrights, the productivity of black playwrights strikes a staggering blow.[1]

The road stretches before us. I must blaze the trail. This overview will provide the reader with a body of dramas selected at random from a cross-section of the black plays of the '70's and then categorized, with succinct introductory and transitional passages as needed interspersed between numerous lists. These lists, when viewed as the collective voices of the '70's, should leave the reader with "a feeling" for black drama of the past decade without trying to persuade him about anything, except, perhaps, its diversity and vitality. The omission of critical comments is deliberate; even annotation of scripts is minimized. Themes and concerns are summarized and trends illustrated by selected writers and groups. I have tried to focus the reader's attention on the many possibilities available to the black playwright, suggest areas with limited alternatives, and provide sufficient data for the reader to draw his own conclusions.

Any honest attempt to view the Black Theatre of the '70's must begin with an examination of the movement of the '60's that set the tone and gave direction to the creative activity of the decade from which we are now emerging. (We are not quite ready to load the care in New York.)

Imamu Amiri Baraka, then known as LeRoi Jones, is the recognized high priest of the Black Revolutionary Theatre. Jones is also as responsible as anybody else for the creation and definition of the entire Movement. It behooves us, however, to remember that only one brief historical moment ahead of Jones was Lorraine Hansberry, who trod with great pride in the footsteps of Richard Wright and Langston Hughes, who were themselves indebted to their predecessors. There are more links in this black historical chain than meet the "myopic eye" of the newcomer. Baraka's plans in 1979 to revive Langston Hughes' 1930 drama, *Scottsboro Limited* illustrates this interdependence more trenchantly than a thousand words could do.

For the purposes of this overview, however, we can begin in the Spring of 1964 when LeRoi Jones wrote the plays and initiated the activities that opened the Black Arts Repertoire Theatre School in New York City. This act, more than any other, ordered the revolutionary thinking of black artists, caused black writers from coast to coast to re-examine their sensibilities, ignited the fuse of self-determination and black consciousness in audiences as well as writers, and thrust "culture" into the spotlight of the struggle for self-realization.[2]

Token black plays had appeared sporadically on the American scene in the decades preceeding the '60's, but now there came a deluge composed primarily of dramas that refused to flow into the mainstream and that formed a separate channel of their own. While the general American public was trying either to ignore or control this flood, Blacks who had never dreamed of being playwrights were becoming aware that their voices lifted in protest could provoke spiritual as well as social change in black and white America. They created dramas that became living microcosms for the awareness and development of new sensibilities. As Hughes had predicted thirty years earlier: "Someday somebody'll stand up and talk about me ... And put on plays about me! I reckon it'll be me, Myself! ... [3] The black playwright's time had come, like it or not, and LeRoi Jones wasted no time and few words letting everybody know that:

> WALKER: (*to his former white liberal friend*) The point is that you had your chance, darling, now these other folk have theirs.
>
> — *The Slave* [4]

The black revolutionary playwrights left a legacy for the writers of the 70's. This summary provides a birdseye view:

1. Art (theatre) as a weapon for change/revolution — spiritually, psychologically, or actual blood revolution.
2. Self-determination.
3. Black consciousness and black identity.
4. Art that functions; not "art for art's sake, but art for people's sake.
5. Art and politics as one: emphasis on liberation.
6. Rejection of western aesthetics, of western forms, if possible; a continuing search for forms appropriate to black expression and experiences.
7. Writing that speaks to, about, for, and by Blacks. [5]
8. Urgent need and desire to speak to the black community.
9. Growing skepticism about "protest literature" since by its very nature of appeal, it suggested "being at the mercy of the 'superior.' "
10. Re-evaluation of the black man's presence in America; broad thematic material covering everything from folk heroes to confrontation between black and white America; any phase of the black man's struggle for survival, but always relevant to and growing out of the life experiences of black people in America.

Almost nobody regretted the end of the 60's. And then the 70's came — a decade in defiance of a single label, despite journalistic efforts to compress all of us neatly into "The Me Generation." (We're loading the car, now.) Most of us will concede that this tag suggests the presence of one strong trend toward individualism, narrow self-interest, even narcissism for some, but it fails to leave space for the eclecticism of the years that withstood the bombing of Cambodia, Kent and Jackson State student deaths, Watergate, cultist deaths in Jonestown, nuclear power scares, rising inflation, and the seizing of American hostages in distant places. It had been a simple matter to call the 60's a "decade of revolution," but for Blacks, particularly, the 70's is yet without a simple name.

This should not be construed to mean that Blacks were not drawn into all the crises of the decade; they were, sometimes unwillingly. They shared on one level the Country's fear, neurosis, pain, shame, and increasing frustrations over national and international events. On another level they kept one eye on Bakke and Webber, on the undercover moves of the FBI and the CIA, the increasing use of the term "minority" as an all-inclusive term for burgeoning ranks of people, on the resurgence of the Klansmen, and on other groups and activities that mitigated against small gains earned in human rights in the 60's. When the gears shifted near mid-decade, it became apparent to most Blacks that ideology was losing the race to pragmatism. Black playwrights, in an effort to stay relevant, and yet imbued with the spirit of their 60's legacy, constantly re-evaluated and re-defined their out-pouring. The dramas of the 70's reflect the changes in society and in themselves and the writers' attempts to cope with them.

Sometimes referred to as a tapestry, the Black Theatre of the 70's more accurately resembles a patch-work quilt when the variety of themes and treatments are viewed together; one can scarcely detect a basic design, but somehow the pieces all fit together and, when bound by a border of common experiences, quite amply cover the desired area. (We're moving now!) While many black plays defy categorization, the following arbitrary headings and selected plays suggests the most prevalent "forms" of the black playwright and provide a view of the patch-work of themes and treatments.[6]

MUSICALS — REVUES

1. *PURLIE* (mod minstrel show according to some critics) Ossie Davis
2. *BILLY NO NAME*, Bill Mackey
3. *DON'T BOTHER ME I CAN'T COPE*, Vinette Carroll
4. *I AM* (blues musical done by Ricker's Island inmates), Ann Early
5. *THE PRODIGAL SISTER*, Micki Grant and J. E. Franklin
6. *BUBBLING BROWN SUGAR*, Rosetta LeNoire
7. *RAG TIME BLUES*, Rosetta LeNoire
8. *CHARITY SUFFERETH LONG* (Gospel musical), Evangelist Mattie Wilson
9. *MASKS IN BROWN*, Al Fann Theatre Ensemble (billed as brief history of Blacks with music, dance etc.)
10. *NIGGERS*, Valarian Smith (billed as musical theatre piece)
11. *NIGGER COWBOY*, Judi Mason
12. *SEASONS REASONS* (billed as a 40-voice "a capella" musical and set for Inner City Cultural Center's opening (L.A.) in early 1980, Ron Milner

13. *BUT NEVER JAM TODAY*, Vinette Carroll
14. *SPARROW IN FLIGHT* — Charles Fuller, conceived by Rosetta LeNoire
15. *MEET ME ON BROAD STREET*, New Freedom Theatre Writers (Phila.)
16. *SISTUHS*, Saundra Sharp

OPERA

1. *Treemonisha* — special production of Scott Joplin's 1907 opera (theme: education as the salvation of Blacks)

HISTORICAL DRAMAS AND DRAMAS OF BLACK HEROES (contemporary & historical)

1. *SLAVESHIP*, Amiri Baraka
2. *MIDDLE PASSAGE*, J. P. Clarke
3. *EL HAJJ MALIK*, The Life and Death of Malcolm X, N. R. Davidson
4. *MISS TRUTH*, Glory Van Scott (on Sojourner Truth)
5. *FREDERICK DOUGLAS, IN HIS OWN WORDS*, (?)
6. *THE MOTION OF HISTORY*, Amiri Baraka (4 hour drama written in 1975–76; one of two plays he wrote in that year.)
7. *SCOTTSBORO LIMITED*, Langston Hughes; Baraka's revival of the 1932 drama (in late 70's)
8. *JOHN BROWN*, Lorraine Hansberry's unfinished script revealed in 1979
9. *PAUL ROBESON IN CONCERT*, Phillip Hayes Dean (a mono-drama)
10. *MAHALIA*, Don Evans (Mahalia Jackson)
11. *THE BROWNSVILLE RAID*, Charles Fuller (on a regiment of Black soldiers stationed in Texas in 1906.)

RITUALS — TOTAL THEATRE

1. *NATIONAL BLACK THEATRE* under Barbara Ann Teer's direction performed several "Blackenings," as they were called, patterned after the traditional church set-up; no specific titles.
2. *THE REVIVAL—NBT* with dance, music, drama, rappings, trappings, Teer and her "Liberators" (name given to actors)
3. *A BLACKENING* based on travel to Oshgo, Nigeria, with African forms, images, ideas — NBT
4. *A HAND IS ON THE GATE*, Roscoe Lee Browne (became known as a "classic:" music, dance, dialogue, folk games, poetry)

5. *SOUL JOURNEY INTO TRUTH* (music, chants, dance, audience participation etc.) NBT
6. *RITUAL*, New Lafayette Company (recorded as a 1970 production)

COMEDIES — SATIRES — SPOOFS (most are treatments of black/white relationships or an area/activity of the Black Revolutionary Movement)

1. *PURLIE VICTORIOUS*, Ossie Davis' drama before it became a musical.
2. *ROSALIE PRITCHETTE*, Carlton and Barbara Molette
3. *CONTRIBUTIONS*, Ted Shine
4. *HAPPY ENDING AND DAY OF ABSENCE*, Douglas T. Ward
5. *THE UPS AND DOWNS OF THEOPHILUS MAITLAND* (billed as one of three comedies with music), Micki Grant and J. E. Franklin (?)
6. *FAT TUESDAY*, Roger Furman
7. *PLANTATION*, Ted Shine
8. *CANNED SOUL*, Sharon Stockard Martin
9. *FIVE ON THE BLACK HAND SIDE*, Charles Russell
10. *MADAME ODUM*, Louis Rivers (billed as "black drawing-room comedy)
11. *ON STRIVERS ROW*, Abram Hill (revival of 1939 satire on black social climbers)
12. *COTILLION*, comedy based on John Killens novel (?)
13. *SING A SONG OF WATERGATE*, Margaret Taylor Snipes
14. *OLE JUDGE MOSE IS DEAD*, Joseph White
15. *LIVIN' FAT*, Judi Ann Mason
16. *INACENT BLACK AND THE FIVE BROTHERS*, A. Marcus Hemphill (a new spiritual mystery comedy)
17. *DON'T ROCK THE BOAT*, Margaret Taylor Snipes (comedy from Biblical story of Noah and the Ark)

BLACK REVOLUTIONARY DRAMA (reflecting the politics of the 60's movement or primarily protesting racist society)

1. *MAD HEART AND JUNKIES ARE FULL OF SHHHH ...*, Imiri Baraka (69–70)
2. *PERRY'S MISSION* (at Negro Ensemble Company, 1971; on the destructive influence of whites on the movement.) (?)
3. *THE BLACK TERROR*, Richard Wesley
4. *THE TAKING OF MISS JANIE*, Ed Bullins
5. *LES BLANC*, Lorraine Hansberry's drama of a Mau-Mau type rebellion in an African country (published in 70's)
6. *THE DEVIL CATCHER*, Ed Bullins

7. *DEATH LIST*, Ed Bullins (1971)
8. *RUN-AROUND*, Ben Caldwell (1970)
9. *THE LEADER*, Joseph White
10. *JOB SECURITY*, Martie Charles (1970)

SERIOUS DRAMAS OF BLACK LIFE

1. *KING HEROINE*, Al Fann
2. *BAPTISM*, Amiri Baraka
3. *ROOTS*, Gil Moses
4. *FLOWERS FOR THE TRASHMAN*, Marvin X
5. *WINE IN THE WILDERNESS*, Alice Childress
6. *DUPLEX, A BLACK LOVE FABLE*, Ed Bullins
7. *AIN'T SUPPOSE TO DIE A NATURAL DEATH,* Melvin Van Peebles
8. *DREAM ON MONKEY MOUNTAIN*, Derek Walcott
9. *THE FABULOUS MISS MARIE*, Ed Bullins
10. *BLACK GIRL*, J. E. Franklin
11. *IN NEW ENGLAND WINTER*, Ed Bullins
12. *BEHOLD! COMETH THE VANDERKELLANS,* Bill Mackey
13. *MOON ON A RAINBOW SHAWL*, Vinette Carroll
14. *THE LONG BLACK BLOCK*, Roger Furman
15. *THE RIVER NIGER*, Joseph Walker
16. *THE STY OF THE BLIND PIG*, Phillip Hayes Dean
17. *SOMETIMES A HARD HEAD MAKES A SOFT BE-HIND*, J. F. "Sonny" Gaines
18. *SISTER SONJI*, Sonia Sanchez
19. *STRIKE HEAVEN ON THE FACE*, Richard Wesley
20. *WEDDING BAND*, Alice Childress
21. *DON'T PLAY US CHEAP*, Melvin Van Pebbles
22. *WHAT THE WINE SELLERS BUY*, Ron Milner
23. *WHAT IS GOING ON*, Ben Caldwell
24. *REQUIEM FOR BROTHER X*, Bill Mackey
25. *TOP HAT*, Paul C. Harrison
26. *GALVINANTIN HUSBAND*, Milburn Davis
27. *ELTON*, Lou Ferguson
28. *ON BEING HIT*, Clay Goss
29. *THE DILEMMA OF A GHOST*, Christina Ama Aidoo (Ghanaian playwright on what happens when a black American wife goes home with her Ghanaian husband.)
30. *HOUSE PARTY*, Ed Bullins
31. *A SOULFUL HAPPENING*, Ed Bullins
32. *THE PAST IS PAST*, Richard Wesley
33. *THE SIRENS*, Richard Wesley

34. *THE GREAT MCDADDY*, Paul C. Harrison (inspired by African novel of Amos Tutola, *The Palm Wine Drinkard*; billed as a musical, one critic called it a "dirge.")
35. *ARIFE AND PENDABUS*, Ernie McClintock (West Indian theme)
36. *MIDDLE CLASS BLACKS*, Herbert Campbell
37. *TOE JAM*, Elaine Jackson
38. *SECTION D*, Reginald Johnson
39. *AN EVENING WITH DEAD ESSEX*, Adrienne Kennedy
40. *SONG OF A GOAT*, J. P. Clarke
41. *DON'T CALL ME A MAN*, Howard Moore
42. *DO UNTO OTHERS*, Samm Williams
43. *THE SQUARE ROOT OF EVIL*, Adolph Ceasar
44. *MALICE IN WONDERLAND*, Mars Hill
45. *THE FIRST BREEZE OF SUMMER*, Leslie Lee
46. *WAITING FOR MONGO*, Silas Jones
47. *LIBERTY CALL*, Buriel Clay
48. *SUGAR MOUTH SAM DON'T DANCE NO MORE*, Don Evans
49. *THE LAST STREET PLAY*, Richard Wesley
50. *EVERY NIGHT WHEN THE SUN GOES DOWN*, Phillip Hayes Dean
51. *SUMMER SCREEN*, Lennox Brown
52. *NO PLACE TO BE SOMEBODY*, Charles Gordonne
53. *FOR COLORED GIRLS WHO HAVE CONSIDERED SUICIDE/WHEN THE RAINBOW IS ENUF*, Ntozake Shange
54. *A STAR AIN'T NOTHIN' BUT A HOLE IN HEAVEN*, Judi Mason
55. *THE BALLAD OF CHARLIE SWEETLEGS VINE*, Farrell J. Foreman
56. *BLACK PICTURE SHOW*, Bill Gunn
57. *THE BOOK OF LAMBERT*, Leslie Lee (Bible-flavored parable about man's search for self-knowledge and self-definition)
58. *NEVIS MOUNTAIN DEW*, Steve Carter (called by critics "an astounding adult piece of work of universal significance; NEC will tour 1980)
59. *THE MOVING VIOLATION*, Sharon Stockard Martin
60. *ADDIS ABABA*, James Bronson (invasion of Ethiopa in 1936)

SPECIAL CATEGORY

1. *SHANGO DE IMA* — Yoruba Mystery Play, Pepe Carril

2. *SISYPHUS AND THE BLUE-EYED CYCLOPS*, Garland Thompson (billed as an "illusory mind play.")
3. *THE FACTORY*, Amiri Baraka's revolutionary poetry readings, music, sounds etc. for The Yenan Theatre Workshop in New York at the end of the decade.)

SUMMARY

The fire that ignited in Jones and the Revolutionary black writers of the 60's became a bonfire in the 70's. The legacy that had spawned black consciousness inspired great gains in quantity and quality in only ten short years of nourishment. The proliferation of black playwrights made black theatre available to the black community and to the world. It should be remembered that at this same time, Alex Haley's *ROOTS* was changing the viewing habits of millions of Americans, *Miss Jane Pitman* was proudly walking her way into the hearts and minds of movie goers, and *THE WIZ* was taking over Broadway.

THEMES AND CONCERNS TREATED IN THE DRAMAS

Martin Esslin, in what he refers to as "an outsider's view of new playwrights in America," declares that American playwrights of the 70's have many problems: severely limited outlets for serious dramatists to develop their craft; absence of a training ground in a highly professional surrounding; no secure market for their plays; plays having to be written in a vacuum; relative sparseness of good theatre in broad areas of the country; the inability of serious drama to maintain a foothold on Broadway; almost total absence of serious drama on mass media which should be serving as a training ground for dramatists; apparent lack of background and historical dimension; and serious deficiencies in the educational system. He further cites American playwrights' obsession with "family matters" and "topical subjects that tend to appear in waves" as evidences of their lack of ideology, philosophical thought or historical reflection. Calling all of this "adolescent," he excuses some of it by the admission that a young civilization may, indeed, lack archetypes and myths that are not too shallow to provide deeper applicability ... Recognizing that the stuff of great drama tends to arise when a society is in a profound crisis — WWI brought Expressionism; WWII, Existentialism/Absurdism; 1930's American Depression some splendid drama, he turns his attention to an area of immediate concern to us:

> It is surely significant that the one area where one can speak of an upsurge of creativity in drama, comparable to the British New Wave, is that of Black drama, where the civil rights movement has produced a revolutionary situation and a restructuring

of society. Some brilliant playwrights have emerged among
American Blacks, but they have inevitably, suffered from some
of the handicaps I mentioned earlier, and to an even greater
degree: lack of educational background, absence of a rich field
of historical or cultural reference, and a woeful lack of opportunities to acquire professional skills. And even the Black playwrights seem to lack the desire, or the ability, to produce or
to refer to an interesting ideological framework: ... [7]

There are black playwrights who have their own views about what is
wrong with American playwriting in the 70's, and a few more who would
like to tell Esslin what is wrong with his perceptions of black playwrights.
Amiri Baraka, the high priest of the 60's and a voice being heard again in the
late 70's, is one of them. In the same year in which Esslin made his
comments (1978), Baraka was explaining his interest in reviving Hughes'
drama on the infamous Scottsboro Boys Case from the 1930's. Heard
together, the two voices strike similar notes:

This is the time to bring that back [Hughes' drama]. The
Depression that's here is not going to let up, it's going to get
worse. Beyond that real deep Depression there's a war, another
war. [8]

He reinforces Esslin's statement about American drama lacking depth
and historical perspective, but uses this belief to put black drama into
proper perspective. Crediting O'Neill, Howard and Rice with initiating
American drama at the same time they began to talk about Blacks realistically, he scores another hit:

American drama didn't exist in any human dimension at all
before that. It's not until they can talk about Black people in any
kind of way approximating humanity or reality that American
theater exists. It doesn't exist just because of that — it's the fact
that they've managed to disconnect themselves from European
models sufficiently to create an American drama. An American
drama has to deal with America, and you cannot deal with
America without the question of the Afro-American, you cannot deal with America without the question of slavery, because
the country's built on it.

Now if the slave master's culture does not develop a theatre
until 1918 or 1920, then Black theater will have to develop a
little later. [9]

Another black articulate voice is that of a young woman playwright
who shook the black theatre world in the late 70's with her drama on black
male/female relationships that dared to defy the age-old taboo placed on

women and started a new trend in black subject matter—Ntozake Shange. Her desire for and insistence on "freedom" strikes a different note from either of the male voices and, perhaps, best exemplifies how the new playwright of the 70's took a long look at his legacy, chose that which could best serve him and moved to the beat of his own drummer:

> I moved from New York in 1970 and went to California because at that time there was no space for an independent woman's voice; women were expected to be quiet and have babies, no matter what kind of training they had ... "[10]

Objecting to the "traps" set by the early writer's attempt to make all black people fit a mold, she postulates:

> This monolithic idea that everybody's the same, that we all live the same lives. That the Black family, the Black man, the Black female are the same thing. A one image. A one something. It's not true, but its very difficult to break through some of that ... [11]

Within the parameters established by these three individual perceptions, we can now consider the possibilities heard in the collective voices of the black playwrights of the 70's.

1. Affirmation of black people's humanity.
2. The black family and black manhood.
3. Black female life and survival; black male/female relationships.
4. Middle class aspirations.
5. Drug addiction in the black community.
6. Inner city life and related problems.
7. Anti-Vietnam War.
8. Religion and "old-fashioned" morality.
9. Watergate and its consequences on black life.
10. Education of Blacks.
11. The social life of Blacks.
12. Survival of black urban characters — pimps, prostitutes, etc.
13. Politics and involvement with the system.
14. Discovery of black roots/images/life styles.
15. Survival techniques in the North and South.
16. Second look at the Black Revolution; the role of women in it etc.
17. Pan-Africanism.
18. Another view of contemporary and historical black heroes.
19. Father-son relationships.
20. Broken marriages/homes.

21. Some Blacks' rejection of their own traditions; necessary adjustments.
22. Black social-climbers.
23. Nostalgia for the days gone by.
24. Fantasy/parables/proverbs that relate to the black experience.
25. Lack of freedom and the presence of evil.

CONCERNS INSPIRING ACTION BUT NOT NECESSARILY CONTENT OF PLAYS

1. Audience development; getting more blacks to attend the theatre.
2. Continuing need for relevance to black experience on stage.
3. Financial problems and ways to get into the higher levels of control.
4. Suitable showcases for black writing.
5. Unity/cooperative spirit among black groups; sharing of physical facilities etc.
6. Assuring both quality and quantity in black theatre.
7. Effect of Women's Movement on the black struggle.
8. Using black vision to move beyond telling it like it is to how to break through the cycle and move on.
9. Finding satisfactory news forms to fit the needs of black plays.
10. Getting more black hero plays before the public.
11. Fear that in depicting some urban characters — superfly, prostitutes etc. they may become "romanticized."
12. Continuing battle against stereotypes on mass media.
13. Need to establish cultural relationships with Blacks in other areas of the world.
14. Preparation of directories; more careful documentation and distribution of black theatrical activities.
15. Providing input into Broadway plays (actors, producers, writers, subject matter); removing barriers that deny Blacks access to the popular platforms of expression — mass media.
16. Overcoming black apathy; getting and keeping black audiences.
17. Need for developing theory, criteria for critical assessment of dramas as black art.
18. Need for clarity of purpose and direction in black theatre.
19. Need for straight, dramatic stories about Blacks — people placed against an historical background; need to go beyond the slave experience.

20. How to use theatre more effectively in moving toward a fuller recognition of our whole selves.
21. Integrating all the dramatic elements in black folks lives into their dramas — song, dance, drums, imagery etc.

TRENDS/DIRECTIONS

1. Continued growth and development of community-based theatre groups.
2. Tenor changing from anger to celebration; efforts to channel anger and frustration of black youth into self-affirming, expressive modes.
3. Effort to make the human figure predominate.
4. Move toward the integration of all elements into total theatre; looking at black art as a total experience.
5. Development of black scholars, critics, theorists in whom the black playwright could place his trust — persons who can examine accomplishments, share feelings, give clarity and direction to black theatre.
6. Conducting of research into black heritage and transforming this research into performance.
7. Efforts to pool resources in producing works of playwrights.
8. Emergence of women writers who broke through the taboo of women being able to criticize men.
9. Effort to instill love for and habit of attending the theatre.
10. Shift from overtly topical and political writing to writing that is critical of its own efficacy.
11. Efforts to work outside the commercial world that is controlled by a few capitalists.
12. Pragmatic nationalism instead of insular nationalism of the 60's.
13. Efforts to provide a safe place where new playwrights' works can be treated seriously, compassionately, and with respect.
14. New cultural outlooks.
15. Providing escape for audience (from economic realities, in musicals).
16. Theatre based in the realities of the present rather than the myths of the past.
17. Insistent on the freedom to be different and varied.
18. Sharing of communal identity (through musicals, particularly).

BRIEF PROFILES OF EXEMPLARY PLAYWRIGHTS

The brief profiles of five new playwrights who made their appearances on the 70's scene illustrate the diversity of writers taking up their pens for black theatre and, perhaps, preview what to expect in the 80's.

MARCUS A. HEMPHILL

Created *INACENT BLACK AND THE FIVE BROTHERS*, a New Spiritual Mystery Comedy, 1979. Born in Forth Worth, majored in Music at Huston-Tillotson College in Austin, Texas. Following an army tour of duty in Korea and Japan, he pursued a musical career as a member of the Jazz-Duo, "The Par Extraordinaire," recorded four albums for Liberty Records and toured with Bill Cosby. In 1968, Hemphill turned his attention to writing, went to New York in the mid-seventies, completed a novel and became involved with the Frank Silvera Writers Workshop where he learned all he could about theatre. *Inacent Black* was completed in one year and first read in April, 1978. Hemphill had written one short theatre piece before this, "I Killed Him," a one-character "satirical-curtain-raiser and closer" in 1976. *Inacent Black* was given a later production at Teachers College, Columbia University where it ran for five performances. The Billie Holiday Theatre, Brooklyn's Professional Resident Black Theatre Company closed its 1978–79 season in May with a production of the drama.

SHARON STOCKARD MARTIN

One of six winners of the Black Playwright Project Award, sponsored by The John F. Kennedy Center for the Performing Arts. Her winning play was *THE MOVING VIOLATION*. A writer/editor, Ms. Martin is a native of Nashville, Tenn., but has lived in New Orleans since 1962. She attended Howard University and Bennington College (Vermont); earned a B.A. Degree at Southern University in Baton Rouge and an M.F.A. in Playwriting from Yale University School of Drama in 1976. She was an intern with Ed Bullins at Harlem's New Lafayette Theatre Workshop (68–69), a Shubert Fellow in 75 at Yale, recipient of a Eugene O'Neill Playwriting Award in 75, and a CBS Foundation Prize in 76. Her plays have been produced at Free Southern Theatre, Dashiki Theatre, Yale University, Clinton-Hill Repertory, Harlem Performance Center, and Yale/Cabaret. Author of a folk play, *CANNED SOUL*, one-act. In 1977, she wrote and directed SOS: *AN EVENING OF ANXIETY PIECES FOR THE CON-*

TEMPORARY AMERICAN STAGE. In addition to several articles and plays published in magazines, periodicals and newspapers, she is currently Associate Editor of The Black Collegian Magazine and Director of Communications for the Urban League of Greater New Orleans, Inc.

JUDI ANN MASON

24 year old winner of The American College Theatre Festival's Norman Lear Comedy Playwriting Award in 1975 for her play, *LIVIN' FAT,* and of The Lorraine Hansberry Award in 1977 for *A STAR AIN'T NOTHING BUT A HOLE IN HEAVEN.* She enrolled at Grambling College in Louisiana with the theatre on her mind, obtained a job as feature editor for the college newspaper and decided to mix writing with drama. Her first play, a long one-act entitled *BEFALLEN ANGEL* won Best Directed play at The National Association of Dramatics and Speech Arts Annual Conference. She then wrote *Livin' Fat* and entered it in the ACTF. As a Lear winner, she received membership in the Writer's Guild of America, was invited by Mr. Lear to Hollywood to write a teleplay for the then popular series *Good Times*, and had her play selected by The Negro Ensemble Company in New York for performances in that famous theatre. *Glamour Magazine* selected her as one of their Ten Top College Women of the Year, 1977. "The S. Randolph Edmond Award was given Ms. Mason for her play, *RED, WHITE, AND DEAD*, one of twelve plays she has written since graduating from Grambling. Her plays reflect Southern black life, echoing history, dreams, hopes, faith, aspirations, and human struggles for survival . . . She tries to reach down into the depths of black life and pull out things that people have never seen and usually don't want to accept."[12] Judi is currently a term writer for TAT, Norman Lear's Production Company and working with Alex Haley on a new television show, *TUMBLIN' BUTTS.*

GLORY VAN SCOTT

Actress, dancer, singer, published author and playwright of *MISS TRUTH*, a musical tribute to Sojourner Truth; Ms. Scott also played the title role in the New York production of *Miss Truth* at the Apollo Theatre in 1978. A graduate of Goddard College, Vermont (B.A. and M.A.), she received a Ph.D. in Education and Theatre Arts from Union Graduate School, Ohio. Her written works are part of the Black Writer's Collection of New York City College. Her plays include, *POETIC SUITE* and *THE*

SYLVILLA SUITE. She had recently completed scripts, music, and lyrics for three children's theatre productions which she has also directed and choreographed: *THE BENCHER, CHILDREN's CEREMONY*, and *I AM*. Her work has been presented at the Lincoln Center and the Sylvan Theatre in Washington, at NEC, on CBS Repertoire Workshop. As an actress, she has appeared in numerous Off-Broadway productions and as principal dancer in *PORGY AND BESS*; she has been a member of the Katherine Dunham Dance Company, the American Ballet Theatre, principal dancer with Agnes de Mille Heritage Dance Theatre, and is an Affiliate Artist.[13]

VALERIAN SMITH

He should, perhaps, not even be listed with "Black Playwrights," inasmuch as his main preoccupation is with music and lyrics for black shows which he calls "new musical theatre pieces." He represents, however, one of the "new breed" of black creators of the 70's. He has other things which set him apart also. He is a practicing dentist by day and an artist "every time he gets the chance." His chief performing group is the Baton Rouge Community Chorus. He views his "pieces" as a "loud voice calling the man to stop his inhumanity." It's a lament for the lost black man and a hope that the future will listen and be better. For Smith, the beginning of hope lies in the South. Even though the black man has been subservient, there is a closeness among Blacks and whites that needs to spread within the nation. "Southern Vibrations" are Smith's words for affinity:

Southern vibrations going to save the nation Y'all wait and see.

Valerian Smith's music is his entire being. It radiates from his handshake, his laughter, and his constant urge to share his creativity. His pieces are *CHANGES, NIGGERS, NEW BALLET* and an unfinished piece for PBS T.V. Production. He has recorded for Columbia, Stax Enterprise, Black Blood Records, and Vee Records.[14]

SELECTED GROUPS EXERTING INFLUENCE ON THE DRAMATISTS OF THE 70's

The Black Theatre Alliance (BTA)

In 1969, under the inspired leadership of Jean Sandler, sixteen black theatre groups in New York City came together to form this consortium and to bridge the gap between the black community and the theatre world. It was the first group to respond to the plea for unity among black theatre groups that were born of the Revolution, and its purposes were: to aid in audience development, to act as a clearing house for theater and related information, to develop new theater programs and forms, to promote activities of member companies, to provide technical theater training, to establish a graphic pool to service members at low or no cost, to establish a technical lending pool to be shared by member companies, and to provide touring assistance and information to member companies.

In less than five years it had sponsored three annual Black Theatre Festivals and published an information and service directory on Black Theatre that listed 130 noncommercial black theatres in the United States. Its latest effort (Spring, 1979), in support of The Richard Allen Center's 10th Anniversary, was "Black Theatre Festival—USA," a month-long arts revival held at the prestigious Lincoln Center in New York. 20,000 persons participated either as performers or audience and plans are underway to make it an annual affair.

The Audience Development Committee (AUDELCO)

AUDELCO is a voluntary organization formed in 1972 "to stimulate interest in and appreciation of the arts in the Black community through the development of new audiences." Its primary goal is to make the black community more aware of opportunities to attend the theatre; thus, the dissemination of information about the arts and the giving of theatre parties for interested groups became two of its major activities. A third activity begun in 1973 and continued annually since then, The AUDELCO Recognition Awards, inspired and promoted black dramatists and other practitioners in black theatre.

The Frank Silvera Writers Workshop

This writers workshop was founded in 1973 by playwright Garland Lee Thompson in memory of the late actor-director-producer Frank Silvera and reflected the support and efforts of the BTA. It was originally intended to provide new playwrights with a place to have their scripts read and discussed by outstanding people in the black theatre. Seminars were led by people like Owen Dodson, Ed Bullins, Phillip Hayes Dean, Richard Wesley, A. Marcus Hemphill, Alice Childress, Ntozake Shange and many others. By the end of the decade, writers from the workshop were winning many of the AUDELCO awards, and dramas were being staged in the Writers/Directors Series at the New Leonard Davis Center for the Performing Arts at City College and in black theatre facilities throughout the City.

*The John F. Kennedy Center Commission on Blacks — Black Theatre and
Playwrights Project*

Grants totalling $56,000 were awarded to six black theatre companies
across the nation in April, 1978, by The J.F. Kennedy Center for the
Performing Arts, Washington. The companies, selected from a field of
nearly 200 eligible groups by a task force of seven, used the grants to
commission new plays and to stage them within 18 months.

The six theatres selected and the winning plays performed were:
Karamu Performing Arts Theatre, Cleveland, Ohio—*DON'T ROCK THE
BOAT* by Margaret Ford-Taylor; Dashiki Project Theatre, New Orleans,
LA — *THE MOVING VIOLATION* by Sharon Stockard Martin; New
Freedom Theatre, Philadelphia, PA—*MEET ME ON BROAD STREET* by
Staff Writers; Amas Repertory Theatre, Inc., NY — *SPARROW IN
FLIGHT* by Charles Fuller; Urban Arts Corps, New York—*BUT NEVER
JAM TODAY* by Vinette Carroll; Inner City Cultural Center, Los Angeles,
CA—*ADDIS ABABA* by James Graham Bronson.

A NOTE ON SOURCES AND ACCESSIBILITY OF SCRIPTS FROM THE 70's

Access to many of the black plays of the 70's is still limited although
many dramatists are now being picked up by the two major play agencies/
distributors. Single copies of plays occasionally appear in paperback form
and a few are anthologized; fewer anthologies are coming out now, however, than in the late 60's and early 70's and some of those published then
are no longer in print, an unwelcomed, but anticipated occurrence in a
society obsessed with the promotion of new products. Black theatre is no
longer "a fad." Catalogs and play lists will be sent upon request from:

Samuel French, Inc.
25 West 45th Street
New York, N.Y. 10036

Dramatists Play Service, Inc.
440 Park Ave. South
New York, N.Y. 10016

Drama Book Specialists
150 West 52nd St.
New York, N.Y. 10019

Three bibliographies published at the end of the decade are the best known sources for locating information about black playwrights and their works and should be consulted for information up through 1977–78:

BLACK AMERICAN PLAYWRIGHTS, 1800 to the Present: *A BIBLIOGRAPHY* by Esther Spring Arata and Nicholas John Rotoli (Metuchen, N.J.: Scarecrow Press, 1976) and

MORE BLACK PLAYWRIGHTS, by Arata, published in 1978; this is a followup of the first volume and contains information on 490 playwrights, 190 of whom appeared in the first volume. (In these two volumes, sources for obtaining copies of the scripts themselves are not given.)

BLACK PLAYWRIGHTS, 1823–1977 (N.Y.: Bowker, 1977) by James Hatch and Omanii Abdullah lists publication facts when they are known, although they note further that pursuing some of the recommended routes may lead to blind alleys; frequently publication is promised but never fulfilled.

Five other important bibliographies are noted in Hatch's preface to the above book, but all were prepared in the first three years of the decade and are of little value to the student of theatre who needs a complete picture of the decade.

The Annual Round-up of Black Theatre in America, prepared annually by Peter Bailey for *BLACK WORLD* (April Issue) from 1970 to 1976 when Black World ceased publication, lists and gives brief critical comments on selected productions in New York; in this same annual issue, information on some of the leading regional theatres across the nation is also given.

VeVe Clark attempted to fill the gap left by Black World's cessation for the year 1978 in her article, "Enough of the Blues, the Year's Work in Black Theatre, 1978: A Biblioreview," *Black Scholar*, Vol. 11, #1, Sept/Nov., 1979.

SUMMARY

The ten-year trek has been completed; of necessity, much of importance has been omitted. There should be sufficient evidence here, however, to prove that black dramatists were not idle in the 70's. They helped black theatre to define its goals; they brought new and varied images to the stage and screen; they encouraged and were strengthened by a growing crop of community based theatre; despite continuing constraints, they sought and took advantage of new/more opportunities; they brought awareness and truth to many Blacks. ·

"About us, by us, for us, and near us"..."and someday, somebody'll stand up and talk about me...I reckon it'll be me, Myself!" Black dreams from 10, 20, 30, 40, 50 years ago were realized in the 1970's. Black dramatists can and must continue to dream — and to work in the 1980's; despite gains, there is much to be done in the years ahead.

NOTES

1. Twenty years ago it was difficult to count more than 15 active black playwrights at any one time in America.

2. Jones' early plays included: *Dutchman, Jello, Experimental Death Unit # One,* and *Black Mass.* See, also, the writings of Larry Neal, Ron Karenga, Ed Bullins, Richard Wesley, and LeRoi Jones for details on the Black Arts Movement.

3. Lines from Langston Hughes' frequently quoted poem, "Note on Commercial Theatre," in *Selected Poems of Langston Hughes* (New York: Alfred A. Knopf, 1973), p. 190.

4. LeRoi Jones, *Dutchman and The Slave, Two Plays by LeRoi Jones,* (New York: William Morrow and Company, 1964), p. 73.

5. The idea for this phrase is attributed to W. E. B. DuBois, Editor of *The Crisis* (N.A.A.C.P. journal) who is credited with an article entitled "Krigwa Players Little Negro Theatre," *The Crisis,* Vol. 32, #3, (July, 1926), p. 134. The original read: "The plays of the real Negro theatre must be: 1. *About us....* 2. *By us....* 3. *For us....* 4. *Near us....*"

6. Plays were selected from production lists, programs, reviews, press releases, year-end reports and other sources; not all the dramas listed are new plays of the 70's — some were revivals of old plays. A few African playwrights are included. At times, categories are selected on the basis of one critic's viewpoint; if seen in production, some categories would probably change.

7. Martin Esslin, "New Playwrights in America," *Theater,* Vol. 9, #2 , (Spring, 1978), p. 40.

8. Amiri Baraka, "On Black Theater," *Theater,* Vol. 9, #2 (Spring, 1978), p. 59.

9. *Ibid,* p. 60.

10. Henry Blackwell, "An Interview With Ntozake Shange," *Black American Literary Forum,* Vol. 13, #4 (Winter, 1979), p. 136.

11. *Ibid,* p. 135.

12. Taken from ACTF Playwriting Awards Newsletter, #22 (Winter, 1980).

13. Taken from Stagebill, The Apollo Theatre, "Miss Truth."

14. Taken from Program, "Niggers, A New Musical."

Sam Shepard:
Today's Passionate Shepard and His Loves

RUBY COHN

Lithe and charismatic, Sam Shepard resembles the movie cowboys and rock musicians who populate several of his plays. Growing up on ranches, playing percussion instruments, Shepard is an improbable blend of nature lover and media freak. Even more improbable is his commitment to theater, that province of an elite that does not usually follow the masses to cowboy movies and rock concerts. Most improbable of all, perhaps, is Shepard's idiomatic range — not only Western colloquialisms and rock slang, but also the vernaculars of sports, drugs, the underworld, science fiction, and the mass media. Shepard fuels his dramatic dialogue with these vocabularies, creating the most energetic language of today's American theater.

Thirty-six years old, Shepard has written more than that number of plays, and he has also produced poems, film scripts, and a journal of a rock band tour. Young as he is, his plays span fifteen years, and I classify them in three groups: 1) Spare and sparely set collages in which the characters talk past one another; 2) Plays with a story-line that involves fantastic or mythological characters; 3) Rather realistic dramas — ordinary setting, sociological and psychological credibility. Committed to an almost surrealistic "pure writing" (Shepard's phrase to me), he rarely revises. Through his three main styles run a few main themes — skewed family relations, the plight of the American artist, the commercialization of America, the riches and limits of pop culture. Never doctrinaire, Shepard has his own version of myth, which, he told me, "short-circuits the intellect and hooks you up with feeling." Through his three phases, which I abbreviate as collage, fantasy, realism, Shepard's signature is visible in what have been variously called arias, verbal trips, rock riffs, volcanic monologues. These passages are associative, image-laden, grammatically simple, occasionally paced by a telling refrain. Although these monologues

161

are analogues to traditional soliloquies, they are rarely spoken when a character is alone on stage; although these monologues resemble soliloquies in exploring a character's inner life, that life bears obliquely on the stage action, and behind the individual's inner life, the monologue sometimes attains a wider truth. The monologue is Shepard's entry into the core of his characters, and occasionally the monologal character leaps imaginatively outside himself.

The Rock Garden, Shepard's first extant play, builds to a self-centered monologue rendered famous (or infamous) in *Oh! Calcutta*. The speech announces old themes in a new idiom — the sexual pressure of adolescence and the loneliness within a family. In this *Spring's Awakening* the first of the three scenes is wordless; a man reads a magazine while an adolescent boy and girl sip milk; the scene ends when the girl spills her milk. In the second scene a woman lies in bed with a cold, and the adolescent boy in his underwear sits in a rocking chair. The woman speaks at length — a monologue except for the boy's occasional laconic questions about her father and her husband. Three times she likens one of the boy's features to one of theirs. She keeps sending the boy out for a blanket or a glass of water, and he returns with clothing over the inherited feature. She complains so repetitively of the draft that the boy finally wears an overcoat and leaves when a man in overcoat arrives. Soon the man sits in the rocking-chair in his underwear; who is imitating whom in the drafty room?

The third scene presents man and boy, father and son, in underwear in the living-room. Like the woman in the second scene, the man speaks a virtual monologue which the boy punctuates with laconic questions. Once, father and son sustain a Pintersque duet about painting a fence. The burden of the man's speech, however, is his fantasy rock garden. After a long pause, the boy spews forth a manic monologue about sexual pleasure; that is his rock garden, which knocks the man off his couch.

Despite inclusion in *Oh! Calcutta*, the finale is shocking not so much because of its explicit sexuality as because of its sudden eruption, after a collage of images rather than a coherent narrative. First the father is oblivious to the sexual stirrings of brother and sister; then the mother is oblivious to sexual implications of her own alternating requests for coolness and warmth — water and blanket — while she fixes the boy in his male lineage. Finally, stripped to their underwear, father and son carry on a dialogue of the deaf, the father projecting a fantasy garden and the son projecting fantasy orgasms. Woman, man, and boy keep stuttering the same refrains: "I don't know." "You know?" They do not know.

In spite of this example of generational insularity, most of Shepard's early plays engage young people. In 1967, a veteran of three years of playwriting, Shepard designed plots for four different fantasies of my second grouping — a blend of pop and ritual in *La Turista*, a rock music melodrama in *Melodrama Play*, a play not so much within as with a play in *Cowboys #2*, and science fiction in *Forensic and the Navigators*.

La Turista is Shepard's first effort at a sustained plot, but the second act precedes or recapitulates the first; chronology yields to pattern. Shepard's title puns on the Spanish word for tourists and the diarrhea that often afflicts them. In a brightly colored Mexican hotel-room an American couple, Kent and Salem, suffer from this malady and from severe sunburn. A native shoeshine boy irritates them further, and when Kent faints in illness, Salem telephones for a doctor. What arrives is a native Mexican Witch-doctor with his son and esoteric paraphernalia. The Witch-doctor conducts an elaborate ceremony, and the boy translates its traditions into tourist-guide idiom. With Kent inert and Salem suffering from turista, the native boy dons Kent's cowboy costume, and Salem auctions him off as though the theater were a slave-market. When Act I closes, Kent lies unconscious before the chanting Witch-doctor and his son, while Salem woos the resistant boy to return with her to the States.

In Act II Kent and Salem are again in a hotel-room, but this one is plastic American. Kent's illness is sleeping sickness, although he behaves as if in a trance. Salem's request for a doctor brings a father-son team dressed like doctors in Westerns, with idiom to match. On Doc's orders, his son and Salem walk Kent around, but the drama gradually narrows to a verbal duel between Kent and Doc. While facing off with guns — Kent's is imaginary — they build a monster verbally. Leaping off the stage, Kent becomes that beast. He describes Doc tracking the beast in the jungle as he runs to the back of the theater. Doc on stage orders his son and Salem to corner Kent at the back of the theater. When they lunge at Kent, he swings out over the audience and back on to the stage. Running to the backstage wall, he "leaps right through it, leaving a cut-out silhouette of his body in the wall."

Kent and Salem, named for well-known American cigarettes, are tourists abroad and in their own country. Suffering from the food and climate of Mexico, they cannot be cured by the traditions of that country, to which they feel superior. In the United States, however, suffering from the patently metaphoric sleeping sickness, Kent cannot be cured by outworn popular models and rhetoric of his own country. Both father-son doctors are rooted in coherent cultural ground, which proves to be quicksand for the contemporary Americans. Kent and Salem are products of American industry and culture. Kent perhaps escapes that contemporary prison through assuming pop roles — macho cowboy in Act I, and in Act II gangster, monster, Tarzan. It is not clear whether Kent's final actions show self-recognition and flight from plastic anonymity, or a violent declaration of independence. What is clear is the inventive stage imagery with which Shepard delineates the cultural poverty of modern American youth.

Although *Melodrama Play* also glances at this theme, it looks more directly at the artist's plight. Unlike dramas about writers — *Chatterton, Tasso, Long Day's Journey* — this play thrives on popular forms such as Grade-B adventure films and rock songs. The stage is dominated by large eyeless photographs of Bob Dylan, king of rock, and Robert Goulet, king of crooners. Duke Durgens, a fictitious rock star, wears "extra long hair, shades, jeans, boots, vest, etc." Four members of a rock band dress identically as do Duke's brother Drake and his friend Cisco.

Having composed a hit song, Duke is pressured by his manager Floyd to compose another one (as Shepard's Horsedreamer will be pressured to name a winner, and his Rabbit Brown will be pressured to create a hit movie). Actually, however, it is not Duke but his brother Drake who composed the hit song, which Duke then sold to Floyd. Ordering his girl-friend Dana to cut his hair, Duke moves from the Dylan to the Goulet image, whereupon Floyd orders his strongarm man Peter to guard Duke, Drake, Dana, and Cisco until a hit is produced, no matter who composes it. With melodramatic violence, Peter shoots Dana, knocks Duke and Cisco unconscious, and bars Floyd from the room. While Peter plays cat-and-mouse with Drake, the actual composer, Duke's voice is heard on the radio, singing the hit song: "So prisoners, get up out a' your homemade beds." One by one, Duke, Cisco, and Dana get up from their homemade beds, and leave the stage. In the final image Peter raises his club to hit Drake, and there is a loud knock on the door. Commerce knocking outside, thug bludgeoning inside — that is the position of today's artist, in Sam Shepard's view. Although *Melodrama Play* does not quite synthesize its stereotypes — rock star, artist, thug, manager — it served to limber Shepard up for such defter artistic bouts as *Mad Dog Blues, Cowboy Mouth, Angel City*, and especially *The Tooth of Crime*.

From his earliest lost play about cowboys Shepard thrives on Camp, with its nostalgia for the kitsch of another era. Shepard loves the stereotypes of popular culture, and yet he can no longer accept them naively. In *Cowboys #2* two young men play at being old cowboys (as Shepard and a friend evidently did in the streets of New York City). At play's end two other men in business suits read the play's opening cowboy dialogue from scripts, without Camp nostalgia, and the idiom turns to dust on their tongues. Shepard loves the West and lives there, but his cowboys come straight from Grade-B films — slow-spoken, hard-riding, straight-shooting, buddies to the death as we see them in *Cowboys #2, The Unseen Hand, Killer's Head*. Cowboys are absent from his most spectacular play, but their landscape is the background of *Operation Sidewinder*.

Like other Shepard titles *Operation Sidewinder* is a pun; the sidewinder is both rattlesnake and military computer. Like other Shepard plays of the fantasy group, *Operation Sidewinder* is coherently (if incredibly) plotted. John Lahr summarizes: "A six-foot sidewinder, which is really an escaped military computer; black, white, and Indian renegades plotting to capture Air Force planes by putting dope in a military reservoir; a Hopi snake dance whose ritual transforms the sidewinder computer from military property to religious icon."[1]

Each group has its own parodic idiom. The Young Man speaks hippy slang of the 1960s; Honey, who becomes his girl, speaks like a movie ingénue; Mickey Free, the half-breed who returns to his native roots, at first speaks pidgin English and later biblical prose. Dr. Vector, who derives from *Dr. Strangelove,* sounds like that film character. The Air Force officers also sound like film parodies, and the Black Power rebels utter their own clichés. Even peripheral characters have their own language: film Western lingo of the old gold prospector, S.D.S. rhetoric of the car bellhop, specialized jargon of the illfated automobile mechanic, fabulous imagery of the Spider Woman.

Unlike hippies of the 1960s, the Young Man is not attracted by religious mysticism, but he is attracted to Honey, who enters the final Indian ritual. The play closes on that ceremony, with its full stage. Full not only of people but of chanting, dancing, and a theater technology that deploys smoke, wind, and sharp shifts of light. John Lahr was appreciative, showing that the play's final image "brings the outlandish plot to a brilliant epiphany," where the world of spirit (the Indians) is challenged by the material world (the military)."[2] As in Shaffer's *Royal Hunt of the Sun*, however, or Hampton's *Savages*, professional actors in native rituals are embarrassing on stage. The grand finale resembles a Disneyland version of New Comedy — boy gets girl against a fantasmagoria of costumed gestures, billowing breezes, and colored lights.

A year later, however, when Shepard ends *Mad Dog Blues* on song and dance, it is a revel after a nightmare. Apparently written in a drugged state, the "two-act adventure show" nevertheless deploys nine characters loved by an undrugged Shepard; in addition to old cowboy Waco Texas, we have a rock star, a drug addict, and cult figures of fact and fiction. On a bare stage the characters venture far and wide, through ocean and desert, within an island and on a frontier, past one another although they are close enough to touch.

Two friends, Kosmo the rock star who "leads with his cock" and Yahoudi the drug addict who "sucks in the printed word" leave New York City separately. In Frisco Kosmo conjures up Mae West, and in a jungle Yahoudi finds Marlene Dietrich. Each Camp prima donna has her dictum:

MAE WEST:	Big surprises come in small packages.
MARLENE DIETRICH:	A mango in the morning is sometimes better than a man.

Kosmo and Mae meet cowboy Waco Texas, and Yahoudi meets Captain Kidd of the legendary treasure.. As all characters seek the treasure, they tumble through swift adventures that are faintly familiar from films. Marlene leaves Yahoudi for Paul Bunyan, lonely without his blue ox Babe. Act I closes on a manic monologue by Waco Texas to a silent Ghost Girl — a cowboy's penance to Indians?

Act II opens on Yahoudi's threats to Captain Kidd, courtesy of John Huston's *Treasure of the Sierra Madre*. As swiftly as film cuts, Shepard moves his characters around the treasure island. Yahoudi shoots Captain Kidd and then shoots himself, falling on the treasure, where Kosmo and Mae discover him. Soon Jesse James robs Kosmo of treasure and Mae. Kosmo implores his friend Yahoudi to return to life and help him dispose of the other characters, and yet the two separate in hostility. Each character is locked in his own myth but seeks a partner. Except for Jesse James and Mae West with the treasure-bags, "The OTHERS keep searching for each other but never meet, even though at times THEY may pass right by each other." When Jesse James and Mae West are stopped by a Customs Inspector, they mount Paul Bunyan's ox and stampede across the border: "That was a custom he wasn't accustomed to." The famous treasure proves to be a mass of bottle-caps. When Jesse decides to go home to Missouri, Mae invites the others to join them. Singing "Home," "THEY join hands and dance and march together around the stage, through the audience, and out into the street." Written early in 1971, the play ends in an abrupt celebration, but Shepard's vision has darkened since then.

With *The Tooth of Crime*, written in England in 1972, Shepard renounced the broad span for the deep probe. Shepard later verbalized his achievement: "Many of my plays center around a character in a critical state of consciousness."[3] The consciousness in *The Tooth of Crime* is that of Hoss, a blend of rock star, sports aficionado, and Mafia ruler. Shepard's invented language endows *Tooth* with effulgence: a law-abiding ruler is conquered by an anarchist usurper, an old champion is bested by a younger athlete, a classical heritage is exploded by an amoral avant-garde — in a world synthesized from rock, crime, sports.

Sam Shepard, rock musician, hears his characters before seeing them. He recalls the origin of *The Tooth of Crime:* "It started with language — it started with hearing a certain sound which is coming from the voice of his character, Hoss."[4] He can no longer remember whether he heard that voice before writing *Mad Dog Blues* in which Yahoudi calls out to his rock star friend: "Kosmo! I had a dream! I dreamed I was Crazy Horse! I was leading a raiding party against the Crows." In *The Tooth of Crime* the names change roles; Crow becomes a gypsy outlaw who raids the territory of Hoss, but like Crazy Horse, the latter dies rather than live imprisoned.

Mallarmé's *Angoisse* provides Shepard's title: "A heart that the tooth of crime cannot wound." Mallarmé's sonnet contrasts the vulnerable persona with his invulnerable partner in vice, and Shepard contrasts vulnerable Hoss with invulnerable Crow. Shepard's subtitle is "A play with music in two acts," and the acts move as cleanly as a blade. Music takes the form of eight songs, whose function Shepard describes: "I wanted the music in *Tooth of Crime* so that you could step out of the play for a minute, every time a song comes, and be brought to an emotional comment on what's been taking place in the play." Or Brechtian estrangement. Brecht was Shepard's preferred playwright when he wrote *Tooth*, and he has described *In the Jungle of Cities* as "a bout, between these two characters, taken in a completely open-ended way, the bout is never defined as being anything but metaphysical," The summary is not inappropriate for *Tooth*.

Like classical tragedy, *The Tooth of Crime* opens close to its crisis: Hoss needs a kill. He fondles the array of guns displayed by Becky, his servant-mistress-tutor. Wiser than Shakespeare's Caesar who ignored the stars, Hoss consults his Star-Man and is advised against moving. Wiser than Shakespeare's Richard II, he seeks counsel, and Galactic Jack reassures him: "A shootin' star, baby. High flyin' and no jivin'. You is off to number nine." But Hoss is not reassured and is almost relieved to have his fear take shape. Becky reports that a Gypsy has been "sussed" — Shepard's polyvalent borrowing from Cockney slang. Hoss sounds out his Chauffeur Cheyenne about "cruising," but this faithful retainer is reluctant to violate the code. Lacking support, Hoss seeks an ally in the East, only to learn of his suicide. Distraught, Hoss sends for the Doc to give him an injection, but this does not tranquilize him. Only to Becky does he reveal his full dread. Warned against cruising, he nevertheless seems soothed by Becky's cruising song, while Gypsy Crow continues to cruise closer. Hoss stalks and knifes a dummy, then recalls the cameraderie of his youth. Alone on stage, he engages in an imaginary dialogue with his father: "They're all countin' on me. The bookies, the agents, the Keepers. I'm a fucking industry." His father responds: "You're just a man, Hoss. Just a man." Once Hoss accepts that, he can accept the arrival of Crow, but he postpones their duel till the following day. Weary, enthroned under a huge shadow of Crow, Hoss absorbs Crow's song "Poison" to close Act I.

Act II reveals Crow alone on stage, dressed in the hard rock fashion of the 1960s. As Prince Hal tried on his father's crown, Crow sits in Hoss's thronelike chair — violently chewing gum. When Hoss arrives, Crow speaks in clipped, metaphoric phrases: "Got the molar chomps. Eyes stitched. You can vision what's sittin'. Very razor to cop z's sussin' me to be on the far end of the spectrum" From his royal isolation, Hoss asks Crow for news of the outside world, then orders him off the throne. Hoss teases Crow by swiftly switching roles — cowboy, 1920s gangster — before summoning a referee who will judge their agon. With the rest of the cast as cheerleaders, the two combatants circle one another "just talking the words in rhythmic patterns, sometimes going with the music, sometimes counterpointing it." In Round 1, Crow attacks Hoss with a capsule biography of a cowardly loser; Ref awards the round to Crow. In Round 2, Hoss accuses Crow of denying his musical origins in the blues of black people, but Crow counters: "I'm in a different time." The Ref declares it a draw. In Round 3, Crow ridicules Hoss's outdated music, and the Ref calls it a T.K.O. An infuriated Hoss shoots him.

Having violated the code, Hoss thereby becomes a Gypsy, and he needs survival instruction from Crow. In a digression that recalls a scene from *Alphaville*, Becky enacts a seduction-rape of her youth, with Hoss perhaps the aggressor. Defeated, Hoss cannot learn to talk, walk, and sing as a Gypsy. Like classical heroes, he prefers death to dishonor: "Now stand back and watch some true style. The mark of a lifetime. A true gesture that won't never cheat on itself 'cause it's the last of its kind. It can't be taught or copied or stolen or sold. It's mine. An original. It is my life and my death in one clean shot." He falls upon that clean shot, and Crow pays him homage: "A genius mark." Crow's reign begins, and his final song is a prayer for supremacy, like Hoss's plea to his advisers at the play's beginning. Embracing earlier Shepard themes — swiftly changing modes of art, commercialization of the artist, mechanization of America, father-son relations — *Tooth* reaches a new depth. Through their self-exploring monologues in condensed imagery and compelling rhythms, we come to know Hoss and Crow more intimately than any other Shepard characters. Because we do, we intuit aspects of raucous contemporaneity.

Having attained tragedy, Shepard gravitated toward realism, his third main phase, but he did not immediately forsake fantasy. *Angel City* and *Suicide in B Flat* (1976) revolve around the plight of the artist in contemporary America. The Angel City artist is Rabbit Brown, shabbily dressed, traveling by buckboard, tied to magic bundles. He is invited to Angel City to invent a disaster that will rescue a movie in the making. The Suicide artist is jazz composer Niles, who is the titular suicide or a victim of murder. By the end of *Angel City* Rabbit is fanged and long-nailed, and he oozes green slime; he has metamorphosed into the mogul who summoned him. The B flat possible suicide has responded to pressure by repeating his creations; he has to simulate his own death in order to escape to his own original music. At first invisible to musicians and detectives in B flat, he is finally apprehended and handcuffed.

Each of these artists is seen against a background of fantasized stereotypes, *Suicide* more complex than the Hollywood of *Angel City*. Two detectives from crime fiction seek to solve a mystery of murder or suicide, while two musicians play unconcernedly and inaudibly, refusing even to acknowledge a death. The musicians are witty and sophisticated, whereas the detectives are foolish parodies. Invisible to them, Niles and his guide Paulette enact roles of cowboy-Indian, bigtime operators. Disparate myths try to communicate, but they can no longer fulfill the imagination of the contemporary artist.

In 1976, the year of these satiric fantasies, Shepard also turned to realism. In 1974 he had already confessed: "I'd like to try a whole different way of writing now, which is very stark and not so flashy and not full of a lot of mythic figures and everything, and try to scrape it down to the bone as much as possible." Shepard's repetition of "try" hints that he might be working against the grain.

Still mythic in reach, *Curse of the Starving Class* (1976) and *Buried Child* (1978) are realistic in setting, straightforward in plot, and coherent in character. The starving class is a Western family on an avocado farm with some cattle; the child is buried on a Midwestern farm gone to seed. Both Western and Midwestern families are cursed, even as the House of Atreus. In *Starving Class* the curse is Emma's first menstrual period, but it is also the explosive blood of the family: "We inherit the curse and pass it down, and then pass it down again. It goes on and on like that without us." The very names announce heredity: father Weston and son Wesley, mother Ella and daughter Emma — the same names, except for a letter or two. Although the family members claim not to belong to the starving class, they do. Each of them keeps opening and closing the refrigerator door: "All it's good for is slamming." Much like John Donne's bell, it slams for thee. Middle-class Americans, the family is so debt-cursed that their home is prey to predators. Only the son Wesley understands the magnitude of that curse: "So it means more than losing a house. It means losing a country." At the end of the play, mother and son recite a parable of the cat and the eagle, clawing at one another high in the air: "And they come crashing down to earth. Both of them come crashing down. Like one whole thing." Greedy America has seized its own killer, a domestic animal driven berserk.

No parables and no imaginative monologues relieve the lower depths of Midwestern farm life in *Buried Child*. Grandfather Dodge (a pun) is a sedentary cougher solaced only by whiskey and television. Grandmother Halie in Whistlerian black, flirts with a clergyman to promote a statue for her dead son. More or less alive are her sons Tilden, an ex-football star and present half-wit, and Bradley, a sadistic cripple before whom the others cower. Home to the family bosom comes grandson musician Vince with his California girlfriend. As Wesley becomes conscious of the starvation of his class, Vince becomes conscious of the corpse in his family yard. His father Tilden digs up carrots, then corn, then the buried child. Realistically, Dodge has evidently murdered his wife's illegitimate infant, but symbolically youth has been buried by an American family that is idiotic, sadistic, moribund.

This essay is concerned with Sam Shepard playwright, but he is also a rock composer and theater director. When he moved to the Bay Area in 1975, he intended to form an acting company. After directing his *Killer's Head* and *Action*, he guided eight actors and eight musicians through improvisations culminating in a performance, *Inacoma*. As an exercise, it was apparently useful, but as theater, the performance lacked cohesion and precision.

Coherence, precision, and intensity distinguish Shepard's next director/playwright projects. Passionate about trying "to find an equal expression between music and the actor,"[5] he collaborated with actor/director Joe Chaikin on performance pieces that do not fit into my three grouping of Shepard's plays. *Tongues* (1978) and *Savage/Love* (1979) were not originally conceived as a whole, but the later piece clung to the earlier mould. Written by Shepard through discussion with Chaikin, each piece is a monologue, the Shepard trademark, full of swift character transformations, Chaikin's Open Theater trademark. In Shepard's program note, he writes of them: "Connections somehow arise & a story seems to be told." I would modify that to a theme rather than a story.

The two pieces are usually performed in inverse order of writing — *Savage/Love* and then *Tongues*. Unlike most monologues, which pivot on "I," *Savage/Love* drives through "you." For some half-hour the speaker reveals glimpses of that congeries of emotions we summarize as love. More varied than the couple in Albee's *Counting the Ways*, Shepard's personae range from a spastic inarticulate to a sophisticated actor. Mercurially, the speaker "transforms" from an unconfident lover — "I'd invent the one you'd have me be " — to a guilty lover who mentally murders his partner, to an egomaniacal lover primping for a love he has not yet met, to a tender lover gazing at his sleeping partner, to a grateful lover for whom love is a raison d'être. One vignette dramatizes a lover's transitions from humility to hostility. The final persona returns to the initial quiver, but the words are enriched by the intervening personae: "I was shaking, you gave me your hand — from your fingers I returned: You, you, you, you."

In this piece Shepard denies himself the flashy lexicon of Kent in *La Turista*, of Hoss and Crow in *The Tooth of Crime*. And he denies himself such mythic personae as cowboys, rock stars, amassers of hearts and fortunes. All these lovers are ordinary, familiar yet dissimilar and convincing. Not all the love is savage in *Savage/Love*, but all of it is savaged — by the next scene, or mood, or lover. The brief piece demands versatile acting, but it offers versatility for the acting.

Tongues, about a dozen sections, or half the number of *Savage/Love*, is even more exacting, since it imposes immobility on the actor, while giving free rein to his associations. As originally performed, Chaikin sat at stage center, a gray blanket covering his feet, hands motionless on his knees. Shepard, seated back to Chaikin's back, was invisible except for his bare arms caressing the tympany into subdued sound (of his own composition). The two were "a fused iconic presence."[6]

Savage/Love starts at the birth of love, But *Tongues* starts in medias res: "He was born in the middle of a story which he had nothing to do with ... " But he, the nameless persona, is dependent on, connected to, moulded by "the people," and he soon dreams of death. Except for a brief, delicate voice of a woman after childbirth — "my arm is his bed" — the dozen tongues belong to men, several of them aware of the power of the voice. A few comic personae provide relief near the end of the piece, but most of the tongues speak pathos. A funny, Pinteresque duologue — the only vignette with two voices — about going out for a bite to eat, graduates into a monologue about a hunger so vast that it eats hunger itself. With verbal simplicity but rhythmic complexity, Shepard hints at religious incantation: "with the people" in the first passage; the hiss of "lapse" cumulates into terror; in the hunger duet the brief clause "when it comes back" engulfs a void; the repetition of "between" trembles at the boundary of living and dying; incredulity at the death of a loved one grows through a refrain of "why isn't ... " Most haunting is the superpersonal range of reactions to the generalization "when you die."

"Be absolute for death," counsels Shakespeare's Duke in *Measure for Measure*, but Shepard's tongues give us a relative measure of death. Achieving resonance through the blend of the verbal and the musical, Shepard's final lines subvert their own loveliness: "Today the river lay open to the sun/Tonight I hear it speaking./ Today the people talked without speaking./ Tonight I can hear what they're saying./ Today the wind roared through the center of town./ Tonight I hear its voice./ Today the tree bloomed without a word./ Tonight I'm learning its language."

Like his persona, Shepard hears beneath words, but he finds words for translation into our common tongue.

NOTES

1. John Lahr and Jonathan Price, eds. *The Great American Life Show* (New York: Bantam, 1974) 108

2. *Ibid.*, 109

3. Bernard Weiner, "Sam Shepard Goes into a Trance of his New Play," *San Francisco Sunday Examiner and Chronicle* (March 20, 1977) 6

4. Unless otherwise noted, quotations from Shepard are taken from an interview in *Theatre Quarterly* (August–October, 1974)

5. Program note for *Savage/Love* and *Tongues*, Eureka Theatre, San Francisco

6. William Kleb, "Shepard and Chaikin Speaking in *Tongues*," *Theatre* (Fall, 1978) 66–9. I am grateful to Kleb's insights and to Irene Oppenheim for her tape of *Tongues*; above all to Sam Shepard for his unfailing grace.

The Plays of David Rabe:
A World of Streamers

JANET S. HERTZBACH

The title and central metaphor of David Rabe's most recently produced play, *Streamers* (1976), provides a retrospectively useful way of describing the dramatic contexts of his four preceding plays as well. A streamer is a parachute which fails to open, and the thin ribbon of silk merely trails the hapless jumper as he plummets towards certain death. As he leaps out of the safe womb of the airplane, he is born, after a few moments, into a brief life governed by the terror of circumstance, the rule of irrationality, and the absence of alternatives to the destruction awaiting him. There is no opportunity for reflection or insight, and there is no reality except for the immediacy of personal disaster. Like the parachutist, the main characters in *The Basic Training of Pavlo Hummel* (produced 1971), *Sticks and Bones* (produced 1971), *The Orphan* (produced 1973), *In the Boom Boom Room* (produced 1973), and *Streamers* itself are busy, in their varying ways, discovering death.

Rabe's body of work thus far is very closely linked, thematically, to the time in which he was writing, the late 1960s and early 1970s in America. He transmutes this turbulent era of the war in Vietnam, racial conflict, the Manson murders, the generation gap, and the sexual revolution into a dramatic world of irreconcilable conflict. For the individual, its most salient features are racial and sexual violence, family strife, social isolation, and personal inarticulation. Whether the setting is an Army barracks room, a middle-class American home, the ancient Greece of Aeschylus' *Oresteia*, or a sleazy go-go bar in Philadelphia, Rabe's characters live in the midst of a metaphorical battlefield. His plays, then, are war plays; his protagonists are destined to lose their separate struggles. The violence and disorder in their lives is figured, institutionalized, and sometimes justified by ritualistic expressions symbolic of their lack of choice.

Although *The Basic Training of Pavlo Hummel, Sticks and Bones,* and *Streamers*, with their episodes of ritual violence a direct product of the Vietnam war, are often tied together as Rabe's "Vietnam trilogy,"[1] they are not doctrinaire antiwar plays. Only *Pavlo Hummel* includes combat action, and the scene is fleeting. Rabe uses the war in Vietnam as a generalized backdrop for his reflections upon the inevitable, natural violence of American life.[2] In *Pavlo Hummel*, the controlling metaphor emanates from the timeless ritual of Army basic training itself: the four-beat cadence of a basic training company's marching and singing, the rhythmic thrusts of bayonet practice, the scheduled trainee proficiency test. Into this arena Pavlo Hummel comes eagerly, the classic loser, leaving his uncaring family and dreary existence behind in New York and searching for the tough, masculine validation of physical courage and sexual prowess which he expects military heroism to afford him.

The two-act play opens with Pavlo's senseless, non-heroic death. He is "fragged" in a Saigon whorehouse by an Army sergeant with whom he argued over a prostitute. Appropriately, he takes the grenade squarely in his lap as the explosion comes. The play then flashes back to portray the stages of Pavlo's journey to this grim end. A constant reminder to the audience of Army ritual, the drill sergeant's tower dominates the stage. The drill sergeant himself promises the recruits that, by completely incorporating them, the Army will become their family: "You gonna see so much a me, let me tell you, you gonna think I you mother, father, sisters, brothers, aunts, uncles, nephews, nieces, and children — if-you-got-'em — all rolled into one big black man" (p. 13).

The trainees step smartly off, to the first of the several four-beat marching songs that, regularly interspersed throughout the play, will govern the pace of their lives: "The Men. LIFT YOUR HEAD AND LIFT IT HIGH ... /Sgt. Tower. ECHO COMPANY PASSIN' BY!" (p. 19). This first song anticipates the last, when Ardell, a black sergeant who surrealistically accompanies Pavlo, functioning as interpreter and commentator, ends the play over Pavlo's coffin with a subdued "Lift your heads and lift 'em high ... Pavlo Hummel ... passin' by ... " (p. 109).

Unfortunately for Pavlo, his pathetic ideals and expectations about Army life clash with everything the audience sees about the Army and the war. His enthusiasm for a career as an Army "lifer" and his desire to excel in the community superficially symbolized by Army ritual actually exclude him from his fellow recruits and from a realistic perspective on the war itself. Army "grunts" such as Pavlo get along by going along, by doing the minimum of activity, and by never volunteering. In short, there is no community, and the war itself is an emblem of cowardice and despair.

As a foil to almost everyone else in the play, Pavlo is most clearly exemplified by his consistent naivete and stupid enthusiasm. In the hallowed manner of the basic trainee, Kress bitterly complains about everything and has a single-minded interest in staying alive. Pavlo persistently volunteers for menial duties and performs supplementary physical training. In his zeal, he recites his General Orders to no purpose, takes solitary bayonet and port arms practice when he should be in formation, and anxiously studies the Army "Code a Conduct" (p. 45) for the impending proficiency test. When the exhausted trainees stagger into the barracks after a five-mile run, Pavlo drops to the floor for yet more push-ups. He is like the grenade which kills him because he spreads disorder and disbelief everywhere in his dumb effort to become the perfect combat infantryman. This frenetic physical activity is countered by an absence of corresponding mental activity. When Ardell gives him a surrealistic, nauseating lesson in chemical warfare, Pavlo protests, "But I'm too beautiful to die." Ardell comments succinctly, "But you the only one who believe that, Pavlo" (p. 31).

In despair about the prospects for his military career, Pavlo attempts suicide. The squadmates who rescue him clothe him in his military dress uniform for his home leave following basic training; and the silent, slow action parodies the arming of a young knight. As the stage directions indicate, "It is a ritual now; Pavlo must exert no effort whatsoever as he is transformed" (p. 61). The scene suggests, by its chilling intensity, the preparation of the sacrificial victim.

In Act 2, Pavlo enjoys the sexual experience which eluded him on his leave, despite his dress uniform.[3] Sergeant Tower drills the men on one side of the stage as Pavlo makes simultaneous four-beat love to the prostitute Yen on the other. Reluctantly serving as a medic in a field hospital, Pavlo refuses to heed the vivid example of Sergeant Brisbey, blown into a "living, feeling, thinking stump" (p. 86) with no legs and one arm. Only after he is actually wounded in combat does Pavlo recognize the truth of Ardell's earlier, mocking commentary on the combat soldier's plight: "I'm talkin' about what your kidney know, not your fuckin' fool's head. I'm talkin' about your skin and what it sayin', thin as paper. We melt, we tear and rip apart" (p. 96).

Whereas he formerly identified acts of violence in the barracks or on the field with the affirmation of manhood, Pavlo simply wants to go home after his third wound. Rewarded, instead, with a Purple Heart, he repairs to the whorehouse for a dalliance with Yen and the assignation with the grenade. From a stretcher, having taken four days to die, Pavlo responds to Ardell's question, "What you think a bein' R.A. Regular Army lifer?" with "It all shit!" (p. 107). He has achieved limited insight, but it is only in terms of what the Army has done to him rather than what he has done to himself.

From beginning to end, as trainee, medic, or combat infantryman, Pavlo Hummel is doomed. Army ritual overtly offers community, song, and some humor as both mask and excuse for the violence which awaits

Pavlo. Life for the enlisted man in Vietnam, however, actually means every-man-for-himself. The interweaving of past and present time, the use of simultaneous action, the play's surrealistic and absurdist elements, and the choric if sometimes gratuitous presence of Ardell function primarily to demonstrate Pavlo's persistent, self-centered confusion and failure to develop. It is nearly impossible to identify with him throughout the action and difficult to maintain sympathy for him.[4] We need only remember Lieutenant William Calley, however, to know that, in some respects, Pavlo Hummel lived.

Like *The Basic Training of Pavlo Hummel, Sticks and Bones* begins with the ending, the shocking ritualistic suicide of the protagonist, David, a blinded Vietnam veteran. He is encouraged by his father, mother, and younger brother. Just as Pavlo's Army "family" rebuffs him, Ozzie, Harriet, and Ricky reject David. One of the many differences between Pavlo and David, however, is that David denies his family, too. They mutually repel each other. In his naming of the characters, Rabe deliberately parodies the Nelsons of *Ozzie and Harriet* the popular radio and later televison situation comedy. Rabe's middle-class American family is the direct antithesis of the radio's comic Nelsons, for it resembles a potential minefield rather than an electronically transmitted vision of harmony. David is injected into its midst, something like a grenade. Verbal and physical violence are inevitable.

The ritual matter of *Sticks and Bones* emanates from what Rabe considers to be the emblems of modern American culture: television and racism. Both preclude communication and, as such, indicate the mutual alienation of David and his family. Television offers a fantasy life vastly preferable to reality, and its catchy commercials appeal to middle-class America's obsession with money and material possessions. Racism answers the need to feel superior to some group, and, more deeply, it is related to sexual fear and insecurity.[5] From the instant when David is literally delivered home, he and his family are strangers to one another. Ozzie denies that David is his son: "Sgt. Major: Your son./Ozzie: No./Sgt. Major: But he is. I have papers, pictures, prints. I know your blood and his" (p. 127). David also resists this predicament: " ... Sergeant ... nooo; there's something wrong; it all feels wrong. ... I don't know these people! ... I AM LONELY HERE!" (p. 132). In Act 2, Ozzie considers checking David's dental records to verify his identity.

Although physically blind, David's moral vision has been expanded by his experiences in Vietnam and also by his sense of guilt over the Vietnamese girl whom he loved but left behind. The wraith-like Zung appears intermittently throughout the play, until the climax "seen" only by David, as a symbol of continuity between his past and present. She embodies the justification for the mission he assumes in his parents' home. Zung speaks only once and, unlike the often intrusive Ardell, is neither an instructor nor a commentator. The moral blindness of David's family is represented by their virulent racial and sexual prejudice. In order to expiate his own guilt over Zung and as an indication of his revulsion against typical American family life, David endeavors to force Ozzie, Harriet, and Rick to recognize their moral emptiness: "They will call it madness. We will call it seeing" (p. 216).[6]

Ozzie's and Harriet's racist contempt for the Vietnamese recalls that of the soldiers in *Pavlo Hummel* in its perverted preoccupation with sex. A corporal in *Pavlo Hummel* boasts, "You give 'em a can a bug spray, you can lay their fourteen-year-old daughter. Not that any of 'em screw worth a shit" (p. 41). Ozzie shrieks to David, "You screwed it. A yellow whore. Some yellow ass"; and Harriet struggles for a plausible explanation: "You were lonely and young and away from home for the very first time in your life, no white girls around—" (pp. 144–45). Neither can tolerate the thought that David might have fathered children with yellow faces and, worse, that he might have brought them home. Both in the field and at home, Rabe charges, the Vietnamese are despised by the Americans who purport to help them.

In response to his parents' ugly racism, David asserts, "We make signs in the dark. You know yours. I understand my own. We share . . . coffee!" (p. 163). His threatening presence and his accusations cause their superficial layer of middle-class respectability to deteriorate. Ozzie is deeply troubled that his combat experience has been confined to his childhood, when he regularly beat up "Ole Fat Kramer." During World War II, his Army service involved truck maintenance. Further operating as a catalytic agent, David releases his father's latent capacity for violence. Oppressed by his lack of independence, Ozzie looks longingly at his past: "How I'd like to cut her tongue from her mouth. . . . I was nobody's goddam father and nobody's goddam husband! I was myself!" (p. 150). He is morally and materially trapped: "I grew too old too quick. I had no choice" (p. 168). As the pressure intensifies, Harriet reveals a streak of quiet savagery that contrasts with the comfortable television jargon typical of her pose as the perfect mother. "It'll give you the sleep you need, Dave" (p. 134) and "Meyer Spot Remover . . . leaves the fabric clean and fresh like spring" (p. 201) are opposed by her gesture of revenge against Ozzie for having taught David about sports and fighting: "Aspirin makes your stomach bleed" (p. 165). Although she appears to take some comfort from the spiritual nostrums of the parish priest, Harriet, like Ozzie and David, is filled with hatred. As for the priest, his glib sanctimony veneers cynicism and racism. The empty-headed, guitar-strumming Ricky stays away as much as possible but incredibly announces his entrances with "Hi Mom. Hi Dad."

David nears an intellectual conquest of his family and vows to actualize the results of Vietnam in their home: "I want them all here, all the trucks and bodies" (p. 215). Zung becomes visible to Ozzie, who asserts, "I will be blind" (p. 216) and strangles her. Rick suggests that David cut his wrists, and Harriet helpfully provides pans and towels to catch the blood. With this ritualistic self-sacrifice, the reality of David and Zung is defeated. They are exorcised from the mainstream of the middle-class consciousness, and the self-deluded American way of life prevails.

Rabe demonstrates that domestic American violence is as terrible as the literal violence in Vietnam. Through language and action, he indicates the immutable division in the family and makes the point that racism was a basic cause of the war in Vietnam. The polarization of the family, at the same time, is a source of the play's most serious flaw. The playwright would have us accept that a blinded Vietnam veteran has greater moral stature than his parents and that he is qualified, because of his experience, to teach them how they should think and live. David is at least the equal of his parents, however, in self-righteous arrogance, and he confesses as he is dying that "I wanted ... to kill you ... all of you" (p. 222).[7] David's sufferings have not increased his capacity for tolerance and compassion; they have only enhanced his ability to hate. Like Ozzie, Harriet, and Rick, he does not develop. Despite his ordeal in Vietnam and the evident truth of much of his indictment of American life, David emotionally remains his parents' child.

The names of the characters finally detract from Rabe's message as well because they isolate the characters from us. The radio and television Nelson clan is such a distinct target that the playwright's intended generalization about middle-class America becomes increasingly difficult to believe as the play progresses. Rabe's Ozzie, Harriet, David, and Rick are simply very unappealing people. Nonetheless, taken in conjunction with *The Basic Training of Pavlo Hummel, Sticks and Bones* presents a disturbing portrayal of the divisive implications of American military and domestic experience in the late 1960s.

The Orphan is Rabe's most intellectually complex play, but it is troubled by its thematic diffuseness. Instead of using war as the background, the playwright employs Aeschylus' *Oresteia*, with its informing theme of violence within the family, as a framework for his reflections upon the related phenomena of Vietnam and Mylai, governmental apathy, commercial preoccupation, and the Manson murders. As in *Sticks and Bones*, the source of all corruption is in the family. Touchstones of modern American culture are sex, drugs, business, and killing. Men are totally enslaved by the rigid progression of cause to effect; past becomes present. Men and women seem literally born to kill. As Apollo says of Orestes, "And it will not be his story that will matter, nor will it be his hatred, but only the knife."[8] Knives are pervasive; Clytemnestra 2 actually gives birth to one. In this world, murder is so common that it achieves the stature of ritual, and its rites can be found in governmental policy statements, the entrails of birds, current scientific explanations, or hallucinatory drug rampages. It is all the same and all inescapable. As a part of this ritual, language itself becomes automatic and thus debased. Rather than furthering human communication, language helps to isolate people from one another by preserving the distinctions between them. As such, it is an instrument of destruction.

Act 1 concerns the sacrifice of Iphegenia over the impassioned opposition of Clytemnestra 1 and Agamemnon's resultant murder by Clytemnestra 2 and Aegisthus; Act 2 entails Orestes' revenge upon his mother and her lover. The character of Clytemnestra is divided into two separate roles. Clytemnestra 1 endures the ritual sacrifice of her daughter; an older Clytemnestra 2 murders her husband Agamemnon and must confront the consquences of this deed. This division allows the two Clytemnestras to be on stage simultaneously, confirming the veritable identity between past and present. For example, the sacrifice of Iphegenia is also the murder of Agamemnon:

AGAMEMNON:	I sacrifice! I sacrifice! I do not slaughter! *(He is fleeing).*
CLYTEMNESTRA 1:	I SACRIFICE!
CLYTEMNESTRA 2:	*(As The Figure plunges his knife into Iphegenia)* I SACRIFICE! *(And Clytemnestra 2 plunges her knife into the tub and Iphegenia screams.)* You have murdered children that I loved...
CLYTEMNESTRA 1:	You have murdered children that I loved... (p. 45)

From the tub in which Agamemnon is slaughtered, Orestes is born in Act 2, wrapped in the placenta-like net in which his father died and covered with blood. Life's violent course is preordained from the moment of birth: "Through the flesh of the father to the hand of the son falls the sword" (p. 14). In this same tub, the bound Clytemnestras will be killed by Orestes. The womb, then, is not so very different from a grave.

Agamemnon, dressed as a contemporary general, is interested in power and efficiency. Desperate for the wind to blow so that the Greek ships can sail to Troy, he officiously tells the incredulous Clytemnestra 1 that Iphegenia can be replaced by other children. After all, Calchas, a national security adviser complete with briefcase, has read the decree in birds' entrails. A Speaker appears occasionally to offer modern scientific explanations for these ancient mythical occurrences; they possess the same dubious plausibility as Calchas' pronouncements. Clytemnestra is sensual, maternal, and vicious in her revenge. Aegisthus worries about the condition of his investment portfolio. He provides the only instance of welcome hilarity in the play when he is warned by messengers that the invisible Orestes has invaded his house, is creeping closer, and is finally in the same room. He moves from complacency to panic in his "dance of death" and, business-like, tries to strike a desperate bargain: "... you can have that side of the room over there ... " (p. 88).

Apollo, as Manson, offers hallucinatory mushrooms to the already confused Orestes, promising smoothly that they will impart knowledge and freedom. The Girl, an acid-freak member of Manson's gang, recalls the interlocking strategic and sexual exhilaration that accompanied the Tate-LaBianca murders: "I mean, we went in and we went out as natural as the wind that took us there.... If they weren't supposed to die we wouldn'ta been there" (p. 84). She assists Orestes in his revenge in a scene guilty of symbolic overkill. The capitalist pig Aegisthus, told to "Think of yourself as a Vietnamese!" (p. 90), dies impaled upon a fork and with an apple stuffed in his mouth. The revenge thus reiterates the Manson murders and Mylai, and depravity and murder are almost sanctified by regularity in this world. Tainted by violence, Orestes is left literally suspended between the uncaring gods of heaven and the waiting Furies on earth, abandoned and ultimately deluded: "I have killed my mother and there is no punishment" (p. 96).

Although *The Orphan* makes provocative statements about modern American society, it founders upon its diffusion of images and upon its categorical position that America is a murderous wasteland. If, in the myth, Orestes' revenge is justifiable, surely the Manson murders and Mylai were not. The authority of the play depends upon our doubtful acknowledgement of such sensational aberrations as the mythically endorsed norm. We further withdraw because, to an even greater extent than in *Pavlo Hummel* and *Sticks and Bones*, the characters are totally manipulated in the service of the prevailing doctrine. Without alternative or ambiguity, they and *The Orphan* become morally artificial and intellectually confused. The flowing, spurting gore fails to affect us.[9]

With *In the Boom Boom Room*, the scene shifts to a deteriorating, neon-lit section of Philadelphia in the mid-1960s. Once again, sex, violence, racism, self-deception, and inarticulation are the interrelated themes. Although Vietnam is not a factor in this play, the characters live in an urban jungle where the weak are not merely defeated, but are also brutalized, by the strong. Chrissy, an aspiring go-go dancer who wants to become good enough to succeed in New York, is doomed in her pathetic struggle for individuality because she is a vulnerable, confused woman in a man's world. Ironically, the lives of the various men in Chrissy's sphere are as rigidly determined and as hopeless as hers. Chrissy is Rabe's only female protagonist and this play the only one in the corpus in which murder is not a staple. Past time and present time intermingle, however, to demonstrate that Chrissy is victimized, in a steady procession, by everyone she knows: her parents, her boyfriends, her lover, her homosexual neighbor, and the bisexual dance captain at the Boom Boom Room. Like Rabe's other characters, her self-awareness remains very limited; and she is forced, at last, to acknowledge the death of her dreams for a better life.

The go-go cages, with their simultaneous associations of physical and mental imprisonment, spiritual isolation, and sexual exhibitionism, provide the continuous backdrop for the action. The controlling metaphor — and the ritual — emanates from the animalistic, solitary go-go dance itself. To be able to perform the Monkey and the Jerk fluidly and sensually will enable Chrissy to transfer to the big time of the go-go world, but the names of these dances symbolize the dehumanization and the degradation that is her present and future lot instead.

The lesson in the Jerk that Susan gives to Chrissy is significant as it relates to Chrissy's experiences:

> Intake. Up. You're high.
> *(And then Susan drives her fist into Chrissy's stomach and Chrissy doubles over.)*
> And then you're hit in the stomach. You come down. Arms working against one another. Opposite. You're up. You're high.[10]

Chrissy's inarticulate desire to succeed — "I gotta be golden" (p. 61) — is at odds with her lack of self-knowledge — "But that's what I don't know what it is!" (p. 69). Every human interaction she has takes on an aspect of the Jerk: a body blow to the stomach which leaves Chrissy gasping, disabled, and weaker than before. Everyone wants something from her, most frequently sex, but no one loves her, starting with the mother who nearly aborted her.

Her father Harold is probably the first man who sexually molested her. Chrissy has dim childhood memories of a "funny kinda finger" (p. 92); and Harold, still fascinated by his daughter, opens the play by symbolically picking the lock to her apartment. Despite her vague dreams of being "golden," Chrissy defines herself most cogently in sexual terms: "I just keep thinkin' what if they didn't want me for anything? ... What else could they want me for?" (p. 32). Passive and without self-esteem, she is a textbook victim for whom every personal relationship is a grim repetition of the last. Her homosexual neighbor, Guy, who makes his living as a sperm donor and thus is a literal father to many children, wants to use her as a prop in his fantasy life. When she balks, he disparages her sexual technique and further claims, "...I'm a better dancer than you!" (p. 58). Susan wants to go to bed with her. The spoiled, rich Eric from Bryn Mawr sees in her a conflation of all of his immature dreams of woman as goddess, mother, and whore.

A thief and a drunk like her father, the brutal, emotionally impotent Al destroys Chrissy's professional hopes and, concomitantly, her ability to "be gettin' some order in my life" (p. 37). He leaves her when he tires of her, eliciting a wan response that encapsulates her pathetic self-concept: "I could be harder, Al. Whatever you wanted. If I knew what you wanted" (p. 48). Later, in an argument suffused with the sexism and racism also fundamental to *Pavlo Hummel* and *Sticks and Bones*, Al beats Chrissy bloody, "...his fist digging into her stomach" (p. 112), much like Susan's in the go-go lesson. In the final scene of the play, Chrissy has come to New York, but as a topless dancer, something she swore never to be. Hooded because of the beating, she is billed as the "Masked Rider." The emcee's introduction points up the ironic, savage contrast of her present situation with her former dreams of being golden: "Now she's been workin' real hard all her life to get this just right. You give her your undivided attention" (p. 113). Chrissy is completely isolated, anonymous, and degraded.

In the Boom Boom Room is like *The Orphan* in its despair about the human condition, but it lacks the intellectual gamesmanship which is the major interest of *The Orphan*. Rabe's reflections on violence in modern America as seen through an Oresteian glass invite the audience — or more effectively, perhaps, the reader — to become sufficiently engaged by his comparisons between ancient and contemporary, mythical and mundane to reject them ultimately. The action of *In the Boom Boom Room*, however, adheres to a simultaneously static and linear structure in which Chrissy does not develop as a personality but in which the quality of her life inexorably deteriorates. Although it is finally difficult for us to sympathize with Pavlo and David, we can at least discern a measure of tension and vitality in their lives. Pavlo and David, and even Orestes, to varying degrees try to resist the arbitrary forces which subdue them. Chrissy never has a chance. Perhaps this play is primarily evidence of Rabe's difficulty in imagining and projecting character, situation, and milieu not directly associated with the war in Vietnam. *In the Boom Boom Room* is only superficial sad; it is, finally, tedious.

Rabe returns to the thematic backdrop of the American experience in Vietnam in *Streamers*. It is Rabe's most persuasive play because it is the most straightforward. It concentrates exclusively upon the present interactions of four young Army enlisted men, each embodying a different facet of American society.[11] Without the flashbacks and the resorts to special effects of his previous plays, Rabe creates a sharp, sustained focus. The four characters each claim equal attention from the audience as they form a sort of desperate family of man in the barracks room.

Their conflicting ideas about war, sex, and racism transform this barracks crucible into a battlefield upon which violence is as certain, and as deadly, as the violence which awaits them in Vietnam. Their metaphorical parachutes have failed to open, and the matter of the play chronicles their fall to earth, streamers floating uselessly above them. The two older "booze-hound" sergeants, Cokes and Rooney, one suffering from leukemia and the other an alcoholic, represent the way that the four recruits are destined to go. As the doomed and exhausted members of the previous generation of cannon-fodder, they introduce the song, set to the tune of Stephen Foster's "Beautiful Dreamer," which provides the ritualistic foundation of the play: "Beautiful streamer,/Open for me,/The sky is above me,/But no canopy."[12]

Like the parachutist and like Rabe's other characters, Roger, Billy, Richie, and Carlyle have no control over their lives. For them, there is no escape from the barracks except through the agency of violence. If they survive the battlefield in the barracks, then they are destined for the jungles and elephant traps of Vietnam. Roger speaks of his predicament with a sense of bewildered wonder: "...this NCO's up there jammin' away about how some a us are goin' to be dyin' in the war. I'm sayin', 'What war?' " (p. 11). They are isolated from the external world; and they find that there is no philosophical, racial, or sexual comradeship inside the Army either. Cokes and Rooney are embittered career men whose actual experiences of combat in World War II cause them simultaneously to envy, admire, and despise the two-year recruits. Blacks, represented by Roger and Carlyle, and whites, represented by Billy and Richie, live together warily, with ready recourse to a switchblade or a racist epithet. The homosexual Richie belongs to the Army's smallest, least visible, and most defensive minority. Rabe clearly establishes these categories within the Army of the Vietnam era, but he manages to transcend them to an extent that he does not achieve in *Pavlo Hummel* or *Sticks and Bones*: the Army in *Streamers* is a credible microcosm of American society at large. The major difference is that human encounters in the Army are more intense because they are both swift and temporary.

Roger and Billy, black and white, exemplify the conventional middle-class stance. They ambitiously want to get out of this holding company, a "goddamn typin'-terrors outfit" (p. 9), as Roger calls it, and into the real Army. Yet it is understandably difficult for them to absorb the fierce reality of Vietnam into their lives. Billy, a former high school track star, maintains a sympathetic curiosity about others and says of his parents in Wisconsin: "I mean, my mom and dad are really terrific people" (p. 58). Roger holds that a game of basketball can do much to cure spiritual malaise. He likes to be busy physically, as his frequent floor mopping reveals; and he hates arguments and fights.

Carlyle is a ghetto black terrified of the deadly fate which the Army obviously, and casually, reserves for him, and Richie is a spoiled white in the process of adjusting to his homosexuality. They constitute the counterpoint to Roger and Billy, and their personal relationship inspires the crisis. Carlyle is the patented Rabean grenade who destroys the precarious equilibrium achieved by the other three; his function is similar to Pavlo's and to David's. He is alienated by his race, education, and social status and thus is filled with hatred for American society in general and the war in particular: "It ain't our war nohow because it ain't our country, and that's what burns my ass — that and everybody just sittin' and takin' it" (p. 22). Richie is also spiritually isolated from his barracks companions. Billy's overly vehement rejections of Richie's coy advances suggests the possibility of some sexual ambivalence in his own past.

The two outcasts, Carlyle and Richie, deserted by their fathers and by conventional society, connect in a sexual pact born at least as much out of loneliness and despair as from physical craving. Roger can accept what exists: "It been goin' on a long damn time, man. You ain't gonna put no stop to it" (p. 82). Billy, on the contrary, is enraged by this desecration of his barracks "house"; perhaps this overt homosexual activity threatens him in his personal psychological "home." His aggressive cries of outrage — "you gay little piece a shit cake" to Richie and "SAMBO! SAMBO!" to Carlyle (p. 88) — are abruptly silenced as Carlyle repeatedly stabs him in the stomach in a bloody, fatal parody of the sexual act. The drunken Rooney, having regressed with Cokes to a game of "hide-and-seek," literally stumbles into the fight's aftermath and inadvertently becomes Carlyle's next victim. Carlyle's valedictory, "I have quit the army!" (p. 100), writes an ironical, pathetic finish to this gruesome barracks scene.

Irrational violence has triumphed. Unaware of what has happened, Cokes ends the play with reminiscences of combat and an inarticulate rendition of "Beautiful Streamer," which he sings in "a makeshift language imitating Korean": "Yo no som lo no/ Ung toe lo knee/ Ra so me la lo/ La see see oh doe" (p. 109). Richie and Roger, white and black, homosexual and heterosexual, have survived the barracks; but Vietnam, with its myriad opportunities for the unanticipated situations which produce streamers, awaits. And if they survive Vietnam, there is always the home front.

There are no simple explanations for the characters' motivations and actions in *Streamers,* and thus Rabe surpasses his earlier work. He blends the themes of war, sex, racism, family, and resultant general chaos without reliance upon a schematic, predictable plot, exhibited at its least effective in *In the Boom Boom Room*. Richie, at least, attains some self-awareness. Circumstances force him to concede the necessity of Roger's demand for honesty: " ... all the time you was a faggot, man; you really was. You shoulda jus' tole ole Roger. He don't care" (p. 102).

Although *Streamers* is a sounder play, structurally, then Rabe's previous dramas, it nonetheless partakes of a full measure of their characteristic cynicism and despair. In all of the plays, the dramatist establishes some expression of ritual as a reflection of disorder. Men live in a world so irrational that there is no order to subvert. This ethos contributes much to the spectacular, bloody stageworthiness of the plays and is a direct function of their topicality. Their effectiveness depends heavily on an audience's knowledge, appreciation, and preferably, experience of American political, social, and cultural history in the mid- and late 1960s and early 1970s. This topicality is, however, a source both of the strength and weakness of David Rabe's plays. For those who experienced the Vietnam era, the plays have a visceral, emotional impact that compensates, to some extent, for the stylization of the characters, their lack of alternatives, and their failure to develop.

On the other hand, like Rabe's characters, the plays become victims of this topical isolation. With the exception of *Streamers*, they cannot transcend the special, tortured time and place that was America in the middle of the twentieth century. Rabe's reflections on the interrelatedness of war, sex, racism, the family, past, and present as they define the contemporary American battlefield are frequently shocking and often provocative. His dramatic world of streamers is, however, all of a piece; and lacking texture and amplitude, it finally fails to convince.

NOTES

1. See, for example, Bonnie Marranca's "David Rabe's Viet Nam Trilogy," *Canadian Theatre Review*, 14 (1977), 86–92.
2. In his introduction to the edition, *The Basic Training of Pavlo Hummel and Sticks and Bones: Two Plays by David Rabe* (New York: Viking Press, 1973),

Rabe, who served in the Army in Vietnam, specifically rejects the "antiwar" label:

> ...an "antiwar" play is one that expects, by the very fabric of its executed conception, to have political effect. I anticipated no such consequences from my plays...I have written them to diagnose, as best I can, certain phenomena that went on in and around me (p. xxv).

Quotations from these two plays refer to this edition and will be noted parenthetically by page number within the text of this essay.

3. It is interesting to note that, in order to increase the trainees' dependence upon the military, Army ritual also plays upon their sexual insecurity, as one of "E" Company's marching songs reveals: "AIN'T NO USE IN GOIN' HOME./... JODY GOT YOUR GAL AND GONE" (p. 30). As a further measure of his isolation, however, Pavlo has no sweetheart at home.

4. In "The Basic Training of American Playwrights: Theater and the Vietnam War," *Theater*, 9 (Spring 1978), 30–37, Robert Asahina contends that *Pavlo Hummel* deals with the "... progressive dehumanization of someone scarcely human to begin with ... " (p. 35) and that, therefore, Pavlo's brutal death is meaningless.

5. In his introduction, Rabe asserts that "... I consider the root of racism to be sex, or more exactly miscegenation" (p. xxiii).

6. Thomas P. Adler notes that in this relationship between physical blindness and moral sight, Rabe is indebted to *King Lear* for some symbols, character configurations, and thematic motifs; " 'The Blind Leading the Blind': Rabe's *Sticks and Bones* and Shakespeare's *King Lear*," *PLL*, 15 (1979), 203–206.

7. Robert Brustein criticizes "the facile guilt-mongering of our accusatory playwrights" and posits the thesis that " ... the crude caricaturing of Ozzie and Harriet at the same time that David and Zung are drawn as sanctified victims suggests that the tolerance and compassion called for in the play are not always felt by the author himself"; "The Crack in the Chimney: Reflections on Contemporary American Playwrights," *Theater*, 9 (Spring 1978), pp. 29 and 24.

8. *The Orphan* (New York: Samuel French, 1975), p. 47. All succeeding references to this edition are noted parenthetically by page number.

9. The first production of *The Orphan* in New York in 1973 ran less than a month. Rabe revised the play extensively, and it is published in its final form. See Barnet Kellman, "David Rabe's 'The Orphan': A Peripatetic Work in Progress," *Theatre Quarterly*, 7 (1977), 72–93, for an account of the play's development. Kellman directed the play in its last production in Philadelphia in 1974 and holds, mistakenly I think, that "We have come to care for [Orestes]. His struggle against corruption has been our struggle" (p. 93).

10. *In the Boom Boom Room* (New York: Knopf, 1975), p. 19. All subsequent citations refer to this edition.

11. Robert Asahina asserts that *Streamers* is superior to *The Basic Training of Pavlo Hummel* and *Sticks and Bones* because "It is the only one of the three that exhibits real dramatic movement" (p. 37).

12. *Streamers* (New York: Knopf, 1978), p. 41. All succeeding citations refer to this edition.

America's Women
Dramatists, 1960–1980

PATTI P. GILLESPIE

As Ellen Moers notes in her excellent volume, *Literary Women*, it is altogether remarkable that, as critics, we have examined — and re-examined — artists according to race, ethnic heritage, nationality, religion, politics, historical period, and even state of health, but that "by some accidental or willed critical narrowness, we have routinely denied ourselves additional critical access to the writers through the fact of their sex — a fact surely as important as their social class or era or nationality, a fact of which women writers have been and still are conscious. How, as human beings, could they not be?"[1]

How, indeed, could they not be? And yet Moers is quite correct that women artists generally, and women playwrights in particular, have seldom been considered as a group. True, Brander Matthews in *A Book About the Theatre* (1916) briefly dealt with them and concluded that, as a group, they failed to attain greatness because they had "only a definitely limited knowledge of life" and tended "to be more or less deficient in the faculty of construction," presumably because they did not customarily "submit themselves to the severe discipline which has compelled men to be more or less logical."[2] Joseph Mersand in "When Ladies Write Plays" (1937) acknowledged that over a hundred women contributed successful plays to the American theatre during the late 1920s and early 1930s but concluded that they succeeded best as "reporters for the stage" rather than as philosophers or artists: "They rarely philosophize, their social consciousness is rarely apparent; they don't preach sermons; they don't raise you to the heights of aesthetic emotions. This is true of even the best of the daughters of the Muses."[3] The *New York Times*, apparently baffled by the meagre offerings of American women dramatists to the contemporary theatre, asked in 1972, "Where are the Women Playwrights?" and learned that by then no one agreed on the question, much less the answer.[4]

Indeed, the number of women writing for the American stage has always been modest. Although the names of Mercy Otis Warren, Anna

Cora Mowatt, and Julia Ward Howe are sprinkled through accounts of the eighteenth- and nineteenth-century American stage, not until the twentieth century could American women playwrights be said to contribute on a regular basis to the literature of the theatre.

By 1960, however, several American women had earned sizeable reputations as dramatists. Pulitzer Prizes had been awarded to *Miss Lula Bett* (Zona Gale, 1921), *Alison's House* (Susan Glaspell, 1931), *The Old Maid* (Zoe Akins, 1935), and *Harvey* (Mary Cole Chase, 1945). The New York drama critics had honored *Watch on the Rhine* (Lillian Hellman, 1941), *The Member of the Wedding* (Carson McCullers, 1950), and *A Raisin in the Sun* (Lorraine Hansberry, 1959). *Abie's Irish Rose* (Anne Nichols, 1922) had set Broadway records. *Machinal* (Sophie Treadwell, 1928) had been hailed as a supreme example of American expressionism. *The Women* (Clare Booth Luce, 1936) had infuriated the critic Heywood Broun. Rose Franken and Gertrude Stein had perplexed and annoyed critics and audiences; and Bella Spewack (in collaboration with Samuel) had delivered wacky farces in such profusion that a descriptive term, "Spewackian comedy," came into the language of show business. Significant contributions to the corpus of American drama had been made as well by Rachel Crothers, Edna Ferber, and Jean Kerr. The range, if not the number, of works by American women was impressive. Prior to 1960, they had offered both commercial and experimental pieces, both propagandistic and escapist plays, and they had viewed their dramatic characters (female as well as male) through both cynical and sentimental eyes. Like the male playwrights of the same period, women dramatists were mostly white and middle- (or upper-middle) class; and, like their male counterparts, they treated social issues (including those of particular interest to women) when society at large seemed interested in such issues.[5]

The decades of the 1960s and 1970s, however, saw significant shifts in these patterns. Three new trends, in particular, became evident. First, women playwrights tended to cluster in alternative, non-commercial theatres. Second, black women playwrights emerged as a major new voice in the American theatre. And third, after 1970, feminist playwrights began to surface and find production.

In 1960, Lillian Hellman won the Critics Circle Award for *Toys in the Attic*, but for the next twenty years no woman playwright was honored with either this, the Tony, or the Pulitzer Prize. Instead, women's dramatic activity shifted to the Off- and Off-Off-Broadway theatres, where their success was astonishing. In 1964, Rosalyn Drexler and Adrienne Kennedy won Obies for their respective plays, *Home Movies* and *Funnyhouse of a Negro*. Rochelle Owens (*Futz*, 1967), Julie Bovasso (*Gloria & Esperanza*, 1969), Megan Terry (*Approaching Simone*, 1970), and Micki Grant (*Don't*

Bother Me I Can't Cope, 1972) also won Obies. Corinne Jacker (*Bits and Pieces* and *Harry Outside*, 1974) and Maria Irene Fornes (*Promenade* and *Successful Life of 3*, and *Fefu and Her Friends*, 1976) won multiple Obies.

Many of the women dramatists writing for these alternative theatres defied categorization, but two clearly recognizable groups did emerge. As a part of the civil rights struggles and the (later) Black Arts movement, black women began writing plays in unprecedented numbers, influencing the direction of the American theatre to an unprecedented degree. By the early 1970s, some women were writing and producing plays specifically for women about the experience of growing up female in America. Thereafter, discussions about women dramatists would necessarily distinguish between those women who write self-consciously about women's issues (the feminist playwrights) and those who write about a wide range of topics for a general audience. And, by 1980, there were even indications that women playwrights might be re-joining the commercial mainstream.

Perhaps the richness and diversity of women's contributions to the American drama during the decades of the 1960s and 1970s can be suggested by placing the major authors in their theatrical contexts and by pausing to consider three benchmark plays.

By the time *Toys in the Attic* opened in 1960, Lillian Hellman had already enjoyed several commercial and critical successes: *The Children's Hour* (1934), *The Little Foxes* (1939), *Watch on the Rhine* (1941), *Another Part of the Forest* (1946), and *The Autumn Garden* (1951). Hailed by established critics as "one of Miss Hellman's most substantial hits," *Toys in the Attic* was credited with bringing "the theatre back to life" and with jolting it "out of its childishness."[6] As the list of plays suggests, however, *Toys* came at the end of Hellman's career as a playwright; her style and attack were of the '40s and '50s not of the '60s and '70s.

Toys in the Attic is an excellent example of traditional American realism, but as such it exploits none of the subjects or structures that would characterize the sixties and seventies. The play gains unity through its action, a domestic intrigue driven by a few strongly drawn characters. Structurally, the play moves from beginning to end through a tightly controlled sequence of events: in the first act questions are raised, altered, and replaced by others that find ultimate answers only in the play's closing scenes.

When the play opens, Anna and Carrie Berniers are fretting over the whereabouts of their younger brother Julian, whose recent marriage to Lily has joined their poor but proud family to that of the wealthy and iconoclastic Albertine, a woman who flaunts southern society by maintaining a liaison with a black man. Julian, a personable failure with a history of unwarranted extravagance, has apparently suffered yet another business collapse, this time losing his new wife's money. The spinster sisters are perplexed and troubled because he has not yet sought their aid. Their concern accelerates when they learn from Albertine that the young couple is already in the city but is seemingly in hiding. Both families prepare to offer Julian and Lily a place to live and additional money, but Julian arrives laden with expensive gifts and promising still greater wealth from a mysterious new business deal. When both Lily and Carrie seem more troubled than pleased by his recent good fortune, Julian is baffled: "What's the matter with everybody? We're not having a very nice party. What's the matter?"[7]

During the second act it becomes increasingly clear that Julian's success has thrown the delicate family relationships askew, exposing abandoned dreams, childish dependencies, incestuous desires, and latent hostilities. Lily says she is unhappy because her husband's new fortune seems to involve his entanglement with another woman, and Carrie says she is unhappy because Anna intends to accept Julian's gifts and go abroad as planned. It is evident, however, that the real source of unhappiness for both women is that a rich and successful Julian seems not to need them. Although Albertine and Anna understand the emotional dynamics of the changed circumstance, neither is able to control the new situation because neither can force her understanding on others. By the second act's end, Anna has accused a horrified Carrie of incestuous love, and Albertine has tried to shield Lily from the destructiveness of her own innocence.

In the final act, the extent of the family ruptures is evident. Despite Anna's warnings, Carrie's lust grows; and despite Albertine's advice, Lily blunders into Julian's business dealings. The distintegration of the fragile network of relationships is made inevitable when Carrie, now wily because desperate, manipulates Lily into betraying Julian's real-estate venture. The play ends with Julian again broke and helpless and again in the care of a delighted Lily and Carrie, neither of whom realizes that their truce is necessarily temporary and uneasy and that things can never be as they once were.

For *Toys in the Attic* Hellman contrives a taut, suspenseful story. The characters, both male and female, are deftly drawn and fully developed. Their frailties, neuroses, and bewilderment are balanced by their strength, innocence, and hopefulness. Their portrayal is at once hardheaded and compassionate, leading audiences to be simultaneously sympathetic and disapproving. The prose dialogue is conversational and clear; it has as its primary purpose to move the action forward by the proper characterization of the dramatic agents. The play's ideas inhere in its action, cloaking the playwright's view beneath those expressed or implied by the characters. In sum, *Toys in the Attic* is a realistic play of the sort prepared by Scribe, transformed and developed by Ibsen, and adapted and popularized in the United States by O'Neill, Williams, and Miller.

For almost twenty years after Hellman's *Toys in the Attic*, however, Broadway produced no particularly successful serious plays by women; some women continued to work there in musicals and comedies. Jean Kerr, building on her successes of the 1940s and 1950s, thrived early in the sixties when *Mary, Mary* (1961) became the decade's longest running sex comedy; her *Poor Richard* (1964) was a failure only by comparison. Despite the success of Kerr and a few others, however, it was not on Broadway but Off that women playwrights exerted the most influence for the remainder of the 1960s and 1970s.

After Joe Cino pointed the way with his small cafe-cum-theatre, a flurry of such spaces opened and offered homes to developing plays and playwrights. Free from the economic pressures strangling Broadway, young dramatists experimented in these non-traditional theatres with both controversial subjects and innovative dramatic structures. Since the 1960s was the era of the Vietnam war, civil rights struggles, and decay of the inner cities, many of the plays dealt with these issues, often taking positions at odds with the law and therefore abhorrent to many American citizens. For their controversial ideas, many authors sought release from familiar dramatic forms and styles as well: some tried to incorporate the audience into the theatrical event; some questioned the importance of dramatic illusion; some abandoned continuity of dramatic character; some manipu-lated scenery, costumes, and lights in new and intriguing ways while others eliminated them altogether; some strove to enrich the theatre by combining it with film, music, dance, poetry, and the visual arts, either singly or in several combinations. Because the plays departed from accepted ideas and familiar forms, they were not welcomed into the commercial theatre — at least not for a time.

In these avant-garde theatres many women artists gained a promi-nence unknown to them before. Ellen Stewart, the founder and primary artistic force behind the Cafe La Mama, was the most influential of all Off-Off Broadway producers, presenting 175 plays by 130 playwrights during the theatre's first six years.[8] Judith Malina, with Julian Beck, man-aged The Living Theatre, the most controversial and important of the many political theatres of the decade. Viola Spolin developed and published (*Improvisation for the Theatre*, 1963) the techniques and games that under-lay the acting and producing styles of several emerging avant-garde groups. Nola Chilton guided the early acting careers of scores of young people. Julie Bovasso, Rosalyn Drexler, Maria Irene Fornes, Rochelle Owens, and Megan Terry all launched their playwriting careers in the artistic ferment offered by these alternative theatres.

These women writers formed no cohesive group. Drexler in *Hot Buttered Roll* (1963), *Home Movies* (1964), and *Skywriting* (1968) revealed herself as a comic artist of great exuberance, one whose world is faintly scatalogical and often "camp." Fornes, "a dramatist of almost pure imagination,"[9] ranged freely in subjects and styles from *The Successful Life of 3* (1966, a vaudeville produced by the Open Theatre) to *Dr. Kheal* (1968, the obvious forerunner of Roberto Athayde's *Miss Margarida's Way*) to *Promenade* (1969, a musical done in collaboration with Al Carmines). Owen's *Futz* (1967), *Beclch* (1968), or *Homo* (1969) bear scant resemblance to Bovasso's *Gloria & Esperanza* (1969) or *The Moondreamers* (1969). Indeed, perhaps the most intriguing trait of women dramatists of the 1960s is that their plays shared few features and that they were not aware of themselves as women; neither they nor their works gave any indication of a latent feminism.

Megan Terry, resident playwright with the Open Theatre, was an exception. In fact, it may be persuasively argued that this alternative theatre provided the most certain link between the avant garde of the 1960s and the developing feminism of the 1970s. Terry, best known for her anti-war play *Viet Rock*, wrote three other plays for the Open Theatre between 1963 and 1968 that presaged issues of the coming decade. *The Gloaming, Oh My Darling, Keep Tightly Closed in a Cool Dry Place*, and *Calm Down Mother* specifically addressed problems of sexual identity, gender stereotyping, and systemic sexism in America.[10] Terry, however, was not the only member of the Open Theatre to confront in the sixties the feminism of the seventies. From the outset, women comprised at least half of the group's membership and figured prominently in all areas of production. Perhaps for that reason, much of the group's work stressed self-exploration, including the relationship between gender and social expectation, making the Open Theatre, according to its founder Joseph Chaikin, a "fertile place to bring up feminism." Significantly, more than half of the women active in this alternative theatre contributed importantly to the feminist theatres that exploded into prominence after 1970.[11]

"There is one ultimate revolution which encompasses them all, and that is the liberation of the female of the species so that the male of the species may be freed forever from supermasculine compulsion and may join his sister in full and glorious humanity. And fuck marriage."[12] With these words Myrna Lamb described, in 1970, the newest social convulsion. With the war in Vietnam winding down, and with major victories already won by blacks in their struggle for civil rights, the issue of women's place in society became the focus of social conflict — and of an entirely new movement in the American theatre.

When *The Mod Donna* was first produced by Joseph Papp at his Public Theatre, it was both condemned and praised; indeed, the play soon found itself at the center of a controversy over social, as well as dramatic, issues. *Newsday's* reviewer was sufficiently irritated by the play to wonder in print if "maybe we were wrong in allowing women to vote;" and a New Jersey reviewer predicted that the play would "spur a drive for male supremacy the like of which has never been seen before." But Clive Barnes of the *New York Times* seemed charmed by Lamb's "neat and funny way of eviscerating male supremacy," and the reviewer for *Time* magazine thought the play "a bracing tonic" and Lamb "a deft lyricist with barbed wit and a no-nonsense lucidity about contemporary man-woman relationships."[13]

In truth, the play is an odd assortment of ideas and actions that do not coalesce to produce a great, or even a good, work of art. Still, its importance is indisputable. *The Mod Donna* adopted many of the techniques developed and nurtured by the avant garde of the 1960s and turned them to a new subject — feminism. It is now considered the first important feminist play and, as such, the harbinger of the vigorous feminist theatre movement of the 1970s.

Described as "A Space-age Musical Soap Opera with Breaks for Commercials," the play lurches through eight short narrative episodes that are embedded in twice as much song, movement, and poetic rumination. The story presents unpleasant people in a harsh and unsparing light. A wealthy couple is desperately bored with their marriage, a sterile arrangement that is occasionally enlivened by furtive affairs. At the woman's insistence, the couple invites Donna, the voluptuous and worldly wife of an employee, to form a ménage à trois. She readily accepts because, as she twice confesses, "I give. I mean I am the type that goes to bed with guys because I can't bear to say no when they've asked me so politely."[14] When Donna's husband comes to fetch her home on the first morning after, their relentless bickering and recriminations reveal another marriage that is a trap to be escaped rather than a haven to be sought.

Predictably, the ménage à trois fails to bring satisfaction: "Something's missing. It hasn't worked. Something's missing."[15] Again at the woman's urging, the couple persuades Donna to serve them: this time she is to bear a child for the three of them. After Donna conceives, however, the wealthy couple reconciles and plans a second honeymoon. When Donna discovers their intention, she appeals angrily to the man's love and the woman's promises but earns only a check for her expenses and a picture album of their sexual encounters.

The story stops, ambiguously, with a symbolic execution of Donna by her husband. The chorus then finishes the play with a bitter song that begins, "We are the whores/The dictated whores/Whore-hating whores/ We collect as they inspect us on the shrine they call 'respect us'," and ends with the chorus crying out for "LIBERATION LIBERATION LIBERATION."[16]

The story, however, is relatively inconsequential. Both in length and impact, the play's commercials and songs dominate. A chorus of women, described alternately as androgynous, sexually ambivalent, and unisexual, talk freely with the audience, themselves, and the play's four characters to expand and reinforce the play's strident didacticism. The chorus opens the play, for example, with a rousing stanza of the Liberation Song and then explains: "We are bringing you the pilot show of a new series. Tomorrow's soap opera today with appropriate breaks for tomorrow's commercials today."[17] Accordingly, the chorus sings and dances its way through an introduction of Donna, a survey of the female's assigned role in American society, and the preparation for an elaborate party (including a recipe for cheese logs) — all before the play's story commences. Thereafter, the narrative episodes are interrupted by a variety of "commercial breaks" that range from songs about female desirability and consumerism/ capitalism ("Invitation") to those about masturbation fantasies and rape ("Incantation"). Some, like the commercial "Creon," demonstrate the failure of many women to support their own liberation; others, like "Charlie's Plaint," talk of the role that military and economic pressures play in warping male behavior. Some, like "Astrociggy," swipe at motherhood, war, pollution, overpopulation, the church, and capitalism; others, like "Now," treat female sexuality almost exclusively.

The play's unity, such as it is, derives from its didactic purpose. The insistence with which Lamb presents issues provides the momentum that moves the play from start to finish. Capitalism is vaguely aligned with sexism, and both are blasted within and between episodes. The characters are didactically conceived and are made only as specific as the ideas of the play require. Dramatic illusion is alternately maintained and shattered. The commercials, like the narrative, are only loosely connected with one another and with the whole. The use of music, dance, and placards, like the manipulation of dramatic illusion, clearly echoes Brecht's Epic Theatre. Although *The Mod Donna* may be considered representative of the avant garde in several ways, its subject matter — radical feminism — made it innovative and therefore pivotal in any study of contemporary American theatre.

The issues raised by Lamb in *The Mod Donna* found expression in her other works (*Scyklon Z, Apple Pie, Crab Quadrille*) as well as in the plays of women like Martha Boesing, Gretchen Cryer, Corinne Jacker, Tina Howe, Karen Malpede, and Eve Merriam. With feminist theatres erupting nationwide during the 1970s (more than fifty by the end of the decade), new plays by, for, and about women suddenly had outlets in unprecedented numbers. Some of the oldest and best-known of the feminist theatres, like Women's Interart in New York, were showcases for the works of talented women. They offered, on a regular basis, plays by women artists, particularly such plays as presented women in non-stereotyped ways and offered strong roles for actresses. Works produced in such theatres tended to be taken seriously, to be reviewed by the established media, and to find their way into (usually women's) anthologies. Far more numerous and less known, however, were theatres like Rhode Island Feminist and the short-lived Its All Right to be Woman, which favored improvised pieces, collectively developed scripts, and authored works too radical in content or structure to find acceptance by general audiences, even the liberal patrons Off-Broadway. Usually ignored and occasionally ridiculed by established reviewers, such groups nevertheless nurtured scores of women writers, serving as a source of ideas and inspiration and, finally for some, as a springboard to better-established theatres or to publication and eventual acceptance by reviewers.[18] Any survey of American women dramatists must acknowledge the importance of these feminist theatres during the 1970s in soliciting and welcoming new plays by women, just as any such survey must acknowledge those alternative theatres that launched the careers of women for whom feminism was not an issue.

Just as the artistic ferment Off- and Off-Off-Broadway gave rise to a theatrical avant garde of the 1960s and forged links with the developing feminist playwrights and theatres of the 1970s, so too was it crucial in the rise of black women playwrights. When Alice Childress's *Gold Through the Trees* opened Off-Broadway in 1952, it was the first play by a black woman to gain a professional New York production. From then until 1980, with few exceptions, black women playwrights (like white) remained outside the commercial mainstream; but unlike their white counterparts, black women dramatists did constitute a recognizable group from the outset: their subject was black people and the problems they encountered because of their race.

Among the black women playwrights of the 1960s and 1970s only Lorraine Hansberry was primarily a Broadway author. When her first play, *A Raisin in the Sun*, opened at the Ethel Barrymore Theatre in March 1959 to rave reviews, she became the first black woman ever to achieve a Broadway production. Still "the best-known and most popular drama ever written by a black American,"[19] *Raisin* depicts the struggles of a black family against racism and its correlative, economic deprivation. The family's goal, achieved by the play's end, is to leave the ghetto, settle in a middle-class (white) neighborhood, and live with dignity. The play shares with *Toys in the Attic*, its contemporary, the virtues of a strong story line, interesting and believable characters, and a traditional dramatic structure. Indeed, except for the author's race and sex and the play's serious treatment of a black family's problems, *A Raisin in the Sun* resembles other carefully wrought realistic dramas of its era.

With the failure of Hansberry's second play, *The Sign in Sydney Brustein's Window* and her early death from cancer in 1965, activity among black women playwrights returned to the alternative theatres where Childress was soon joined by several new voices, chief among them Marti Charles, Micki Grant, Elaine Jackson, Adrienne Kennedy, and Ntozake Shange.

When *Funnyhouse of a Negro* by Kennedy opened Off-Broadway in 1964, it was only the third play by a black woman to be professionally produced in New York. Unlike Childress and Hansberry, Kennedy did not write realistic plays organized through action. Her three most famous works, *Funnyhouse, The Owl Answers* (1965), and *The Rat's Mass* (1969) all featured a young black woman torn by conflicting claims: black and white, good and evil, love and hate. In each, Kennedy presented poetic and allusive excursions into worlds of dream and nightmare, worlds occupied by people and animals who change identities, places, and points of view with dizzying speed and without accompanying explanation. The cast list of *The Owl Answers*, for example, calls for a character named "She who is Clara Passmore who is the Virgin Mary who is the Bastard who is the Owl" and another named "The White Bird who is Reverend Passmore's Canary who is God's Dove." Kennedy's poetic flights often result in dialogue that is incancatory and obscure, likened by one critic to "a storm of ambiguities that blow and swirl into a pool of liquid sunlight and shadow."[20] Indeed, Kennedy's plays suggest, rather than show, and therefore demand audiences willing to reach understanding through unfolding images rather than through developing narratives.

Within the range defined by Hansberry and Kennedy rest the plays of other black women authors. Most resemble Hansberry more than Kennedy in preferring a realistic style for their sympathetic portrayals of the peculiar frustration of black people. Elaine Jackson's *Toe Jam* (1971), for example, treats the passage of a young girl from aloofness to involvement, while Marti Charles' *Job Security* (1970) presents a chilling tale of a ghetto student who murders teachers in retribution for their callous ineptitude. Micki Grant's commercially successful musical, *Don't Bother Me I Can't Cope* (1972), diverges from realism and causality in many details, but not until the work of Ntozake Shange did the experimental techniques of the alternative theatres, the power of the Black Arts movement, and the vitality of contemporary feminism converge. The result was stunning.

Without elaborate scenery, without a narrative line, without a well-known star, without indeed any of the usual trappings of a commercial success, *for colored girls who have considered suicide/when the rainbow is enuf* moved onto Broadway and captured audiences and critics alike. Clive Barnes of the *New York Times* called the piece "extraordinary and wonderful ... a lyric and tragic exploration into black women's awareness."[21]

Its author, Ntozake Shange, did not begin as a playwright but as a dancer and poet, an artist influenced heavily by a curriculum in Women's Study and by teachers who glorified anything African and everything colloquial. In the summer of 1974, Shange began a series of numbered poems that were "to explore the realities of seven different kinds of women." Beginning in December 1974, in a woman's bar outside Berkeley, California, and moving through various clubs and bars in Los Angeles, San Francisco, and New York's Greenwich Village, several versions of *colored girls* appeared before Shange even envisioned the "twenty-odd poems as a single statement, a choreopoem."[23] Once the unity of the pieces was perceived, Shange relinquished staging responsibility to Oz Scott, who shaped the versions that appeared in Joseph Papp's Public Theatre in June and in Broadway's Booth Theatre in September, 1976. The final production was, according to Shange, "as close to distilled as any of us in all our art forms can make it."[24]

Colored girls is a compelling piece of theatre, visually exciting, aurally stimulating, thematically coherent. It is not, however, a play in the sense that Ibsen or Hellman would have understood. There is no unified action, no logical beginning or end, no sustained character development, no exposition or preparation. Rather, seven women, simply garbed in strong colors, move about a stage that is set starkly and lit boldly. The performers interpret, through voice and dance, singly and in dissolving and forming clusters, a series of poems imagistically rich and linguistically imaginative. The women change characters and identities easily, transforming their own persons without changes in costume or scenery. *Colored girls* is a celebration of being black and being woman. The play's lady in yellow puts it best: "bein alive & bein a woman & bein colored is a metaphysical dilemma/ i havent conquered yet/ do you see the point/my spirit is too ancient to understand the separation of soul & gender/ my love is too delicate to have thrown back on my face."[25]

The poem treats the lives, dreams, and fears of various women. For the black woman in yellow, "It was graduation nite & i waz the only virgin in the crowd," but by the end of the party "in the backseat of that ol buick/ WOW/ by daybreak/ i just cdnt stop grinnin."[26] For the black lady in blue whose "papa thot he was puerto rican" came the bittersweet confession that "we waz just reglar niggahs wit hints of spanish."[27] The black lady in red painfully discovered that for unthinking people "a rapist is always to be a stranger/ to be legitimate/ someone you never saw/ a man wit obvious problems."[28] For the black lady in purple who fell in love with a dream and went to bed with a reality, "1955 was not a good year for lil blk girls."[29] The black lady in blue describes the horror of life in a ghetto, beginning with "I usedta live in the world/ then i moved to HARLEM/ & my universe is now six blocks."[30] The black lady in orange gropes for a solution to the dilemma of black women: "ever since i realized there waz someone callt/ a colored girl an evil woman a bitch or a nag/ i been tryin not to be that...i cdnt stand it/ i cdnt stand bein sorry & colored at the same time/ it's so redundant in the modern world."[31] And as the black lady in green sagely observes, "stealin my shit from me /dont make it yrs/ makes it stolen."[32]

Through solo and choral presentations, the piece moves to the most powerful poem of all — a bitter and frightening portrait of Crystal and her boyfriend, Beau Willie, as told by the black lady in red. "He kept tellin crystal/ any niggah wanna kill vietnamese children more n stay home & raise his own is sicker than a rabid dog," but all the while Beau Willie beats and threatens Crystal, the more so since she has become pregnant for the second time but steadfastly refuses to marry him. When he threatens the children, though, "crystal grabbed the lil girl & stared at beau willie like he waz a leper or somethin/ dont you touch my children/ muthafucker/ or i'll kill you."[33] But Beau Willie succeeds in enticing the babies away from Crystal and, while people from the street look on in horror and Crystal watches piteously, Beau Willie drops them out of the fifth floor window.

At the end of this poem, the theatrical piece moves to a cry of joyful self-discovery as first one, then several, and finally all of the black women say and sing: "i found god in myself & i loved her/i loved her fiercely."[34] With all of the performers repeating these lines, first to the audience and, when exhausted, back to one another in an ever-tightening circle, the words become a hymn of joy, a celebration of being black and woman. The lady in brown then ends the piece simply with the lines, "& this is for colored girls who have considered suicide/but are movin to the ends of their own rainbows."[35]

In *colored girls*, subjects previously believed too controversial and theatrical techniques thought too incoherent to be commercially successful find expression in a form acceptable to Broadway's theatregoers. Its images and language proclaim the author's race and sex. Its lyric form and flowing style of production capture the qualities prized by the avant garde, who have long strived to free theatre and drama from the shackles of domestic realism. Although Shange wrote other plays before the decade's end (*A Photograph: A Still Life with Shadows/ A Photograph: A Study of*

Cruelty; In the Middle of a Flower, Spell#7), none achieved the success of *colored girls* and none earned the critics' acclaim.

The friendly reception of *colored girls*, however, seemed to open more theatres to plays by women that dealt with dramatic subjects and used theatrical techniques previously thought unpromising: Gretchen Cryer's *I'm Getting My Act Together and Taking It on the Road*, Eve Merriam's *The Club*, Marsha Norman's *Getting Out*, and Elizabeth Swados's *Runaways*, to cite only the most obvious. Too, groups other than feminist theatres and Papp's Public Theatre began actively to encourage women playwrights. Among the most notable was the American Place Theatre which, in 1979, began an ambitious new project to discover and air works by women. By 1980, the indications, although tentative, were promising that perhaps serious women playwrights would soon rejoin New York's commercial mainstream in significant numbers.

After an examination of women dramatists as a group, some conclusions are possible. Certainly, Mersand's earlier generalizations prove absolutely false: contemporary American women dramatists were not primarily reporters for the stage; they did philosophize; they did preach; and their social consciousness was readily apparent. Matthews likewise sounds merely quaint as he patronized women dramatists for the flawed construction of their plays and the deficient experiences of their lives. In obvious contradiction to his observations, some contemporary women excelled in realistic plays unified through action even as others forged new forms that won commercial acceptance. And social consciousness, often combined with political awareness, was a distinguishing feature of most of their works.

Three trends are apparent. First, after 1960, most American women dramatists produced their plays Off- rather than On-Broadway, and most abandoned the dramatic structures typically associated with American realism in favor of those modelled on the epic, the argument, or the lyric poem. Second, after 1960, black women dramatists exerted leadership and achieved successes unprecedented in the history of the American theatre; and they offered the major exception to the first generalization, since, although working Off-Off-Broadway, they continued to write plays unified by action and rooted in social and domestic problems. Third, after 1970, increasing numbers of women turned to the fact of their womanness for a new perspective, indeed for a new subject. Thereafter, American women dramatists would be routinely described with respect to their identification with feminism as well as their preferences for certain dramatic and theatrical techniques.

Such a survey of female dramatists, however, appears to raise at least as many questions as it answers.

Why, for example, after establishing a strong foothold in the commercial American theatre of the 1920s and 1930s, did women dramatists retreat from this forum? Several different explanations have been advanced, but none has been proved. Some argue that social forces during the 1940s and 1950s reversed the movement toward emancipation and replaced it with a period of adjustment to women's "proper sphere." Rachel Frank, for example, proposed that women abandoned careers and returned home in large numbers because of the pseudoscientific support given "The Cult of True Womanhood" by the publication of Helene Deutsch's book (*The Psychology of Women*, 1944), the widespread dissemination of these views by the popular press, and the general intellectual repression that set in after World War II.[36] To her list of social factors could well be added the state of a post-war economy that again drove women from the work force in order to make way for returning veterans. Some propose instead that the retreat was due to changes in the structure of the American theatre itself, a triumph of the forces that led to the hit-or-flop syndrome on Broadway and the consequent development of alternative theatres Off-Broadway. Lillian Hellman, Jean Kerr, and Clare Booth Luce all described economic pressures that made the effort of producing plays on Broadway not worth the toll it took on their personal lives. Rosalyn Drexler angrily indicted Broadway's commercialism, and Rochelle Owens implied that women, in particular, needed freedom from its "horrible economic entanglements."[37] Still others complained that women dramatists were the victims of a barely disguised misogyny among established literary and theatrical critics[38] and that males excluded women from the camaraderie so essential to the production of plays on Broadway.[39]

Why, among women dramatist of the 1960s and 1970s, did blacks exert so profound an influence? The early success of Lorraine Hansberry may have created a climate particularly receptive to the efforts of other black women. Again, the anger and power of the then-recent Black Arts movement may have been strong enough to open theatre doors to all blacks and to sweep its women (along with its men) into prominence. Or perhaps in their race, black women dramatists found a serious subject for their plays, a subject that they knew intimately and one that society had already legitimized.

But most significant and puzzling of all, why were women dramatists so late in discovering their womanness as a suitable subject for serious plays? Why did not "the fact of their sex" (to use Moer's phrase) give them a subject until 1970 or later? Again, different theories have been advanced. Marcia Lieberman observed that until recently all accepted literary conventions were based on a view of life and society that was masculine.[40] Susan Koppelman Cornillon urged that society had conditioned women to view their own experiences as atypical, abnormal, or trivial, but, in any case, not as suitable subjects for serious art.[41] Joanna Russ argued convincingly that an active heroine is a contradiction in terms ("What Can a Heroine Do? Or Why Women Can't Write")—and thus implied that women were left with the option of writing about men or of not writing for the stage.[42]

The questions remain. They must persist, unanswered, until a new perspective resolves them. Their existence, however, is proof of the vigor and importance of the American woman as dramatist.

WOMEN DRAMATISTS

List of Plays Cited, and Source

Bovasso, Julia.
  Gloria & Esperanza. Mailman and Poland.
  The Moondreamers. Samuel French, 1979.
Charles, Marti.
  Job Security. Hatch and Shine.
Cryer, Gretchen.
  I'm Getting My Act Together and Taking It On the Road. Samuel
    French, 1979.
Drexler, Rosalyn.
  Home Movies. Mailman and Poland.
  Hot Buttered Roll. Benedikt.
  Skywriting. France.
Fornes, Maria Irene.
  Dr. Kheal. Fornes. France.
  Fefu and Her Friends. Script at American Place Theatre, 111 W. 46th
    St., New York, New York 10036.
  Promenade. Fornes.
  Successful Life of 3. Ballet, II. Orzel and Smith.
Grant, Micki.
  Don't Bother Me I Can't Cope. Samuel French, 1978.
Hansberry, Lorraine.
  A Raisin in the Sun. Cerf. Hansberry.
  The Sign in Sydney Brustein's Window. Hansberry.
Hellman, Lillian.
  Another Part of the Forest. Hellman.
  The Autumn Garden. Hellman.

The Children's Hour. Hellman. Sullivan and Hatch.
The Little Foxes. Hellman.
Toys in the Attic. Cerf. Hellman.
Watch on the Rhine. Hellman.
Jacker, Corinne.
Bits and Pieces. Moore.
Harry Outside. Dramatists Play Service, 1978–79.
Jackson, Elaine.
Toe Jam. King and Milner.
Kennedy, Adrienne.
Funnyhouse of a Negro. Oliver and Sills.
The Owl Answers. Hatch and Shine. Hoffman. Ashley.
The Rat's Mass. Couch.
Lamb, Myrna.
Apple Pie.
Crab Quadrille.
The Mod Donna. Lamb.
Scyklon Z. Lamb.
Scripts at New York Public Theatre Archives, 150 W. 65th St., New
York, New York 10023.
Merriam, Eve.
The Club. Samuel French, 1978.
Norman, Marsha.
Getting Out. Dramatists Play Service, 1979–80.
Owens, Rochelle.
Beclch. Owens.
Futz. Hoffman. Owens.
Homo. Owens.
Shange, Ntozake.
*For colored girls who have considered suicide when the rainbow is
enuf*. Shange.
A Photograph: A Still Life with Shadows/
A Photograph: A Study of Cruelty.
Spell #7.
Scripts at New York Public Theatre Archives, 150 W. 65th St., New
York, New York 10023.
Swados, Elizabeth.
Runaways. Samuel French, 1980.
Terry, Megan.
Approaching Simone. Terry.
Calm Down Mother. Orzel and Smith. Sullivan and Hatch.

The Gloaming, Oh My Darling. Bain.
Keep Tightly Closed in a Cool Dry Place. TDR 1966.
Viet Rock. Samuel French, 1979.

List of Anthologies and Collections

Ashley, Leonard R.N., ed. *Mirrors for Man: 26[sic] Plays of the World Drama.* Cambridge, Mass.: Winthrop Publishers Inc., 1974.

Bain, Carl E., ed. *The Norton Introduction to Literature: Drama.* New York: W. W. Norton and Co., Inc., 1973.

Ballet, Arthur H., ed. *Playwrights for Tomorrow.* Vol. II. Minneapolis: University of Minnesota Press, 1966.

Benedikt, Michael, ed. *Theatre Experiment.* Garden City, New York: Doubleday and Co., Inc., 1967.

Cerf, Bennett, ed. *Six American Plays for Today.* New York: The Modern Library, 1961.

Couch, William, ed. *New Black Playwrights.* New York: Avon Books, 1970.

France, Rachel, ed. *A Century of Plays by American Women.* New York: Richards Rosen Press, Inc., 1979.

Fornes, Maria Irene. *Promenade and Other Plays.* New York: Drama Book Specialists, 1973.

Hansberry, Lorraine. *A Raisin in the Sun.* New York: Random House, 1959. _____. *The Sign in Sydney Brustein's Window.* New York: Random House, 1965.

Hatch, James V. and Shine, Ted, eds. *Black Theatre U.S.A.: Forty-Five Plays by Black Americans, 1847–1974.* New York: The MacMillan Publishing Co., Inc., 1974.

Hellman, Lillian. *The Collected Plays.* Boston: Little, Brown and Co., 1972.

Hoffman, William M., ed. *New American Plays.* Vol. II. New York: Hill and Wang, 1968.

King, Woodie, and Milner, Ron, ed. *Black Drama Anthology.* New York: Columbia University Press, 1972.

Lamb, Myrna. *Plays of Women's Liberation: The Mod Donna and Scyklon Z.* New York: Pathfinder Press, 1971.

Mailman, Bruce, and Poland, Albert, eds. *The Off-Off Broadway Book: The Plays, People, Theatre.* Indianapolis, Ind.: Bobbs-Merrill Co., Inc., 1972.

Moore, Honor, ed. *The New Woman's Theatre*. New York: Random House, 1977.

Oliver, Clinton S., and Sills, Stephanie, eds. *Contemporary Black Drama: From "A Raisin in the Sun" to "No place to be Somebody."* New York: Charles Scribner's Sons, 1971.

Orzel, Nick, and Smith, Michael, eds. *Eight Plays from Off-Off-Broadway*. Indianapolis, Ind.: Bobs-Merrill Co., Inc., 1966.

Owens, Rochelle. *Futz and What Came After*. New York: Random House, 1968.

Shange, Ntozake, *For colored girls who have considered suicide/when the rainbow is enuf*. New York: MacMillan Publishing Co., 1977.

Sullivan, Victoria, and Hatch, James, eds. *Plays By and About Women*. New York: Random House, 1974.

Terry, Megan. *Approaching Simone*. Old Westbury, N.Y.: The Feminist Press, 1973. *Tulane Drama Review*, 10, 4 (Summer 1966): 177-213.

NOTES

1. Ellen Moers, *Literary Women: The Great Writers* (Garden City, New York: Anchor Press/Doubleday, 1977), p. xiv.

2. Brander Matthews, *A Book About the Theatre* (New York: Charles Scribner's Sons, 1916), pp. 124–125.

3. Joseph Mersand, "When Ladies Write Plays," *Players Magazine*, 14, 1 (September/October 1937): 8.

4. "Where Are the Women Playwrights?" *New York Times*, 20 May 1972, sec. 2, pp. D1, D3.

5. See, for example, Yvonne B. Shafer, "The Liberated Woman in American Plays of the Past," *Players Magazine*, 49, 3–4 (Spring 1974): 95–100.

6. Bennett Cerf, Richard Watts, Jr., of the New York *Post*, and John Chapman of the *News*, respectively, as quoted in Bennett Cerf, ed. *Six American Plays for Today* (New York: The Modern Library, 1961), p. 599.

7. *Ibid.*, p. 540.

8. According to Oscar G. Brockett and Robert R. Findlay, *Century of Innovation: A History of European and American Theatre and Drama Since 1870* (Englewood Cliffs, N.J.: Prentice-Hall, Inc., 1973), p. 711.

9. See Phyllis Jane Wagner, "On Megan Terry," *Approaching Simone: A Play* by Megan Terry (Old Westbury, New York: The Feminist Press, 1973), pp. 30–35.

10. For this information I am indebted to Betty Moseley Davis, "Women at the Open Theatre," paper presented at the annual convention of the Southern Speech Communication Association, Knoxville, TN, April 1977. Davis cites as her source, Joseph Chaikin, telephone interview, 19 July 1976.

12. Myrna Lamb, "Introduction," *Plays of Women's Liberation: The Mod Donna and Scyklon Z* (New York: Pathfinder Press, Inc., 1971), p. 28.

13. *Ibid.*, back cover.

14. *Ibid.*, pp. 35, 55.

15. *Ibid.*, p. 93.

16. *Ibid.*, pp. 138–139.

17. *Ibid.*, p. 35.

18. Patti P. Gillespie, "Feminist Theatre: A Rhetorical Phenomenon," *The Quarterly Journal of Speech,* 64 (1978): 284–94.

19. According to Darwin Turner, ed. *Black Drama in America: An Anthology* (Greenwich, Conn.: Fawcett Publications, Inc., 1971), p. 13.

20. Ted Shine, "Introduction to *The Owl Answers,*" *Black Theatre, U.S.A.*, ed. James V. Hatch (New York: The Free Press, 1974), p. 756.

21. As cited on dustcover, Ntozake Shange, *for colored girls who have considered suicide/when the rainbow is enuf* (New York: MacMillan Publishing Co., Inc., 1977).

22. Shange, p. xi.

23. *Ibid.*, p. xiii.

24. *Ibid.*, p. xiv.

25. *Ibid.*, p. 36.

26. *Ibid.*, pp. 4, 7.

27. *Ibid.*, p. 8.

28. *Ibid.*, p. 13.

29. *Ibid.*, p. 21.

30. *Ibid.*, p. 28.

31. *Ibid.*, pp. 33–34.

32. *Ibid.*, p. 40.

33. *Ibid.*, pp. 44, 46.

34. *Ibid.*, p. 51.

35. *Ibid.*

36. Rachel Frank, "Introduction," *A Century of Plays by American Women*, ed. Rachel Frank (New York: Richard Rosen Press, Inc., 1979), p. 21.

37. As quoted in "Where are the Women Playwrights?" See footnote 4.

38. See, for example, Fraya Katz-Stoker, "The Other Criticism: Feminism and Formalism," *Images of Women in Fiction*, ed. Susan Koppelman Cornillon (Bowling Green, Ohio: Bowling Green University Popular Press, 1972), pp. 315–327, but especially pp. 324–326; Marilyn Stasio, "The Night the Critics Lost Their Cool," *Ms*, 4 October 1975, pp. 101–104.

39. Honor Moore, "Introduction," *The New Women's Theatre: Ten Plays by Contemporary American Women*, ed. Honor Moore (New York: Vantage Books, 1977), p. xiv.

40. Marcia R. Lieberman, "Sexism and the Double Standard in Literature," *Images of Women*, pp. 328–340.

41. Susan Koppelman Cornillon, "The Fiction of Fiction," *Images of Women*, pp. 113–130.

42. Joanna Russ, "What Can a Heroine Do? Or Why Women Can't Write," *Images of Women*, p. 3–20.

David Mamet: The Plays, 1972–1980

STEVEN H. GALE

David Mamet's plays are about relationships. Throughout dramatic history, of course, the theme of interpersonal relationships has been a primary concern, yet Mamet's examination of the intercourse between individuals is more intimate and more human than that of most of his forerunners or his American or British contemporaries. In part this is because he is extremely perceptive and in part it is because he is an accomplished craftsman.

Well grounded in theatre history and theory, Mamet is also gifted in bringing common experiences alive for his audience. His situations are sometimes realistic and sometimes symbolic, but they all contain a universal kernel around which the action is built and with which the audience identifies. In addition, he creates characters who are both believable and human; and the phrasing, clichés, and cadences of his dialogue are so accurate that when his plays first opened in New York, many reviewers compared his work to that of Harold Pinter.[1] He is not just an American Pinter, though. While there are similarities in content and technique, essentially Mamet's approach is less intellectual, philosophical, or theoretical than Pinter's as his narrower focus generally deals with the superficial aspect of his subject. By this I do not mean to denigrate his work, for he is extremely successful at what he does, and his writing is far more easily accessible than is much of Pinter's—and he is still a young dramatist developing his skills. Where Pinter deals with the deepest levels of the psyches of characters who have desperate needs in order to expose those needs and the strategies employed to fulfill them, Mamet shows ordinary human beings caught in the immediacy of stipulated needs for various kinds of social interaction. As a result, Mamet's plays are not as deep and dark as Pinter's; at the same time they ring truer for a less sophisticated audience.

The Duck Variations was first staged by the St. Nicholas Theatre Company at Mamet's alma mater, Goddard College in Plainfield, Vermont, while he was teaching drama there in 1972. It later played in Chicago where it met critical acclaim, and then moved to the St. Clements Theatre in 1975 and later that same year to the Cherry Lane Theatre, both in New York City.

The play deals with two men in their sixties. They often come together during lunch to talk—about life and death, the perils of leadership, fate, sex, the environment and pollution, or whatever else comes to mind. Because of their age they have the wisdom and perspective on their subjects that comes with experience, but sometimes they are the butt of their own societal satire, too, and exhibit the foolishness of those whom they both envy and find ridiculous.

Each of the fourteen variations is about a different topic, though they are all connected by the common denominator of the ducks and each is somehow related to the preceding variation and prepares for the variation that follows. Mamet's stage directions are minimal; he suggests that there be a slight interval between variations and "any blocking or business is at the discretion of individual actors and directors."[2] The opening line or two establish the topic for each variation, as the men link a series of clichéd stories and commentaries about ducks that become allegories for serious protests about life, nature, mankind, and society. As Emil and George alternate in setting the topic, they try to top one another and their personalities emerge; ultimately, the seemingly slower-witted George is seen as the more perceptive. The characters become believable, recognizable; they remind us of our favorite grandfathers. In spite of the fast delivery of short one-line dialogue, the characters know each another well enough to communicate, sometimes responding to unfinished thoughts, though ironically, too, sometimes not being able to pick up the most obvious clues.

While the philosophical stances assumed by George and Emil regarding their numerous, shifting subjects carry revelations about the nature of the universe and man's place in it, ultimately the importance of their conversation lies not in occasional insights but in the fact that they are conversing. When they come together it is clear that they know each other and that they have met here previously, perhaps for years. They are familiar and they use their familiarity as a basis for much of the mental gymnastics that they engage in. They have achieved a stable relationship, one that is vital to their mental well-being. Every day at lunch time they meet to talk, to share the time together, to create an imaginative break in their mundane day. Indeed, this may be the high point of their day—the companionship that both need and relish. As Emil says in the "Seventh Variation," "A man needs a friend in this life."[3]

Sexual Perversity in Chicago was first produced in the summer of 1974 by The Organic Theatre Company in Chicago where the play received the Joseph Jefferson Award for best new play. In December 1975 it was part of a double bill with *The Duck Variations* in an off off-Broadway production and then on off-Broadway and the plays were listed among *Time* magazine's ten best plays of 1976. As with *The Duck Variations*, reviewers stressed the accuracy of Mamet's language and the reality of the play's situation, comparing the dramatist's talents favorably with Pinter's.

At first glance *Sexual Perversity* seems less mature than *Variations*. The language is certainly coarser, being filled with four-letter words, and the sexual imagery that abounds is sophomoric in tone. The subject, too, seems to be more college blackout material than the earlier drama[4]: two young men talk about their sexual exploits and describe the women they see as sexual objects in very graphic, though limited, terms. Actually, however, the play is more subtle than a simple plot summary suggests, for the sex is not important *per se* as it really functions metaphorically to carry the author's meaning. The physical act supplies Mamet's terms for discussing his underlying theme. While he comments on the relationships between one man and another and between one woman and another, this is incidental and only a by-product of his main concern. His focus is on the relationship between men and women.

There are two couples involved, though the members of each recombine with a member of the other to form two additional pairings. Dan and Bernie are filing clerks; Dan is twenty-eight and Bernie somewhat older. They are paralleled by Deborah, a twenty-three-year-old illustrator, and her older roommate, kindergarten teacher Joan. As the play progresses, Dan and Deborah pair off, as do Bernie and Joan. From the composite conversations between the members of the various groupings, together with occasional monologues, the individual nature of each character emerges.

Although there are few direct statements of theme, a Gestalt forms from Dan and Bernie's constant comments and observations about women in general and their sexual relationships with women. It is important to note that the drama opens with just such an exchange:

DANNY: So how'd you do last night?
               . . .
BERNIE: Are you fucking kidding me?
               . . .
BERNIE: So tits out to here. (p. 9)[5]

There follows an improbable Pinteresque story of Bernie's exploits that winds up with the suggestion that the girl involved can be sexually stimulated only if a friend she telephones makes noises like an anti-aircraft battery while she and Bernie have sex—and the climax comes when she sets the room on fire and sings "Off we go into the Wild Blue Yonder." This scene is countered by one in which Deborah and Joan conclude that men are "all after only one thing" (p. 18). But amusingly, "it's never the *same* thing."

The two commentaries come together in the next scene when Joan and Bernie meet at a singles bar. He tries a line on her, claiming to be a meteorologist for TWA, but she rejects him—"I do not find you sexually attractive" (p. 20). Bernie fights back, calling her names and forcing her to realize that just as he treated her as a sex object, she has treated him the same; and, now that she can see an individual behind her easy categorizing, she realizes that he is as much a person as she is, and that she has hurt him.

This recognition may be the high point in the relationship between the sexes in the play, for thereafter everything is largely downhill. In the next scene, for instance, Bernie details one of his fundamental principles of life: "The Way to Get Laid is to Treat 'Em Like Shit" (p. 22). As Danny observed earlier, "Nobody does it normally anymore." Herein lies the key to the play. The relationship between the sexes, Mamet says, is not natural. It may be that this stems from the very setting of modern urban society, something implied in the drama's title. It may be that life in a big city causes people to become perverted as a consequence of sharing lodgings with members of the same sex, artificially separating the sexes and reenforcing their biases and prejudices about one another through the kinds of bull sessions that fill the play. Whatever the reason, male bonding and female bonding have replaced heterosexual relationships and understandings.

The thematic content is most clearly expressed through the characters of Dan and Bernie. The themes are reflected through Deborah and Joan, too, though Mamet either does not understand women's fears of men as well as he understands men's fears of women, or he feels that he is making his point through male characters and that since the females' fears are the same, they can be seen mirroring those fears without much development. Thus, the theme of the play is simply fear of trusting the opposite sex. This fear leads to feelings of bitterness, pain, resentment, and, finally, to despair and desperation. Bernie, the older male, talks around the subject of women and meaningful (i.e., more than purely sexual) relationships with them and he tells stories about women degraded by men (as in his tale about King Farouk's habits), yet the way he talks about the things that he talks about indicates the importance of what he cannot talk about. He resorts to clichés, the idiom of the barroom, the barracks, and pornographic movie houses to avoid straightforward communication. He cannot express his needs and fears. We hear him talk about how he treats women (the radio-throwing episode, for instance), but when we see him with Joan his actions do not match his words.

What we have, then, is a picture of a man who wants and needs a relationship with a woman, but whose experience has shown him that he cannot trust them. Unfortunately, his need makes him vulnerable to rejection, and it appears that there have been frequent rejections. So he cuts himself off from others in an effort to avoid a repetition of previous pain, thereby isolating himself further as the vicious circle progresses. He lies to others because he has been lied to. He sets up self-protective walls, defense mechanisms, in the form of rituals and clichés. He plays roles in attempting to conquer women, who are worthy of nothing more, but they do not respond correctly, so he gets madder. Sex becomes an instrument of revenge: " ... when she's on her back, her legs are in the air, she's coming like a choo-choo and she's screaming 'don't stop' ... that *power* means *responsibility*" (p. 31). Bernie's thoughts, couched in the terms of the *Playboy* mentality, seem immature. Seen as a reaction to the source of his vulnerability and humiliation and to his powerful fear of rejection, however, these actions are understandable.

Joan, as Bernie's counterpart, fears being "used" sexually. This is a different fear from Bernie's, but essentially it is the same; she fears rejection as a person. Dan and Deborah are younger, so they have not met as much rejection, but it exists, as is apparent in Dan's patterns of noncommitment or exposure in his relationship with her: "So, look, so tell me. How would you like to eat dinner with me tomorrow. If you're not doing anything. If you're not too busy. If you're busy it's not important" (p. 25).

Bernie and Joan are harder, more fearsome, than Dan and Deborah. They serve as mentors to the younger pair—who are too shallow to perceive the mistakes of their instructors, who will follow the older pair's lead, and who will probably end with similar attitudes and approaches in their relations with the other sex.

American Buffalo was first produced by the Goodman Theatre Stage Two in Chicago on November 23, 1975, moved to the St. Clement's Theatre in New York in February 1976, and subsequently became Mamet's first play to appear on Broadway when it was mounted at the Ethel Barrymore Theatre on February 16, 1977. It won the New York Drama Critic's Circle award for best play of 1977 and Mamet received an Obie as best playwright.

The plot is simple. In Act I, Don, owner of the shop where the action takes place, and his gofer Bob discuss a burglary that Bob plans to commit. The intended victim had visited the shop earlier and bought a buffalo-head nickel for ninety dollars, and Don thinks that the customer's apartment may be filled with valuable coins. A friend of Don's called Teach becomes involved in the planning session and tries to persuade Don to use him for the job. There is little action and the play's interest derives from psychological tensions and the constant flow of slang and the strong language used (certainly a natural idiom for these circumstances and characters).

Act II might be subtitled "Waiting for Fletcher," since most of the tension until the end of the drama revolves around whether the mysterious Fletcher will appear and the burglary be committed. Ultimately, the three men turn on each other; Teach strikes Bob in the head with a piece of junk and the play ends with the two older men about to drive Bob to the hospital.

In an interview,[6] the dramatist claims that he meant for the play to be an indictment of the American business ethic and that his hoodlum characters are lower-class respresentatives of the levels of corporate employees. "We excuse all sorts of great and small betrayals and ethical compromises called business," he says. The basis for this drama, then, is that "There's really no difference between the *Lumpenproletariat* and stockbrokers or corporate lawyers who are the lackeys of business. Part of the American myth is that a difference exists, that at a certain point vicious behavior becomes laudable."

The play definitely can be read in this light, and it makes sense, though it is not sufficiently developed or epic enough to be as convincing as it might be. However, the concept of relationships is again crucial. Where *Sexual Perversity* was about the fear of establishing relationships, *American Buffalo* is about the fear of losing a relationship.

Essentially, Don is concerned with the business venture at hand. His relationship with Bob is business oriented, though there is affection displayed—he treats Bob kindly, offers Polonius-style advice, and trusts him to perform his function adequately; he lends Bob money, shows some concern over the young man's drug habits (getting upset when Teach refers to "the kid's ... skin-pop"), and worries about the blood coming out of Bob's ear. Don makes distinctions, however, as he points out to Bob early in the play, "there's business and there's friendship" (p. 7).[7] This distinction allows Don to deal with Bob in a way that does not involve a change in his relationship with Teach. Furthermore, Don's emotional range is limited to pride that his shop is a focal point for activity in the neighborhood. Otherwise he is passive. Apparently his relationship with Teach has never been verbalized and he is too contented and unconcerned to worry about it now. That he is not overly involved emotionally with Bob is demonstrated by his lack of a vehement reaction to Teach's attack.

When Teach enters, there is a change in tone. Teach perceives his relationship with Don as threatened by Bob, if Bob and Don have gone so far as to form an alliance for the burglary, and Teach's seeming anger at the way Grace and Ruth treat him really masks his feelings about Bob. His immediate reaction when he enters the shop is to begin a tirade deriding the two women, but when his explosion comes, near the end of Act II, it is directed against Bob—because of the implications of the newly emerging relationship between Bob and Don.

Teach has his definition of friendship: "I pop for coffee ... cigarettes ... a *sweet roll*, never say word ... and [I] don't forget who's who when someone gets *behind* a half a yard or needs some help ... or someone's sick" (p. 10). And he insists on certain distinctions: "We're talking about money....We're talking about cards. Friendship is friendship, and a wonderful thing....But let's just keep it *separate*" (p. 15). In the final analysis, Teach wants to maintain the *status quo*. Whether his relationship with Don is based on business or friendship, it demands the exclusion of Bob.

Bob is caught in the middle. He both works for and likes Don, as evidenced by his distress at having bungled the job and his buying another coin to please his boss (p. 99). He is not perceptive enough, however, to realize his position vis-à-vis either Don or Teach, whatever the basis of the competition that he is unwittingly engaged in with Teach. Ironically, he is a threat to Teach only in Teach's mind.

That none of those relationships is as fully developed as that of George and Emil in *Duck Variations* is evident from the characters' dialogue, which is incomplete. These characters are more futile than those drawn by Mamet previously, and their fragmented dialogue reflects their lives. It also indicates that their thoughts and words are relatively insubstantial or unimportant, so they do not bother to finish them.

The title of the play is interesting. Obviously it may refer to the coin, which serves as a plot device and has little intrinsic value, regardless of the consequences of its existence. It might also refer to American business, which because of its excesses may be on the verge of extinction, as the buffalo has been. Or it may have significance in reference to the characters, for buffalo are large, bumbling, fairly unattractive animals and normally we do not attribute to them the same emotions and sensitivity that we might project onto other creatures. Don, Bob, and Teach end up as innocents in regard to their planned crime. But the crime is incidental anyway. More important is their innocence in terms of being able to recognize relationships, emotions, or the connection between relationships and emotions.

The Water Engine was written in 1976 as a radio drama for National Public Radio's *Earplay*. It was first produced as a stage play by Mamet's St. Nicholas Theatre Company in Chicago on May 11, 1977 and subsequently was mounted at the New York Shakespeare Festival Public Theatre on January 5, 1978 and then at the Plymouth Theatre on Broadway on March 6, 1978.[8]

In spite of Richard Eder's contention that in comparison to Mamet's earlier plays the action here is "both more overt and more complex" and the drama is "less intense, more complex and more spacious," resulting in the playwright's "most beautiful play,"[9] *The Water Engine* is probably Mamet's weakest full-length published work, amounting to little more than a 1930s radio melodrama. Subtitled "An American Fable," *The Water Engine* is epitomized by the quotation that preceeds the published text: *"The mind of man is less perturbed by a mystery he cannot explain than by an explanation he cannot understand."*[10] Mamet's basic premise is that business is willing, even desperate, to suppress inventions that otherwise are beneficial to mankind if they endanger profits. There is a whole sub-genre of popular literature that supports this theory, of course, and the dramatist has drawn on all of its clichés. Essentially he is dealing with public distrust of business and the business ethic.

In Act One it is disclosed that a young inventor, Lang, has "built an engine which used distilled water as its only fuel" (p. 8). After some pseudoscientific gobbledygook that is supposed to support this possibility,[11] there are two sources of tension in the play. Briefly there is concern over whether Lang will be able to make his marvellous machine available to the public. At the end of Act One and throughout the second act the tension gains momentum as the concern becomes whether Lang and his sister Rita will be murdered by business interests in order to silence them. By the end of the play Lang's laboratory has been wrecked, he has been lied to and cheated, and he and Rita are kidnapped and murdered.

Throughout the play there are three thematic threads. First is the pervasive undercurrent of rumor ("Lindbergh came in with this *Doctor's bag*") that reflects the intermixings of society and suggests that public speculation is wildly imaginative and completely inaccurate—but is contrasted with events in the play. Many of these expressions are Whitmanesque or Sandburgian in tone. Second is the linking of trust and money in American business, as evidenced by Lang's need to pay his patent attorney, thereby insuring the lawyer's honesty — but naturally he is sold out to a higher bidder. This theme is carried by the voice over Chainletter ("we are characters within a dream of industry" p. 23) and the Soapbox Speaker, who points out that business gets its authority from its victims: "The power of the torturers comes from the love of Patriotic Songs ... where is the *wealth?* ... The ownership of the land./These things do not change./They don't change with give aways and murals" (pp. 26, 34). The corruption and malevolence of business is ironically apparent in the contrast between

Murray's expounding on "the great essential strength of the Free Market" (p. 63) and the Speaker's rhetorical "What happened to this nation? Or did it exist?...It was all but a myth. A great dream of avarice" (p. 64). The third thematic thread is the connection between trust and the survival of civilization. As stated in the chainletter, "All civilization stands on trust./ All people are connected. ... Technological and Ethical masterpieces decay into folktales" (pp. 61, 71).

Water Engine is Mamet's most ambitious work in terms of the large number of characters (there are eight main roles and thirty-two supporting parts) and the interweaving of subplots and themes. It is almost epic or heroic in its treatment of society and in the action's of Lang. It is also more accessible and more acceptable to a general audience than most of the playwright's pieces since *Duck Variations*. The theme is traditional, shallow, and melodramatic (with a thirties' tone; B-grade Odets), and relatively straightforward. It is cinematic in nature, possibly because of its radio origins; there is more action, a different kind of suspense and general tone, almost like a Charlie Chan movie. And the language is not flavored with Mamet's typical spice of four-letter words.[12]

Where in all of this are the interpersonal relationships? Nowhere. Not every play has to be a serious endeavor and for Mamet this drama was an exercise rather than a statement. It lacks the emotional intensity and involvement of his other works. The style is diffuse and there is little significance in the play, but the author probably enjoyed writing it, just as he enjoys working on children's dramas.

Mr. Happiness was produced as a companion piece to *Water Engine* and was first produced at the Plymouth Theatre on March 6, 1978. It is a short, slight play, a filler. Some obvious connections exist with *Water Engine* in theme and event ("a fellow with a smoking gun is standing over the proprietor of some poor candy store" p. 79): mankind needs love, someone to listen, traditional values, etc. Nothing very deep or inspiring—merely an entertainment.

Reunion was first staged by the St. Nicholas Theatre Company on January 9, 1976 and opened in New York in 1979. It is the playwright's most affecting and human work since *Duck Variations*. The situation is simple. After a separation of twenty years, fifty-three-year-old Bernie is reunited with his twenty-four-year-old daughter, Carol. As they talk about their lives and bring each other up to date, it is evident that the father needs and wants to reestablish a relationship with his daughter and the daughter needs and wants to reestablish a relationship with her father. Mamet's drama beautifully depicts the touching way in which they communicate, hesitatingly, as a renewed bond is formed.

The conversation realistically bounces from thought to thought about the past and the present. The two are not sure what they have in common or whether the other will reciprocate emotionally. We learn a lot through the play's fourteen scenes: Bernie was a machine gunner in World War II, he was hospitalized for back trouble, worked for a van line and the phone company, he had a second wife and a son, is a Democrat, has friends, works in a restaurant, was an alcoholic, and is thinking about remarrying; Carol has been married for two years to a man who already had two sons, but she is unhappy in the marriage because her husband is "a lousy fuck" (p. 28).[13] More vital, though, is their need for each other. Naturally they display curiosity about what the other is like and has been doing (pp. 11, 36), but the crux of the play is that they need to overcome their separation. Bernie recognizes that their meeting is a "very important moment" (p. 5) and recalls that he felt like crying when Carol's husband contacted him (p. 17). His philosophy of life is uncomplicated: "I spent a couple of days in jail once./ What it taught me, you've got be where you are. . . . While you're there./ Or you're nowhere" (p. 36). His needs are simple, too: friends, an enjoyable job, perhaps the companionship of marriage. But his tentative relationship with his daughter has become supremely important — because, after all, "Having your own kids is . . . indescribable" (p. 19) and "what's between [the two of them] isn't going nowhere, and the rest of it doesn't exist" (p. 37).

Carol's needs are similar. She has been deprived. As important as marriage is to her ("The most important institution in America"), coming from a broken home has altered her marriage (p. 29), yet that result may not be as significant as the fact that a husband cannot take the place of a father. When Bernie notes that she smokes too much and states that Gerry should set an example for her, she replies, "He's my husband . . . not my father" (p. 20). Later she informs Bernie that she sent Gerry to set up the meeting because "I felt lonely. . . . You're my father. . . . I felt cheated. . . . I never had a father. . . . And I don't want to be pals and buddies; I want you to be my father. . . . I'm entitled to it" (pp. 38–39).

The final scene is appropriate. Out of his love for his daughter Bernie has gotten her a gold bracelet. Human fallibility intrudes, for the present is marred — there is an error in the inscription. Yet despite the flaw, the message is clear; the gift is intrinsically too valuable to be damaged by superficialities. As Bernie said earlier when he recalled Carol's birthday, "I was going to call you up./ You probably don't believe it./ It's not important. The actions are important./ The present is important" (p. 36). It is fitting that the time of the play is early March, the beginning of the season of renewal, for the relationship between father and daughter has been reestablished.

Dark Pony was first mounted as a companion piece with *Reunion* in a Yale Reperatory production in New Haven, Connecticut on October 14, 1977 and then moved to New York in October 1979. Very short, it is a sketch consisting of a father telling his four-year-old daughter a story about an Indian and his friend Dark Pony as they drive home at night.

As in *Reunion*, the two characters are very human and the play is a powerful theatrical moment. The father and daughter have shared the ritual of this story in the past—they announce the brave's name simultaneously when it is time to do so in the story (p. 48). The daughter is a typical four-year-old—literal minded; when Rain Boy is described as running "like a deer," she wants to know if he hopped (p. 47). The father becomes engrossed in his mythmaking and is moved by the plight of an Indian who thinks that he has been deserted by a magical horse, a feeling with which the father identifies.

On the one hand, the play shows the closeness of the father and daughter. On the other, the generation gap is apparent, for the daughter's involvement in the story ceases when she recognizes that they are almost home, but she does not realize her father's emotional reaction. He is concerned with the need for a father-like companion who helps when needed, she with the security of home. The father's final words, "Dark Pony, Rain Boy calls to you," may be a call for help in the dark—and his daughter's final words may be the answer: "We are almost home" (p. 53).

A Life in the Theatre premiered at the Theatre de Lys in New York on October 20, 1977. Its critical reception was more enthusiastic than for any of Mamet's other plays—perhaps due to its subject matter, the theatre. Because of this favorable reaction, the drama became the first of the playwright's plays to be filmed. On June 27, 1979 the WNET (New York) production was telecast nationwide by the Public Broadcasting System.

In twenty-six scenes[14] the dramatist displays veteran actor Robert and relative newcomer John solo and interacting, on stage during performances and off-stage between scenes, performances, or productions. Ostensibly about the theatre, the day to day life of two characters, the play obviously uses its subject to discourse dramatically on life in general, the role of art in society, the relationships between teacher and pupil, the generations, and man and man. Throughout the play a number of statements clearly draw superficial parallels between the theatre and life. For example, Robert lectures John on how time is spent: "this is a wondrous thing about the Theatre [note capitalization]. . . . one of the ways in which it's most like life . . . .That in the *Theatre* (as in life—and the Theatre is, of course, a *part* of life. . . .)" (pp.78, 81). Similarly, he refers to the concept of "Beauty in the

Theatre" (p. 78) and he declaims on the history and aspirations of the theatre, concluding that "We [the theatre] *are* society" (pp. 35–36).

This reversed Shakespearean statement seems to be the drama's controlling metaphor; the philosophy expressed in scene five animates all that these two actors do and the idea of control discussed in scene fourteen fits the aesthetic theory of drama that states that drama functions to create a momentary and repeatable order out of universal chaos. But Mamet undercuts his metaphor, too. Scene thirteen is filled with self-mockery as Robert discovers the pseudoserious illuminations (the "leitmotif") in the O'Neill-like script for the "famous lifeboat scene." Further undercutting the importance of applying to life the lessons learned from the theatre are the laughable production bits seen. Six scenes are supposed to be performances, and a number of other scenes refer to these and other plays. The range of genres represented is wide: a World War One melodrama,[15] an Elizabethan sword and costume piece, a 1930s British melodrama, a "Chekovian" death scene, the O'Neill-like lifeboat scene, a speech on the barricades during the French Revolution, a Civil War period piece, and a modern melodrama set in a hospital operating room. About the only thing that these plays have in common is that they are bad plays. If there are any lessons to be learned, they are superficial truisms at best—and it is fitting that the theatrical clichés expressed (a performance is fulfilling, "The show goes on," acting makes them "glad to be alive") are on a par. The quality of the play that these men perform in is not as important as the fact that they are in a play. Thus the juxtaposition of life and the lessons provided by the theatre is ironic.

Related to the theatre as life theme is the teacher/student subtheme. Besides the phenomena control idea, Robert tries to impart wisdom on a wide variety of subjects. He speaks about self-control, initiates John into the theatre's superstitions (knocking on wood),[16] holds forth on the importance of developing voice control and keeping a straight back, reflects middle-class values in his comment about his younger colleague's admirable care of his tools, and offers advice about whose advice should be heeded. Robert is basically a contemporary Polonius. Conservative, a traditionalist who opts for law and reason in the theatre and in life, his lessons are essentially inconsequential. He affects a liberal artistic stance, yet he decries artistic experimentation. As a result, his role as teacher is a hollow one.

As was the case with *American Buffalo*, though, there is both less and more to this play than might be assumed from the foregoing. It is too episodic and sketchy to develop the theatre/life metaphor fully. Some critics have complained about the stereotypes, clichés, and superficialities, and there is an incompleteness about the characters because they are always playing roles, on stage and off. At the same time, while there is no specific indication of the passage of time, taken together the scenes create a time-lapse montage that is sufficient to trace the stages of development in the relationship between the two men. When the play opens John is in awe of Robert. He does not know the other actor well enough to predict his reactions, but he wants to please the older man. The conversation regarding the doctor scene in that evening's performance exposes John's uncertainty and his shifting evaluation of an actress's looks betrays his toadying attitude. Caught off guard by Robert's responses, John makes a comment about the table scene that is much less expansive, for he is apprehensive and wants to know which way to jump before he commits himself to either praise or criticism. Robert postures through this and many of the following scenes, alternately playing with and patronizing John, though it is not until scene seven that he is willing to antagonize his younger companion when he reacts defensively to the other's actions on stage, and even then this is done under the guise of offering a neophyte advice based on the wisdom of experience. In scene nine, however, Robert's grand posture is weakened when he confuses a line on stage and John saves him. By scene thirteen John is beginning to find Robert's pose tiresome and is unimpressed by the insights that the older man gleans from the lifeboat script; the opening scene's atmosphere of ingratiation is gone by scene seventeen when John can yell at Robert to stop his inane babbling. At this point the relationship begins to shift again. Robert has taught John about snobbery and decorum by example and by declamation; now he relates John's "breach of etiquette" not just with society and by extension with the theatre but also with "our personal relationship with each other" (p. 66). In scene twenty-two that relationship appears to be becoming an unhappy one when Robert reacts jealously to some of John's reviews and John responds in a pique, and scene twenty-three reenforces this assessment as John is put out by Robert's watching him rehearse from the wings. Robert's attitude is different from what it has been, though. In this scene his concern with the ongoing traditions of the theatre becomes personalized and he watches with the fondness of a proud father as John performs. Scene twenty-five reveals that John likewise is genuinely concerned with Robert when the older man cuts himself. In the final scene even petty jealousies over each other's lives outside the theatre have been put aside as the relationship has matured and the men can part for the evening with shared respect and affection.

In part *A Life in the Theatre* delineates the decline of one actor and the concurrent rise of another, but more importantly through a variety of circumstances and over a long period of time it shows how two men overcome obstacles to form a solid relationship. Scene twenty-four serves as a miniature of the play and of the relationships: there are muffed lines, attempts to help each other, displays of misplaced self-confidence, and anger: As in life, in the theatre parts run over into other plays and into life itself. But through it all there is an underlying sense of good humor and, ultimately, proportion that binds the men together.

The Woods was first produced by the St. Nicholas Theatre Company on November 11, 1977. In it Mamet returns to the theme of relations between the sexes that operated in *Sexual Perversity,* but this play has been tempered by the theme of love that moves through *Reunion* and *Dark Pony,* producing a more intimate, personal, and closer view than that of *Sexual Perversity.* As a result, the characters and situation are more fully drawn and the rendering is more accurate—and maybe more typical.

The three scenes follow the logical construct of thesis, antithesis, and synthesis. In scene one, we learn what the characters want and need from a relationship and that their desires are similar. Nick has brought Ruth to his family's cabin in the woods. She is in love with him and enthusiastic about life. We find out in scene two that Ruth believes that his having brought her means that he is committed to their relationship (p. 62)[17] and she is expansive and philosophical: "So little counts....Just the things we do.... To each other. The right things" (p. 11). The cabin is a pleasant sanctuary where she finds security and happiness in her lover's companionship. "This is the best thing two people can do. To live through things together" (p. 23), she says. Later she expands on her romantic dreams and the idyllic nature of their situation: "When I'm with you...I feel so strong. I feel like I know everything.... I wish I could stay up here forever" (p. 29). The woods are especially attractive because they are clean and quiet (pp. 18, 30) and because she feels freed from the masks and trappings of society[18]: "That's why I like the country. In the city we can never know each other really.... It's clean out here. ... You can see the way things are" (p. 30).

Nick seems content in their relationship, too, though more taciturn and even a little apprehensive: "All we have are insights. ... Who *knows* what's real?...They exist all independent of our efforts to explain them.... We cannot know it" (p. 27). Still, they retire peacefully.

Scene two take places at night. Now the needs of the two are patently at odds. Ruth is still verbalizing her dream: "I always wanted it to be like this.... With my lover. In the country. In the middle of the night. This is so beautiful." (p. 38). Nick's dream, "we would meet and we would just be happy" (p. 53) is more barren in detail and he has begun to tire of her constant talk, so he tries to take what he wants—and she has given freely previously. He tries to force her sexually. When she rejects his physical attack, Nick complains that there is nothing to do in the woods, even though Ruth has been cataloguing activities throughout the play. She has become a sexual objective for him and he cares about little else, thus becoming frustrated, bored, and uninterested in her. Ruth responds that he cannot force something merely because he wants it and that he does not treat her with respect; Nick tells her that she talks too much (pp. 61–63). Ruth tries to reverse the mood, presenting Nick with a gold bracelet as a symbol of her eternal love, but he rejects her. When he refuses her offer of sex as proof of her love, she feels that she must leave.

Reconciliation is at the heart of scene three. Nick does not want to break off the relationship completely, but Ruth does. Having wanted to know all about him, she now knows too much: "The worst part, maybe, is just learning little *things*. ... about each other" (p. 80). One thing that she learns is that the basis of his relationship with her is limited: "I want to fuck you" (p. 86). This statement brings a tirade from her in which she accuses him of not being a man, of having "bizarre" fantasies, and of being afraid (pp. 87–88); and in anger she tries to strike him with an oar. Instead, he strikes her, knocking her off the porch. This is the turning point in the play. The recognition of his physical violence causes Nick to regard Ruth as human again and for the first time he can expose his own vulnerability. His shock at having hit her brings a revelation of his dream which parallels the one that she articulated in the first scene: "All my life I thought that I would *meet* a person... She would say, 'Let us be lovers. ... /I know you./I know what you need./ I want to have your children.' ... I would fall down and thank God. ... We'd sit here in the Winter and we'd talk and watch the snow" (p. 94). He claims that he needs time to separate himself from the influence of the city, that he needs her and he equates being alone with death. Having expressed this understanding of himself, Nick admits that he brought Ruth to the cabin because he loves her and he can finally say "I love you." Ruth can now accept him and the relationship and the play ends with them hanging on, partly in love and partly in a desperate need to be together. The title of the play is taken from its setting, of course, but it also has reverberations with the Grimm fairytale of the two children who become lost in the woods and huddle together in each others arms in a vain attempt to comfort and support one another as they die.

Mamet is still young (he was born November 30, 1947), yet his work is consistently more imaginative, sensitive, and technically superior to the dramatists of his own generation and it surpasses in promise that of the previous generation. In the eight years that he has been writing he has produced several minor gems as well as a body of solid work. Clearly his style improves as he becomes more certain of his major themes. As he progresses, his plays reflect a more and more accurate and personal rendering of interpersonal relationships. As he becomes more concerned with his characters as people and less concerned with them as symbolic representations, his dramas become less abstract and more moving. His characters become less desperate and as a result more normal and real. And it is here that Mamet's greatest promise lies, for he has had an ability to write effective theatre from the beginning. His future looks bright; he is likely to become a standard against which his contemporaries will be measured.

NOTES

1. See T. E. Kallem, "Pinter Patter," *Time,* 12 July 1976, p. 68, for example.

2. David Mamet, *Sexual Perversity in Chicago and The Duck Variations* (New York: Grove, 1978), p. [73].

3. *Ibid.,* p. 97.

4. This is reenforced by the fact that there are thirty-four scenes.

5. *Sexual Perversity in Chicago.* Page numbers indicated parenthetically after references.

6. Richard Gottlieb, "The Engine That Drives Playwright David Mamet," *New York Times,* 15 January 1978, Sect. 2, pp. 1ff.

7. *American Buffalo* (New York: Grove, 1977). Page numbers indicated parenthetically after references.

8. Even though the chronology becomes slightly skewed here, I have chosen to consider *The Water Engine* and *Mr. Happiness* together since they were produced as companion pieces. The same choice was made in considering *Reunion* and *Dark Pony.*

9. David Mamet's New Realism," *New York Times Magazine,* 12 March 1978, pp. 40ff.

10. *The Water Engine and Mr. Happiness* (New York: Grove, 1978), p. [vii]. Subsequent references to the plays appear parenthetically in the text.

11. See the commentary in connection with the 1934 Century of Progress Exposition in Chicago, pp. 6, 11, 54, etc.

12. It is interesting that in the television production of *A Life in the Theatre* there were alterations made in the language to accommodate a non-theatrical audience: "cunt" became "witch," "Christ" and "shit" became "God," and "fucking" was deleted or changed to "silly."

13. *Two Plays by David Mamet: Reunion/Dark Pony* (New York: Grove, 1979). As noted above, I have chosen to deal with *Reunion* and *Dark Pony* together in spite of chronological problems because they were produced as companion pieces and published together. References to the plays appear parenthetically in the text.

14. In the television production scene 20 was incorporated into scene 21. *A Life in the Theatre* (New York: Grove, 1978). Page numbers are indicated parenthetically after references.

15. The back of the scenery in the television production indicates that the play is called *Doughboys*.

16. In the television production John knocks on wood after his audition in scene 14.

17. *The Woods* (New York: Grove, 1979). Page numbers are indicated parenthetically after references.

18. See her comments about clothing, p. 78.

Images of the Past
in the Plays
of Lanford Wilson

HENRY I. SCHVEY

With more than thirty plays to his credit since he began writing for the stage in 1963, Lanford Wilson is almost certainly the most prolific of the younger generation of American playwrights and among the very few who have made the transition from Off-Off Broadway experimental theaters (the Caffe Cino and La Mama Experimental Theatre Club) to widespread commercial and critical success. However, despite the largely favorable reviews his plays have enjoyed since 1973 (when he won the New York Drama Critics Circle Award for Best American Play with *The Hot L Baltimore*) and despite his continuingly productive relationship with New York's Circle Repertory Company of which he is a founder member and resident playwright, Wilson's plays have not yet received serious critical attention.

Wilson presents the literary critic with the uninviting paradox of a contemporary writer who has already produced a large body of work, yet is young enough to be characterized as a "developing" artist whose best plays have probably not yet been written. Nevertheless, in the plays that have appeared, certain distinct stylistic and thematic preoccupations are evident, particularly in the five plays written from 1973–79, which not only permit but invite detailed examination. Therefore the present essay, while making occasional reference to various plays written before 1973, will stress the essential thematic unity in Wilson's work from *The Hot L Baltimore* to *Talley's Folly* (1979).

Nearly all of Wilson's plays are about people who are outcasts or misfits of some sort. Thus, there is an obvious connection between early plays such as *Balm in Gilead* (1965), set in an all-night bar frequented by heroin addicts, prostitutes and homosexuals on Upper Broadway in New York, or the *Rimers of Eldritch* (1966), about the conservatism and prejudice in a small midwestern town, with later works such as *The Hot L*

Baltimore (1973) or *5th of July* (1978). All of these works have large casts and are essentially peopled by characters who have no definite place in society. But whereas the two early plays conclude with an essentially melodramatic act of violence (the stabbing of Joe, the shooting of Skelly), the later plays rely more heavily on concision, scenic imagery and detailed characterization; this is particularly true of Wilson's most recent work, *Talley's Folly,* which indicates a major development in the playwright's ability to create a work of delicacy and beauty.

Perhaps Wilson's most effective use of setting comes in *The Hot L Baltimore*, where the play's title (referring to the burnt-out "e" from the hotel marquee) is particularly suggestive of its theme. The hotel itself is a once fashionable establishment which has fallen into disrepair and is awaiting demolition.

> The Hotel Baltimore, built during the late nineteenth century, remodeled during the Art Deco last stand of the railroads, is a five-story establishment, intended to be an elegant and restful haven. Its history has mirrored the rails' decline. The marble stairs and floors, the carved wood paneling have aged as neglected ivory ages, into a dull gold...
>
> The lobby is represented by three areas that rise as the remains of a building already largely demolished.[1]

In an interview Wilson explained that the play was originally intended as a trilogy with the same rundown set to be used for each part, with each play set in a different American city. However the Circle Repertory needed a play immediately and the idea of the trilogy was abandoned. The present reference in the title to Baltimore and the importance of the declining history of the railroad in the play was described by Wilson as follows:

> Baltimore is the epitome, to me, of a city that was once really great and is now going to hell in a handbag. Do you know that Baltimore was once the first railway center in this country? That's why the lament for the railroad goes through the play.[2]

On one level the play is a lament for a bygone and beautiful past, for an America that has lost its vision and direction, and whose glorious past has been replaced by a decaying present:

> GIRL: Baltimore used to be one of the most beautiful cities in America.
>
> APRIL: Every city in America used to be one of the most beautiful cities in America.
>
> GIRL: And this used to be a beautiful place. They got no business tearing it down. (p. 129)

This sense of the present as wavering between an impressive past on one hand, and an uncertain future on the other, emerges as a central theme in Wilson's next two plays, *The Mound Builders* and *5th of July*; it is to be found, however, in *The Hot L Baltimore* as well, at the moment when the characters are speculating on the future of the doomed hotel:

> I wonder what's gonna be where my room is? I mean in that space of air? That space will still be up there where I lived. We probably walk right under and right past the places where all kinds of things happened. A tepee or a log cabin might have stood right where I'm standing: wonderful things might have happened right on this spot. (p. 41)

The hotel is, as one would expect, inhabited by outcasts and people who have not found their vocation in life; prostitutes, the old and weak, and the poor and homeless. In writing about this cross-section Wilson is exploring territory familiar to him from his earlier plays (*Balm in Gilead, The Madness of Lady Bright*, etc.). However, in *The Hot L Baltimore*, Wilson's focus is not so much on these helpless outcasts themselves, as on the glowing contrast between the world as it is (dramatically conveyed by the shabby decaying hotel), and a community of people who need to believe in something—whatever the odds. Although this may remind us of the central situation in Eugene O'Neill's *The Iceman Cometh* (a play with which *The Hot L Baltimore* has obvious similarities), it should be observed that while O'Neill concentrates on the unfortunate necessity of illusions and pipe dreams as a means of survival for the inhabitants of Harry Hope's saloon, Wilson stresses the importance of hope among his lost souls. As Wilson himself has said: "For me, *The Hot L Baltimore* is about losers refusing to lose".[3]

Nearly all the characters in the play are searching for something, "a relative, a memory, a fantasy or just some fugitive happiness",[4] yet most if not all their dreams are either worthless or fraudulent, like Jackie and Jamie, a domineering young woman with the "manner, voice and stance... of a young stevedore", and her weak, impressionable younger brother who are planning to practice organic gardening on a plot of land they have bought from a radio advertisement, only to discover that what they have acquired is worthless salt desert. Nonetheless, as Jackie screams when it is discovered that she has robbed Mr. Morse, an old resident of the hotel: "I got dreams, goddammit! What's he got?" Although the theft is not seen as justified within the context of the play, the dreams are. As a result, despite its almost unanimously favourable reviews and wide public appeal (a short-lived television series grew out of the play), its simple message wears thin, and its characterization is ultimately superficial.

The *Hot L Baltimore* is divided among those who can dream and those who cannot, and the author's own position being as unequivocal as it is, the result is highly schematic. One of the chief actions in the play concerns the attempt of a young man named Paul Granger III to locate his grandfather, who apparently at one time stayed in the hotel. However, as soon as he gets close to finding a clue, he mysteriously gives up the search. Having come to the hotel full of hopes ("I want him! I have room for him!") he suddenly leaves ("Doesn't really matter ... I got things to do"). The unmotivated decision to give up his search need not have been ineffective dramatically, but in this instance it feels too decidedly like the contriving hand of the dramatist.

In contrast to Paul's unwillingness to pursue his dreams to the end are the three prostitutes (each endowed with a heart of gold) who insist on following theirs. In particular, the character of the Girl (because she has not yet decided on a name) seems to be Wilson's representative of the need for hope, regardless of circumstances; as she says, "I want some major miracle in my lifetime!" (p. 92). Although she is clearly intended to be full of "romantic enthusiasm" as it says in the play's dramatis personae, none of the hazards of such an attitude toward life are shown, only its positive features. As a result, the character seems flat, sentimentalized and unconvincing, particularly given her chosen profession.

Characteristically, when Paul is about to give up his search ("He could be anywhere") she replies, "He could be somewhere", anticipating her speech near the end of the play which links Granger's unfinished search with the image of the decaying hotel and, by extension, with the declining values of the country as a whole:

> I could just kill Paul Granger. That's why nothing gets done; why everything falls down. Nobody's got the conviction to act on their passions ... I don't think it matters what someone believes in. I just think it's really chicken not to believe in anything! (pp. 140–41)

The play ends with a hymn to the need for belief as April, another of the prostitutes, takes Jamie, who has been deserted by his older sister, aside and teaches him to dance: "Come on, you're so shy, if someone doesn't put a light under your tail, you're not going to have passions to need convictions for (Jamie walks uncertainly to April)" (p. 144).

Jamie's last line, "Tell me how", indicates that not only has he finally broken free of his sister's domination, he is willing to begin to live. April's reply, the final speech of the play, accompanied by "a positive song with an upbeat" (p. xiv) from the radio, points to the play's essence, the need for vitality and hope even in a world where no hope exists: "Come on, they're gonna tear up the dance floor in a minute; the bulldozers are barking at the door. Turn it up Bill, or I'll break your arm. Turn it up!" (p. 145). As Wilson himself has said, "There is a lot of hope [in the play]. The image of April and Jamie drinking champagne and dancing, turning round and round in circles in the middle of a hotel that is to be torn down . . . that has to do with the acceptance of life, of mortality, but not defeat".[5]

In a work of art, however, an upbeat message full of hope is not sufficient, particularly when that message is as straightforward and superficial as it is in *The Hot L Baltimore*. The play is ultimately weakened by its overly schematic and sentimental approach to character, and by the author's insufficiently critical attitude towards his dreamers. When all is said and done, the fact of the hotel's demolition is far less felt dramatically than his characters' unreasonable faith, and as a result there is never a single moment of dramatic tension. A simple comparison with a play like Chekhov's *The Cherry Orchard*, (perhaps ultimately closer to Wilson's intention than *The Iceman Cometh*) in which something old and beautiful is similarly demolished to make way for something new, is revealing. In the Russian play, everything is complex and double-edged; and our response to the loss of what is beautiful is weighed against the uselessness and decadence of that beauty. In Chekhov's work, the characters' hopes for the future (even those like Ania and Trofimov who are young and "romantic") are always balanced against our awareness that these hopes are fragile and possibly doomed, and we are always aware that the characters exist in a world where hope is not always enough.

Unlike the naturalistic *Hot L Baltimore*, Wilson's next play *The Mound Builders* (1976) offers a far more complex structure in order to reveal the play's theme: the relationship of the past to the present on various different levels. The play opens in the study of Professor August Howe, an archeologist who is dictating into a tape recorder his remembrances of the failed archeological expedition of the previous summer to unearth an ancient Indian civilization in the hills of Southern Illinois. As his thoughts move into the past, the old farmhouse in which the archeologists and their families lived and worked is gradually revealed, first as a slide projected against the back wall of the study, then, as the stage lights shift and we move into the past, the house itself becomes the focal point of the action of the play.

Nothing in Wilson's previous dramatic work has prepared us for the complex time structure of the *Mound Builders*: a play about a search for an ancient past by the archeologists on one level, the play is itself presented as past action in the mind of Professor Howe, who is both one of the characters in the past as well as the narrator in the present. In addition, the juxtaposition between past and present time is suggested by the fact that the excavation site is within earshot of the construction of Blue Shoals Dam, so that the "scenes in the house are accompanied by a dense orchestration of sounds", including the "sounds of bulldozers and workmen preparing the lakebed, which will flood the valley".[6] As a result, Wilson poses a continuous series of questions simply by means of the play's setting: what is the relationship between the ancient "mound builders" and the archeologists who are trying to piece together their world in the present? In what way is our own civilization (suggested by the sounds of building which counterpoint the scenes inside the farmhouse) equally doomed to extinction just as was the legendary civilization of the "mound builders"?

Surely the fact that we know from the beginning of the play that the expedition has ended in failure, suggests that this play is heavily ironic, and that the hopes and dreams of the scientists eager for the fame of a great discovery is constantly undercut by the audience's awareness that this discovery will somehow never come to fruition. This sense of futility is also reflected in the set of the old farmhouse in which most of the action takes place, a structure not seen with photographic realism but with the mind's eye as a "house that lifted up like an ark as the lake flooded the valley and floated down some great floodstruck current, wrecking in another place" (p. 4). This image of the farmhouse as an 'ark' floating 'down some great flood-struck current', obviously suggestive and linking the deliberate flooding of the valley with the Flood in the Bible, is an accurate representation of Wilson's perspective in the play. On one level the play is about man's need to discover and to create, both in the past and in the present ("every society reaches the point where it builds mounds") while on the other it is about the inevitable futility that accompanies all such endeavors, whether in extinct prehistoric cultures, or in our own, which one day (it is suggested) may become as remote and mysterious as the Mississippian.

This basic dichotomy regarding human achievement — revealed in the ironic structure of the play — makes it apparent that Wilson is writing not only about a once glorious prehistoric civilization that is now extinct, but about our own "mound builders" as well; "the species crawls up out of the warm ocean for a few million years and crawls back to it again to die" (p. 88). Since these words are spoken by Delia Eriksen, the sister of Professor Howe, a writer who is now unable to create and has come to the excavation site as an invalid, they gain special significance for the audience.

Resounding through the entire play is the sense of the discrepancy between the limitlessness of human aspirations and the limitations of human achievement. When told that the lost Indian civilization he is searching for has "vanished without a trace", Dan Loggins, the young archeologist who is Professor Howe's assistant on the expedition, enthusiastically exclaims that: "Cochise did not disappear without a trace. I think we have palpable evidence of his craft, of a subtle skill and imagination, of his care and conscientousness" (p. 107). On the other hand, Dan himself has earlier quoted an anonymous Aztec poem which ironically stresses the transience of the achievements of which only scattered traces remain;

> Here are our precious flowers and songs
> May our friends delight in them,
> May the sadness fade out of our hearts.
> This earth is only lent to us.
> We shall have to leave our fine work.
> We shall have to leave our beautiful flowers.
> That is why I am sad as I sing for the sun. (p. 52)

If this ironic contrast between the dreams and achievements of mankind is the focus of *The Mound Builders*, it is an irony which must of necessity escape the archeologist who clutches each bone awl and shard of pottery as tangible evidence of the reality of glorious past; similarly, it is beyond the conciousness of the materialist who cannot learn from the past but can only think of the possibilities of the future.

In the *Mound Builders* this theme of the contrast between the need to build and the inevitable end to all building is relevant not only to the mysteries of the past but to our present culture as well. Wilson illustrates this not only through the fact that the dig fails or that the mound builders of the past are contrasted with the Dam builders of the present, but through his two central characters in the play, Dan, the young archeologist, and Chad, the acquisitive and materialistic son of the landowner who has leased the land to the university supervising the dig.

These two characters, one idealistically searching for keys to the past, the other, for the key to his own future, seem complete opposites but are in fact, intended as analogues for one another. Despite the differences in their education and background, they both enjoy fishing and getting drunk together, and both are in love with the same woman (Dan's wife Jean). More importantly, both see the digging site as bound up with themselves. For Dan, "they built the mounds for the same reason I'd build the mounds. Because I wanted to make myself conspicuous... For an accomplishment, honey, to bring me closer to Elysium; to leave something behind me for my grandchildren to marvel at. To say I'd built something!" (p. 22). Similarly, for Chad, the mounds represent fulfillment, not for what they contain, but as a means to wealth; "My land, baby! MY LAND! MY LAND! It don't belong to your Indian God... The mounds are going to be under about forty tons of highway interchange. They're going to be under a tennis court" (pp. 131, 130).

At the end of the play, these two opposing forces are brought into conflict through the sudden discovery of the grave of a god-king; "the most important find in forty years of work. We do not allow ourselves to dream of what we might find and dream every sweep of a trowel" (p. 113). But the discovery which offers potential fulfillment to the archeologists, threatens to destroy the dreams of Chad, and when he realizes that Professor Howe has secretly filed a report to the State Legislature having the site declared a national monument (thus re-routing the interstate highway on which he had pinned his hopes of wealth), his fear turns to panic: "Where do you get off thinking you're better than the people around here and can take over and take away everything we hope for—where—laughing about my god-damned island—what do you care. Millions! You're trying to steal from me!" (p. 133).

During the following night, Chad (wearing the mask of the god-king which Dan had earlier tried on as a joke: "Tell me I look like a god-king") lures Dan outside and kills him, commits suicide, and ruins the excavation by running over the site with a bulldozer. Thus the salvage operation which has suddenly yielded the treasure of a lifetime, ultimately salvages nothing. As Professor Howe remarks (in the present) while examining a slide depicting Dan: "prepared to conquer lost worlds with a doctorate in one hand and a trowel in the other. A man's life work is taken up, undertaken, I have no doubt, to blind him to the passing moon" (p. 113). The sense of futility suggested in these words is further conveyed by the fact that the bodies of Chad and Dan cannot be recovered. As a result, the phrase "vanished without a trace" which was often sceptically applied to the Mississippian Culture earlier in the play, is now ironically applicable to the two men themselves who for reasons of their own, have sought to make use of the mounds, either to mine or to flatten them. In the end, not only is the lost culture of "Cochise" an archeologist's dream, but the remains of Chad and Dan are now perhaps destined (with the deathmask) to provide a startling discovery to some future civilization.

In direct contrast to the life-affirming dance which concludes *The Hot L Baltimore*, *The Mound Builders* ends with the characters silent, the final words coming from the disembodied voice of Professor Howe's tape recorder; "In my mind's eye the river's currents swept the house before it as a great brown flood...The house looked more scuttled than inundated. The lake rises as a great long hand-shaped pond, slowly" (p. 148). This final haunting image of civilization washed away by the flood suggests once more the identity of past and present, and echoes the Aztecs' disturbing warning: "The earth is only lent to us".

The *Mound Builders*, a far more sophisticated and serious work than the more popular *Hot L Baltimore*, is nonetheless not without its problems for the audience. Indeed, its complexity has been paid for at a heavy price, and *The Mound Builders* is a play that is heavily flawed. This is not, however, a result of the intricacy of its symbolism as much as it is due to the turgid quality of the dramatic texture (especially in the first act) and the thinness of some of its characterization. Neither Professor Howe's wife Cynthia, nor Dan's wife Jean ever really emerge as convincing portraits, and their only excuse for being in the play seems to be related to Chad's having an affair with the former and a frustrated desire for the latter which is partly responsible for his hatred and jealousy of Dan. No such justification can be found for the presence of Professor Howe's child, who seems a totally irrelevant and wasteful indulgence. The other woman's role, that of Professor Howe's sister, Delia Eriksen, is carefully and concisely contrived, but her own artistic frustrations are only vaguely and unsatisfactorily linked with the play's theme. As a result, *The Mound Builders*, despite the interest of its theme and the breadth of its scope, is only partially successful as a work of art.

In *5th of July*, his next full-length play (in the interim he wrote the short one-act play *Brontasaurus*, a thin work which does not require extended exegesis), Wilson moves toward a far greater concentration in both structure and characterization. The play is set in 1977 and, although it has a large cast of characters ranging in age between fourteen and sixty-seven, is most particularly concerned with the generation who were in college during the turbulent years of upheaval in American universities in the late 1960s, the years of Vietnam, drugs and flower-power. Wilson's particular concern in the play is the changing attitudes of that generation from radical commitment to frustration, and from protest marches on the White House lawn to materialism. Although in some respects, as in *The Hot L Baltimore*, he verges dangerously close to caricature, on the whole Wilson is able to convincingly capture the language, style and manner of 1960s enthusiasm, now soured into the cynicism of the 1970s. Like *The Hot L Baltimore* and *The Mound Builders*, this play is about the past and its relationship to a tarnished present, as one of the characters says of that vanished era to her daughter: "You've no idea of the country we almost made for you. The fact that I think it's all a crock now does not take away from what we almost achieved".[7]

The four principle characters, survivors from Berkeley in the late 1960s, are now in their mid-thirties. John and Gwen are married and have replaced the world of flower-power ("I remember once we bought twenty dollars worth of daffodils and June and I ran up and down, giving them to all the stalled drivers on the Nimitz Freeway") and drugs ("How can you take that many drugs... and not have your brains fried?") with the materialism of the American dream; ("Look around you, wake up, for God's sake. You can buy anything!") (p. 120). June and Ken, who are brother and sister, have become equally disillusioned, but instead of materialism, have covered their frustrations with a mask of cynicism. Ken Talley, who has not resisted the draft and gotten both legs blown off in the Vietnam war, is clearly the play's central figure. Unlike Gwen and John who have pursued financial success, albeit with an "acceptable" counter-culture life-style as a pop singer and producer, Ken has entered the seventies a physical and emotional cripple, unable to come to terms with his past or to commit himself to beginning a new future. As his sister points out to him, "You're the only person I know who can say 'I'm not involved' in forty-five languages". Formerly, a successful secondary school teacher, Ken is afraid to place his crippled body in front of a class again:

> By prancing and dancing and sleight of hand, I actually managed
> to get their [his students'] attention off sex for one hour a day.
> They became quite fascinated by trochees, thrilled by Cyrano
> de Bergerac. But now I'm afraid my prancing would be quite
> embarrassing to them. (p. 42)

Nevertheless, beneath his fears and frustrations, Ken wants to return to teaching, as is apparent from the play's opening moments when he is found listening to a tape-recorded story by a pupil with a communication problem. Thus, the opening words of the play, sarcastically spoken by John, "Hey, teacher" reveal that Ken is as yet afraid to acknowledge his true vocation.

On one hand the play's theme is Ken's gradual acknowledgement of his fear of involving himself in life and of commitment to his true vocation, it is also about his acceptance of the past. The latter is visually conveyed by the contrast in the conclusion to Acts One and Two. The first act ends with Ken lying on the floor, doing sit-ups and being carried upstairs by his lover, Jed Jenkins. The act ends on a note of Ken's helplessness and defeat: "I really ...have done myself...in. I cannot teach those kids, Jed...We can't stay here...I can't walk into a classroom again..." (p. 72).

The second act also concludes with Ken on the floor, having been pushed over by his former friend John. Initially, Ken's reaction is one of complete terror, which quickly modulates into his particular brand of self-deprecating humour; "(Ken is nearly crying. Jed sits beside him, holding his hand) Jesus. That scares me. (Fighting tears) Falling backwards is the one thing the guys always — sometimes I think I'll never dance Swan Lake again" (pp. 125–26). But having experienced this fall and surviving seems to bring about a sudden decision to return to teaching ("I haven't worked out a syllabus"). At the end of the play he reads aloud from the young pupil's story which began the play, and expresses his own, newly discovered awareness of the need for commitment as the only justification for life:

"After they had explored all the suns in the universe and all the planets of all the suns, they realized that there was no other life in the universe, and that they were alone. And they were very happy, because then they knew it was up to them to become all the things they had imagined they would find." (p. 127)

This final plea for commitment to life echoes the circular dance at the end of *The Hot L Baltimore*, and reflects the playwright's own viewpoint on the need for involvement. But this scene is far more effective than its earlier counterpart, largely because the character of Ken Talley is so much more convincingly drawn as a human being than any of the hopeful outcasts in the earlier play.

Ken's dilemma about coming to terms with the past is not only expressed through the symbolism of his crippled legs (at a moment when accused of showing cowardice in front of a class he conspicuously says, "June, could you hand me my-crutches") but through the play's setting as well, which, as in the two plays previously discussed, has an important function in *5th of July*. The play is set in a large properous Southern Missouri farmhouse built around 1860, the Talley Place, which Ken now owns. The principal action of the plot of the play is Ken's desire to sell the house to his former friends, John and Gwen, who want to turn it into a mammoth recording studio. By focusing our attention on the sale of the house, Wilson suggests through visual means Ken's desire to flee from himself. Early in the play, Ken's Aunt Sally indicates that John and Gwen are not really interested buyers and that the real issue is Ken's responsibility to himself:

SALLY:	Oh, they aren't serious about the house. You're just going to have to stay down here and teach like you're supposed to.
KEN:	(*Overlapping*) Under no circumstances will I teach, and they are very serious about it, and you are not to say anything that will gum it up. (p. 16)

The character of the apparently senile Sally, who will return as one of the two characters in Wilson's second play about the Talley family, *Talley's Folly*, is included in the play to point out Ken's true vocation to him. Throughout most of the play she is bewilderedly searching for something, usually the ashes of her late husband Matt Friedman (the other figure in Wilson's next play). But instead of functioning as mere comic relief, the box with Matt's ashes which she intends to strew out over the lake, is symbolically connected with the importance of the "spirit of place" which is one of the play's chief motifs, and with Ken's decision to stay on and accept life as it is. As she says near the end of the play, anticipating Ken's own moment of self-awareness shortly afterwards: "Matt didn't believe in death and I don't either ... There's no such thing. It goes on and then it stops. You can't worry about the stopping, you have to worry about the going on" (p. 114).

Ironically, it is the apparently batty Aunt Sally who with these lines comes closest to Wilson's own point of view; and it is therefore significant that, having earlier said that "if Gwen and John are going to buy the Talley place, then Matt doesn't belong here", we learn, just prior to Ken's fall and subsequent decision not to sell the house that she has, aided by Jed, "scattered Matt all over the rose garden early this morning". Thus, Ken's final decision is complemented, as it were, by the ashes of Matt which serve as a "blessing" on the home he has decided not to abandon. Not only the place, but the time (Independence Day) is significant to the play's theme; and at the end of the play Ken has indeed achieved independence by accepting his past and for the first time in the play, talking with enthusiasm about tomorrow ("I've got to talk to Johnny Young about the future") and working his way, unassisted, although not without difficulty, toward the door.

In Wilson's most recent play, *Talley's Folly* (1979), the second part of a projected trilogy about the Talley family of Lebanon, Missouri (Lanford Wilson's own birthplace), he continues the development towards compact dramatic structure and increasingly convincing characterization already in evidence in *5th of July*. Unlike the plays previously discussed, *Talley's Folly* has a small cast of only two characters, and at first sight appears slight and even trivial in comparison with the scope of the earlier plays. However, the apparent simplicity of this one-act play is misleading, and "the fineness of its details makes up in penetrancy and persuasiveness for what it may lack in weight and impact".[8] In *Talley's Folly* Wilson emerges for the first time as a craftsman in complete control of his tools.

The play, which has no pretensions other than being "a waltz, one-two-three, one-two-three; a no-holds barred romantic story"[9] is about the romance which develops between Matt Friedman, a forty-two year old Jewish accountant from St. Louis, and Sally Talley, a thirty-one year-old nurse. Both these characters are familiar to us from *5th of July*, in which the aging Sally returns to the Talley Place bearing the box containing Matt's ashes. *Talley's Folly* is set thirty-three years earlier in July, 1944, and the setting, as in all of Wilson's recent works is of the utmost importance.

Having had a brief romance the previous summer, Matt has come back to seek Sally but has been run off the Talley farm with a shotgun by Sally's brother. He takes refuge in a gazebo-like structure built by one of Sally's eccentric ancestors Whistler Talley (known as "Whistler" not as a tribute to his artistic ability but because he sang and whistled), a man who "did exactly what he wanted to do" and built similar follies all over town "the way people used to build Roman ruins for their gardens" (p. 28). As the title of the play indicates, the appearance of the folly sets the tone for the entire work, poised as it is midway between the romantic and the absurd. It is "a Victorian boathouse constructed of louvers, lattice in decorative panels and a good deal of Gothic gingerbread", yet "nobody has any use of it anymore. You couldn't get materials now if you wanted to". Matt himself suggests, his interrogative tone betraying his own uncertainty, that "it isn't really grand, it's just silly. Is it not silly?", but as he comments elsewhere: "it isn't bombed out, it's run down, and the difference is all the difference'. As in *The Hot L Baltimore* where the stage set of the dilapidated hotel was instrumental in revealing the play's theme, in *Talley's Folly*, a play about two charmingly eccentric outcasts who fall in love, the set also has a vital function.

The contrasting elements juxtaposed in the folly's appearance are present in other aspects of the play as well. The lighting, for example, "should be very romantic: the sunset at the opening, later the moonlight slanting into the room ... the river reflected in lambent ripples across the inside of the room". On the other hand, the opening stage directions deliberately counteract this potentially excessive sweetness: "all this is seen in a blank white work-light; the artificiality of the theatrical set quite apparent". In addition, Wilson further undercuts the tendency towards overly simple romance by using Matt at the beginning of the play as a most un-romantic narrator (reminiscent of the Stage Manager in Thornton Wilder's *Our Town*) who deliberately makes us aware of the play's artifice; "we have everything to help me here. There's a rotating gismo in the footlights ... because we needed the moon out there on the water". In addition, Matt further makes the audience conscious of the dramatic illusion by repeating his opening monologue, at break-neck speed, "for the late-comers" (p. 2). The effect of this deliberate "Verfremdung" is not, as Walter Kerr suggests, simply to prove that "so long as the people on stage are alive and warm and breathing and warmly full-bodied, we don't require anything else to believe",[10] but rather to place the audience intellectually on its guard against the snares of romantic love, and then, in spite of ourselves to force us into believing in its truth.

Despite all its pretensions to the contrary, *Talley's Folly* is not a simple love story of boy gets girl, but as with Wilson's other plays written since 1973, it is a study of the characters' confrontation with the past and with themselves. The play begins with the narrator's setting the play at a time

(1944) when " 'peace and prosperity' are in the air; when that 'hope' the people had known (following the Great Depression) had been changed into the enemy. Peace, and more to the point . . . prosperity, is our ally" (p. 2). Both of the play's central characters, as in so many of Wilson's other works (most notably *Balm in Gilead* and *The Hot L Baltimore*) are outcasts. Sally, at thirty-one is the black sheep of her conservative, WASP Missouri home: "everyone is always saying what a crazy old maid Emma Goldman I'm becoming" (p. 22). Matt Friedman, the German-Jewish immigrant who has a "reading vocabulary" rather than a "speaking vocabulary" and has been chased off the Talley Place with a shotgun (you're Sally's Jewish friend, ain't ya? . . . Did you ever hear that trespassing was against the law?" p 8.) is seen as a "Communist traitor infidel" (p. 4) by the Talley clan.

In its simplest form, the play may be seen as the gradual unfolding and acknowledgement of the love between Sally and Matt which takes place in an environment as outlandish, extravagant and passionate as the lovers themselves. But at the center of this simple, innocent, and deliberately old-fashioned romance, is the reminder that people are essentially closed off to one another, and it is only through breaking down those barriers that real communication and love become possible. Thus behind both Matt's endless stream of wit, and Sally's apparent priggishness, lies pain caused by their experiences in the past. Like Ken in *5th of July* who must come to terms with his fears about the past before he can commit himself to the future, both Matt and Sally must make a confession before their love can be sealed.

Matt embarks on his confession about his past in the only way he can, by concealing it behind an apparent joke:

MATT:	This guy told me we were eggs . . . All people. He said people are eggs. Said we had to be careful not to bang up against each other too hard. Crack out shells, never be any use again. Said we were eggs. Individuals. We had to keep separate, private. He was very protective of his shell . . .
SALLY:	And you think he's right or you think he's wrong?
MATT:	. . . I told him he was paranoid. Ought not to worry too much about being understood. Ought to work at it. We . . . got our work cut out for us, don't we? I told him . . . What good is an egg? Gotta be hatched or boiled or beat up into something like a lot of other eggs. Then you're cookin'. I told him he ought not to be too afraid of gettin' his yoke [sic] broke. (p. 32)

Following this preface which reveals the purpose behind the story to follow, Matt narrates to Sally the history of his arrival in America. The story is told in a detached, ironic tone in the third person to mask its significance. But when Sally objects: "Matt, you're maddening — I don't know if this is a story or a — ", Matt replies firmly, "I will tell this, Sally, in the only way I can tell it" (p. 34). The narrative culminates in the truth about his past: the arrest, persecution and "indefinite detainment" of his parents by the Germans, his sister's being tortured to death by the French police, and his own arrival ("Norway to Caracas to America") on a banana boat.

Although Matt's bitterly ironic tone remains intact to the end of this third person autobiographical narrative ("There is always something thrilling about the broad canvas of a European story, isn't there?"), he deliberately reveals the reasons why he can never let his mask drop completely: "No allegiances would claim him any more, no causes" and his deep resolve not to "bring into this world another child to be killed for a political purpose". Matt's confession — "what I told you I have never before spoken for the same reason that you speak nothing to anybody, — because we are terrified that if once we allow ourselves to be cracked" — has been stimulated by his love and his knowledge that this is probably his last opportunity to secure Sally's love: "I said, Matt, go down, tell Sally who you are. Once in your life risk something. At least you will know that you did what you could" (p. 39).

Following Matt's confession, Sally is goaded into delving into her past: her abortive engagement to Harley Campbell, the tuberculosis which forced the engagement to be postponed, and finally the ensuing medical complications which meant that she could not bear children and caused her isolation from her family who saw in her marriage to Harley Campbell (now abrogated due to her forced childlessness) a prosperous merger of the two wealthy families: "Everyone came to the hospital. Everyone said it made no difference. By the time Harley graduated, the Campbells weren't speaking to the Talleys. By then Dad was looking at me like I was a broken swing" (p. 56). Following these parallel revelations of the facts behind their mutual isolation from other people and from one another, the "no-holds barred romantic story" is free to conclude romantically, as the band in the distance begins to play "Lindy Lou", and the lovers agree to go off together that very night. Both Matt and Sally are now fully aware of what the audience has known all along; that "we are a lot alike, you know? To be so different. We are two such private people" (p. 31).

If *Talley's Folly* seems a minor work in length, breadth and scope, this should not diminish its place as Wilson's best crafted work. Paradoxically, by trying to do less, the playwright has actually accomplished far more; by paring the work down to its bare essentials and creating two such convincingly alive characters as Matt and Sally, Lanford Wilson indicates for the first time the promise of a major talent. At the same time as it suggests a new development in Wilson's career as a dramatist, it is apparent that *Talley's Folly* is thematically and stylistically related to the other plays discussed in this essay. All of these works are concerned with the relationship between the individual and the past, and all of them (in contrast to Wilson's earlier works) use the stage setting metaphorically to suggest a special relationship between the characters, their past, and their hopes for the future. Thus, there are obvious connections between the soon-to-be demolished hotel in *The Hot L Baltimore* and the faded grandeur of the boathouse in *Talley's Folly*, just as there is a point of connection between the need for convictions celebrated by music and dance in the former work, and the act of communication which is accompanied by distant band music in the latter. What distinguishes Wilson's two most recent works, however, are his careful avoidance of clichéd sentimentalized characterization, and his willingness to refine, to hone, his dramatic world down to its bare essentials.

NOTES

1. Lanford Wilson, *The Hot L Baltimore* (New York: Hill and Wang, 1973), p. xiii. Subsequent references will be to this edition.

2. Patricia O'Haire, "That Seedy old 'Hot L' is still Packin' 'em in", *New York Daily News*, 30 Nov., 1975, Sec. L, p. 16.

3. Guy Flatley, "Lanford is One 'L' of a Playwright" *New York Times*, 22 April, 1973, p. 21.

4. Clive Barnes, "Lanford Wilson's *Hot L Baltimore*", rev. in *The New York Times*, 23 March, 1973.

5. In Flatley, p. 21.

6. Lanford Wilson, *The Mound Builders* (New York: Hill and Wang, 1976), p. 4. Subsequent references will be to this edition.

7. Wilson, *5th of July* (New York: Hill and Wang, 1978), p. 62. Subsequent references will be to this edition.

8. John Simon, "Folie à Deux," rev. of *Talley's Folly, New York Magazine*, 21 May, 1979, p. 77.

9. Wilson, *Talley's Folly* (New York: Hill and Wang, 1979). Subsequent references are to this edition.

10. Walter Kerr, "Three New Plays, One a Treasure", rev. of *Talley's Folly, The New York Times*, 13 May, 1979.

Mexican-American Drama

JOHN W. BROKAW

Before the Pilgrims landed at Plymouth, Spanish language theatre and drama came to stay in what is now the United States. Beginning in the sixteenth century conquistadors and priests used theatre to amuse, impress, and instruct themselves and their Indian subjects. The tradition they started continued under Mexican tutelege after Independence. Even after 1845–48, though perhaps with diminished force and altered form, the productions formed an important part of Mexican American culture. This chapter treats Mexican American theatre and drama; hence, the focus will be on the tradition since 1845 but one must appreciate the rich heritage from whence it came.[1]

Ancestors of Mexican Americans had lived in the area currently comprising the southwestern States of Texas, California, New Mexico, Arizona and Colorado for more than two hundred years before the Mexican War led to their absorption into this country. Before this, they had not had very close ties to the regime in Mexico City. Most scholars who have investigated this early period note the isolation of the northern settlements from the central government, a fact which explains those settlers' independent attitude, self-reliance, and pride in accomplishment.[2] They were for the most part left to their own devices both by the Spanish Viceroys and, after the revolution of 1810, by the Mexican government. To a large degree, especially in New Mexico, the society cleaved to tradition, developed apart from the rest of New Spain and revealed its distinctive culture through its art. Wood-carving, painting, music, and theatre all were supported by rather large popular audiences.

After annexation by the U.S., these communities remained more or less isolated from the Anglo American regime, partly by choice and partly by discrimination.[3] At all events, the Mexican American communities depended on their arts to maintain their cultural identity in the face of uncontrollable social upheaval which came at the end of the Mexican War. One of the more interesting ways they found to do this was in the production of plays which involved the participation of numerous persons in the community; thus they were a cohesive force in their lives.

The plays of the period before 1845–48, like those afterward, derived much from the Spanish *autos*.[4] Although the number of productions has declined in recent years, they continue to be produced to the present day. These religious plays since their inception were performed by amateurs—members of the parish in which the pieces were done, in the churches, and they treat religious subject matter. The most enduring and also the oldest of these is a Christmas play variously titled but commonly called *Las Pastorelas* which depicts the events of the Nativity. In addition to the Christmas play, other religious celebrations motivated Saints' plays and, perhaps most important, those of the Easter season when Passion plays were performed with such exuberance by the Penitentes, a group who depicted Christ's Passion with actual bloodshed, and by others with less illusionism.

Besides the religious drama which dominates the stage of the period, there were occasional secular amateur productions which featured illustrious historical events such as the defeat of the Moors in Spain. Along with such inspiring works, important visitors might be received with allegorical conceits performed as part of the welcome, but these occasional events reflect, rather than augment, the developing dramatic tradition. Significant productions were done in the religious sphere, not the secular, and their significance derives from their longevity and their reflection of the culture.

In addition to the plays, what some call the narrative line—the story of the people—was maintained in song (e.g., *los corridos* which are ballads whose popular topics reflect the attitudes and aspirations of the singers and their audience) and story (e.g., *los cuentos* or stories in the oral tradition some of which have been recorded in recent years). In the face of so few surviving plays from the nineteenth century, one infers much about them from the other parts of the folk tradition—the corridos and cuentos, at least with respect to the cultural values to which the communities subscribed. In this regard, we are indebted to such folklorists as Professor Americo Paredes who brought to light and print so much of the oral tradition, particularly that of the Texas Borderlands.[5] It is his contention that an important basis of Mexican American folklore, as evidenced by this narrative tradition, lies in cultural conflict with the English speaking majority in the southwest. Moreover, he suggests that this conflict stems from a growing sense of nationhood among Mexicans on the northern frontiers long before it existed elsewhere in Mexico. "Mexican nationalist feeling does not define itself until the last third of the Nineteenth Century," he says:

> and owes a great deal to the French occupation during the reign
> of Maximilian of Austria. In the northern frontiers, however,

and in the parts of the United States recently taken from Mexico, nationalism begins to be felt toward the end of the 1830's, if we may take the folklore of those regions as an indication. It is a blaze stirred up by the daily conflict between the quietism of the Mexican and the power, aggressiveness, and the foreign culture of the Anglo-American.[6]

Among the features of the corridos and cuentos from that time which Paredes identifies as indicative of growing nationalism are insulting labels for Anglos, hostility to their culture leading to rejection of it, and firm adherence to those values which clearly distinguished the Mexican American from the Anglo. "Under those circumstances," Paredes writes, "for a Mexican to accept North American values was to desert under fire," because, "the Mexican saw himself and all that he stood for as continually challenging a foreign people who treated him, for the most part, with disdain. Being Mexican meant remaining inviolable in the face of...attack of one's personality."[7] The relationship of the plays to this attitude perhaps can best be discovered in their close association with the Roman Catholic Church in the face of a Protestant Anglo society. One may wonder whether that association at times was more a refuge than a redan, but there can be no doubt that during the nineteenth century the majority of Mexican Americans derived most, if not all, their personal mores from the Church and her teachings. And those mores form the thematic spine of the early plays: devotion to family, subordination of self to legitimate superiors, and acceptance of God's will in all things. One notes the contrast between the rather fatalistic attitude in the plays and the more contentious one expressed in the corridos.

In the corridos, one finds indignation at the injustice Anglo society visited on Mexican Americans, bewilderment at the strangeness of that society, but at the same time a resignation toward the first and condescension toward the latter neither of which connotes a particularly belligerent attitude. The question would seem to be was there continuing and intense conflict from the first between Mexican Americans in general and the rest of American society or were the tensions between the two intermittent and localized? The evidence from the corridos would weigh on the side of continuing and general conflict; the plays would weigh on the other. Perhaps, however, we should note that, to paraphrase Lewis Carroll, a person may have six contradictory opinions before breakfast and hold them all at the same time. One may not, of course, dismiss as unimportant to their culture the opposition of Mexican Americans to discrimination and exploitation at the hands of Anglo American society; by the same token, it is no less important that Mexican Americans hold other and sometimes contradictory values which also played a role in the formation of that culture. And these latter values are most clearly seen in the religious plays.

Beyond the amateur theatricals of the years between 1848–1910 there were also professional players touring productions of dramas from the international repertory.[8] As early as the 1860's in California and Texas, troupes of strolling players appeared occasionally to entertain those in the community who had a taste for literary art. Texas especially had a relatively large population of Mexican exiles during this decade when the French occupied their country. San Antonio, during Juarez' struggle against Maximilian, had an inordinately large population of exiled Mexican intellectuals and artists in residence who patronised these performances. Because these troupes were in the neighborhood, so to speak, they also performed at other cities and towns in Texas. In so doing, they cultivated an interest in and market for their productions among the smaller population centers in south Texas as well as northern Mexico. In the process, they built circuits which they continued to tour until the second quarter of the twentieth century.

Theatre historians have hitherto paid little attention to these circuits or troupes; consequently, research has barely scratched the surface of their operations and their contribution to Mexican American culture. What we do know, however, leads us to believe that they made three such contributions: first, they brought to popular audiences dramas from a variety of European and Anglo American cultures which presented a relatively more sophisticated spectrum of attitudes, values, and ideas than one could find in the religious drama of the day; second, since they performed throughout the year, the troupes provided rather more theatre and drama than the churches thus making their performances a more extensive part of the cultural fabric than the one or two church performances each year could have done; and third, as a consequence of their appeal and accessibility, the troupes built a large enthusiastic audience among Mexican Americans for theatrical art of a rather high order. The manner in which these contributions were made had just recently been discovered and bears brief retelling here.

The troupes themselves, as a rule, were family enterprises headed by the senior member. That person arranged the tours which included bookings, transportation, and logistics. Before and during the tours, he or she also supervised the training of younger members of the company and rehearsal and performance in general. In this regard, they were not directors in the sense that the term is used today, nor was one necessary then. An actor prepared his roles, all much alike, as a combination of techniques and methods that remained more or less constant through all the plays in which he appeared.

This was not unique to Mexican companies; ordinarily, professional actors throughout the Western World in the nineteenth century, prepared a "line of business" and played that line of characters during their careers. The names and requirements of the lines might vary from country to country and time to time, but they had much in common. For example, in the sort of small touring company that one finds in south Texas in the nineteenth century, an actor had to have two lines or more: one for serious plays, one for comic ones, and perhaps an entertainment speciality into the bargain such as singing, dancing, playing a musical instrument, or all of them together, The same would have been true of strolling players in Britain, Russia, or for that matter Anglo companies in Texas. Since the bill offered several items in addition to plays, namely corridos and other entertainments, the actors had to be both versatile and energetic; that is, they had to contribute to a variety of productions and to do so with sustained enthusiasm. The bill, however, changed frequently; sometimes each performance differed from the last. One result of this was the distilling of an actor's many characters into an amalgamation—in short, he intended to do more or less the same things from role to role. Each role might have certain unique features, but in contrast to our own day had more in common with its fellows than not.

Actors who achieved success in their careers did so in part by capitalizing on their natural gifts—namely, physical attractiveness, vocal presence, and talent—and in part by cultivating performance skills through assiduous practice. The surviving members of these troupes speak of the arduous rehearsal periods in which the manager would repeat a scene again and again until the actors reached his expectation. During these rehearsals, the actors overcame or at least minimized their deficiencies, carefully constructed their performances, and developed a capacity to play for a variety of tastes.

Many of their performances on both sides of the border were for persons in the lower classes; e.g., agricultural and urban workers and their families. This last is an important point: the Mexican professional theatre in the United States was a family enterprise on both sides of the footlights. It served to reinforce those cultural values associated with family life characteristic of Mexican Americans. As such, instead of having to quiet opposition, these companies were welcomed heartily by all sections of the Mexican American community. This stands in stark contrast to the Anglo American troupes who frequently met implacable hostility from religious groups especially who saw the theatre as a threat to morality.

In addition to supervising rehearsals, the manager also ordered costumes and scenery, saw that they met the criteria set forth, and oversaw their maintenance and storage. Much of the wardrobe came along on tour in the wagons; the same is true of the scenery. Attrition wore away at both; hence, replacements had to be acquired on the road and the manager saw to this.

In order to facilitate the troupe's operations, an advance man usually was hired to precede the company by a day or two. He arrived at the next town in time to secure licenses, permits, materials, and performance space. Few occasions saw these troupes in theatres: most often they rented and refurbished a hall. The preliminaries taken care of, he built a playing space in the hall to accommodate both the performers and their auditors as conveniently and commodiously as possible. The stock of scenery or that part needed for the first performance usually accompanied him and, after erecting a platform at one end of the playing space, he arranged the scenery on stage. So that the audience could appreciate the scenery and the performance, the advance man cum stage manager also arrayed lights in appropriate locations about the house. Although on some occasions after the turn of the twentieth century electric lights were available, most of the time before and afterward the lights were kerosine lamps. After he set the stage, lighted the lamps, and saw to it that the technical side of the production was ready, the advance man might also take a role in the performance before he set off on the next leg of the itinerary.

The relatively elaborate production efforts supported a cosmopolitan repertory. Plays from Europe, especially Spain and France, outnumber those from Germany, England and other countries. One even finds an occasional piece from the United States, but not many. Since cataloging of the plays is in its early stages, our evidence concerning the general repertory is based on that of only the most prominent troupes rather than on a list of all the plays performed. Still, some tentative conclusions are possible beyond saying most of the plays came from Europe. For example, most of the plays depict thrilling melodramatic actions which threaten the heroes and heroines with great danger, but through perserverence, faith in God, and good luck, they vanquish their enemies to end the plays on happy notes. Such melodramas formed the bulk of most nations' repertories during the nineteenth and early twentieth century; thus, the Mexican American community was not completely an island. By and large, it was part of the main, thanks to the theatre. That its performances were conducted in Spanish and that most of the foreign plays originated in Spain differentiated it from Anglo American theatre; that it was performed outside Mexico and included corridos and cuentos from the Borderlands differentiated it from the metropolitan theatre of Mexico City.

Generally since the Second World War, scholars have noted that the area for hundreds of miles on either side of the political frontier between

Mexico and the United States has geological, climatic, and social cohesion. In most places along its route, the frontier itself is merely an imaginary line which can be and regularly is ignored. So this zone has come to be called the Borderlands and incidentally forms the territorial limits of the professional Mexican theatre troupes in the southwestern United States. During a typical nineteenth-century tour, a troupe would begin in the small towns of Tamaulipas, Nuevo Leon, or Coahuila in the spring of the year. As the weather moderated, it would cross the Rio Grande to southern Texas appearing at various locations in that State and then return to Mexico late in the fall. Such a tour would last eight to nine months and have between one hundred to one hundred-fifty performances. The majority of these performances took place in different towns, but in such cities as Reynosa, Monterrey, and San Antonio the companies might stay as long as a week. During such a week, they would stage as many as four performances, but more often only three. The titles changed daily and more or less the same audience came to see each production.

This relationship between the Mexican theatre and Mexican Americans might have gone on much longer than it did but for two events: the first was the Mexican Revolution of 1910 which forced large numbers of Mexicans to flee their homes for refuge in the United States. In the chaos that followed, the itinerant troupes found that they were better off in the United States than in Mexico and the best of the lot settled in cities with large Mexican and Mexican American populations such as San Antonio and El Paso. There they found sufficiently large audiences to justify prolonged resident seasons, restricting their tours to a few weeks each year. Those marginal troupes not capable of competing for audiences with these metropolitan companies either disbanded or continued to tour through the year providing a continuity for the rural audiences. The second event which marked the end of this theatre occurred in the 1930's: the Depression. This economic disaster struck hard at the Mexican American community and there was little money left after the necessities for tickets to the theatre.

After having become part of the Mexican American communitues and providing resident theatrical fare for over twenty years, the companies went out of business. Many of the members, however, continued to work in the amateur productions staged in the churches and by civic associations. Their expertise raised the esthetic quality of these occasions. For the next generation, however, there were only a few productions of a professional nature in the southwestern states and those, as they had been a hundred years before, came from Mexico. The most important of these tours was managed by Virginia Fabregas, the famous actress and director from Mexico City, who conducted a brief tour in 1931. But this and the others were fleeting and evanescent manifestations of the Mexican theatre. The movies imported from Mexico played a more important role in maintaining the dramatic ties between the Mexican American community and Mexico.[9]

Between the 1930's and the 1960's, the imported movies and the continuing amateur productions formed the bulk of Hispanic theatrical fare available to Mexican Americans; there was Anglo American theatre in abundance, of course, but it is difficult to know in the absence of research what effect this had on Mexican American tastes and attitudes. In 1965, however, Mexican American theatre reemerged in the fields of California and spread quickly throughout the southwestern States.

The spark that ignited this rebirth came from the agricultural workers' strike led by César Chávez. Many Mexican Americans, disenchanted with American society's discrimination against them, saw *la huelga* (the strike) as the opportunity to redress grievances. Among the most active in support of Chávez, Luis Valdez came to the picket lines at Delano and began producing theatrical events, using student actors and the strikers themselves, improvising the dialog and action to depict those incidents in which the issues of the strike were clearly evident. "Anything and everything that pertained to the daily life, la vida cotidiana, of the huelgistas [the strikers]," Valdez wrote, "became food for thought, material for the actos."

> the reality of campesinos [farm workers] on strike has become dramatic ... and so the actos merely reflected the reality. Huelgistas portrayed huelgistas, drawing their improvised dialogue from real words they exchanged with the esquiroles (scabs) in the fields everyday.... The first huelgista to portray an esquirol in the teatro did it to settle a score with a particularly stubborn scab he had talked with in the fields that day. Satire became a weapon that was soon aimed at known and despised contractors, growers, and mayordomos. The effect of the early actos on the huelgistas de Delano packed into Filipino Hall was immediate, intense, and cathartic.[10]

Valdez used his "weapon" quite effectively in support of the strike, but when it was won, he continued his work apart from the United Farm Workers, as the union was then called, by founding a cultural center in San Juan Bautista, California which housed a group of actors—el Teatro Campesino, and others who shared their esthetic and philosophical interests. Since 1966, Valdez has written several actos in finished form and has turned to other dramatic styles and types. None of these other plays, however, has surpassed the effect or the attraction of his actos.[11]

"The Acto," Valdez stated, "developed into its own structure through five years of experimentation."

It evolved into a short dramatic form now used primarily by Los Teatros de Aztlán [that part of the United States which was ceded by Mexico during the nineteenth century], but utilized to some extent by other non Chicano guerilla theater companies throughout the U.S. including the San Francisco Mime Troupe and the Bread and Puppet Theater. (considerable creative crossfeeding has occurred on other levels, I might add, between the Mime Troupe, the Bread and Puppet, and the Campesino.) Each of these groups may have their own definition of the actos, but the following are some of the guidelines we have established for ourselves over the years:

ACTOS: Inspire the audience to social action. Illuminate specific points about social problems. Satirize the opposition. Show or hint at a solution. Express what people are feeling.[12]

After the success of Teatro Campesino at Delano, scores of other Teatros sprang up in most Mexican American communities in the Southwest. Modelled on Campesino, they used Valdez' actos, improvised on themes of local importance, and gave voice to numerous grievances they had concerning injustice, discrimination, and exploitation by American society in general. Most of their members were young students who had the interest and capability to operate such demanding ventures as a teatro. The zenith was reached during the years from 1966 to 1976; afterward the number of troupes has declined. Even today however, there are several excellent troupes including Campesino who make up in quality of production what Teatro Chicano now lacks in numbers. What initiated the movement to organize Teatros and held it together for so long is the acto. It formed the basis of every Teatro's repertory. Valdez notes that many antecedents precede Teatros Chicanos in seeking to realize these goals. He and others have identified groups and traditions which begin in the ancient world, extend through the medieval period, the Renaissance, and more recently can be seen in the works of Shaw, Brecht, Odets, and a host of other dramatists with a social message. Like his most recent antecedents, Valdez pictured himself as part of a social movement which aimed at the transformation of American Society into a more congenial place for Mexican Americans, among others, to live. His drama put in immediate and powerful form his views of present injustice, discrimination, and exploitation in American society. His purpose was to change it, but he said only by the dramatist developing a "social vision, as opposed to the individual artist or playwright's vision" can the acto achieve its purposes.

At the outset of his career as a playwright, Valdez set his sights on the victory of the campesinos in the vineyards of Delano. After that triumph, he aimed much higher, namely at transforming the whole of American society. Some of the effects of his shift in goals can be seen in the actos he chose to publish in 1971 in *Actos: El Teatro Campesino* which was the first published anthology of Chicano drama.

In that volume Valdez placed nine pieces written between 1965 and 1971. Their subject matter includes the farm workers' strikes *(Las Dos Caras del Patroncito, Quinta Temporada,* and *Huelgistas),* assimilation of Mexican Americans into Anglo American society *(Los Vendidos* and elliptically *La Conquista de México* which draws parallels between the Spanish devastation of the indigenous Aztec culture and the Anglo American assaults on Mexican American culture), the dysfunctional schooling of Mexican American children *(No Saco Nada de la Escuela* and *The Militants),* and the last two treat the impact of the Vietnam war on Mexican Americans *(Vietnam Campesino* which points out the similarities between Mexican American and Vietnamese farm workers, both of whom are being exploited by Anglo American business interests and *Soldado Razo* which depicts the events in the life and death of a Mexican American draftee).

Among these plays, one finds a variety of subjects, themes, and approaches. For example, although Valdez began improvising actos in the fields of Delano which dealt with quite localized incidents, six years later his concerns had broadened to include urban and international as well as rural issues; moreover, he composed his scripts rather than depending on the inspiration of the moment. These changes reflect other, quite fundamental ones in his view of his work. During the first years of his career, Valdez was at pains to set his actos in a political, rather than an esthetic context. He said in an interview published in 1967, "art" was not a consideration in his plays and his only concern was "political,"[13] and yet this was not entirely true even then. "We know," he remarked in that same interview, "when we're not turning on the crowd. From a show business point of view that's bad enough, but when you're trying to excite crowds to go out on strike . . . it gains added significance."[14] It might be more accurate, then, to say that his purpose was obviously political but was served by artistic means consciously from the first and that he worked for six years to refine them, as evidenced by the anthology itself.

By 1971, in fact, he had reversed political purpose and esthetic effect in his work. Instead of direct agit-prop, he then saw a different kind of theatre:

> Not a teatro composed of actos or agit-prop but a teatro of
> ritual, of music, of beauty and spiritual sensitivity. A teatro of

legends and myths. A teatro of religious strength. This type of theater will require real dedication; it may, indeed, require a couple of generations of Chicanos devoted to the use of the theater as an instrument in the evolution of our people.[15]

As a consequence of this altered attitude, Valdez began writing a new kind of play. The acto remained the mainstay of the repertory of the teatros, but drama of a more mystical sort began to appear. Valdez went to Aztec mythology, Christian doctrine, and Mexican folklore. Out of this came what some have called an idealization of the past, but which Valdez called mito, a mythical depiction of the Mexican American's past, present, and future as seen in a microcosm of the play. The mito was not to displace the actos, but in Valdez' words "the two forms are, in fact, cuates [twins] that complement and balance each other as the day goes into night, el sol la sombra, la vida la muerte, el pájaro la serpiente." He then explains that his rejection of white western European types of theatre requires him to invent new ones: "thus, los actos y los mitos; one through the eyes of man; the other, through the eyes of God."[16] Whatever one cares to believe about the conceptual originality of either actos or mitos as dramatic types, clearly the blending of them in the same play as Valdez does in *La Gran Carpa de los Rasquachis* is unusual.

La Gran Carpa has gone through several versions through the years as Valdez responded to criticism directed at its weaknesses; thus, being a work in progress, it defies final judgment. Still, one may catch a glimpse of the conception of acto-mito at work. It is divided into three parts: the first and last are mitos and the middle is an acto. The play opens with the protagonist, Jesús Pelado de Rasquachi encountering the Virgen de Guadalupe and other characters from the pre-colonial period who perform a dance of conquest which depicts the popular historical uprisings among the people of Mexico against their oppressors down to the time of Pelado de Rasquachi. The stage is then set for the acto in which Jesús, a farm worker, confronts a series of incidents in the fields and is forced to choose between joining the union and its strike or scabbing for the growers. He chooses the growers and by so doing betrays his predecessors among the Aztecs and Indians who fought oppression in the first part, loses his family, and descends into misery and despair.

The third part or final mito begins with Jesús' death. The Aztec Sun god resurrects him and Jesús asks if his life is now over to which the god replies, "what do you say?" Jesús shouts, "No!" and the scene reverts to the occasion of his defection from the workers' cause. He has another chance to join the union and this time he does, is reunited with his family, and becomes a part of the historic parade of mestizos who have fought against oppression, first against the Spaniards and now against the Anglo Americans.

There is obviously a fusion of the thesis piece and mythologizing in this play. The nature of the myth, its meaning, and function are not so clear. In fact, when the play was presented at the Fifth Festival of Chicano Theater Groups (Mexico, 1974) the audience was confused to some degree by the changing identities of some of the characters: The Virgen de Guadelupe, for instance, becomes at times the Aztec goddess Tonantzin and other Christian figures become Aztec mythological ones.[17] The point of this was to fuse the two traditions into one and the inclusion of stereotypical — others might say archetypal—Chicano characters in the play was an attempt to transcend the limitations of time and space and place the action in an intellectual context somewhat broader than the daily polemics of the Chicano Movement. Opinions vary as to the degree of his success or failure in this regard.

Some charged that he had lost touch with the Chicanos' past; that in fact he was idealizing it by ignoring the rather unsavory parts and exaggerating or inventing the good. A superficial knowledge of the Aztecs includes the facts that a small elite class ruled the vast majority; tribes conquered by the Aztec forces were ruthlessly subjugated and exploited; human sacrifice in prodigious quantities kept the lower orders of society both amused and controlled; and social mobility was nil. In light of this, at least one commentator was moved to ask what place would Chicanos have in such a society; hence, what interest should they have in this part of their past?

On the other hand, some found the idealization useful in placing the Mexican in a broader historical and philosophical context. There were, they argued, useful parallels between Aztec mythology and Christian faith; thus, the European missionaries in a sense brought coals to Newcastle. Beyond that, it was asserted, the pre-Hispanic Indian realized the Christian ideal in his daily life. He lived in a spirit of freedom, but he was committed to a social and communal life rather than to one of selfishness and individualism. In this society, all individuals had full equality; thus, love and brotherhood dominated their cultural values. This Utopian view of the Aztecs does not mention social flaws, such as they were, because the point seems to be that this society was superior to that European one which replaced it. Today, therefore, Chicanos ought to realize what they once had and seek to restore it through communal action emphasizing love and brotherhood, at least for one another if not for their oppressors.

The controversy has not been resolved between the two points of view, and of course cannot be until American society finally does succeed in ending oppression of minorities, offer genuine equality to all its people, and achieve a just balance between individual freedom and social imperatives by implementing one or the other plan. In other words, the goals are clear and widely accepted by society at large, but the means to achieve them remain a subject of controversy.

At all events, Valdez has moved on to other equally controversial experiments in drama. Most recently, he wrote and produced *Zoot Suit,* a musical piece concerned with an incident which occurred in California during World War II involving the brutal beating of a Mexican American youth by members of a rival gang who are put on trial for the crime. The judge, an Anglo American, exhibits a virile racial prejudice against the accused, so skewing justice that even though they are convicted in his court, the higher court reverses the him and frees the defendants. The play opened at the Mark Taper Forum in Los Angeles to enthusiastic reviews and audiences. It was seen as a poetic expression of high quality of the Mexican American point of view. Although it was large, the play's appeal was not universal.

Some commentators saw caricatures instead of characters, simplistic instead of symbolic issues, and more intention than realization in the drama as a whole. Be this as it may, the play ran for many months in California and Valdez was moved to stage a version of the piece in New York at the Winter Garden Theatre. It opened there to unanimous condemnation from the press, tepid audience response, and it closed quickly. Still, it is the first play to reach Broadway by a Mexican American dealing with that ethnic group's particular point of view. Those who do not share that viewpoint may see it as self-serving or sophomoric, but it would probably be an error to dismiss it out of hand.

Beyond question, Luis Valdez today is the most respected Mexican American dramatist. His development as a writer and director has taken him from the fields of California to Europe, from the back of a flatrack truck to the Broadway stage. He has combined his skill as a performer with his insights into the Mexican American culture to generate a different type of theatre for our day; one that cannot be found among any other ethnic group in this country although the Black theatre comes close. He has done much of this on his own, but not all; he comes from a long and illustrious line. Despite his and others' general acknowledgement of Teatro Chicano's debt to the past, few realize either the nature of that debt or the dimensions of the tradition of Spanish language theatre in the Southwestern States.

Most ethnic groups who immigrated to the United States brought a type of their native theatre with them. Those transplanted institutions flourished for a time, but as succeeding generations lost interest in "the old country" the non-English speaking theatre companies closed their doors forever. The Germans, Italians, Scandinavians, Jews and others all had their days of theatrical activity on the American stage and then passed into fond memory. The Spanish language theatre in the Southwest alone has continued to produce dramas of significance to their audience, generation after generation, from the sixteenth century to the twentieth. There have been, of course, changes through the years, but a remarkably stable core remained constant. For example, the religious amateur dramas were the first plays to be staged and they continue to be staged today. The appeal they have for the community lies partially in their involvement of so many members of it as actors, scene-costume-prop makers, and auditors. In addition to the social cohesion this provides, the plays also present in an enjoyable manner a number of truths which the community holds dear. And finally, the plays represent a tradition, a continuity with the past that the communities are proud of and wish to maintain.

The Mexican American communities have been hospitable to travel-ing professional companies from Mexico over the years. These troupes kept open the conduits of Hispanic culture in the Southwest, especially the literary and artistic aspects of it. Since they traveled from town to town, they were able to subsist on relatively small capital investments and could thus keep their ticket prices low enough to exclude few who wanted to see them. As a consequence, persons from all social classes patronized the Mexican troupes whose bills give ample evidence of that fact in the spec-trum of entertainment they offered of an evening: dramas, farces, corridos, dances, and monologues. No matter what one's taste might be, something on the bill would appeal to it. Moreover, since these enterprises were family affairs and since their dramatic fare promoted family life, they offered one of the very few forms of recreation in which the entire Mexican American family could participate together. The other, of course, was the Church.

When one looks at the nature of Teatro Chicano, one sees several important parallels with this rich theatrical past. First of all, the use of music and dance along with the play has been a part of the Mexican American tradition from the first. The fact that most of the present Teatros use corridos merely reinforces a past practice. Corridos have been an important part of the Mexican American theatrical performance since the first professional companies began touring in this country. They used the familiar songs as a means to draw their audiences into a closer, more congenial relationship with themselves — strangers in town. It would be useful to know how many of the corridos, or verses of them, were origi-nated by the troupes themselves; however, corridos being folk songs have no known authors. In any case, the professional actors employed the corridos to enliven their productions, just as the Teatro Campesino does today. In fact, the format of the Teatros today is arguably the same as that of the professional companies of seventy years ago.

This is not to say that there are no differences between the Teatros of today and the amateur and professional troupes of the past. Obviously, there are major philosophical differences which in turn produce differences in practice. For example, a contemporary Teatro would perhaps be less concerned with the artistic or esthetic aspect of their productions than the professional actors; however, they probably have no less than that of the amateurs in the Church plays. In both amateur traditions, the message is more important than the means of its presentation. There is a key point to be made here: as long as a Teatro remains an amateur venture, it may do more or less as its members wish without considering consequences to any great extent. If the members of such groups have political goals for their productions, they must of course consider how best to motivate their audiences and not alienate them. It is certainly easier, however, to gain adherents to strong, not to say radical, political solutions to social problems if the audience is composed of strikers than it is if the audience is composed of casual observers in an East Los Angeles park or community center. This may account for the success of Teatro Campesino at Delano with respect to its stated purposes and its and other teatros relatively failure afterward. Some Teatros continue to repeat the actos from the sixties or variations of them, but many including Teatro Campesino have developed different means and new styles and types of drama. The best of the latter, including the Teatro Campesino, have turned professional and now have commercial as well as political goals, at least to the extent of earning sufficient money to allow them to work full time in the theatre.

Like their professional predecessors, these Teatros see themselves as repositories of dramatic art, resources for their audiences to draw upon for sustenance and pleasure. For awhile, they were content to work exclusively for the Mexican American community. But like their predecessors who sought patronage from all sections of the community because, one assumes, they welcomed everybody's money, Valdez and his associates evidenced a broadening perspective in the matter of audience when they opened *Zoot Suit* in the Mark Taper Forum and the Winter Garden. With this event, one can see an important change in Valdez' thinking about his audience and therefore his purposes, but more important than that is the fact that now Americans generally and not just Mexican Americans will have the opportunity to participate in the senior theatrical tradition in our country.

NOTES

1. At the outset one should realize that seemingly clear term — Mexican-American — is in fact not clear at all nor is it acceptable to many citizens of the United States with Mexican forebears. Through the years, several alternate terms have been advanced including: Spanish American, Mexican, Chicano, not to mention those who prefer to be called simply Americans. Each of these terms has political, sociological, or economic overtones which tend to cause signal reactions; therefore, for purposes of this study I propose to use "Mexican American" operationally as the most descriptive of the subject under scrutiny — namely, the theatre and drama of those who have Mexican antecedants and who live in this country.

2. See for example Cary McWilliams, *North From Mexico* (Philadelphia: J. P. Lippencott, 1961), pp. 63ff.

3. W. D. Altus, "The American-Mexican: The Survival of a Culture," *Journal of Social Psychology*, XXIX (1949), 211–220.

4. Arthur L. Campa, *Spanish Religious Folktheatre in the Southwest* (Albuquerque: University of New Mexico Press, 1934). This is the standard reference work on the religious drama and this study leans rather heavily on it.

5. See for example his *With a Pistol in his Hand* (Austin: University of Texas Press, 1958).

6. "The Folk Basis of Chicano Literature," *Modern Chicano Writers: A Collection of Critical Essays*, edited by Joseph Sommers and Tomas Ybarra-Frausto (Englewood Cliff, NJ: Prentice-Hall, Inc., 1979), p. 9.

7. *Ibid.*, p. 10

8. Much of this information has appeared in two of my articles: "A Mexican-American Acting Company: 1849–1924," *Educational Theatre Journal*, XXVII (1975), 23–29; and "The Repertory of a Mexican American Theatrical Troupe: 1849–1924," *Latin American Theatre Review* (fall 1974), 25–35.

9. Luis Reyes de la Maza, *El cine sonoro en México* (Mexico: UNAM, 1973).

10. Luis Valdez, *Actos: El Teatro Campesino* (San Juan Bautista, CA: La Cucaracha Press, 1971), p. 5.

11. There are, of course, other Chicano playwrights, but Valdez is the only one of national stature. He provides the leadership which all others acknowledge even when they do not follow it. There are currently four anthologies of Chicano drama on the market: Valdez' *Actos*; Roberto Garza, *Contemporary Chicano Theatre* (Notre Dame: University of Notre Dame Press, 1976); Jorge Huerta, *El Teatro de la Esperanza* (Goleta, CA.: El Teatro de la Esperanza, Inc., 1973); and Leon de Nepthali, *5 Plays* (Denver; Totinem Books, 1972).

12. Valdez, p. 6.

13. TDR, 11 (summer 1967), 78.

14. *Ibid.*

15. *Actos*, p. 3.

16. *Actos*, p. 5

17. Theodore Shank "A Return to Mayan and Aztec Roots," *The Drama Review*, XVIII (1974), 56–70.

Luis Valdez, Chicano Dramatist: An Introduction and An Interview

DIETER HERMS

I. Introduction

The interview that follows this introduction is history. It was conducted on December 14, 1978, in the small town of San Juan Bautista, California, where the Teatro Campesino has had its base since 1971 and where Luis Valdez now lives with his family. The interview took place at the hitherto high point of Valdez' career as the leading Chicano dramatist of today. His play *Zoot Suit* had then been running successfully since April 1978 in three different theatres of Los Angeles. I myself had seen it at the Aquarius Theatre, Hollywood, prior to the interview.

The interview consequently focussed on the genesis, on the shaping and the making of *Zoot Suit*, at a time when preparations began for taking the production to Broadway. While I was staying with the Teatro December 11–19, 1978, Valdez — although personally involved as director/actor in the Christmas productions of *La Virgen del Tepeyac* and *La Pastorela* — kept flying to Los Angeles to cast replacements in the Los Angeles *Zoot Suit* production for those actors who would be taken to New York. The interview is history, for *Zoot Suit* did run on Broadway, at the Winter Garden Palace, March — May 1979 for 58 performances. It closed at a loss of $825,000, clearly a "flop" by the tough economic Broadway standards. Thus the high hopes and aspirations expressed in the interview have been partly frustrated.

A fair amount of critical writing on the work of the Teatro Campesino as a whole has appeared in recent years[1]; so my introduction will shift its emphasis on Valdez as a person; although his own development as a writer and a dramatist is totally inseparable from that of the Teatro as an aesthetic instrument of political change and a cultural institution of Chicano philosophy. Valdez was born in Delano, California, in 1940. His parents were then migrant farmworkers, and Luis — along with his nine brothers and sisters — had to follow the crops around California. He started picking grapes when he was six.

Formal education was difficult under the conditions of the nomadic life-style of farmworkers. Yet Luis eventually managed to enter San Jose State College from which he received a degree in English and Drama in 1964. Luis' interest in theatre goes back to his early youth. "I was supposed to play in a Christmas program in the first grade but I never played in it because my family moved away before we performed."[2] By the time he was 12, he was already producing puppet shows.

Valdez wrote his first full-length play in college: *The Shrunken Head of Pancho Villa*, visibly under the influence of the San Francisco Mime Troupe's *commedia del arte* style, where the author had studied practical political theatre under the direction of R. G. Davis. *The Shrunken Head*, about the social struggle of a Chicano family, a kind of a "Chicano *Death of a Salesman*", received the acclaim from Valdez' fellow playwrights John Howard Lawson and William Saroyan. It was the historic grape pickers' strike in 1965 that afforded Valdez both the return to his birthplace Delano and the bringing together of his farmworker heritage and his dramatic interest: the founding of El Teatro Campesino.

The struggle of the United Farm Workers to establish the first union in the area of Agribusiness in the history of U.S. labor has been dealt with extensively.[3] El Teatro dedicated the first two years of its existence exclusively to the survival of the Union: theatre by, for, and about farmworkers, played from the back of trucks and in the fields, labor camps, and towns wherever the strike was, where campesinos had to be persuaded of the necessity of strikes in order to force the growers into the acceptance of the new union as the bargaining partner. Valdez wrote and directed the plays which were called *actos*, sharp satirical skits that were aggressive and funny; dramatizing the confrontation of patroncito and campesino; satirizing working and living conditions, exploitation, the grower-teamster alliance, the situation of the Mexican "wetback".

Simple popular devices were employed: signs, typical costuming, ropes, el cortito, the paper plane distributing pesticides, the allegorical personification of seasons, self-irony, "liberation through laughter"[4]. The *actos* were modified and expanded in the process of playing them until they were eventually published by the Teatro through their own distributing apparatus, El Centro Campesino Cultural.[5] One of the typical *actos* of the early phase is *Las Dos Caras del Patroncito* ("The Two Faces of the Boss")[6]. Valdez here juxtaposes capital and labor, grower and farmworker in a broad slapstick comedy wherein the two antagonists exchange clothes, accessories, and finally their respective roles. The political and educational objective of the piece (the farmworker audiences are meant to recognize themselves and their own existence in the farmworker on the stage; they are meant gradually to acquire self-awareness, dignity, and liberation from the authoritarian power of the patron) is achieved through the growing confidence of the actor in assuming the boss's pose, the cunning transfer of the boss's characteristics. But he doesn't take over the farm in the end; he only keeps the cigar — symbolic indication that the antagonism of property and exploitation will only be solved in negotiation, in the recognition of Cesar Chavez' farmworkers' union.

As early as in *Los Vendidos*[7] Valdez broadens the subject matter of his *actos* into the Chicano experience as such under the conditions of U.S. imperialism in the Southwest. Again, acting within the *acto*, exaggeration, satire, and farce are the pervading elements of the dramatic force. With biting irony Valdez ridicules the ready availability of the Chicano in his diverse functions to the "infinite variety" of needs and demands exerted by the white Anglo capitalist society. The completely Americanised secretary Miss Jiminez from Governor Reagan's office, looking for a "Mexican type for the administration" is confronted in Honest Sancho's "Mexican Curio Shop" with Mexican models: the farmworker model who lives on beans, ten in a shack, picks grapes, melons, cotton, who strikes and scabs, leaves for Mexico in the fall and returns in the spring, is rejected because he doesn't speak English. The urban Pachuco model used for the training of cops in the Los Angeles Police Department, is bilingual, riots, can be kicked, has an inferiority complex, and is rejected because he also steals. "We can't have any more thieves in the State administration." The "standard Revolucionario and/or Early California Bandit type" is rejected because he is not a genuine American product. Finally the Mexican-American model ("we had to melt down two pachucos, a farmworker, and three gabachos to make this model") is bought, but soon after explodes into revolutionary shouting. All models together chase the secretary away and Honest Sancho turns out as "the best model we got".

The cynical self-irony (the selling-out reproach among Mexicans in the U.S.; the recurring automobile metaphor in advertising the products) renders *Los Vendidos* a durable piece (it was also televised) which transcends the simple agitprop technique of the early *actos* and is still valid today. Valdez has repeatedly stated that his and the Teatro's work evolved in cycles. The first was the cycle of the *actos*, characterised by the close cooperation with the UFW and Cesar Chavez. But starting in 1967, Valdez — who sporadically taught drama at different California colleges and had always been in touch with the Chicano Student Movement — embarked on a new search for Chicano identity from which emerged the cycle of the *mitos*.

Mito means "myth" and represents the theatrical reflection of the Chicano's research into his indigenous past. Like the Native Americans of today, Chicanos are viewed by Valdez as the proud successors of the pre-Columbian American population whose culture has to be sought and regained, appropriated, as it were, as one's own heritage: "...the gringo is trying to impose the immigrant complex on the Chicano, pretending that we 'Mexican Americans' are the most recent arrivals. It will not work. His melting pot concept is a sham... We did not kill, rape, and steal under the pretext of Manifest Destiny and Western Expansion. We did not, in fact, come to the United States at all. The United States came to us."[8] Valdez' stance of cultural nationalism has been criticised as a retreat into religious cult. What is being neglected is that a growing awareness of national and personal identity is a necessary prerequisite of class consciousness of a lasting character, beyond the concrete struggle of the farmworkers against agribusiness.

The farmworker's base, the base of the Chicano *rasquachi*, is not lost in the *mito, corrido,* and *historia* cycles, it is simply put on a higher plane of historical complexity. The campesino and the pachuco are viewed as the more modern successors of the Mexican pelado, the "lumpen" who cuts through five centuries of oppression and emerges as the conscious Chicano who is now capable of recapturing his roots. Thus, *Bernabe, La Virgen del Tepeyac, La Carpa de los Rasquachis, Fin del Mundo, Zoot Suit*[9], have to be judged in terms of complementary elements of a both spiritual and realistic totality, all expressing in a corresponding manner the more complex reality of the U.S. Mexican today who is becoming aware of the specifics of his own philosophy and history. "*La Carpa*", Valdez explains in a letter to a friend, "exists on three planes; one involves the pre-performance setting-up the carpa time period, during which the actors appear as naturally as possible as la familia Rasquachi... The portrayals here are supposed to be realistic, in the tradition of naturalism (without the constraints of the proscenium box). The interludes between corridos, in which Jesus Rasquachi and later Maria Rasquachi (the mother) give speeches, are also realistic. The style of acting here is supposed to contrast greatly with the caricatures in the corrido, and the ritualistic movements of the mitos."[10]

La Carpa, the most mature piece of Valdez and El Teatro, developed collectively over a period of six years, has, after all, as its realistic base, the life and death of a bracero farmworker who — and this is the spiritual element — is inspired to join the Union, only in a resurrection scene, by the appearance of Quetzalcoatl, a technique, Brechtian in form, and Aztec in content.[11] Reviewers who criticise the seeming lack of politics in the Teatro of the 70s; fail to realise that in the long run, Valdez' new cultural nationalism is probably more radical and revolutionary than the merging with the short-term political struggle in his campesino agitprop art.

Myth and history are then, first and foremost, rediscovered and re-gained in Valdez' theatre of the 70s, in order that the producers themselves (El Teatro) and the audiences learn about their own cultural heritage and organize and structure their lives according to the new awareness. The revolutionary potential should be obvious. Aztec culture and the Mexican history of the oppressed under Spanish colonial rule may very well become an instrument of resistance and rebellion vis-a-vis the U.S. neocolonial power structure. For several years the Teatro has performed the old Mexican play (shortened and adapted by Valdez) *La Virgen del Tepeyac*, which shows the spiritual rebellion of an indio against the dogmatic rule of the Spanish Catholic bishops, inside the mission of San Juan Bautista, a mission built in 1797 to Christianize and repress the native Indian population of California.

History, furthermore, signifies for Valdez the critical artistic representation of Chicano life within the gabacho capitalist power system of the U.S.A. The subject matter spans from the early phase of U.S. appropriation of California in 1848 *(The Rose of the Ranchos)* to the life and acculturation of a bracero family *(La Carpa)* and finally the historical documentation of a murder case, riots, and a specific urban life-style in the Los Angeles of the early 40s *(Zoot Suit)*. These are segments of a more recent history that have yet to be integrated into a sense of continuity, as yet elements, fragments rather than a tradition.

Myth and history, of course, meant for Valdez the discovery of a richness of new aesthetic forms and devices. *La calavera*, the skeleton as a dramatic realization of the death figure was the most important single device to be reshaped from Aztec mythology. In 1972, El Teatro produced a play in collaboration with the "Mascarones" from Mexico City, entitled *Calaveras*, where the skeleton mask is founded in the mythical figure of Coatlicue, the Aztec goddess who represents the double principle of life and death, of the material and the immaterial, of decay and rebirth.[11] In *La Carpa* the death represents in conjunction with *el diablo* all those evil forces and powers the campesino is confronted with in U.S.: border control, contratistas, growers, teamsters, bureaucrats, businessmen, whores. In *El Dia de los Muertos* and *Fin del Mundo* (the "calavera" version) the skeleton becomes the central image of the play. The corrido, the Mexican folk ballad traditionally sung by the pelado is the most significant form for the Teatro to emerge from Mexico's history of the oppressed. Corridos are the "running commentaries" in *La Carpa*; they create historical depth, with regard to the life history of Jesús Rasquachi as well as Mexican history as such. This is heightened by the Aztec dances, expressive element of the

Chicano *historia* as well as the Indio/Spanish *historia* of the *Virgen* play. The swing big band sound and the caló lyrics of the Zoot Suit era form the folklore background of *Zoot Suit*. The Zoot Suit fashion originated in the black ghetto, but became rapidly a national phenomenon, and also seized the barrio. Valdez blends this all-American experience with the Chicano caló of the dialogue and the lyrics.

Mestizo Chicano history and mythology in its collision with Anglo imperialist culture and economy, ultimately, however, becomes a problem for Valdez. "We are translating all the research on Mayan philosophy we've done all these years in order to lay a philosophical base, and apply it to our approach to reality these days. It explains our aggression into the professional world. We are aggressively moving into the professional world; into film, into television, and of course, into the professional theatre."[12] The professional world — this of course also means: the commercial world. It means: the world of recognition by the Anglo establishment. It means: the ultimate step of "taking over". It is the grand vision — inspired by the old culture — of instrumentalizing the Anglo world (including its commercial aspects) for the far-reaching goal of reversing the US-americanisation of the *Mestizo indio* into a process of "indianizing" the U.S. Americans.

In California, Valdez is today a figure of public reputation. He serves as a member of the California Arts Council, appointed by Governor Brown, Jr. Sponsored by the National Endowment for the Arts, Valdez is a member of an advisory group to produce a study on the needs and conditions of U.S. theatre. He was virtually "commissioned" to write *Zoot Suit* by the "playwright in residence" award granted from the Rockefeller Foundation. Some of this shows its effects in the content of *Zoot Suit* and in the method of the play's commercial advertising for the Broadway production.

In the play itself Valdez fails to show the full political potential of the defense committee by reducing the Jewish Communist Alice McGraw to a protagonist in a trivial "private" love story and by overemphasizing the role of the white lawyer who binds the defendants to exactly that class justice machinery which had been responsible for their imprisonment. This "internal" evidence finds its corollary in an incident of cynical proportions when "selling" *Zoot Suit* in New York. As the *New York Times* reported, "Now, promotion efforts are branching out into the business world. Coca Cola has gotten into the act. In a few weeks, 50,000 Coke bottles will turn up on supermarket shelves wearing *Zoot Suit* collars. These collars will advertize what Coke is calling 'a night on the town', offering in exchange for six bottle caps discount tickets to the play plus a free dinner at one of six Riese Brothers restaurants..."[13] This must leave a bad taste in the mouths of those who know about the Coca Cola conglomerate's responsibility for exploitation, misery, and unemployment of Chicanos in the Agribusiness of the Southwest.

So there are controversial issues.[14] Leaving these controversies out of the interview provided an atmosphere of openness and trust, an opportunity for Valdez to speak out. His final statement, however, about Broadway being "part of the national expression right now" deserves a concluding comment. I believe that this assessment is out of proportion. Dependant on commercial profit only, Broadway, over the past years, has mostly produced musical comedies of a flat and purely entertaining nature. Relevant national drama, on the other hand, has emerged from the many community and university theatres all over the country and from New York ventures which must be labelled "off-off Broadway". Recent news has it, that the Teatro Campesino plans to take *Zoot Suit* on tour; a far more appropriate method to publicise relevant Chicano drama, which the play still represents, despite its faults.

II. Interview

Question

Luis, what made you choose the case of the Sleepy Lagoon murder in Los Angeles as a central example of Chicano experience in the United States?

Valdez

The case itself involves an image of the Chicanos and Latinos that persists to this day, an image that has been fostered in the national media for the last 35 years, the image of the Latino or Chicano as a street punk, a hoodlum, a juvenile delinquent. I think that racism is about anything, it's about the stereo-typifying of an entire group of people into a single superficial one-sided image. In this country, for instance, we have the Irish cop, or super-flying the blacks, and we have the juvenile delinquent, the Latin. There are other images that have served in the past, images such as the Mexican bandit, the farm worker, and then very little in between in terms of a national scope. And this image of the Chicano as a street punk is perpetrated and used in movies, on television, and it's in the popular imagination of the people of the United States. One of the curious things about this image is that it can be linked, I think, directly back to the Sleepy Lagoon case in 1942, because there was such an enormous publicity that was given to this case across the country, and particularly on the West Coast. It left a tremendous lasting impression of Chicanos as pachucos, who were young street guys who dressed in zoot suits and spoke their own particular form of language, of patois, slang, a thing called caló, which borrowed from the English and the Spanish, it's a patois all to itself, complete. It has other variations in other parts of Latin America. And so the reason that I dealt with it in *Zoot Suit* was because I wanted to attack it directly, I wanted to attack the stereotype of the Latin in this country directly, as the Teatro Campesino for the last 13 years has been attacking the image, the stereotype, of the farm worker. We were showing farm workers in social action, which was already changing the image of the passive, dazzled farm worker.

Question

You did a lot of research into the Sleepy Lagoon case. How did you go about that?

Valdez

You know, I have known about the Sleepy Lagoon case for almost 20 years or you might say: I have known about it all my life, because I was 3 years old and in Los Angeles with my family at the time of the *Zoot Suit* Riots, and I learnt from my parents later that we left Los Angeles, for one, because we were migrant workers, and we came up North to work on some crops and also because the situation in Los Angeles was very hard. I have known pachucos all my life. I learnt about the Sleepy Lagoon case in a book written by Carey McWilliams back in the 40s. A book called *North of Mexico*. I read that about 20 years ago. I was tremendously impressed with it. Some 10 years later, I saw a copy of a pamphlet that dealt with the case, and had more specifics, and a photograph of the guys. And I saw the tremendous theatrical potential in the material. But it wasn't possible to work on it then, for one thing: there were too many things to write about anyway in 1968, too many things to deal with the present reality and not to go back 20 years; and so last year, when I was approached by the Mark Taper Forum to write a play to be produced in their house, I began to think about a play on the Sleepy Lagoon case and the question of how to research came up, and we discovered that in the special collections branch of the library of UCLA there was a Sleepy Lagoon file and also Carey McWilliams' files were there. Also, the whole judicial structure of Los Angeles had records of the case as well as the newspapers, and so we were able to uncover a great deal of material in a very short period of time. A major decision came with regard to the transcript of the trial, which was available at UCLA, but which was 12 volumes numbering 6,000 pages of testimony.

So the Taper provided a young woman who went to UCLA and xeroxed the whole 6,000 page transcript, which was sent to me regularly in the mail — 12 volumes — and once I got my hands on it I began to read that thoroughly, completely, backwards and forwards. I also, through contact with the lawyers — some of the lawyers that worked on the case, the appeal lawyers, George Shibley was one, who became one of the characters in the play — managed to get hold of additional materials including the appeal brief, which summarized the trial and the violations of judicial procedure, and it showed why the appeal was granted.

Question

You also interviewed people, right?

Valdez

And then there was a whole series of interviews, in which we went around and talked to living members. The one thing that is curious is that we weren't able to contact any of the guys who were actually in the case. They seemed to be shying away from us. I understand that better now, because even to this day there are some of the actual guys who were in the case — they are in their 50s now — who don't want any publicity. In many cases the families don't even know that their father, or uncle, or grandfather, was in this case, and they don't want it exposed. So I am trying to respect that. Some of them were willing to talk, but that came a little bit later. In the meantime we talked to lawyers, we talked to people in the community that worked in the case, went to New York to McWilliams, interviewed him, and he brought up the name of Alice McGraw, the executive secretary, and we did not know where she was, but we finally contacted her in Ventura and went to her house. And she had also a whole file of personal material. As a matter of fact, her file was the one that was in UCLA. But she had kept some personal items, letters and stuff. And then, as I began to talk to her, and she began to trust me more, because she had been approached over the years by many different people, she began to open up and tell me more about the background of the case. The human side of the story. She described the guys as she remembered them. It was clearly obvious to me that she was speaking out of love, out of a personal human dedication to the guys in the case, rather than an intellectually abstract relationship, you know. She was very realistic about the fact, and very political. She was a member of the Communist Part at the time. The Communist Party was indirectly involved in the case. She wasn't there as a member of the CP, she was there as a volunteer, but as it turned out, later on, the House Un-American Activities Committee made a great deal of the connection.

Question

The subtitle of the play is: A new American play". What is so specifically American about it?

Valdez

I remember just from memory that music is a very important part of the Pachuco era, and that it was the Big Band Sound of the 40s, of the swing era. And it so happens that there is a musician in the 40s by the name of Lalo Guerrero who became famous because of the Pachuco songs. Lalo Guerrero was also my father's cousin, you know. A Latin musicologist, a friend of ours, sent us some tapes, some cassette tapes of Lalo's old Pachuco songs. And when I heard them I said: That's incredible, this is the musical heart of the material, and so the music became an important part. Now the thing that is distinctive about the music, as to your second question: It is that it is American swing with *calo* lyrics. It is truly unusual, I think, that on the one hand you have a very universal expression that everyone can understand American swing music, and on the other hand you have this very specific language which only a very few people can understand, the guys in the street. And for me it was a powerful combination. I thought it had to be used precisely as written, and certainly the first version of the play came out almost as a musical document. But it did open up the theme to the point where we were no longer just dealing with the Chicano experience, we were dealing with an American experience; and certainly as we began getting the material, I was very surprised, for instance to find that the language of the guys was very American, more American let's say than Chicanos speak today. They didn't tend to mix the Spanish English quite so much as we do. And when they spoke English, they spoke a more black English, and they used words you hear in the movies all the time. You know: "Copper", and "I didn't do it, see!" And they used nicknames that were also very American. Like Hank for Henry. So I quickly began to see the theme as the theme that involved the whole nation. And the problem, I thought, was also a national problem of a national stereotype.

Question

The situation of the case, this phenomenon in the history of American class justice, of accusing so-called 'Un-Americans' of committing the crimes; it is like Haymarket, Joe Hill, the Rosenbergs, Angela Davis, Sacco and Vanzetti. These are all cases of Americans who did political work and were falsely tried by means of a frame-up situation. Do you see any parallels?

Valdez

Definitely. I think we were dealing with a crucial period in the development of the American image. World War II brought about a real crisis in the U.S. Of course, everyone wanted to be patriotic, and yet there were people that had been systematically excluded: the Blacks, the Chicanos, the Asians, and when they tried to move into the center of the country they were rejected. Of course, the Japanese-Americans were placed in relocation camps and then the focus on the West coast reshifted to the Mexicans, to persecute the Mexican, and what was called into question was the whole notion of what the United States is, what is America? And the nation has always had certain ideals. But there has also been a certain amount of hypocrisy in relation to these ideals. And these "non-Americans" were challenging those ideals, trying to put them into practice. And the response by the nation, the first response, was not pretty, was ugly, was very ugly. And Mexicans were put in their place, Blacks had already been continually put in their place, and so were the Asians. And all of that is part of the evolving concept of what the United States of America is. It's also always been associated with the politics of the country. One of the important background features to the whole Sleepy Lagoon case and Sleepy Lagoon riots is that in the 1930s during the depression Mexicans were repatriated. They had trainloads leaving Los Angeles to take Mexicans back to Mexico, just to get rid of them, and sometimes by force. And certainly in terms of the politically active people, there was a certain amount of deportation that took place, even if they had been born here; and that's our background to the case. By the time 1942 rolled around there was a nervousness in the barrio about being political and then, everybody wanted to be more American rather than political. They didn't want to be identified. The Pachuco started out as an apolitical phenomenon in some ways, that turned political because it had to be. Eventually I think you're talking about a human expression that takes on all of the color of the society whether people like it or not. It brings into play all of the relevant themes: politics, racism, culture, all those things come in.

Question

You are using the life-style of the Zoot Suit and the Pachuco as a figure, as the central image of the play. What is the significance, the aesthetic significance of El Pachuco as a figure in the play? He is the commentator, he is the epic narrator, he is also the one who inspires the thinking of Henry Reyna, the gang leader.

Valdez

One of the things the Pachuco represents first of all, I think, is an urban consciousness, and, in terms of the Mexican experience, there had been no urban figure that we could relate to. Mexicans had been by and large a peasant population and certainly in terms of the waves of immigration that came from Mexico starting 1910, that was largely a peasant population. But it became urbanized in 20 to 30 years. And the first generation to grow up in the streets of the cities, and the final urban expression, was the Pachuco generation. They latched on to style, the style of clothing, the style of behaviour, the language that may have seemed shocking and ugly to an older generation, but to the young people it represented everything that they needed to have in order to survive in the city. It was their values that they had learnt in the streets. So the *Zoot Suit* phenomenon as a national phenomenon arose; it was very strong with the Blacks and all the minorities in the country, including also the white minorities. It really caught on among Chicanos, they picked up on it and they saw it as the uniform of their own particular generation, and they crossed certain barriers; the girls adopted a form of dress that was complementary to the Pachuco style. The Pachuco had baggy pants, and a floppy hat, and the long coat. The women, on the other hand, went in short skirts, and black net stockings.

Question

And you portray this in the play, when the parents are shocked at their daughters showing too much leg?

Valdez

It was ridiculous. They did not understand that this was an urban system of values that was being established and I think that if you look at the history of the development of cities, that an urban style that develops and catches the fire of the imagination also allows for urban survival, and people wanted to survive. That is why the Pachuco to this day among Chicano youth is still a symbol, because he represents all of those qualities that they need in order to go on in the streets. The Pachuco today who calls himself a Bartoloco is more modest in his dress because of the tremendous repression that the Zoot Suit Riots brought about. He went 'underground', so to speak, and he went to khaki pants and a handkerchief as a headband and was contented with that. And in the meantime he spruced up his car. It was his car that took on all of the flash and the color and the style of the *Zoot Suit*. But I think it stands a chance of coming back in that sense, because the meaning has always been there. So that is the urban experience. The Pachuco is an urban figure. A lot of people do not know that 80% of Chicanos in this country live in cities. They are not farm workers, by and large.

Question

But what about the epic narration of El Pachuco in the play? What about his function within its internal aesthetics?

Valdez

The Pachuco is a theatrical figure. I saw him as an actor in life, and much of city life involves that sort of acting in life. The fact that he was also considered to be dangerous, I think, just adds to the excitement of his figure. Dangerous in what way? He was vaguely associated with drugs, certainly associated with sex, and most definitely associated with violence. And this makes him an enormous theatrical figure. He is something of a *lumpen*; many people are asking me: "Why are you making him heroic?" But what I am dealing in the play with, is his very theatricality, that he comes from that consciousness. The uses of language, the uses of body movements, the use of a costume. And since he is also a symbol of resistance I decided to use him as the 'touch-point' of reality. The story is being told from the Pachuco's point of view.

Question

So he is the one who makes fun of the audience, who has a critical attitude towards the action. But he is also the one who, at a very specific point in the play, the point when the appeal has come through and the accused are acquitted, says: "Now we could have a happy ending. And the play could be finished. But that is not what life is like." And then the play goes on and we have quite a strong conflict scene within the family at the party; at the house of Henry Reyna's parents. Are we back now in the barrio with all its complications and problems?

Valdez

What I was trying to deal with in that last part, which we started to call the 'coda', is the human side of Henry Reyna and through his humanity the question of his loyalty to the barrio. At the beginning of the play, when Henry wants to join the navy and go off to war, the Pachuco asks him: "Why do you want to go off, you know, when they are kicking you in the ass here? Is this your country?" And the Pachuco says: "No, it's not your country." And so that last scene, the 'coda', really deals, specially in terms of the triangle, with the love relation between Henry, Della and Alice. It is a little corny in a sense; however, when you understand it in terms of the social issue of loyalty, it assumes a different value. And there is nothing wrong actually with Henry loving Alice. I tried to make that clear. At the same time there is a larger issue at hand: is he going to be the type of Chicano that leaves the barrio and marries into a non-Chicano part of the country and disappears. Or is he the type that stays behind and holds on and tries to deal with it; recognizing that staying behind would expose him to the same old problems, and the same old frustrations. Let me say this about the fake ending of the play, the winning of the appeal. Just as a dramatist I go from the solitary theme in which Alice and Henry make contact into the winning of the war, and the winning of the appeal, dramatically there is deliberately no build-up there in the sense of suspense of about winning the case. While it may seem, in terms of the story, like a logical place to end the play, dramatically this really doesn't answer the questions, it doesn't really satisfy. When I was doing the research, there was a part of me that wanted to end at that positive point: they won the case, and it is a happy ending, how great! But 35 years of additional history have told us that the problem is not resolved, that you still have gangs in the city, that there are still people like Hank Reyna being born and raised in the barrios and going to prison and getting the drugs or, as the end of the play suggests, going off to the service or becoming union organizers. It's a living, breathing problem. So I didn't want to stop at that point. I thought that the social point had somehow been undermined by individual problems and I wanted to deal with Henry's individual embroilment there. And I wanted to show that life goes on, and in fact Henry Reyna's life did go on and provided him other challenges. We know too much, in other words, about the Pachuco just to stop at a happy ending, it couldn't be a happy ending. Also what makes the sort of change possible, that sort of slight of hand possible in terms of the theatre is that the essence of Pachucismo has to do with a thing called 'el bacilon', which means — kidding around, means: don't take life that seriously. That's part of what the pachuco is telling you. And that's what the essence of Pachucismo has been.

Question

A device which makes the impact probably even stronger. As in epic theatre, where disillusioning is supposed to heighten the effect. But I would like to shift the emphasis of our conversation toward that institution where your political and artistic roots are: El Teatro Campesino. In which way does *Zoot Suit* reflect the style of the Teatro?

Valdez

Well, one of the things again that may not seem evident is that in 1942 the Pachuco to some extent was also a rural figure. He was born in the streets — but often had to go into the fields for a job. So the Pachuco patois is easily recognizable among Campesinos. In the smaller towns the Pachuco phenomenon lasted into the late 1950s.

Question

And you use El Pachuco in the early *actos* of the Teatro.

Valdez

He appears very early in our work, in terms of language and as an actual figure. In *Bernabe* he is the moon. It is a theme that has been kept warm by the Teatro all these years. The other connection is the method of acting that the Pachuco himself employs. It is very mimetic; he is using his whole body when he moves, and his arms. The actor (*in Zoot Suit*) discovered the Pachuco through our rehearsals in Los Angeles, in which I had to employ some Teatro techniques and Teatro exercises. Once he had discovered that, he moved with it.

Question

What were those particular techniques?

Valdez

It had to do with moving to the music. It had to do with a concept of the actor as a sphere that we use in developing actors. The individual actor sees himself as a sphere capable of establishing a center and then moving throughout this sphere. In other words: if you rotate your arms and your legs in every direction that you can, you would cruise out of the inside wall of the sphere and also should be able to move your sphere like a ball rolling. And it's that continuity of a ball rolling across stage, either quickly or slowly, that gives your movements power on the stage. So that is in the Pachuco as well, on the stage. The singing, the uses of music, the dance scenes, are elements that have begun to enter our work continually now for the last 10 years. They allow the actions to float better.

Question

Let us talk about the work of the Teatro in 1978. You did the international tour in the summer, and there was a tour of the North West of the United States after that. And there is the community work here. And I get the feeling now being here that *La Carpa, Fin del Mundo*, and the Christmas Plays seem to be the center of your present work, of course, it has grown, gradually evolved over a period of years. *La Carpa* has been around for almost 8 years now.

Valdez

We've been finished with *La Carpa* actually for about a year and a half. We discovered many things as a result of doing *La Carpa*. Things which we started to put into practice in other forms of work. Our major piece that we're working on, of course, is *Fin del Mundo*. This is one that has been evolving over a period of years as well as the Christmas Shows that you saw. Another piece has to be mentioned here: *The Rose of the Rancho*. They are all like the roots of other material that is developing. In talking about *Fin del Mundo* I have to point out that there are many different versions. The "calavera" version is what we call *Fin* 3. You know, we began *Fin* 1, *Fin* 2, *Fin* 3. *La Carpa* 5 was the version we toured through Europe last time.

Fin 2, which we did in the Spring of 1976, was a realistic play that dealt with the microcosm, with the specifics of daily life in a farm worker community. We used the carpa as the backdrop, but eventually discarded that, because the major element that we used were the fruit picking boxes. It became our set, and we moved fruit picking boxes and created the set that we needed. (There is that relationship with *Zoot Suit*, by the way. The set of *Zoot Suit* is composed out of newspaper bundles; the use of a newspaper.) There is also the connection between *Fin* 2 and *Zoot Suit*, that the central character called Mundo Mata is a symbolic name, of course. Mundo means world and Mata means kilt or plant, and what it involved was a lumpen-proletariat figure, who was a drug pusher, who was asked by the growers to undermine the election campaign of the United Farm Workers. And so he agrees for a certain amount of money — but inside himself he also agrees to betray the growers — so it is a double-betrayal, and where he gets into trouble is that the farm workers believe that he is against them. And he's got enough power in his little community, he's feared by enough people, and he's also loved by enough people to kind of stay on the line for a while; and it deals with a sense of personal corruption as well as the corruption of this one town, it's sort of decaying and changing at the same time.

Question

What were the specific problems and difficulties in working out this play?

Valdez

It wasn't time for us to do the play yet. We needed really to study a method of staging. It took 27 people to do it. We had to take them all out on tour and it just drained our resources in order to be able to do that version. That play is still, let's say, dormant, it's within our work. We will return to it within the next couple of years to rework it. I don't know if it will be called *Fin del Mundo*. One of the things that gets confusing is that we use the same title over and over again and then eventually end up with 3 or 4 different plays. I like, as a playwright and director, to work a bit like a painter, pick out a theme and then do many many different versions of this one theme. *Fin* 1 was an Indian play, dansas, and used animals, and was highly symbolic; I saw it as a sand painting. It was more like a sand painting than anything else, with bright colors, 4 cardinal colors, and then 2 other colors to make up six. And in addition to white. White and black are neutral, and so we ended up with a rainbow effect in the use of colors. It was a short play, 52 minutes long. We used animal masks but the "calavera" base. *Fin* 3 now is based on a corrido; *Corrido de Fin del Mundo* and it kind of tries to go directly into the theme and tell the story of the end of the world. That's a large theme. It's much too big. I really felt that it needed a greater sense of maturity. I felt that I needed to live more in order to be able to attempt that sort of picture of the world. I'm just not old enough, I'm 38. It's presumptuous of me at this age to assume to try to do this.

Question

You mentioned earlier *The Rose of The Rancho*, El Teatro's adaptation of a play by David Belasco and Richard Walton Tully. What is its significance for your work?

Valdez

Belasco was from San Francisco. And he knew about San Juan Bautista. And so he wrote about San Juan Bautista. The play was a big hit on Broadway in 1904. It was revived in 1944, again a big hit. And when we got here, someone directed us to the play. And it was too big again. It had 37 people in it. But we adapted it, broke it down. Cesar Flores adapted it and broke it down to 8 characters, and then we began to work it. We introduced the dance of the period and learned that nobody had really worked on that period of early Californian history of the music. It's not exactly Flamenco, it's not exactly Spanish. They did what they call Xotas. I want to return to that theme and work on a major play on early California history, at the period when Americans were starting to get here. And I want to deal with the theme of Mexican banditry at that time.

Question

You are saying that *The Rose* forms a cycle with *La Pastorela* and *La Virgen del Tepeyac*, the two Christmas shows you have done regularly for the past 6 or 7 years. What impact does the cycle have on the life here in the community of San Juan and the surrounding county?

Valdez

San Juan doesn't only have a past, it also has a future. And even though our existence here has been rather modest, because it's a town that has not too many physical resources, it's a town of around a thousand people, and it's somewhat isolated in its own way, certainly from the great open centers. We figure, since we're a migrant group anyway, a touring group, that it didn't matter where we laid our base. The attraction to San Juan was both its historical and cultural significance. We were trying to evolve a certain kind of cultural life for ourselves as a group and as a part of our community, and as a theatrical company tries to influence just culture in general. It gives us a great sense of identity to come from San Juan Bautista, in its historical sense. By being here, we have the potential of invoking the last 150 years of

American history, which we wouldn't have, if we were in one of the big cities. So we very naturally move into areas of folk theater that fit very well with the spirit of the town. We were in a small town 10 years ago, in Del Rey (that's really the town I am writing about in *Fin* 2, you know.) The difference was that Del Rey was decaying. It was a town with no law. It was a town with no government, and evidence of decay everywhere. Buildings had been abandoned, wretched living conditions with illegal immigrants, etc. It was impossible to do culture under the circumstances, whereas in San Juan you still have the small town, there are still many farm workers here as well as artists. There is an opportunity to represent the spirit of the town, which again invokes those 150 years of history. It's possible to do the *Virgen* play here, because the mission is here, for instance, the mission which was established in 1797, and was used in fact to Christianize the Indians. And so just by invoking the mission, we can invoke the whole history of America in terms of the Spanish or the Portuguese coming to Christianize the Indians. And that makes it a very important symbol. The *Virgen* play is symbolic, I think not only for Catholics and not only for Mexican Catholics and for Indians, it's symbolic for the whole American experience. And it is a doctrinal part of Catholic belief, let me say that. The Virgen de Guadalupe has been accepted as an actual experience by the mother of Christ, and her picture appears in Catholic churches all over. Se is called La Rena de las Americas. She was proclaimed by the Pope. She is a brown version of the mother of Christ. We don't have to go into the extremes that some black radicals did some years ago when they went and painted a statue of Christ black. The Virgen is an Indian already. And it's the same with *Pastorela*. Here we have again an ancient play from the Middle Ages. We have a script which had been handwritten by someone from his memory from Mexico. It was given to us by the mother of one of the actors, and she sat here with us and taught us the songs, and that's how we evolved that piece. We had to cut it down, because we couldn't do the full tradition from Mexico, it takes 12 hours. The people here don't have that kind of time.

Question

You use the whole town for staging it?

Valdez

Yes, we do it in the streets and we take the audience with us, too, on this pilgrimage of the shepherds. So it's a moving audience. We use the lights of the intersection, and we stage these different stops that the shepherds are making on the way to see the Christ child and then, of course, they are disturbed by the devils who come in and disrupt everything.

Question

Are the devils specially conceived with regard to Anglo spectators?

Valdez

We get a bilingual audience, you know. We get many people that are non-Mexicans, coming to see the play. And they come from urban areas from town. They like the story, and they can follow the action. The very spirit of a piece is embodied in the manner of presentation, where you present it. I'm really basically concerned here with the point of origin of a piece, o.k.? As the Teatro Campesino we are involved in the creation of pieces. The ambiance, the environment in which we create a piece, makes it possible then to put it in a place where it might not be created.

Question

So you could also take this on tour?

Valdez

Having done it round here, we could. But with Del Rey or Los Angeles it would be very difficult. There'd be too many disruptions, the values are different. The work with the Christmas plays and our work here in San Juan is the raw earth, in which we can plant seeds and make things grow. Theater must come from a community. We must maintain this very close small town reality in order to be able to relate to all other places. What we discover here could eventually be translated even into film. Certain elements of *Zoot Suit* were discovered here.

Question

And now it's going to Broadway!

Well, the Teatro Campesino today is more than just a theater group. For Chicanos it's a Centro Campesino Cultural and it's also Menyah Productions. What is the organisational structure and what are the specific goals of the entire organisation with regard to the Chicano community at large?

Valdez

The Teatro covers the entire South-West. We have known that we have an audience all over the South-west and now we are reaching the Midwest and even the North-East Coast. Our capacity to serve these areas has always been behind need. The need is enormous. The people could use a lot more from us than we are able to deliver. We have tried to work out a number of different economic schemes in order to grow and develop as a group. Different philosophies have come as we have grown. We used to use words very easily: commune, community, co-operative. We are less reluctant now, because of more experience behind us. We know that we have to exist in this society and that we have to function as a business, as a theater company, and as a family. There are many different ways to describe how we function, what we do. But within that the growing of the individual as well as the group is concerned. Everyone does two or three different things: acting, work in the office, work in the shop, or work at production aspects. Our greatest desire is to be able to expand that staff, to be able to grow, to allow for greater productivity. *Zoot Suit* will enable us to acquire more space. That'll bring more people. We also have to improve our publicity work. It is not only a question of survival, but also of the effectiveness in what you're trying to do. You want people to know what you're doing. You want people to know that your show is on. So that they can come and see it. It must be made as attractive as possible in the promotion. We have been touring for the last 13 years. It gets you to audiences and places you've never seen. We hope to be able to develop the capacity to keep the resident company here, and send a touring group out. That requires a greater sort of organization, and an understanding of what our separate roles are. This is a phase of transition for us. Just as I have made a decision to go back to playwrighting more deliberately and to write a number of plays that I want to write — requiring for instance that I have my own individual hours to work — there are other members in the group that also need to develop specific skills. Some have a greater capacity for being actors than others. The whole music, the studio. It needs more time to expand the studio. In the new building there is a perfect space for it. We want to be able to function at a greater level of productivity and allow everybody the opportunity to grow as artists and as individuals, as well as being with their families at the same time.

Question

Would you be able to expand more easily in a larger city?

Valdez

For one thing: we would be able to find warehouses that are enormous, even theaters. People have offered us theaters. But we resist that because of the faith in the future importance of San Juan Bautista as a symbol. As the cities become more highly urbanized, as the U.S. moves towards a new consensus of itself, what it is, as it begins to deal with its own history, places like San Juan will take on increased significance, will grow.

Question

So with regard to your future plans, San Juan is the ideal base.

Valdez

I want to question the whole thing about the West. It's important that people know exactly how California was acquired. What happened to all the ranchers, what happened to the Indians. These things have to be asked from a position, from a base. And so I see us growing to a point where we can, in fact, function as an organization that serves the nation, that serves Chicanos from all over. We'll have to give up a certain amount of our romantic notion of "rasquachiness". But it's there in our history. It's part of us. And I never want to lose the ability to be able to perform in a labor camp. I never want to lose the opportunity to perform in a barrio. At the same time I don't want us to shy away from the ability of staging a play on Broadway with the Teatro Campesino, if we want to, because that's part of the national expression right now.

NOTES

1. Cf. among others: D. Herms: *Agitprop USA. Zur Theorie und Strategie des politisch emanzipatorischen Theaters in Amerika seit 1960* (Kronberg 1973), passim; D. Herms: "Mime Troupe, El Teatro, Bread and Puppet. Ansätze su einem politischen Volkstheater in den USA", *Maske und Kothurn* 19 (1973), 342–362; F. Kourilsky: "Approaching Quetzalcoatl. The Evolution of El Teatro Campesino", *Performance* 7 (1973), 37–46; J. Harrup, J. Huerta: "The Agitprop Pilgrimage of Luis Valdez and El Teatro Campesino", *Theatre Quarterly* 5 (1975), 30–39; G. Burger, A. Rating, G. Riecke: "Erkenntnisse über den Abfall. El Teatro Campesino und sein Stück 'La Carpa de los Rasquachis' ", *Theater heute* (3/1977), 31–35; B. Novoa, D. Valentin: "Revolutionizing the Popular Image. Essay on Chicano Theatre", *Latin American Review* 5(1977), 43–50; D. Herms: "Zwischen Mythos, Anpassung und Rebellion. El Teatro Campesino 1978", *Iberoamericana* 7 (1979), 14–32

2. "Luis Valdez — A Biography", leaflet compiled by A. Gutierrez (San Juan Bautista 1978), p. 1

3. Cf. D. Herms: "Der Kampf der United Farm Workers of America", *Gulliver, deutsch-englische Jahrbücher* 2 (1977), 123–142 (see additional titles in footnotes of this article)

4. Cf. D. Herms et al: "Das befreiende Gelächter. Interview mit Luis Valdez." *Theater heute* (9/1972), 29–32

5. Valdez, L. and Teatro Campesino: *Actos* (Fresno 1971) Reprinted 1974

6. *Ibid.*; also in German translation in D. Herms: *Agitprop USA*, op. cit., 117–128

7. In: *Actos*; also in: R. J. Garza (ed.): *Contemporary Chicano Theatre* (Notre Dame, London 1976), 15–27

8. Valdez, L.: "Introduction", in Valdez, L. and S. Steiner (eds.): *Aztlan. An Anthology of Mexican American Literature* (New York 1972), p. XXXII

9. None of these have been published yet, except two different sections from *Bernabé* in: Valdez, L. and S. Steiner (eds.): *Aztlan*, op. cit., 353–376 and in R. J. Garza (ed.): *Contemporary Chicano Theatre*, op. cit., 29–58

10. L. Valdez to J. Acevedo, n.d.

11. This being an introduction, but no full-fledged article, I cannot give a detailed analysis of *La Carpa*, nor of *Zoot Suit*, for that matter. Cf. Burger, Rating, Riecke, op. cit. and my own "Zwischen Mythos, Anpassung und Rebellion", op. cit.

12. T. Benitel: "Facing the Issues Beyond 'Zoot Suit'. Interview with Playwright Luis Valdez", *Neworld* 3 (1978), p. 37

13. C. Lawson: "News of the Theater. Selling a 'Suit' ", *New York Times* (2/14/1979), p. C 15

14. The most recent "controversial" critical studies: Y. Yarbro-Bejarano and T. Ybarra-Frausto: "Zoot Suit Mania Sweeps L. A., Moves Toward East", *In These Times* (1/31/2/6/1–79), p. 23; S. Bassnett-McGuire: "El Teatro Campesino. From Actos to Mitos", *Theatre Quarterly* 9 (1979), 18–21; R. G. Davis and B. Diamond: " 'Zoot Suit' on the Road", ibid., 21–25

BIBLIOGRAPHY
KIMBALL KING

The following bibliography has been provided as a convenience to scholars who wish to read more about the playwrights discussed in this volume. A list of books and articles which survey the new American drama from a broader perspective is also included.

EDWARD ALBEE
(1928–   )

All Over, 1971

The American Dream, 1961

The Ballad of the Sad Cafe, 1965 (adaptation)

Box and Quotations from Chairman Mao Tse-tung: Two Interrelated Plays, 1969

Counting the Ways, 1976

The Death of Bessie Smith, 1962

A Delicate Balance, 1966

Everything in the Garden, 1968

The Lady From Dubuque, 1980

Listening, 1975

Malcolm, 1966 (adaptation)

The Sandbox, 1961

Seascape, 1975

Tiny Alice, 1965

Who's Afraid of Virginia Woolf? 1962

The Zoo Story, 1960

Amacher, Richard E. *Edward Albee*. New York: Twayne Publishers, 1969.
    Amacher's first two chapters concentrate on biographical information and present Albee's literary theory. In the remainder of the book, Amacher analyzes each of the plays. He also attempts to relate Albee's life to his works and draws a respectable picture of the man as an important figure in literary circles.

Ballew, Leighton M. "Who's Afraid of *Tiny Alice?*" *Georgia Review*, 20 (Fall 1966), 292–99.
    Reviewers and critics — even Albee himself — have been unable to state the central thematic motif of this play. Ballew suggests that the entire play takes

place in Julian's mind. Blending techniques of reality and fantasy, Albee deals with the amorphous problems of illusion and reality, existential agony, and the nature of God.

Bierhaus, E. G., Jr. "Strangers in a Room: *A Delicate Balance* Revisited." *Modern Drama*, 17 (1974), 199–206.

Bierhaus focuses on the significance of the characters' names, the surprising permutations of the characters, and, finally, the parable of Tobias and the cat. "The Players" in *A Delicate Balance* evoke biblical, historical, and sexual references through their naming and add to the ironic incongruities in the character development. Bierhaus believes that Tobias' parable of the cat is an analogue of the whole play and he further illustrates this point through an in-depth study of its "eleven salient points."

Bigsby, C. W. E. *Albee*. Edinburgh: Oliver and Boyd, 1969.

Bigsby discusses Albee's role as the leading young American dramatist. He focuses on the playwright's early life as a factor in his later development and argues that Albee is not an absurdist; he only exhibits some similarities to this European form in some of his work. Bigsby provides a short biography, bibliography, and briefly analyzes each of Albee's plays and adaptations through *A Delicate Balance*.

_____, ed. *Edward Albee: A Collection of Critical Essays*. Englewood Cliffs, N.J.: Prentice-Hall, 1975.

Bigsby includes essays from a variety of well-known theater critics. Nevertheless he attacks modern academic and theatrical criticism in his introductory remarks, noting that "few playwrights can have been so frequently and mischievously misunderstood, misrepresented, overpraised, denigrated, and precipitately dismissed." The book includes a chronology of important dates in Albee's life and a selected bibliography.

Braem, Helmut M. *Albee* 2nd ed., Velber: Friedrich Verlag, 1977

Braem discusses American theatre as part of show "business", the consequences for American drama (on-, off-, off-off Broadway theatre), analyzes the plays of Albee and their performances on German speaking and American stages.

Brede, Regine. "Edward Albee." *Literatur in Wissenschaft und Unterricht* 8 (1975), 30–46.

Brede reviews Albee's achievements from *The Zoo Story* to *Everything in the Garden*. A biography of the playwright is provided as well as a history of American critical opinion regarding his works. She debates the question of whether Albee is a nihilist or an engaged humanist. Through descriptions of Albee's themes and techniques Brede attempts to show Albee's commitment to intellectual honesty and social reform. There is also a brief bibliography at the conclusion of the article.

Diehl, Digby. "Edward Albee Interviewed." *Transatlantic Review*, No. 12 (Spring 1963), 57–72. Also included in *Behind the Scenes*. Ed. Joseph McCrindle. New York: Holt Rinehart & Winston, 1971. Pages 223–42.

In one of his more informative interviews, Albee asserts that audiences prefer vicarious experience as opposed to genuine involvement. He indicates that although he writes for himself and not for the audience he still "does not wish to leave them indifferent." He compares himself to a musical composer in the manner with which he treats his art and maintains that the playwright should "notate" his lines in such a way "that it's impossible for an actor to say the line incorrectly." Albee reveals his opinion that Americans are too much interested in writers and too little interested in their works. At this point he emphasizes that his dissatisfaction with American society is the motive for his writings and he predicts that there is still a great deal about which he can write.

Gabbard, Lucina P. "Albee's *Seascape*: An Adult Fairy Tale." *Modern Drama* 21 (September 1978), 307–17.

"The play's principal concern is the realization of the proximity of death that comes with the passing of middle age." She explores *Seascape* as a play that uses the language of symbols to communicate various levels of personal reality. Gabbard writes that the play is ultimately positive, accepting death as transcendence.

Goetsch, Paul. "Edward Albees Zoogeschichten: Zur eingelagerten Erzählung im modernen Drama". In: Weber, Alfred und Siegfried Neuweiler, eds *Amerikanisches Drama und Theater im 20. Jahrhundert.* Göttingen: Vandenhoek und Ruprecht, 1975

Goestsch analyzes the function of the "story within the play" in Albee's dramatic work. For him, Albee's motifs and themes have their origin in Jerry's story ("The Zoo Story"), which he considers the key to the meaning of Albee's dramatic work.

————. *Who's Afraid of Virginia Woolf?* In: Goetsch, Paul ed. *Das amerikanische Drama.* Düsseldorf: Bagel Verlag, 1974

Goetsch discusses the reception of Albee's drama *Who's Afraid of Virginia Woolf?*, its relation to European drama, to psychoanalysis, and finally examines the structure of the action.

Hopkins, Anthony. "Conventional Albee: *Box* and *Chairman Mao.*" *Modern Drama*, 16 (September 1973), 141–48.

Here, Albee further refines the techniques and images he has favored in early creations. The box especially intrigues him as a symbol of the constricting forces of modern life. The monologues in *Chairman Mao* are reminiscent of earlier plays and, taken together, they illustrate the failure of American ideals as measured against the pronouncements of Chairman Mao.

Razum, Hannes. "Edward Albee und die Metaphysik", in: Lohner, Edgar und Rudolf Haas, *Theater und Drama in Amerika.* Aspekte und Interpretationen. Unter Mitwirkung zahlreicher Fachgelehrter. Berlin: Erich Schmidt Verlag, 1978.

Good introduction to American drama since O'Neill: the book contains essays to German and American scholars. Razum's article tries an analysis of Albee's most contradictory play *Tiny Alice*.

Scheller, Bernhard. "Der Figurenaufbau in den Stücken Edward Albees." In Bruning, Eberhard, Klaus Köhler, and Bernhard Scheller, eds., *Studien zum amerikanischen Drama nach dem Zweiten Weltkrieg.* Berlin: Rütten and Loening, 1977.

Scheller identifies the certain patterns in Albee's work, discusses his didacticism, his daring, his experimentalism with absurdist techniques and his overall contribution to American theatre in a fine, thought-provoking essay.

Schwarz, Karl. "Edward Albee's *Zoo Story.*" *Die Neueren Sprachen*, 18 (June 1969), 261–67.

In *The Zoo Story*, Albee intends to totally involve the audience with his drama. In part he achieves this by developing "doubly distorted parallels" between Jerry's story concerning the janitoress and the dog and the actual encounter involving Jerry and Peter. In any case, it is the shock of Jerry's death scene which draws the spectators emotionally to the stage.

Stenz, Anita M. *Edward Albee: Poet of Loss*. The Hague: Mouton, 1978.

Since there has been such a misunderstanding and misrepresentation by the critics of Albee, Stenz has endeavored to re-examine his intentions, especially "with respect to the motivation and behavior of his characters," not only within individual works but also with regard to one another. Stenz does not compare his work with that of other playwrights nor does she relate it to movements of drama; she has attempted "to clarify the meaning of each play in the light of descriptions of the original performance." Although she excludes his adaptations because of their experimental nature, Stenz does treat each play from *The Zoo Story* to *Seascape* in an effort to "relate the themes of individual works to the oeuvre as a whole."

IMMAMU AMIRI BARAKA (LE ROI JONES)
(1934–   )

Arm Yourself and Harm Yourself, 1967

The Baptism, 1964

BA-RA-KA, 1972

A Black Mass, 1966

Board of Education, 1968

B. P. Chant, 1968

Chant, 1968

Dante, 1961

The Death of Malcolm X, 1969

Dutchman, 1964

The Eighth Ditch (Is Drama) 1962

Experimental Death Unit #1, 1965

A Good Girl Is Hard to Find, 1958

Great Goodness of Life (A Coon Show), 1969

Home on the Range, 1968

Insurrection, 1968

Jello, 1965

Junkies Are Full of (SHHH . . .), and Bloodrites, 1970

The Kid Poeta Tragical, 1969

Madheart, 1967

The Motion of History, 1976

Police, 1968

A Recent Killing, 1964

S-1, 1976

Sidnee Poet Heroical, 1975

Slave Ship: A Historical Pageant, 1967

The Slave, 1964

The Toilet, 1964

Slave Ship: A Historical Pageant, 1967

The Slave, 1964

The Toilet, 1964

Benston, Kimberly W., ed. *Imamu Amiri Baraka (LeRoi Jones). A Collection of Critical Essays*. Englewood Cliffs, N.J.: Prentice Hall, 1978.
     This is a collection of critical essays on the prose, poetry, and drama of Baraka, also containing a short biography and substantial introductory material on the general impact of Jones' art. The section on drama consists of articles on *Dutchman, The Slave, The Toilet, Madheart*, and *Slave Ship*.

Brady, Owen E. "Cultural Conflict and Cult Ritual in LeRoi Jones' *The Toilet*." *Educational Theatre Journal*, 28 (March 1976).
     "This work is a metaphor for the explanation of the hero's double conscious-ness, his conflict over his roles as a Negro and as an American. Ora represents the black society close to Africa, Foots the part of the black community trying to make a bridge to success in both white and black worlds. Foots' tragic fate and the play's setting are metaphors for American life, and the play's action is a ritual dramatizing the psychic conflict and initiation of Ray Foots."

————. "LeRoi Jones's *The Slave*: A Ritual of Purgation." *Obsidian*, 4 (Spring 1978), 5–18.
     Brady maintains that Baraka's *Dutchman* and *The Slave* are companion pieces, *The Slave* fulfilling Clay's prophesy that a bloody racial war will destroy the existing social order in America. He includes a careful examination of character and symbol in *The Slave*. The self-sacrifice of the protagonist "re-vitalizes the hope for a better life."

Dace, Letitia. "Amiri Baraka" (LeRoi Jones). In: *Black American Writers*: Biblio-graphical Essays. Inge, M. Thomas, Maurice Duke, Jackson R. Bryer, eds. New York: St. Martin's Press 1978
     Dace's bibliographic article is invaluable in that it rewrites the various phrases of Baraka's career and the response of two decades of critics to his work.

Miller, Jeanne-Marie A. "The Plays of LeRoi Jones." *College Language Associa-tion Journal*, 14 (1971), 331–39.
     Miller begins by establishing the moral basis of Jones' art and develops her readings of his plays along ethical lines. A fairly extensive treatment of *Dutch-man* and *The Slave* with shorter attention to *Baptism, The Toilet, A Black Mass, Great Goodness of Life, Madheart: A Morality Play, Slave Ship*, and *The Slave*. Miller maintains that Jones seeks a mental revolution, often punishing the audience.

Schatt, Stanley, "LeRoi Jones: A Checklist to Primary and Secondary Sources." *Bulletin of Bibliography*, 28 (1971), 55–57.

   This is a selective checklist of Baraka's work through 1969. Primary materials include books edited, poems, plays, essays, novels. There are brief selections of annotated secondary materials ranging from articles in *Time* and *Newsweek* to Gerald Weales's book-length study of American drama in the sixties.

Sollors, Werner. *Amiri Baraka/LeRoi Jones: The Quest for a "Populist Modernism."* New York: Columbia University Press, 1978. Chapters 5, 6, 9 are specifically concerned with drama.

   Sollors takes an American Studies approach to Baraka's work and discusses the writer's indictment of racism and oppressive social structures.

ED BULLINS
(1935–   )

Clara's Ole Man, 1965

The Corner, 1971

The Devil Catchers, 1971

The Duplex: A Black Love Fable in Four Movements, 1970

The Electronic Nigger, 1968

The Fabulous Miss Marie, 1970

The Game of Adam and Eve, 1969

The Gentleman Caller, 1969

Goin' a Buffalo: A Tragifantasy, 1968

Home Boy, 1976

House Party, 1973

How Do You Do: A Nonsense Drama, 1965

In New England Winter, 1967

In the Wine Time, 1968

It Bees Dat Way, 1970

It Has No Choice, 1969

Jo Anne!!!, 1976

The Mystery of Phyllis Wheatley, 1976

The Pig Pen, 1970

The Psychic Pretenders, 1972

A Son, Come Home, 1968

Street Sounds, 1970

The Taking of Miss Janie, 1975

Clayborne, Jon L. "Modern Black Drama and the Gay Image." *College English*, 36 (November 1974), 381–84.

This is an indictment of such contemporary black dramatists as Bullins, Herbert Stokes, and Charles Gordone as perpetuating images of the black male as the sole viable expression of masculine power—a notion whose origin may be related to Black Liberation—at the expense of the homosexual, stereotypically viewed, according to Clayborne, as "devoid of masculinity."

Giles, Jas. R. "Tenderness in Brutality: The Plays of Ed Bullins." *Players*, 48 (October/November 1972), 32–33.

Three plays of Bullins, *In the Wine Time, In New England Winter,* and *Goin' a Buffalo,* illustrate the destruction of human aspirations for romance and tenderness by the grim reality of black life as it really is in America.

Grant, Lisbeth. "The New Lafayette Theatre — Anatomy of a Community Art Institution." *Drama Review,* 16 (December 1972), 46–55.

Grant provides a general overview of a black community theatre and on Bullins as its writer-in-residence; performances of his plays at New Lafayette include those of *The Electronic Nigger, Pig Pen, The Duplex, The Fabulous Miss Marie,* and *Clara's Ole Man.*

Tener, R. L. "Pandora's Box: A Study of Ed Bullins's Dramas." *College Language Association Journal*, 19 (June 1976), 533–44.

"The fictive universe of Ed Bullins' dramatic writings is like Pandora's box set within the larger compass of white American cities...

The elements of the social compass in Bullins' vision are the conceptual spatial environment, the nature of order within that space, and the operating fictive values."

As the above quoted material suggests, Tener discusses the emphasis upon the confining nature of environment in Bullins' plays. He shows how physical environment narrows individual power, thus becoming destiny for characters in Bullins' drama.

True, W. R. "Ed Bullins, Anton Chekhov, and the Drama of Mood." *College Language Association Journal*, 20 (June 1977), 521–32.

A comparison of Bullins to Chekhov that maintains: "the prevailing dramaturgical techniques of his plays reflect those of Chekhov's four major dramas." The similarities which True finds are (1) pervasive disconnected dialogue, (2) obscure development of plot, and (3) circularity in plot shape. True defends his findings with a thorough comparison.

Sollors, Werner. "Ed Bullins." In Grabes, Herbert, ed., *Das Amerikanische Drama der Gegenwart.* Kronberg: Anthanäum, 1976.

Sollors evaluates Bullins' career, describes his theatrical techniques and his major themes, finding him a powerful voice in the New American Theatre and a convincing exponent of black power.

LORRAINE HANSBERRY
(1930–1965)

Les Blancs, 1970

The Drinking Gourd, 1961

A Raisin in the Sun, 1959

The Sign in Sidney Brustein's Window, 1964

To Be Young, Gifted and Black, 1969

What Use Are Flowers?, 1967

Bigsby, C. W. E., *Confrontation and Commitment: A Study of Contemporary American Drama 1959–1966*. London, 1967.
    Bigsby provides a very thorough treatment of Hansberry's work as playwright. He claims that *Raisin* is disappointing when viewed in light of her greater achievement in her second play *Sign in Sidney*. He compares the cynicism and nihilism of *Raisin* to *Death of a Salesman* and claims that *Sign in Sidney* is "as much a statement of artistic responsibility as of social inadequacies." He places her in context of other contemporary dramatists.

Brown, Lloyd W. "Lorraine Hansberry as Ironist." *Journal of Black Studies* (Los Angeles), 4 (March 1974), 237–47.
    Hansberry has joined the list of controversial black writers. The article sums up the criticism of her "integrationist" philosophy. Her tendency to isolate questions of structure or technique from those of social or racial significance is explored. Brown maintains that the perceptual conflicts in *Raisin in the Sun* are deliberate, not just evidence of her own confusion. The ultimate irony of the play is that, "despite all the hallowed myths of change and its cherished dream of ideals of human fulfillment, American society allows far less room for optimism about real change than do the despised societies of the so-called underdeveloped world."

Kaiser, Ernest and Rober Nemiroff. "A Lorraine Hansberry Bibliography." *Freedomways*, 19 (Fall 1979), 285–304.
    This is a useful checklist of primary and secondary sources for research in Hansberry.

Turner, Darwin T. *Black Drama in America*. Greenwich, Conn.: Fawcett, 1971.
    Turner offers a very brief treatment of *A Raisin in the Sun*. He places the play in a tradition which develops verisimilitude of characterization and incident. He includes a summary of the action of the play and concludes that *Raisin* is one of the most perceptive presentations of Afro-Americans in the history of American professional theatre.

Willis, Robert J. "Anger and the Contemporary Black Theatre." *Negro American Literature Forum*, 8 (Summer 1974), 213–15.
    Willis views Hansberry's work in light of protest literature. *Raisin in the Sun* is a well crafted, "angry" play that is tempered when compared to Baraka and Baldwin. The play presents an awareness of the changing attitudes of the black man: Mama's world is one of the past. There is some deliberate stereotyping in the play.

ARTHUR KOPIT
(1937–   )

Across the River and Into the Jungle, 1958

As for the Ladies, 1963

Asylum: or, What the Gentlemen Are Up To, 1963

Aubade, 1959

Chamber Music, 1963

The Conquest of Everest, 1964

The Day the Whores Came Out to Play Tennis, 1965

Don Juan in Texas, 1957

Gemini, 1957

The Hero, 1964

Indians, 1968

Louisiana Territory; or, Lewis and Clark – Lost and Found, 1965

Mhil'daim, 1963

Oh Dad, Poor Dad, Mama's Hung You in the Closet and I'm Feelin' So Sad: A Pseudoclassical Tragifarce in a Bastard French Traditon, 1960

On the Runway of Life, You Never Know What's Coming Off Next, 1957

The Questioning of Nick, 1957

Sing to Me Through Open Windows, 1959

Secrets of the Rich, 1977

Wings: a Play, 1978

What's Happened to the Thornes' House, 1972

Jones, John Bush. "Impersonation and Authenticity: The Theatre as Metaphor in Kopit's *Indians*." *Quarterly Journal of Speech*, 59 (1973), 443–51.
   The play's major theme of mythmaking (which consists of impersonation insofar as a mythic representation is a personification on a cosmic plane of a natural characteristic) is related to the question of impersonation v. authenticity. This theme is in large part communicated by the play's formal aspects of "shape," and Jones thinks it "hardly accidental" that the action is constructed out of a complicated series of impersonations within a framework of the theatre itself as a metaphor for the mythmaking process. The brilliance of *Indians* is a direct result of a unity of structure and theme, form and content.

Jys, Vera M. "*Indians*: A Mosaic of Memories and Methodologies." *Players*, 47 (June–July 1972), 230–36.
   Jys treats *Indians* as a patchwork mosaic of 13 scenes at odds with four disconnected stage conventions: theatre of fact, theatre of alienation, expressionist theatre, and naturalist theatre. She concludes that the play is ultimately a failure — interpreted as a history lesson — owing to inadequacy of language, independence of four separate themes in conflict with each other, and the impediment presented to action of the plot by the alternation of scenes.

Lahr, John. "Arthur Kopit's *Indians*: Dramatizing National Amnesia." *Evergreen Review*, 13 (October 1969), 19–21, 63–67.
   Lahr sees *Indians* as a moral snipe at the exploitative "democratic" mythologizing of the American western experience; the West had the potential of the democratic ideal as an idea, but in actual fact, and contrary to received notions, its real use represented a betrayal of that ideal. Buffalo Bill's ambiguous career becomes the vehicle for this re-interpretation.

_____. "*Indians*: A Dialogue Between Arthur Kopit and John Lahr, edited by Anthea Lahr." Unpaginated insert in Bantam ed. of *Indians*. New York: Bantam, 1971.

The play's purpose, says Kopit, was to explore the confused "amorphousness" of history and attempt to locate the madness of Viet Nam in its proper *American* context with respect to that history, and with respect to the usual American way of conducting affairs of national interest, including the mythic rationalization after the ugly fact that is also characteristic. The distortion in the play is in deliberate emulation of the nightmare distortion of sensibilities resulting from Viet Nam, and that is built into the American ideology of justice, which has consistently confounded a vocal (though highly ambiguous) moral ideal with practical politics. The classically shallow position has been that if we do a thing, it must therefore be good, because we are Americans — who are known to be good.

March, A. C. "Genet-Triana-Kopit: Ritual as Danse Macabre." *Modern Drama*, 15 (March 1973), 369–81.

March explores the dramatic properties and cultural significance of ritual action (as opposed to the inaction of the absurdist theatre) in Genet's *The Maids*, Triana's *The Night of the Assassins*, and Kopit's *Chamber Music*. March considers that the analogous relationship of the three plays is illustrative of the use of a global culture, the common note of which, in its western incarnation, is the alienation of the individual.

Rinear, D. L. "*The Day the Whores Came Out to Play Tennis:* Kopit's Debt to Chekhov." *Today's Speech*, 22 (Spring 1974), 19–23.

Rinear suggests that *The Day the Whores Came Out to Play Tennis* may be a conscious, even conscientious, aping of *The Cherry Orchard*. The parallels are carefully noted, well-substantiated and not without interest, but Rinear does not explain why Kopit has done what Rinear claims he has done.

Weiher, Carol. "American History on Stage in the 1960s: Something Old, Something New." *Quarterly Journal of Speech*, 63 (December 1977), 405–12.

Weiher focuses on Martin Dubermann's *In White America* and Kopit's *Indians*, exploring the "special relationship of the historical play to the audience's own past." *Indians* presents "a supressed American heartbreak . . . in an effort to make audiences respond to the guilt locked into the awesome growth of America."

Wilz, Hans-Werner. "Arthur Kopit: *Indians*." In Grabes, Herbert, ed. *Das Amerikanische Drama der Gegenwart*. Kronberg: Athenäum, 1976.

Han-Werner Wilz discusses *Indians* as an example of the mature Kopit's work and praises his handling of the Buffalo Bill legend and its relevancy to current American political and social problems.

DAVID MAMET
(1947–   )

American Buffalo, 1975
Dark Pony, 1977
Duck Variations, 1972

A Life in the Theatre, 1977

Mackinac (children's play), 1977

Marranos, 1972

Mr. Happiness, 1978

The Poet and the Rent, 1974

Reunion, 1976

Revolt of the Space Pandas (children's play), 1977

Sexual Perversity in Chicago, 1974

Squirrels, 1972

The Water Engine, 1977

The Woods, 1977

Eder, Richard. "David Mamet's New Realism." *New York Times Magazine*, (12 March 1978) 40–43.
   Eder describes the warmth and simplicity of Mamet's ethnic urban stage language and compassionate character studies.

Gottlieb, Richard. "The Engine That Drives Playwright David Mamet." *New York Times*, (15 January 1978) sec. 2, p. 1.
   Gottlieb speaks of Mamet as a dynamic new playwright who is impressing theatre-goers with original American dramas of the seventies and eighties.

Kalem, T. E. "Pinter Patter." *Time*, (12 July 1976) 68.
   Kalem discusses the impact of young David Mamet's work and notes its similarity to Pinter in terms of its pared down language and psychological subtext.

ARTHUR MILLER
(1915–   )

After the Fall, 1964

All My Sons, 1947

The American Clock, 1980

The Archbishop's Ceiling, 1976

The Creation of the World and Other Business, 1972

The Crucible, 1953

Death of a Salesman, 1949

An Enemy of the People (adaptation), 1958

Fame, and the Reason Why, 1970

Honors at Dawn, 1936

Incident at Vichy, 1964

The Man Who Had All the Luck, 1944

No Villains (They Too Arise), 1937

The Price, 1968

That They May Win, 1944

Up from Paradise, 1974

A View from the Bridge (revised), 1956

A View from the Bridge, and *A Memory of Two Mondays: Two One-Act Plays*, 1955

Corrigan, Robert W. ed., *Arthur Miller: A Collection of Critical Essays*. Englewood Cliffs, N.J.: Prentice-Hall, 1969.
 Essays by Clurman, Weales, Blau, Warshow, and Driver, among others, evaluate Miller's major works.

Hayashi, Tetsumaro. *An Index to Arthur Miller Criticism*. 2nd. ed. Metuchen, N.J.: Scarecrow Press, 1976.
 The second edition of Hayashi's Miller bibliography has brought up to date a valuable starting place for research on the playwright.

Hogan, Robert. *Arthur Miller*. Minneapolis: The University of Minnesota Press, 1964.
 Hogan's contribution to Miller biography, bibliography, and interpretation to the Minnesota pamphlet series is nearly two decades old but still makes an effective introduction to the young playwright's work.

Huftel, Sheila. *Arthur Miller: The Burning Glass*. New York: Citadel Press, 1965.
 Huftel explores "the questions of guilt and innocence" that take root in Miller's plays. The search for truth and the methods to present truth on the stage are Miller's preoccupations, from *The Man Who Had All the Luck* to *Incident at Vichy*. A list of production casts is provided.

Lübbren, Rainer. *Arthur Miller*. Velber: Friedrich Verlag, 1966.
 Lübbren surveys Miller's work through *Incident at Vichy*. He provides close readings of Miller's major works. The book includes a chronology of the author's works, photographs from a variety of productions, and a brief bibliography.

Merserve, Walter J. *The Merrill Studies in "Death of a Salesman."* Columbus, Ohio: Merrill, 1972.
 This casebook on Miller's most famous play is still a valuable teaching and research book.

The Theater Essays of Arthur Miller. Edited and with an Introduction by Robert A. Martin. Foreword by Arthur Miller. Penguin Books, Harmondsworth 1978.
 Collection of Miller's essays and interviews, which give his views about drama and theater. Includes complete "Bibliography of Works" (1936–1977) by Arthur Miller.

Moss, Leonard. *Arthur Miller*. New York: Twayne Publishers, 1967.
 Moss offers the standard Twayne series approach to Miller with a chronology of his life, an analysis of each individual work by the author, and a selected annotated bibliography. The chapter on *Death of a Salesman* incorporates many critical points of view toward that play and is an effective summary of attitudes widely shared in 1967.

Nelson, Benjamin. *Arthur Miller: Portrait of a Playwright*. New York: McKay, 1970.
 Although Nelson does not praise Miller's plays equally, he is convincing when he speaks of the solidarity of Miller's overall achievement, his conservative

theatrical approach, and his emphasis on enduring moral values. Nelson believes Miller's plays have, however, increasingly emphasized "the absurdist element in human experience." Discussions include Miller's major work through *The Price*.

Rössie, Wolfgang. *Die soziale Wirklichkeit in Arthur Millers "Death of a Salesman."* Freiburg/Schweiz Universitätsverlag, 1970.

Rössie has made an in depth analysis of *Death of a Salesman* which is seen as a kind of landmark American play.

Brüning, Eberhard, "Arthur Miller: Spätbürgerlicher Humanist und Gesellschaftskritiker." In Brüning, Eberhard, Klaus Köhler, and Bernhard, Scheller, eds., *Studien zum amerikanischen Drama Nach dem Zweiten Weltkrieg*. Berlin: Rütten and Loening, 1977, 40–53.

This excellent recent essay surveys Miller's achievement, applauds him as a humanist and fine craftsman. It offers penetrating insights into Miller's evaluation of American life.

DAVID RABE
(1940–   )

The Basic Training of Pavlo Hummel, 1971

Burning, 1974

Boom Boom Room, 1973

In the Boom Boom Room (revised version), 1974

The Orphan, 1973

Sticks and Bones, 1969

Streamers, 1977

Asahine, Robert. "The Basic Training of American Playwrights: Theater and the Vietnam War." *Theatre Yearbook*, 9 (Spring 1978), 30–37.

Asahine approaches the theatre of the 1960s in a broad context of the arts in America and the "link between aesthetic and political radicalism." He looks at *The Basic Training of Pavlo Hummel, Sticks and Bones*, and *Streamers*, which comprise Rabe's trilogy of plays on Vietnam.

Kellman, Barnet. "David Rabe's 'The Orphan': A Peripatetic Work in Progress." *Theatre Quarterly* (Spring 1977), 72–93.

"Barnet Kellman directed *The Orphan* as it reached its final form, and here he describes the creative process through which this re-working of Aeschylus' *Oresteia* was enriched with the seventies through the analogous horrors of My Lai and the Manson murders." This is an extremely detailed article working both from the playwright's point of view and the director's imagination.

Marranca, Bonnie. "David Rabe's Viet Nam Trilogy." *Canadian Theatre Review*, 5 (Spring 1977), 86–92.

Marranca discusses features of a recent production of the trilogy.

RONALD RIBMAN
(1932–   )

A Break in the Skin, 1972

The Ceremony of Innocence, 1967

Cold Storage, 1977

Fingernails Blue as Flowers, 1971

The Final War of Olly Winter, 1967

Harry, Noon and Night, 1965

The Journey of the Fifth Horse, 1967

Passing Through from Exotic Places, 1969

The Poison Tree, 1973

Brustein, Robert. "Journey and Arrival of a Playwright." *New Republic*, (7 May 1966.)

A general review of *Journey of the Fifth Horse* including a summary of the action is presented. Brustein notes that Ribman writes neither out of his own personal life experience nor out of the American experience. While *Journey* preserves the core of Turgenev's *The Diary of a Superfluous Man*, it is unmistakably original. The highly ingenious structure combines the modern and traditional, the grotesque and the lyrical, the world of actuality and the world of dreams. While ambitious in form, it falls short of complete gratification. Ribman shows much promise as a future playwright.

Weales, Gerald. "Ronald Ribman." In *Comtemporary Dramatists*, Vinson, James, ed. London: St. James Press; New York: St. Martin's Press, 1973.

A general discussion of the plays stresses the innovations that the young, untested playwright introduced in *Harry, Noon and Night* and *The Journey of the Fifth Horse*. Ribman took chances and succeeded; the example of his peculiar emphasis on pronouns at crucial times is explored. Ribman does not settle into an attitude or genre, but moves from psychological drama to direct social comment.

SAM SHEPARD
(1940–   )

Action, 1974

Angel City and *Suicide in BFlat* (1976)

Back Bog Beast Bait, 1971

Blue Butch, 1973

Buried Child, 1978

Chicago, 1975

Cowboy Mouth, 1971

Cowboys, 1964

Cowboys #2, 1967

Curse of the Starving Class, 1976

Dog, 1964

4-H Club, 1965

Fourteen Hundred Thousand, 1967

Forensic and the Navigators, 1967

Geography of a Horse Dreamer, 1974

Holy Ghostly, 1970

Icarus's Mother, 1965

Killer's Head, 1975

La Turista, 1966

Little Ocean, 1974

Mad Dog Blues, 1971

Melodrama Play, 1967

Nightwalk, 1973

Operation Sidewinder, 1970

Red Cross, 1966

Rock Garden, 1964

Rocking Chair, 1964

Rolling Thunder Logbook, 1977

Savage/Love, 1979

Shaved Splits, 1969

Tongues, 1978

The Tooth of Crime, 1972

The Unseen Hand, 1970

Up To Thursday, 1964

"American Experimental Theatre, Then and Now." *Performing Arts Journal*, 2
(Fall 1977), 13–24.
  This general article on the experimental theatre contains brief remarks by
Shepard on his attempts to arouse interest in social and moral problems avoided
by "establishment" playwrights.

Bachman, Charles R. "Defusion of Menace in the Plays of Sam Shepard." *Modern
Drama*, 19 (December 1976), 405–16.
  Bachman suggests that Shepard's plays reflect both an abhorrence for violence
and a fascination with it. The article explores the structure which introduces a
threateningly violent character and then defuses the terror they create; he
examines the structures of the major plays, focusing on the dynamics of the
menace of violence.

Cohn, Ruby. "Sam Shepard." In *Contemporary Dramatists*, Vinson, James, ed.,
London: St. James Press; New York: St. Martin's Press, 1973.

Sam Shepard is a prolific writer who, more than any other contemporary American dramatist "weaves into his own dramatic idiom the strands of a youth culture." He has absorbed, and reflects, the pop-media culture. Says Cohn, "At his best — *La Turista, Mad Dog Blues, The Tooth of Crime* — Shepard achieves his own distinctive coherence through beautifully bridled fantasy."

Davis, R. A. " 'Get up Out a' Your Homemade Beds': The Plays of Sam Shepard." *Players*, 47 (1972), 12–19.

Davis surveys Shepard's disturbing plays which are obsessed with the inconsistencies and "barbarisms" of American life. The hollowness and alienation of the present seems to augur an even more brutal future.

Kleb, William. "Shepard and Chaikin Speaking in Tongues." *Theater*, 10 (February 1978), 66–69.

Tongues, a collaborated work, was performed only five times in June 1978. The work demonstrates Shepard's thesis that a more flexible attitude toward time in theater is needed. A short play, it consists of a dozen speeches. The essay examines the work briefly.

LUIS VALDEZ
(1940–   )

Actos, 1970

Bernabe, 1970

La Carpa de los Rasquachis, 1974

El Corrido, 1976

The Dark Root of a Scream, 1973

El Dia de los Muertos, 1973

Las dos Caras del Patroncito, 1974

Fin del Mundo, 1975

The Shrunken Heads of Pancho Villa, 1970

Los Vendidos, 1974

Villa, 1964

La Virgen del Tepeyac (adaptation), 1973

Zoot Suit, The Triumph of El Pachuco, 1978

Bagby, Beth. "El Teatro Campesino." Interviews with Luis Valdez. *Tulane Drama Review*, 11 (Summer 1967), 70–80.

García, Nasario. "Satire: Techniques and Devices in Luis Valdez' *Las dos Caras del Patroncito*." *De Colores*, 1 (1975), 66–74.

García discusses Valdez' unique combination of song, dance, mime, and morality play and links him to both the religious theatre of the Indians and the Roman Catholic Church.

Martinez, Julio A. "Luis Valdez." In *Chicano Scholars and Writers: A Bio-Bibliographical Directory*. Metuchen, N.J.: Scarecrow Press, (1979).

Martinez provides a useful guide to the writings of Valdez and a list of critical studies of Chicano theatre.

Steiner, Stan. "Cultural Schizophrenia of Luis Valdez: Founder of El Teatro
   Campesino." *Vogue*, (15 March 1969,) 112–13.
   Steiner praises Valdez' attempts to span two cultures, to preserve his Chicano
heritage while making a valid commentary on mainstream American experience.
Valdez, Luis. See "Chicano Theatre" above.

TENNESSEE WILLIAMS
(1911–   )

At Liberty, 1968

Auto-da-Fé, 1947

Battle of Angels, 1940

Cairo! Shanghai! Bombay!, 1936

Camino Real, 1953

Candles in the Sun, 1936

The Case of the Crushed Petunias, 1957

Cat on a Hot Tin Roof, 1955

The Dark Room, 1966

Demolition Downtown: Count Ten in Arabic – Then Run, 1976

Eccentricities of a Nightingale, 1966 (a new version of *Summer and Smoke*)

The Enemy: Time, 1959

Fugitive Kind, 1937

Garden District: Something Unspoken and *Suddenly Last Summer*, 1958

The Glass Menagerie, 1944

The Gnädiges Fräulein, 1966 (produced under the title, *Slapstick Tragedy*)

Headlines, 1935

Hello from Bertha, 1961

I Can't Imagine Tomorrow, 1976

I Rise in Flame, Cried the Phoenix: A Play about D. H. Lawrence, 1953

In the Bar of a Tokyo Hotel, 1969

Kingdom of Earth: The Seven Descents of Myrtle, 1968

The Lady of Larkspur Lotion, 1947

The Last of My Solid Gold Watches, 1946

The Long Goodbye, 1940

The Long Stay Cut Short; or, The Unsatisfactory Supper, 1971

Lord Byron's Love Letter, 1947

The Magic Tower, 1936

The Milk Train Doesn't Stop Here Anymore, 1962

The Mutilated, 1966 (produced under the title *Slapstick Tragedy*)

Mooney's Kid Don't Cry, 1946

The Night of the Iguana, 1959

A Perfect Analysis Given by a Parrot, 1976

Period of Adjustment: High Point over a Cavern: A Serious Comedy, 1959

Portrait of a Madonna, 1946

The Purification, 1954

The Red Devil Battery Sign, 1974

The Rose Tatoo, 1951

Slapstick Tragedy, 1966 (includes *The Gnädiges Fräulein* and *The Mutilated*)

Small Craft Warnings, 1972

Something Unspoken, 1958 (produced under the title *Garden District*)

Spring Song, 1938

Stairs to the Roof, 1944

The Strangest Kind of Romance, 1969

A Streetcar Named Desire, 1947

Suddenly Last Summer, 1958 (produced under the title, *Garden District*)

Summer and Smoke, 1947

Talk to Me Like the Rain and Let Me Listen, 1958

Ten Blocks on the Camino Real, 1948

This Is (Entertainment), 1975 or

This Is an Entertainment, 1976

This Property Is Condemned, 1946

Three Players of a Summer Game, 1955

To Heaven in a Golden Coach, 1961

27 Wagons Full of Cotton, 1955

The Two Character Play, 1967

You Touched Me, 1944 (with Donald Windham; adaptation of a story by
  D. H. Lawrence)

Brustein, Robert. "Williams' Nebulous Nightmare." *Hudson Review*, 12 (Summer
  1959), 255–60.
  Brustein discusses the negative aspects of Williams' work: distorted charac-
  terizations, pretentious symbolism, sexual obsessions.

Falk, Signi. *Tennessee Williams*. 2nd ed. Boston: Twayne Publishers, 1978.
  Falk's revision of her 1961 Twayne Series biography provides up-to-date
  information on Williams' career. It contains a chronology of major events in his
  life and his publications, and offers an effective annotated bibliography of secondary sources of major interest. William's plays are discussed individually but
  they are effectively related to major patterns and themes that run throughout his
  work.

Jackson, Esther Merle. *The Broken World of Tennessee Williams*. Madison: University of Wisconsin, 1965.

Jackson's sensitive treatment of the aesthetics of Williams' plays and his particular treatment of myths and antiheroes emphasizes the playwright's preoccupation with a "comprehensive moral structure."

Köhler, Klaus. "Psychodiagnose und Gesellschaftanalyse im Bühnenwerk von Tennessee Williams." In Brüning, Eberhard, Klaus Köhler und Bernhard Scheller eds. *Studien zum amerikanschen Drama nach dem Zweiten Weltkrieg.* Berlin: Rütten und Loening, 1977.
Köhler offers a brilliant psychological study of Williams' major themes and obsessions and accounts for his popularity in the modern theatre.

Link, Franz. H. *Tennessee Williams Dramen. Einsamket u Liebe.* Darmstadt: Thesen Verlag, 1974.
Link explores Williams' view of life and message of love and compassion.

Popkin, Henry. "The Plays of Tennessee Williams." *Tulane Drama Review*, 4 (Spring 1960), 45–60.
Popkin investigates archetypes in Williams' work and examines recurrent patterns of symbolism.

Maxwell, Gilbert. *Tennessee Williams and His Friends.* Cleveland: World, 1965.
Maxwell is not a scholar but a friend of the playwright. His book is valuable for its psycho-biographical insights, but does not attempt to approach the writer's work from a scholarly viewpoint.

Stanton, Stephen S., ed. *Tennessee Williams: A Collection of Critical Essays.* Englewood Cliffs, N.J.: Prentice-Hall, 1977.
This is a Twentieth Century Views Collection offering scholarly essays on individual plays and in general thematic and biographical topics.

Thorpe, Jack, ed. *Tennessee Williams: A Tribute.* Jackson, Miss.: University of Mississippi Press, 1977.
This is a lengthy collection of essays by nearly fifty contributors who mostly praise various aspects of the playwright's work.

Williams, Tennessee, *Memoirs.* Garden City, New York: Doubleday, 1975 Interesting biography, "written by something like the process of 'free association' ", which gives an insight into the author's psyche, also to some extent reveals the psychological condition of the characters in his plays.

————, *Where I live: Selected Essays.* New York: New Directions, 1978.
This book is a mixture of dramatic theory and autobiograhpical recollections by Williams. There are lapses of memories, contradictions, and some self-pity, but mainly the essays provide readers with insights into Williams' dramatic method and into the problems of the American theatre.

LANFORD WILSON
(1937–   )

Balm in Gilead, 1964
Days Ahead, 1965
The Family Continues, 1972
The Fifth of July, 1978

The Gingham Dog, 1968

The Great Nebula in Orion, 1970

Home Free! 1968

The Hot L Baltimore, 1973

Ikke, Ikke, Nye, Nye, Nye, 1971

Lemon Sky, 1970

Ludlow Fair, 1965

The Madness of Lady Bright, 1964

Miss Williams: A Turn, 1967

The Mound Builders, 1975

No Trespassing, 1964

The Rimers of Eldritch, 1965

The Sand Castle, 1965

Serenading Louis, 1970

Sex Is Between Two People, 1965

Sextet (Yes): A Play for Voices, 1971

So Long at the Fair, 1963

Summer and Smoke, 1971

Talley's Folly, 1980

This Is the Rill Speaking, 1965

Untitled Play, 1967

Wandering: A Turn, 1966

Berkvist, Robert. "Lanford Wilson — Can He Score on Broadway?" *New York Times*, (17 February 1980,) Arts and Leisure sec., p. 1, cont'd, p. 33.

   Berkvist presents a thorough background of the playwright and his plays, leading up to the Broadway production of *Talley's Folly*. *Talley's Folly* was Wilson's first Broadway play, a "romantic comedy about the wooing of a hesitant spinster." Berkvist provides a fairly extensive biographical sketch and explores the possibility of Wilson's being a "regional" playwright who is always looking back to his roots in Missouri.

Saner, Arthur. "Lanford Wilson." In *Contemporary Dramatists*, Vinson, James, ed. London: St. James Press; New York: St. Martin's Press, 1973.

   This is a general discussion emphasizing *Hot L Baltimore, The Madness of Lady Bright, Lemon Sky, The Sand Castle*. Saner characterizes Wilson's plays as busy, "peopled" worlds and maintains that Wilson's plays suggest a sense of innocence about life, that there is no bitter grappling with "one's own devils, with the subconscious powers of darkness." He remarks that there are no evil forces in the plays; most of the stage time is spent in "chatter or rumination about the nature of things."

BLACK PLAYWRIGHTS

Fabre, Geneviève. "The New Black Theatre: Achievements and Problems." *Caliban* (Toulouse), 15 (1978), 121–29.

The development of new black theater has reached a state of crisis primarily due to lack of economic support. A fairly general survey of activity in the black theater in the 1960s and early 1970s is placed in a historical context that concentrates on the period before 1900 and in the 1950s.

Johnson, Helen Armstead. "Black Influences in the American Theatre: Part II, 1960 and After." In *The Black American Reference Book*. Smythe, Mabel M. ed., Englewood Cliffs, N.J.: Prentice-Hall, 1976.

Johnson lists eighteen major recurring themes in black drama and discusses the expanding black theatres of the sixties. She concludes with trends among black playwrights of the seventies and suggests problems in black drama and areas where further research and development are needed.

Miller, Elizabeth. "Theatre, Dance, and the Arts." In *The Negro in America*. 2nd ed., revised and enlarged. Cambridge: Harvard University Press, 1970.

Miller provides an excellent historical and bibliographical survey of contributors to Negro theatre.

CHICANO PLAYWRIGHTS

Brokaw, John W. "Teatro Chicano: Some Reflections." *Educational Theatre Journal*, 29 (December 1977), 535–44.

Brokaw presents a history of Spanish-language theatre in the southwest United States, broken down into three periods: (1) the decline of the vestigial Spanish theatre, (2) the birth of a distinctly Mexican theatre, and (3) the replacement of the Mexican theatre by a Mexican-American theatre. [Includes some discussion of Valdez.]

Huerta, Jorge. "Concerning Theatro Chicano." *Latin American Theatre Review*, 6 (Spring 1973), 13–20.

This is one of several articles by Huerta who wrote his dissertation on Chicano theatre. He discusses its cultural and religious origins and its contempt for the material aspects of American life.

Martinez, Julio A. See "Luis Valdez" below.

Valdez, Luis. "Notes on Chicano Theatre." In *Aztlan: An Anthology of Mexican American Literature*. Valdez, Luis and Stan Steiner, eds., New York: Vintage Books, 1972.

Valdez calls for a theatre that will be "revolutionary in technique as well as content." He wants a theatre of ritual, music, of beauty and spiritual sensitivity. A teatro of legends and myths."

WOMEN PLAYWRIGHTS

France, Rachel. "Introduction" to *A Century of Plays by American Women*. France, Rachel, ed., New York: Richard Rosen Press, 1979.

France describes the repression of women playwrights and the critical neglect of those few who were able to contribute to American theatre. She provides an interesting, succinct history of women writers and the stage and explains that the plays in her anthology reveal "aspects of our cultural identity beyond the theatre itself."

Moore, Honor. "Introduction" to *The New Women's Theatre*. Moore, Honor, ed., New York: Random House, 1977.

Moore argues that theatre since the golden age of Greece has been dedicated to the male-god Dionysus but notes that "Dionysian rites had their origins in earlier rites to Demeter, a woman god." She argues that the world is waiting for a theatre which will realistically depict the feelings and ideas of women.

Sutherland, Cynthia. "American Women Playwrights as Mediators of the 'Woman Problem.' " *Modern Drama*, 21 (September 1978), 319–36.

This article focuses on Glaspell, Akins, Gale, and Crothers. It examines their chronicling of the social changes involved in the emancipation of women in America. Sutherland's historical approach explores how theme in drama reflects and affects social change.

CONTRIBUTORS

HEDWIG BOCK is a Lecturer in the Englisches Seminar at the Universität Hamburg. She is the co-editor of this series and has published articles on Edward Albee, Tennessee Williams, Arthur Miller and other American writers.

JOHN W. BROKAW teaches at the University of Texas, where he is an Associate Professor in the Department of Drama. He has written widely on Mexican-American theatre.

PETER BRUCK is Wissenschaftlicher Assistent für Englische Sprache und Literatur und ihre Didaktik at the Westfälische Wilhelms-Universität Münster. He has published articles on James Baldwin, the non-fiction novel, and science fiction. He is the editor of *The Black American Short Story in the Twentieth Century* (1977) and a textbook, *The Frontier and the American West* (1980).

RUBY COHN, who is Professor of Comparative Drama at the University of California, Davis is likely the most distinguished Beckett scholar. Her three important studies of Beckett — *Samuel Beckett: The Comic Gamut* (1962), *Back to Beckett* (1973), and *Just Play: Beckett's Theater* (1980) — have been supplemented by numerous essays on Beckett. Her *Currents in Contemporary Drama* (1969) and *Dialogue in American Drama* (1971) are seminal studies as is her more recent *Shakespeare Offshoots* (1976).

WINONA L. FLETCHER holds a joint appointment as Professor of Theatre & Drama and Afro-American Studies at Indiana University. She is a past President of the University and College Theater Association and was recently elected to the American Theatre Association's College of Fellows. She has played a major role in the study and production of black drama at American universities.

STEVEN H. GALE is Chairman of the Department of English at Missouri Southern State College in Joplin, Missouri. He is the author of an important study of Harold Pinter's plays, *Butter's Going Up: A Critical Analysis of Harold Pinter's Work* (1977), as well as *Harold Pinter: An Annotated Bibliography* (1978). He is the editor of a new textbook, *Readings for Today's Writers* (1980).

PATTI P. GILLESPIE serves as Head of the Department of Theatre and Speech at the University of South Carolina. She has published several essays on nineteenth-century theatre as well as on modern women's theatre.

DIETER HERMS is a Professor at the Universität Bremen. The author of *Agitprop USA: Zur Theorie und Strategie des politisch emanzipatorischen Theaters in Amerika seit 1960* (1973) as well as a more recent study of Upton Sinclair, Prof. Dr. Herms is the editor of *Gulliver, deutsch-englische Jahrbücher* and has published numerous articles on American minority literature.

JANET S. HERTZBACH teaches at Gettysburg College, where she is Assistant Professor of English. She has been an NEH Fellow and maintains a strong interest in Renaissance and medieval drama as well as in American drama.

KIMBALL KING is the new Editor of the *Southern Literary Journal*. A member of the Department of English at the University of North Carolina, Professor King is an authority on American literary manuscripts and is the author of a bibliography, *Twenty Modern British Playwrights* (1977).

HENRY I. SCHVEY, who is Assistant Professor of English at the Rijksuniversiteit Te Leiden in the Netherlands, is the author of *The Playwright's Eye*, a soon to be published study of the plays written by the Austrian painter Oskar Kokoschka. He has published a number of articles on modern literature, Edward Albee, Dylan Thomas, Sylvia Plath, and Eugene O'Neill.

WERNER SOLLORS has taught at the John F. Kennedy-Institut für Nordamerikastudien at the Free University of Berlin and is now Assistant Professor of English at Columbia University. He is the author of *Amiri Baraka/LeRoi Jones: The Quest for a "Populist Modernism"* (1978) as well as articles on Ed Bullins, black theatre, Eugene O'Neill and Stephen Crane.

GERALD WEALES, a distinguished authority on modern American drama, is Professor of English at the University of Pennsylvania. He has published a great many reviews, essays and books on American drama. His *American Drama in the 1960's* (1969) and *Clifford Odets, Playwright* (1971) are among the most well-known and respect studies in American drama.

ALBERT WERTHEIM is Professor of English at Indiana University. A co-editor of this series, he has published widely on Shakespeare, Renaissance and Restoration drama as well as on modern American drama. He is completing a study of the plays of James Shirley.

MARGARET B. WILKERSON is Director of Continuing Education for Women and a Lecturer in Afro-American Studies at the University of California, Berkeley. A playwright and director, she chairs the Black Theatre Program of the American Theatre Association. She has published a number of articles on black writers.

JÜRGEN WOLTER is the author of *Das Prosawerk Thomas Deloneys* (1976) and has written as well on other Renaissance writers, Stephen, Crane, Eugene O'Neill and American drama. He teaches at the Gesamthochschule Wuppertal.

KATHARINE WORTH serves as Head of Drama and Theatre Studies at Royal Holloway College, University of London. Her publications include *The Irish Drama of Europe* (1978) and the seminal *Revolutions in English Drama* (1973). She edited *Beckett the Shape Changer* (1975) and has published articles on modern drama in various journals and symposia.